T0331709

INTRODUCTION TO BISIMULATION AND COINDUCTION

Induction is a pervasive tool in computer science and mathematics for defining objects and reasoning on them. Coinduction is the dual of induction, and as such it brings in quite different tools. Today, it is widely used in computer science, but also in other fields, including artificial intelligence, cognitive science, mathematics, modal logics, philosophy and physics. The best-known instance of coinduction is bisimulation, mainly employed to define and prove equalities among potentially infinite objects: processes, streams, non-well-founded sets, and so on.

This book presents bisimulation and coinduction: the fundamental concepts and techniques, and the duality with induction. Each chapter contains exercises and selected solutions, enabling students to connect theory with practice. A special emphasis is placed on bisimulation as a behavioural equivalence for processes. Thus the book serves as an introduction to models for expressing processes (such as process calculi) and to the associated techniques of operational and algebraic analysis.

DAVIDE SANGIORGI is Full Professor in Computer Science at the University of Bologna, Italy, and Head of the University of Bologna/INRIA team 'Focus'.

INTRODUCTION TO BISIMULATION AND COINDUCTION

DAVIDE SANGIORGI

University of Bologna (Italy)
and INRIA (France)

CAMBRIDGE
UNIVERSITY PRESS

Shaftesbury Road, Cambridge CB2 8EA, United Kingdom

One Liberty Plaza, 20th Floor, New York, NY 10006, USA

477 Williamstown Road, Port Melbourne, VIC 3207, Australia

314–321, 3rd Floor, Plot 3, Splendor Forum, Jasola District Centre, New Delhi – 110025, India

103 Penang Road, #05–06/07, Visioncrest Commercial, Singapore 238467

Cambridge University Press is part of Cambridge University Press & Assessment,
a department of the University of Cambridge.

We share the University's mission to contribute to society through the pursuit of
education, learning and research at the highest international levels of excellence.

www.cambridge.org
Information on this title: www.cambridge.org/9781107003637

First published 2012

A catalogue record for this publication is available from the British Library

ISBN   978-1-107-00363-7   Hardback

Additional resources for this publication at www.cs.unibo.it/~sangio/Book_Bis_Coind.html

Contents

Illustrations

Preface

This book is an introduction to bisimulation and coinduction and a precursor to the companion book on more advanced topics. Between them, the books analyse the most fundamental aspects of bisimulation and coinduction, exploring concepts and techniques that can be transported to many areas. Bisimulation is a special case of coinduction, by far the most studied coinductive concept. Bisimulation was discovered in Concurrency Theory and processes remain the main application area. This explains the special emphasis on bisimulation and processes that one finds throughout the two volumes.

This volume treats basic topics. It explains coinduction, and its duality with induction, from various angles, starting from some simple results of fixed-point theory. It then goes on to bisimulation, as a tool for defining behavioural equality among processes (bisimilarity), and for proving such equalities. It compares bisimulation with other notions of behavioural equivalence. It also presents a simple process calculus, both to show algebraic techniques for bisimulation and to illustrate the combination of inductive and coinductive reasoning.

The companion volume, *Advanced Topics in Bisimulation and Coinduction*, edited by Davide Sangiorgi and Jan Rutten, deals with more specialised topics. A chapter recalls the history of the discovery of bisimulation and coinduction. Another chapter unravels the duality between induction and coinduction, both as defining principles and as proof techniques, in terms of the duality between the mathematical notions of algebra and coalgebra and properties such as initiality and finality. A third chapter analyses the profound implications of the concept of bisimulation in modal logics, with some beautiful results on the expressiveness of the logics. Two further chapters are devoted to the bisimulation proof method, a major ingredient for success of bisimulation: the algorithmic content of the method, showing striking separation results between bisimilarity and other behavioural equivalences; and enhancements of the bisimulation proof method, whose goal is to further facilitate the proof of bisimilarity results. Finally, separate chapters discuss two important refinements of bisimulation, which have to do with probabilities and higher-order linguistic constructs.

Bisimulation and coinduction offer us powerful tools for defining, understanding and reasoning about objects and structures that are common in Computer Science. Today, bisimulation and coinduction are also used in other fields, e.g., Artificial Intelligence, Cognitive Science, Mathematics, Modal Logics, Philosophy and Physics.

Although the history of bisimulation and coinduction is fairly short, interest in them has rapidly grown and will certainly continue to grow in the years to come. However, one does not find textbooks that offer comprehensive treatments, allowing a newcomer to be exposed to the basic concepts and to learn how to use and apply them. I hope that these two volumes can contribute to fill this gap.

I intend to maintain a Web page for general information and auxiliary material about the volumes. At the time of writing, this page is located at

`www.cs.unibo.it/~sangio/Book_Bis_Coind.html.`

Davide Sangiorgi

General introduction

0.1 Why bisimulation and coinduction

Induction is a pervasive tool in Computer Science and Mathematics for defining objects and proving properties of them. *Coinduction* is less known. It has been discovered and studied only in recent years. It is therefore not part of the standard scientific culture. The interest in coinduction is, however, growing: more and more application areas are suggested, and with compelling evidence.

Coinduction brings in tools for defining and reasoning on objects that are new and quite different from the tools provided by induction. This is because coinduction is the dual of induction. Induction has to do with least fixed points, coinduction with greatest fixed points. Greatest fixed points are as natural as least fixed points; in the same way coinduction is as natural as induction.

In the world of induction, constructions are stratified. Objects are hereditarily constructed, starting from basic atoms or primitive objects at the bottom, and then iteratively moving upward through higher or composite objects. Coinduction liberates us from the constraints of stratification. An immediate consequence is that the objects can be circular; more generally, they can be infinite. Examples of infinite structures are streams, as infinite sequences of elements, and real numbers, as infinite digit streams or Cauchy sequences. Another example is a process that continuously accepts interactions with the environment: semantically it is an infinite object, as it can engage in an infinite number of interactions. Indeed, any non-terminating program, as a computation that goes through an infinite sequence of steps, may be viewed as an infinite object. Infinity may also appear in chains of dependencies among the objects. For instance, in programming languages with store, memory cells with pointers to each other may produce cycles in the store. More generally, infinity may arise from cycles in any data structure that can be represented as a graph (as opposed to a tree); the structure could even be finitary, i.e., composed of a finite number of elements. Infinity may even be assumed for convenience when representing the objects, because we are unable to place bounds on them: for instance bounds on the size of a database, of an XML document, or of a stack. Sometimes infinity arises because the objects, or the environments in which they operate, are not fixed or may undergo mutations during their life time. This is frequent in modern distributed systems: a given component may be used in different environments, or may move from an environment to another one, or may be required to adapt itself to modifications in the surrounding environment. The set of possible configurations, as pairs (object state, environment), may be infinite. In all the situations above, if we wish to define the objects, or analyse them (i.e., proving invariance properties), notions and techniques from coinduction can be fruitful.

Coinduction is important in constructive mathematics. The most visible difference between constructive and classical mathematics (and logics) is the treatment of negation. In constructive mathematics, the limitations on the use of negation have led to the introduction of coinductive tools to reason on concepts that in classical mathematics are studied as the complements of inductive concepts. For instance, in classical topology closed sets may be defined as the complements of open sets, and open sets are inductively defined. In intuitionistic topology, one prefers a more informative definition of closed sets, as sets satisfying certain closure properties; coinductive definitions are then very natural and elegant, and particularly convenient for computer-formalised mathematics [Val05, HH06]. Similarly, in constructive formalisation of the λ-calculus, the set of 'divergent terms' is not defined as the complement of the inductive set of 'convergent terms'. One looks for an informative way of describing the meaning of divergence, and for this coinductive methods are very appropriate (see, e.g., Section 2.1.2).

The best known coinductive concept is *bisimulation*. In Computer Science, bisimulation and coinduction have been discovered in Concurrency Theory. Here, the bisimulation equality, called *bisimilarity*, is the most studied form of behavioural equality for processes, and is widely used for a number of reasons, notably the following ones.

- Bisimilarity is accepted as *the finest extensional behavioural equivalence* one would like to impose on processes. An extensional property is one whose definition only takes into account the interactions that the processes may, or may not, perform. An example of extensional property is 'after receiving a query, the process produces an answer'. Examples of non-extensional properties are 'the state space of the process has cardinality 8' (where the state space of a process is the set of states reachable from the process), and 'the set of states of the process has a Hamiltonian cycle'. Being 'the finest' means that one may argue that bisimilarity makes too many distinctions; but it also means that bisimilarity is a robust equality (see, e.g., Sections 5.12 and 5.14).
- The *bisimulation proof method* is exploited *to prove equalities* among processes. This occurs even when bisimilarity is not the behavioural equivalence chosen for the processes. For instance, one may be interested in trace equivalence and yet use the bisimulation proof method since bisimilarity implies trace equivalence and computing bisimilarity is efficient.
- The efficiency of the algorithms for bisimilarity checking and the compositionality properties of bisimilarity are exploited to *minimise* the state-space of processes.
- Bisimilarity, and variants of it such as similarity, are used *to abstract* from certain details of the systems of interest. For instance, we may want to prove behavioural properties of a server that do not depend on the data that the server manipulates. Abstracting from the data may also turn an infinite-state server into a finite one.

Further discussions on the strengths of bisimilarity are found in the book, e.g., in Section 5.14.

Bisimulation and coinduction are indeed considered as one of the most important contributions of Concurrency Theory to Computer Science. Aside from concurrency, coinduction is employed today in a number of areas of Computer Science, including Type Theory, Domain Theory, databases, program analysis and verification. For instance, in Type Theory bisimulation and coinductive techniques have been proposed to prove the soundness of type systems [MT91], to define the meaning of equality between (recursive) types and then to axiomatise and prove such equalities [AC93, BH97] and to define coinductive types and manipulate infinite proofs in theorem provers [Coq94, Gim96]. In databases, coinduction is used to formulate, optimise and decompose queries for nonstructured data [BDHS96, BGMM99, ABS99]. In program analysis coinduction is used to formalise, and reason about, invariance properties [NNH99], e.g., security properties such as confidentiality and non-interference [Sab03, Smi08], to prove compiler correctness and compiler optimisations [LJWF02, LG09], to reason about elements of recursively defined domains and data types [Fio93, Pit94] and to reason about equivalence in sequential programs [Pit97].

In Mathematics, bisimulation and coinduction have been introduced in the study of the foundations of theories of non-well-founded sets. Non-well-founded sets are, intuitively, sets that are allowed to contain themselves; they are 'infinite in depth'. More precisely, the membership relation on sets may give rise to infinite descending sequences

$$\ldots A_n \in A_{n-1} \in \ldots \in A_1 \in A_0.$$

For instance, a set Ω which satisfies the equation $\Omega = \{\Omega\}$ is circular and as such non-well-founded. A set can also be non-well-founded without being circular; this can happen if there is an infinite membership chain through a sequence of sets all different from each other. Bisimulation was derived from the notion of isomorphism with the objective of defining the meaning of equality on non-well-founded sets; in other words, for understanding what it means for two infinite sets to have 'the same' internal structure. A major motivation for the study of non-well-founded sets in Mathematics has been the need of giving semantics to processes, following Robin Milner's work in Concurrency Theory. Similarly, the development of Final Semantics [Acz88, RT94, RJ12], an area of Mathematics based on coalgebras and category theory and used in the semantics of programming languages, has been largely motivated by the interest in bisimulation. As a subject, Final Semantics is today well developed, and gives us a rich and deep perspective on the meaning of coinduction and its duality with induction.

Bisimulation is also popular in Philosophical Logic, specifically in Modal Logics; some of the most interesting results in the expressiveness of Modal Logics rely on the notion of bisimulation [BRV01]. Bisimulation and coinduction have also found applications in Artificial Intelligence, Cognitive Science, Epistemic Logics and Philosophy, mainly when there is a need to explain phenomena involving some kind of circularity. In Physics, coinductive tools have been advocated to model quantum systems [Abr10].

Today, coinduction appears to us so natural that it is surprising that it was discovered so late, roughly at the beginning of the 1980s [San12]. This has probably a lot to do with the fear of circularity and paradoxes, which has been strong in mathematicians and logicians throughout most of the twentieth century. Circularity was perceived as the culprit for paradoxes such as Burali-Forti's and Russell's, which had made the set theory studied by Cantor and Frege shaky, as well as for paradoxes known in other fields. Against circularity, at the beginning of the twentieth century, Bertrand Russell advocated a 'stratified' approach to science, which was followed by all logicians in the first half of the twentieth century, with very few isolated exceptions. Under the stratified approach, the constructions are inductive, and the obvious reasoning techniques are inductive.

Another explanation for the late discovery of coinduction is probably the lack of sufficiently strong motivations. Russell's stratified approach seemed in line with common sense and perception, which denies the existence of circular or infinite objects. On this aspect, the establishment of Computer Science has been influential: as discussed above, Computer Science frequently brings in needs that have to do with circularity and infinity.

0.2 Objectives of the book

This book is an introduction to bisimulation and to the more general notion of coinduction. The book explains what coinduction is, and its duality with induction, using simple mathematical structures: complete lattices. These are sets with an ordering on their elements that satisfies a few simple properties. We need only a few elementary results for complete lattices, dealing with fixed points. A complete lattice is dualisable: turning it upside-down (that is, reversing the order relation) yields another complete lattice. This duality will give shape to the duality between coinduction and induction.

Bisimulation was introduced in Concurrency Theory, and concurrency remains the main application area. The book therefore puts a special emphasis on processes, by presenting the basics of the theory of bisimulation on processes.

Bisimilarity, the equality of bisimulation, is a behavioural equivalence: it tells us what it means for two process behaviours to be the same. Several other forms of behavioural equivalence have, however, been proposed in the literature. The book makes detailed comparisons between bisimilarity and the other main notions of behavioural equivalence, both coinductive and inductive. Thus the book can also serve as an introduction to the topic of behavioural equivalences for processes.

For a better grasp of the theory of processes and of behavioural equivalences, the book introduces a process calculus, essentially Milner's Calculus of Communicating Process. Process calculi are small 'core concurrent languages', embodying the essential ingredients of concurrent systems. Process calculi are useful to provide succinct descriptions of the interaction and synchronization capabilities of processes. In the book, the purpose of introducing a process calculus is twofold. The first reason is to see how inductive and coinductive techniques can be profitably intertwined. The terms of a process calculus – the processes – are defined from a grammar; hence, syntactically, they are inductive objects. The equality on processes will be bisimilarity; hence, semantically, they are coinductive objects. The connection between syntax and semantics is tight; for instance, one needs to show that bisimilarity is preserved by the operators of the calculus. The second reason for introducing a process calculus is that the terms have a structure, resulting from the way they are assembled from the operators in the calculus. We can thus analyse the algebraic properties of bisimilarity. For instance, we will discuss algebraic characterisations of bisimilarity as a set of algebraic laws that allow us to derive all and only those equalities on processes that are valid for bisimilarity.

In summary, the objectives of the book are:

- to familiarise the reader with bisimulation and coinduction, so as to make him/her capable of using and applying them;
- to explain the duality between induction and coinduction;
- to introduce behavioural equivalences, in particular the differences between bisimilarity and other behavioural equalities;
- to initiate the reader to process calculi and their basic operational and algebraic techniques of analysis.

0.3 Use of the book

The book, integrated with parts of the second volume [SR12], could be the basis for courses on bisimulation, or coinduction, or on behavioural equivalences and process calculi.

The reader only interested in bisimulation, not coinduction, may safely skip Chapter 2. Exceptions may be the initial Sections 2.1 and 2.2, which informally introduce coinduction and its duality with induction by means of examples, and Section 2.10, which presents the characterisations of bisimilarity via fixed points and via inductive approximants.

Concerning behavioural equivalences, for an introduction to the topic the more technical parts could be omitted, notably the second parts of Chapters 4 (Section 4.6 to 4.9) and 5 (Sections 5.7 to 5.13), and Chapter 6.

Induction is explained and then applied in many examples and results. The book should therefore also be useful for understanding induction. However, induction in itself is not a goal of the book. We will not dwell on explaining how to write inductive definitions and carry out inductive proofs. Thus a reader that has no experience with induction should integrate the parts on induction with other material, especially examples of applications. An excellent textbook for this is Winskel [Win93]. Aside from this, and some elementary acquaintance with discrete mathematics, the book aims to be self-contained.

Exercises

All chapters contain several exercises. Solutions, or sketches of solutions, to most of the exercises are provided in an appendix; the exercises with a solution in the appendix are marked '↪'. Solving an exercise should not take much time; those that may require a little more time are marked with the asterisk '*'. Sometimes (e.g., Chapter 2) exercises with solutions have been preferred to examples; the less experienced reader may take these solutions as developed examples. This especially concerns the recommended exercises, which are those marked as 'Recommended'. The exercises without solutions are those considered either very easy or not fundamental to the understanding of the contents of the book.

0.4 Structure of the book

In Chapter 1 bisimulation and bisimilarity are gently introduced, as a way of setting equality on processes, beginning with the general question of the meaning of 'process' and of 'process behaviour'. Bisimilarity is compared with trace equivalence from Automata Theory, and with isomorphism from Graph Theory. The basic properties of bisimilarity are explained and the reader begins to get practice with the bisimulation proof method.

In Chapter 2 the bisimulation proof method and bisimilarity are shown to be instances of the broader notions of 'coinductive proof method' and 'coinductively defined set'. Other such instances are discussed. Fixed-point theory is used to explain coinduction and its duality with induction. A number of characterisations of inductive and coinductive sets are derived.

In Chapter 3 some common process operators are introduced. They impose a structure on processes and bring in concepts from algebra. The chapter offers numerous examples of the bisimulation proof method. An important result is an axiomatisation of bisimilarity, that is, an algebraic characterisation of bisimilarity on the term algebra generated by the operators.

In Chapter 4 bisimilarity is relaxed so as to allow some of the internal behaviour of systems to be ignored. The properties of the resulting notion – called weak bisimilarity – are examined and examples of the associated proof method are given. Weak bisimilarity is the form of bisimilarity mostly used in applications.

Chapters 5 and 6 delve into the topic of behavioural equivalences of processes. The main goal is to compare and contrast bisimilarity with other notions, for instance testing equivalence and failure equivalences, but also coinductive relations such as simulation (the asymmetric version of bisimilarity). It is interesting to see the different viewpoints that these other notions take on equality of behaviours. For instance, in testing equivalence two processes are deemed equal unless there is an experiment, or a test, that can separate them. Another goal of the chapters is to show that bisimilarity is mathematically stable and robust. For instance, the bisimilarity between the two processes of a language is not broken – under mild conditions – by extensions of the language; and equalities such as testing and failure equivalences may collapse to bisimilarity if the set of process operators allowed is rich enough. Chapter 6 is specifically devoted to simulation and like notions. In contrast with bisimilarity, similarity is a preorder, which is sometimes more handy than an equivalence. For instance, when comparing a specification and an implementation of a system, it may be that the specification has more non-determinism than the implementation: thus moving to the implementation involves a kind of deterministic reduction of the specified behaviour that is captured by a preorder but not by an equivalence.

The actions performed by the processes in the book are very simple: they just represent process synchronisations. When the actions are more complex, for instance involving exchange of values (e.g., exchange of communication ports, or exchange of processes), the meaning of bisimilarity may not be obvious. In Chapter 7 a method is shown for deriving bisimilarity that can be applied to virtually all languages whose terms are described by means of a grammar. The crux of the method is to set a bisimulation game in which the observer has a minimal ability to observe actions and/or states, and then to take the closure of this bisimulation under all contexts.

The concluding appendix offers solutions to most exercises in the book.

0.5 Basic definitions and mathematical notation

We adopt standard definitions and notations from set theory. A *set* is often defined by a property of its elements, and we write $\{x \mid x \text{ has the property}\}$ to denote the set consisting of all elements that enjoy the property. Moreover, $x \in X$ means that x is an element of the set X. *Set union* and *set intersection* are denoted by the symbols $\cup$ and $\cap$, respectively. The *difference* $X - Y$ between two sets X and Y is the set of elements that appear in X but not in Y. The *cartesian product* of two sets X and Y is written $X \times Y$ and denotes the set of all ordered pairs (x, y) where $x \in X$ and $y \in Y$. For a set X, we write X^n (with $n \geq 1$) for the cartesian product of n copies of X; the elements of X^n are the tuples $(x_1, \ldots, x_n)$ with each $x_i \in X$. We write $\wp$ to denote the *powerset* construct: if X is a set then $\wp(X)$ is the set of all subsets of X. A *predicate*, or a *property*, on a set X is subset of X.

We use the symbol $\stackrel{\text{def}}{=}$ for definitions. For instance, $P \stackrel{\text{def}}{=} E$, where E is some expression, means that P is defined to be, or stands for, the expression E. We use the symbol $=$ for syntactic equality; for instance, if P and Q are process expressions, then $P = Q$ means that the two expressions are syntactically identical. On sets (hence also on relations), equality is the standard set-theoretical notion; thus if X and Y are sets, then $X = Y$ means that X and Y have exactly the same elements.

A *relation* $\mathcal{R}$ between a set X and a set Y is a subset of $X \times Y$, that is, an element of $\wp(X \times Y)$. We often use the infix notation for relations; hence $P \, \mathcal{R} \, Q$ means $(P, Q) \in \mathcal{R}$. We use $\mathcal{R}, \mathcal{S}$ to range over relations. As relations are special sets, *relational inclusion*, $\mathcal{R}_1 \subseteq \mathcal{R}_2$, simply means that $(x, y) \in \mathcal{R}_1$ implies $(x, y) \in \mathcal{R}_2$. The *inverse* of a relation $\mathcal{R}$ is written $\mathcal{R}^{-1}$ and is the set $\{(x, y) \mid (y, x) \in \mathcal{R}\}$; thus if $\mathcal{R} \subseteq X \times Y$, then $\mathcal{R}^{-1} \subseteq Y \times X$. The *composition* of relations $\mathcal{R}_1 \subseteq X \times Y$ and $\mathcal{R}_2 \subseteq Y \times Z$ is the relation $\mathcal{R}_1 \mathcal{R}_2 \subseteq X \times Z$ defined thus:

$$\mathcal{R}_1 \mathcal{R}_2 \stackrel{\text{def}}{=} \{(x, z) \mid \text{there is } y \text{ such that } x \, \mathcal{R}_1 \, y \text{ and } y \, \mathcal{R}_2 \, z\}$$

We often consider *relations on a set* X; these are subsets of $X \times X$. Such a relation is

- *reflexive* if $x \mathrel{\mathcal{R}} x$, for all $x \in X$;
- *symmetric* if $x \mathrel{\mathcal{R}} x'$ implies $x' \mathrel{\mathcal{R}} x$;
- *transitive* if $x \mathrel{\mathcal{R}} x'$ and $x' \mathrel{\mathcal{R}} x''$ imply $x \mathrel{\mathcal{R}} x''$;
- *irreflexive* if there is no x with $x \mathrel{\mathcal{R}} x$;
- *antisymmetric* if $x \mathrel{\mathcal{R}} y$ and $y \mathrel{\mathcal{R}} x$ implies $x = y$;
- *total* if any pair of elements in the set are comparable ($x \mathrel{\mathcal{R}} y$ or $y \mathrel{\mathcal{R}} x$ holds, for all x and y);
- an *equivalence* if it is reflexive, symmetric and transitive;
- a *total order* if it is antisymmetric, transitive and total;
- a *partial order* if it is reflexive, antisymmetric and transitive;
- a *preorder* if it is reflexive and transitive;
- *well-founded* if there are no infinite descending chains

$$\ldots \mathcal{R} \; x_i \; \mathcal{R} \ldots \mathcal{R} \; x_1 \; \mathcal{R} \; x_0;$$

- *non-well-founded* if there are infinite descending chains.

The requirement of totality is the difference between total order and partial order; in the latter totality is replaced by the weaker reflexivity condition (totality implies reflexivity, hence any total order is a partial order). On preorders, antisymmetry is not needed; hence all partial orders are also preorders. Note that if $\mathcal{R}$ is well-founded then $\mathcal{R}$ must be irreflexive. Moreover, if $\mathcal{R}$ is a well-founded relation on X, then any non-empty subset S of X has at least one minimal element (an element x with $x \in S$ and such that there is no $y \in S$ with $y \mathrel{\mathcal{R}} x$). This is an immediate consequence of the well-foundedness of $\mathcal{R}$: if no elements in S were minimal, then $\mathcal{R}$ would not be well-founded, because, starting from any element x_0 of S we could build an infinite descending chain

$$\ldots \mathcal{R} \; x_n \ldots x_1 \; \mathcal{R} \; x_0$$

Special relations are indicated by means of dedicated symbols. For instance, $\mathcal{I}$ will be the identity relation, and $\sim$ the bisimilarity relation. If $\leftrightarrow$ is a relation symbol, then $\nleftrightarrow$ indicates the complement relation. For instance, $P \not\sim Q$ means that P and Q are not bisimilar.

The *transitive closure* of a relation $\mathcal{R}$, written $\mathcal{R}^+$, is the least transitive relation that contains $\mathcal{R}$. It is obtained by composing $\mathcal{R}$ with itself in all possible ways. Thus $x \mathrel{\mathcal{R}^+} x'$ if there are $n \geq 1$ and $x_0, \ldots, x_n$ with $x = x_0$, $x' = x_n$ and $x_i \mathrel{\mathcal{R}} x_{i+1}$ for all $0 \leq i < n$. Similarly, the *reflexive and transitive closure* of a relation $\mathcal{R}$, written $\mathcal{R}^\star$, is the least relation that is reflexive, transitive and contains $\mathcal{R}$. We have $\mathcal{R}^\star = \mathcal{R}^+ \cup \mathcal{I}$.

A *partition* of a set X is a set S of non-empty subsets of X such that each $x \in X$ belongs to exactly one member of S. An equivalence relation $\mathcal{R}$ on X determines a partition on X: a member of this partition is obtained by picking an element x of X and then taking the set $\{x' \mid x' \mathrel{\mathcal{R}} x\}$ (this set is also called the *equivalence class of x with respect to $\mathcal{R}$ in X*).

A *function* f from a set X to a set Y is written as $f : X \rightarrow Y$; then X is the *domain* of the function, and Y its *codomain*. The result of applying f to an argument x is written $f(x)$. A function f may also be seen as a relation, namely the relation with all pairs (x, y) such that $f(x) = y$. This view may be convenient in the case of *partial functions*, that is, functions that may be undefined on certain elements of their domain, as opposed to the *total functions*, which are defined on all elements of the domain. A function $f : X \rightarrow Y$ is

- *injective* if for all $x, x' \in X$, if $f(x) = f(x')$ then also $x = x'$;
- *surjective* if for all $y \in Y$ there is $x \in X$ with $f(x) = y$;
- *bijective* if it is both injective and surjective (that is, it establishes a one-to-one correspondence between the domain and the codomain sets).

An *endofunction* on a set X is a function from X to X. A function $f : X \times X \rightarrow X$ is sometimes written in infix notation as $x \, f \, x'$, in place of $f(x, x')$. The function is:

- *commutative* if for all x, x' it holds that $x \, f \, x' = x' \, f \, x$;
- *associative* if for all x, x', x'' it holds that $(x \, f \, x') \, f \, x'' = x \, f \, (x' \, f \, x'')$.

When f is associative, we can omit brackets in iterated applications of f as in $x_1 \, f \, x_2 \, f \ldots f \, x_n$.

A few times in the book we use constructions that operate on the *ordinal numbers*. We therefore recall here a few facts about the ordinals. These are an extension of the natural numbers to account for infinite sequences of objects. More precisely, they are used to reason on *well-ordered sets*, that is, sets equipped with a relation $\leq$ that is a well-founded total order.

The natural numbers, $\{0, 1, \ldots\}$ are the finite ordinals. The first infinite ordinal is written ω, and is the least ordinal above all natural numbers. It is a *limit* ordinal because it is not the successor of another ordinal: the set of all ordinals smaller than ω does not have a maximal element. From ω we can then go on with the sequence

$$\omega + 1, \omega + 2, \ldots, \omega + n, \ldots$$

which leads to the next limit ordinal, $\omega \times 2$. Similarly we obtain $\omega \times 3$, $\omega \times 4$, and so forth. The first ordinal above all ordinals of the form $\omega \times n + m$, where n and m are natural numbers, is ω^2. We can then continue with ω^3, ω^4, and so on to ω^ω; and then with the sequence

$$\omega^\omega, \omega^{\omega^\omega}, \omega^{\omega^{\omega^\omega}}, \ldots;$$

and then again we can continue indefinitely far towards larger ordinals.

Leaving aside the initial ordinal 0, the ordinals can be divided into *successor* ordinals (those that can be written as $\alpha + 1$, for some ordinal α) and *limit* ordinals (those for which the successor construction does not apply; a limit ordinal is the limit of its smaller ordinals, in a certain topological sense). This distinction is important for definitions and proofs by transfinite induction.

We sometimes use, informally, the term *extensional equality*. An equality on a set is extensional if it equates elements of the sets precisely when no observation can distinguish them. Of course, this hinges upon the meaning of observation, which in turn depends on the intended use of the elements in the set. For instance, on sets of lists of integers, an extensional equality should identify two lists if the sequences of integers they contain are the same. If the set contains processes, then an extensional equality should identify processes that cannot be distinguished by observing them, i.e., by interacting with them. There are different ways, however, of formalising the notion of observation, and these may lead to different equalities; an example is bisimilarity, other examples are discussed in Chapter 5 and the following chapters.

Acknowledgments

I am grateful to the following people for reading parts of a draft of the book and offering comments: Luca Aceto, Ferdinanda Camporesi, Yuxin Deng, Marcelo Fiore, Roberto Gorrieri, Sławomir Lasota, Fabrizio Montesi, Joachim Parrow, Jorge A. Perez, Andrew Pitts, Jan Rutten and Alan Schmitt. A special thank you to Claudio Sacerdoti Coen and to the students of the Bertinoro International Spring School (Bertinoro, Italy, 1–12 March 2010), in particular Livio Bioglio, Valerio Genovese, Lino Possamai and Enrico Scala. Thank you also to Emilka Bojanczyk for the cover design idea.

I would also like also to express my appreciation for the work of David Tranah and his colleagues at Cambridge University Press in guiding the book into print.

1

Towards bisimulation

We introduce bisimulation and coinduction roughly following the way that led to their discovery in Computer Science. Thus the general topic is the semantics of concurrent languages (or systems), in which several activities, the *processes*, may run concurrently. Central questions are: what is, mathematically, a process? And what does it mean that two processes are 'equal'? We seek notions of process and process equality that are both mathematically and practically interesting. For instance, the notions should be amenable to effective techniques for proving equalities, and the equalities themselves should be justifiable, according to the way processes are used.

We hope that the reader will find this way of proceeding helpful for understanding the meaning of bisimulation and coinduction. The emphasis on processes is also justified by the fact that concurrency remains today the main application area for bisimulation and coinduction.

We compare processes and functions in Section 1.1. We will see that processes do not fit the input/output schema of functions. A process has an interactive behaviour, and it is essential to take this into account. We formalise the idea of behaviour in Section 1.2 via labelled transition systems (LTSs), together with notations and terminology for them. We discuss the issue of equality between behaviours in Section 1.3. We first try to re-use notions of equality from Graph Theory and Automata Theory. The failure of these attempts leads us to proposing bisimilarity, in Section 1.4. We introduce the reader to the bisimulation proof method through a number of examples. More examples will be given in the following chapters, in particular Chapter 3, where we introduce a core language of processes. This will also serve us to see how an LTS can be associated with a language defined by means of a grammar. In the same Section 1.4 we establish a few basic properties of bisimilarity such as being an equivalence relation.

1.1 From functions to processes

If we begin investigating the semantics of concurrent languages, it is natural to check first whether we can adapt to these languages the concepts and techniques that are available for the *sequential* languages, i.e., the languages without constructs for concurrency. This is indeed what researchers did in the 1970s, as the work on the semantics of sequential languages had already produced significant results, notably with Scott and Stratchey's *denotational semantics*. In sequential languages, a program is interpreted as a function which transforms inputs into outputs. This idea is clear in the case of functional languages such as the λ-calculus, but it can also be applied to imperative languages, viewing a program as a function that transforms an initial store (i.e., a memory state) into a final store.

The interpretation of programs as functions, however, in general is unsatisfactory in concurrency. Take, as an example, the following two program fragments in an imperative language:

$$\mathtt{X} := 2 \quad \text{and} \quad \mathtt{X} := 1; \mathtt{X} := \mathtt{X} + 1.$$

They yield the same function from stores to stores, namely the function that leaves the store unchanged, except for the variable X whose final value must be 2. Therefore, in this view of programs-as-functions, the two fragments above are 'the same' and should be considered equal.

However, the above equality is troublesome if the language to which the two fragments belong is concurrent. For instance, suppose the language has a construct for parallelism, say $P|Q$, which, intuitively, allows the parallel execution of the two program arguments P and Q (this rough intuition is sufficient for the example). Then we may want to try running each fragment together with another fragment such as $\mathtt{X} := 2$. Formally, one says that the two fragments are used in the context

$$[\cdot] \,|\, \mathtt{X} := 2$$

to fill the hole $[\cdot]$. Now, if we place in the hole the first fragment, $\mathtt{X} := 2$, we get

$$\mathtt{X} := 2 \,|\, \mathtt{X} := 2,$$

which always terminates with $\mathtt{X} = 2$. This is not true, however, when the hole is filled with the second fragment, $\mathtt{X} := 1; \mathtt{X} := \mathtt{X} + 1$, resulting in

$$(\mathtt{X} := 1; \mathtt{X} := \mathtt{X} + 1) \,|\, \mathtt{X} := 2,$$

as now the final value of X can be different from 2. For instance, the final value can be 3 if the command $\mathtt{X} := 2$ is executed after $\mathtt{X} := 1$ but before $\mathtt{X} := \mathtt{X} + 1$.

The example shows that by viewing programs as functions we obtain a notion of program equality that is not preserved by parallel composition: equal arguments to the parallel construct can produce results that are not equal any more. In other words, we cannot define the meaning of a compound term based on the meaning of its constituent subterms. Formally, one says that the semantics is not *compositional*, or that the equality on programs is not a *congruence*.

A semantics of a language that is not compositional would not allow us to exploit the structure of the language when reasoning. We cannot, for instance, use properties of components to infer properties of larger systems, or optimise a program component by replacing it with an equal but simpler component, as the meaning of the whole program might change.

Another reason why viewing a concurrent program as a function is not appropriate is that a concurrent program may not terminate, and yet perform meaningful computations (examples are an operating system, the controllers of a nuclear station or of a railway system). In sequential languages, for instance in the λ-calculus, programs that do not terminate are undesirable; they are 'wrong', perhaps because of a loop for which the termination condition is erroneous. Mathematically, they represent functions that are undefined – hence meaningless – on some arguments.

Also, the behaviour of a concurrent program can be *non-deterministic*, as shown in the examples above. In sequential languages, operators for non-determinism, such as choice, can be dealt with using powersets and powerdomains. For instance, in the λ-calculus, the term $\lambda x.(x \oplus x + 1)$, where $\oplus$ indicates the (internal) choice construct, could be interpreted as the function that receives an integer x and returns an element from the set $\{x, x + 1\}$. This approach may work (and anyhow can become rather complicated) for pure non-determinism, but not for the parallelism resulting from the parallel execution of activities of the kind seen above.

If parallel programs are not functions, what are they? They are *processes*. But what is a process? When are two processes equal? These are very fundamental questions for a model of processes. They are also hard questions, and are at the heart of the research in concurrency theory. We shall approach these questions in the remainder of the book. Without the presumption of giving single and definitive answers, we shall strive to isolate the essential concepts.

1.2 Interaction and behaviour

In the example of Section 1.1, the program fragments

$$X := 2 \quad \text{and} \quad X := 1; \ X := X + 1$$

should be distinguished because they *interact* in a different way with the memory. The difference is harmless within a sequential language, as only the initial and final states are visible to the rest of the world. But if other concurrent entities have access to the same memory locations, then the patterns of the interactions with the memory become significant because they may affect other activities.

This brings up a key word: *interaction*. In concurrency, computation is interaction. Examples are: an access to a memory cell, a query to a database and the selection of a programme in a washing machine. The participants of an interaction are the *processes* (for instance, in the case of the washing machine, the machine itself and the person selecting the programme are the involved processes). The *behaviour* of a process should tell us *when* and *how* the process can interact with the outside world – its *environment*. Therefore we first need suitable means for representing the behaviour of a process.

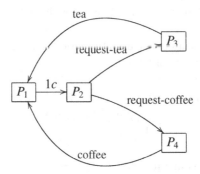

Fig. 1.1 The LTS of a vending machine.

In the book, we will consider a particularly simple case: the interactions of the process with its environment are pure handshake synchronisations, without exchange of values. We hope this will make the material easier to understand. The transport of the bisimulation concept to other interaction models is the main topic of Chapter 7.

1.2.1 Labelled transition systems

As another example of interactions, we consider a vending machine capable of dispensing tea or coffee for 1 coin ($1c$). The machine has a slot for inserting coins, a button for requesting coffee, another button for requesting tea, and an opening for collecting the beverage delivered. The behaviour of the machine is what we can observe, by interacting with the machine. This means experimenting with the machine: pressing buttons and seeing what happens. We can observe which buttons go down and when, which beverages we can get and when. Everything else, such as the colour or the shape of the machine, is irrelevant. We are interested in what the machine does, not in what it looks like. We can represent what is relevant of the behaviour of the machine as a *labelled transition system* (LTS), as shown graphically in Figure 1.1.

An LTS tells us what are the states in which a system can be and, for each state, the interactions that are possible from that state. An interaction is represented by a labelled arc; in the LTS terminology it is called a *transition*. In the case of the vending machine of Figure 1.1, there are four states. Initially the machine is in state P_1. The arc labelled $1c$ between P_1 and P_2 indicates that on state P_1 the machine accepts a coin and, in doing so, it evolves into the state P_2; in P_2 two further transitions are possible, one representing the request for coffee, the other the request for tea; and so on. Other examples of LTSs, in graphical form, are given in Figures 1.2–1.5.

LTSs are the most common structures used to represent the interactions that a system can produce. They are essentially labelled directed graphs. Variant structures that one finds in Computer Science are relational structures (i.e., unlabelled directed graphs) and Kripke structures (i.e., relational structures with an additional labelling function that specifies for each state a set of properties that hold at that state), and it is easy to adapt the concepts we will introduce, notably bisimulation, to them.

Definition 1.2.1 (Labelled transition system) A *labelled transition system* (LTS) is a triple $(Pr, Act, \longrightarrow)$ where Pr is a non-empty set called the *domain* of the LTS, Act is the set of *actions* (or *labels*), and $\longrightarrow \subseteq Pr \times Act \times Pr$ is the *transition relation*. $\square$

In the LTS of Figure 1.1, the domain is $\{P_1, P_2, P_3, P_4\}$, the actions are $\{1c$, request-tea, request-coffee, tea, coffee$\}$, the transition relation is $\{(P_1, 1c, P_2)$, $(P_2$, request-tea, $P_3)$, $(P_2$, request-coffee, $P_4)$, $(P_3$, tea, $P_1)$, $(P_4$, coffee, $P_1)\}$.

In the definition above, the elements of Pr are called *states* or *processes*. We will usually call them processes as this is the standard terminology in concurrency. We use P, Q, R to range over such elements, and μ to range over the labels in Act.

Remark 1.2.2 Sometimes students find puzzling the identifications between states and processes, and possibly also their relationship to the notion of behaviour. For instance, they may find it puzzling, on the vending machine of Figure 1.1, to say that 'P_1 is a process that by an interaction labelled $1c$ becomes the process P_2'. Any interacting system, that is, a system that may interact with its environment, is a process. The behaviour of the process specifies how and when the process may evolve into another one. At the beginning, the vending machine is an interacting system, hence a process, named P_1; after receiving a coin it is still an interacting system, hence a process, named P_2. The two processes P_1 and P_2 have different behaviours because they interact in different ways with the environment. $\square$

1.2.2 Notation and terminologies for LTSs

We write $P \xrightarrow{\mu} Q$ when $(P, \mu, Q) \in \longrightarrow$; in this case we call Q a μ-*derivative of* P, or sometimes simply a *derivative* of P. A transition $P \xrightarrow{\mu} Q$ indicates that process P accepts an interaction with the environment, in which P performs action μ and then becomes process Q. For each μ, $\xrightarrow{\mu}$ is a binary relation on processes; we will therefore apply to it notations and terminologies for relations.

The transition relation is extended to finite sequences of actions in the expected way. If s is the sequence $\mu_1 \cdots \mu_n$, then $P \xrightarrow{s} P'$ holds if there are $P_1, \ldots, P_{n-1}$ such that $P \xrightarrow{\mu_1} P_1 \cdots P_{n-1} \xrightarrow{\mu_n} P'$. In this case we say that P' is a *derivative of* P *under* $\mu_1 \cdots \mu_n$, or simply a *multi-step derivative* of P.

We write $P \xrightarrow{\mu}$ to mean that $P \xrightarrow{\mu} P'$ holds, for some P', and $P \not\xrightarrow{\mu}$ if no such P' exists. Also, $P \xrightarrow{s}\xrightarrow{\mu} P'$ holds if there is some P'' such that $P \xrightarrow{s} P''$ and $P'' \xrightarrow{\mu} P'$.

Definition 1.2.3 Given an LTS $\mathcal{L}$, the *LTS generated by a process* P *of* $\mathcal{L}$ has as states the multi-step derivatives of P, as actions those of $\mathcal{L}$, and as transitions those in $\mathcal{L}$ that relate the multi-step derivatives of P. $\square$

We introduce some special classes of LTSs that we will occasionally use.

Definition 1.2.4 (Image-finite relation)   A relation $\mathcal{R}$ on a set S is *image-finite* if for all $s \in S$, the set $\{s' \mid s\ \mathcal{R}\ s'\}$ is finite. □

Definition 1.2.5 (Classes of LTSs and processes)   An LTS is:

- *image-finite* if for each μ the relation $\xrightarrow{\mu}$ is image-finite (that is, for all P and μ, the set $\{P' \mid P \xrightarrow{\mu} P'\}$ is finite);
- *finitely branching* if it is image-finite and, moreover, for each P, the set $\{\mu \mid P \xrightarrow{\mu}\}$ is finite;
- *finite-state* if it has a finite number of states;
- *finite* if it is finite-state and acyclic (in other words, there is no infinite sequence of transitions $P_0 \xrightarrow{\mu_0} P_1 \xrightarrow{\mu_1} P_2 \xrightarrow{\mu_2} \cdots$);
- *deterministic* when all processes are deterministic, where a process P is deterministic if for each μ, $P \xrightarrow{\mu} P'$ and $P \xrightarrow{\mu} P''$ imply $P' = P''$.

The above definitions are extended to *processes* by considering the LTSs generated by the processes. (For instance, a process P of an LTS $\mathcal{L}$ is *image-finite* if the LTS generated by P is image-finite.) □

Exercise 1.2.6   Show that finite-state implies finitely branching, if the set of actions is finite; and deterministic implies image-finite. Show also that the converse of each such implication does not hold and, similarly, image-finite does not imply finitely branching. □

In the literature sometimes the definitions of 'finite' and 'finite-state' include a finiteness assumption on the actions that can be performed (e.g., the 'finitely-branching' condition). This difference does not affect the contents of the book.

Definition 1.2.7 (Sort)   We say that μ is in the *sort* of P, written $\mu \in \mathrm{sort}(P)$, if there is a sequence of actions s and a process P' such that $P \xrightarrow{s} \xrightarrow{\mu} P'$. □

In the remainder, we usually do not explicitly indicate the LTS for the processes we write.

1.3 Equality of behaviours

LTSs tell us what the behaviour of processes is. The next question now is: when should two behaviours be considered equal? That is, what does it mean that two processes are equivalent? Intuitively, two processes should be equivalent if they cannot be distinguished by interacting with them. In the following sections we try to formalise this – very vague – statement.

1.3.1 Equality in Graph Theory: isomorphism

We have observed that LTSs resemble graphs. We could therefore draw inspiration for our notion of behavioural equality from Graph Theory. The standard equality on graphs

Fig. 1.2 Non-isomorphic LTSs.

is *graph isomorphism*. (In mathematics, two structures are isomorphic if a bijection can be established on their components; on graphs the components are the states and the transitions.) Is this notion satisfactory for us?

Certainly, if two LTSs are isomorphic then we expect that the corresponding states give rise to the same interactions and should indeed be regarded as equal. What about the converse, however? Consider the LTSs in Figure 1.2, and the interactions that are possible from the initial processes P_1 and Q_1. Both processes just allow us to repeat the sequence of interactions a, b, ad infinitum. It is undeniable that the two processes cannot be distinguished by interactions. However, there is no isomorphism on the two LTSs, as they have quite different shapes.

We have to conclude that graph isomorphism is too strong as a behavioural equivalence for processes: it prevents us from equating processes like P_1 and Q_1 that should be considered equal.

1.3.2 Equality in Automata Theory: trace equivalence

LTSs also remind us of something very important in Computer Science: *automata*. The main difference between automata (precisely, we are thinking of non-deterministic automata here) and LTSs is that an automaton has also a distinguished state designated as *initial*, and a set of distinguished states designated as *final*. Automata Theory is well established in Computer Science; it is therefore worth pausing on it for a moment, to see how the question of equality of behaviours is treated there.

Automata are string recognisers. A string, say $a_1, \ldots, a_n$, is accepted by an automaton if its initial state has a derivative under $a_1, \ldots, a_n$ that is among the final states. Two automata are equal if they accept the same language, i.e., the same set of strings. (See, e.g., [HMU06], for details on automata theory.)

The analogous equivalence on processes is called *trace equivalence*. It equates two processes P and Q if they can perform the same finite sequences of transitions; precisely, if P has a sequence $P \xrightarrow{\mu_1} P_1 \cdots P_{n-1} \xrightarrow{\mu_n} P_n$ then there should be $Q_1, \ldots, Q_n$ with $Q \xrightarrow{\mu_1} Q_1 \cdots Q_{n-1} \xrightarrow{\mu_n} Q_n$, and the converse on the transitions from Q. Examples of equivalent automata are given in Figures 1.3 and 1.4, where P_1 and Q_1 are the initial states, and for simplicity we assume that all states are final. As processes, P_1 and Q_1 are indeed trace equivalent. These equalities are reasonable and natural on automata.

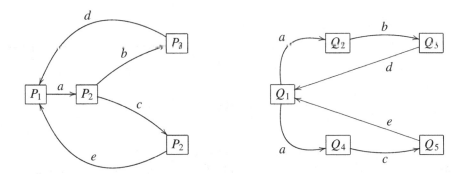

Fig. 1.3 Example for trace equivalence.

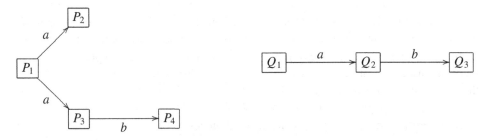

Fig. 1.4 Another example for trace equivalence.

However, processes are used in a quite different way with respect to automata. For instance, a string is considered 'accepted' by an automaton if the string gives us *at least one* path from the initial state to a final state; the existence of other paths that fail (i.e., that lead to non-final states) is irrelevant. This is crucial for the equalities in Figures 1.3 and 1.4. For instance, in Figure 1.4, the automaton on the left has a successful path for the string ab, in which the bottom a-transition is taken. But it has also a failing path, along the upper a-transition. In contrast, the automaton on the right only has a successful path. Such differences matter when we interpret the machines as processes. If we wish to press the button a and then the button b of the machine, then our interaction with the machine on the right will always succeed. In contrast, our interaction with the machine on the left may fail. We may indeed reach a deadlock, in which we try to press the button b but the machine refuses such interaction. We cannot possibly consider two processes 'the same' when one, and only one of them, can cause a deadlock!

As another example, the equality between the two automata in Figure 1.3 is rewritten in Figure 1.5 using the labels of the vending machine of Figure 1.1. It is certainly not the same to have the first or the second machine in an office! When we insert a coin in the machine on the right, the resulting state can be either Q_2 or Q_4. We have no control over this: the machine, non-deterministically, decides. At the end, if we want to have a beverage at all, we must accept whatever the machine offers us. In contrast, the machine on the left always

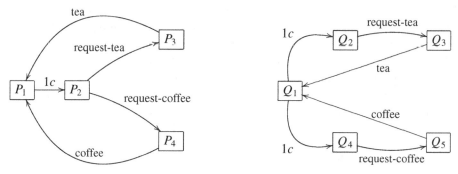

Fig. 1.5 Two vending machines.

leaves us the choice of our favourite beverage. In concurrency, in contrast with automata theory, the timing of a branch in the transition graph can be important.

In conclusion, we also reject trace equivalence as behavioural equality for processes. (Trace equivalence has, however, applications in concurrency. For instance, on deterministic processes and for verification of so-called 'safety' properties, see Exercise 5.7.8.)

1.4 Bisimulation

In the previous sections we saw that the behavioural equality we seek should:

- imply a tighter correspondence between transitions than trace equivalence;
- be based on the information that the transitions convey, as opposed to the shape of the LTSs as in LTS isomorphism.

Intuitively, what does it mean then that two machines have the same behaviour? When we do something with one machine, we must be able to do the same with the other and, on the two states that the machines evolve to, the same is again true. This is the idea of equality that we are going to formalise. It is called *bisimilarity*.

Definition 1.4.1 A *process relation* is a binary relation on the states of an LTS. □

Definition 1.4.2 (Bisimilarity) A process relation $\mathcal{R}$ is a *bisimulation* if, whenever $P \mathcal{R} Q$, for all μ we have:

(1) for all P' with $P \xrightarrow{\mu} P'$, there is Q' such that $Q \xrightarrow{\mu} Q'$ and $P' \mathcal{R} Q'$;
(2) the converse, on the transitions emanating from Q, i.e., for all Q' with $Q \xrightarrow{\mu} Q'$, there is P' such that $P \xrightarrow{\mu} P'$ and $P' \mathcal{R} Q'$.

Bisimilarity, written $\sim$, is the union of all bisimulations; thus $P \sim Q$ holds if there is a bisimulation $\mathcal{R}$ with $P \mathcal{R} Q$. □

Note in clause (1) the universal quantifier followed by the existential one: P, on all its transitions, challenges Q; and in each one of these transitions Q is called to find a match. The same occurs in clause (?), with the roles of P and Q swapped.

The definition of bisimilarity immediately suggests a proof technique: to demonstrate that P and Q are bisimilar, find a bisimulation relation containing the pair (P, Q). This is the *bisimulation proof method*, and is, by far, the most common method used for proving bisimilarity results. It is useful to examine some examples, and to get some practice with the proof method, before exploring the theory of bisimilarity.

Remark 1.4.3 Note that bisimulation and bisimilarity are defined on a single LTS, whereas in the previous (informal) examples the processes compared were taken from two distinct LTSs. Having a single LTS is convenient, for instance to ensure that the alphabet of actions is the same, and to compare processes from the same LTS. Moreover, we do not lose generality, as the union of two LTSs is again an LTS. □

Example 1.4.4 Suppose we want to prove that $P_1 \sim Q_1$, for P_1 and Q_1 as in Figure 1.2. We have to find a relation $\mathcal{R}$ containing the pair (P_1, Q_1). We thus place (P_1, Q_1) in $\mathcal{R}$. For $\mathcal{R}$ to be a bisimulation, all (multi-step) derivatives of P_1 and Q_1 must appear in $\mathcal{R}$ – those of P_1 in the first component of the pairs, those of Q_1 in the second. We note that P_2 does not appear; hence at least we should add a pair containing it. For this, it is natural to pick (P_2, Q_2). Thus we have $\mathcal{R} = \{(P_1, Q_1), (P_2, Q_2)\}$. Is this a bisimulation? Obviously not, as a derivative of Q_2, namely Q_3, is uncovered. Suppose, however, we did not notice this, and tried to prove that $\mathcal{R}$ is a bisimulation. We have to check clauses (1) and (2) of Definition 1.4.2 on each pair in $\mathcal{R}$. As an example, we consider clause (1) on the pair (P_1, Q_1). The only transition from P_1 is $P_1 \xrightarrow{a} P_2$; this is matched by Q_1 via transition $Q_1 \xrightarrow{a} Q_2$, for $(P_2, Q_2) \in \mathcal{R}$ as required. However, the checks on (P_2, Q_2) fail, since, for instance, the transition $P_2 \xrightarrow{b} P_1$ cannot be matched by Q_2, whose only transition is $Q_2 \xrightarrow{b} Q_3$ and the pair (P_1, Q_3) does not appear in $\mathcal{R}$. (Note: if we added to the LTS a transition $Q_2 \xrightarrow{b} Q_1$ this problem would disappear, as $(P_1, Q_1) \in \mathcal{R}$ and therefore the new transition could now match the challenge from P_2; however $\mathcal{R}$ would still not be a bisimulation; why?) We realise that we have to add the pair (P_1, Q_3) to $\mathcal{R}$. We let the reader check that now $\mathcal{R}$ is indeed a bisimulation.

The reader may also want to check that the relation $\mathcal{R}$ above remains a bisimulation also when we add the transition $Q_2 \xrightarrow{b} Q_1$. □

In the example above, we found a bisimulation after an unsuccessful attempt, which, however, guided us towards the missing pairs. This way of proceeding is common: trying to prove a bisimilarity $P \sim Q$, one starts with a relation containing at least the pair (P, Q) as an initial guess for a bisimulation; then, checking the bisimulation clauses, one may find that the relation is not a bisimulation because some pairs are missing. These pairs (and possibly others) are added, resulting in a new guess for a bisimulation; and so on, until a bisimulation is found.

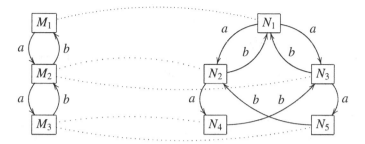

Fig. 1.6 Graphical representation of a bisimulation.

An important hint to bear in mind when using the bisimulation proof method is to look for bisimulations 'as small as possible'. A smaller bisimulation, with fewer pairs, reduces the amount of work needed for checking the bisimulation clauses. For instance, in the example above, we could have used, in place of $\mathcal{R}$, the relation $\mathcal{R} \cup \mathcal{I} \cup \{(Q_1, Q_3)\}$, where $\mathcal{I}$ is the identity relation. This also is a bisimulation, and contains the pair $\{(P_1, Q_1)\}$ we are interested in, but it has more pairs and therefore requires more work in proofs. Reducing the size of the relation to exhibit, and hence relieving the proof work needed to establish bisimilarity results, is the motivation for the enhancements of the bisimulation proof method discussed in [PS12].

When one has little familiarity with the bisimulation method and is trying to understand whether two processes are bisimilar, it may be convenient to draw the connections among the related states of the LTSs. This is done in Figure 1.6, where the bisimulation drawn to prove $M_1 \sim N_1$ is

$$\{(M_1, N_1), (M_2, N_2), (M_2, N_3), (M_3, N_4), (M_3, N_5)\}.$$

Example 1.4.5 Suppose we want to prove $Q_1 \sim R_1$, for Q_1 as in Figure 1.2 and R_1 as below.

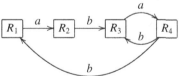

Proceeding as Example 1.4.4, our initial guess for a bisimulation is the following relation:

$$\{(Q_1, R_1), (Q_2, R_2), (Q_3, R_3), (Q_2, R_4)\}.$$

This may seem reasonable, as all the states in the LTS are covered. However, this relation is not a bisimulation: clause (2) of Definition 1.4.2 fails on the pair (Q_2, R_4), for the transition $R_4 \xrightarrow{b} R_1$ has no match from Q_2. We thus add the pair (Q_3, R_1). The reader may check that this produces a bisimulation. □

Example 1.4.6 Suppose we want to prove that processes P_1 and Q_1 in Figure 1.4 are *not* bisimilar. We can show that no bisimulations exist that contain such a pair. Suppose $\mathcal{R}$

were such a bisimulation. Then it should also relate the derivative P_2 of P_1 to a derivative of Q_1; the only possible such derivative is Q_2; but then, on the pair (P_2, Q_2), clause (2) of Definition 1.4.2 fails, as only Q_2 has a transition.

Other useful methods for proving results of non-bisimilarity will be shown in Section 2.10.2, using the approximants of bisimilarity, and in Section 2.12, using games. □

Notation 1.4.7 In the remainder we often depict LTSs as rooted graphs (or just trees) in which the nodes have no names, as in Figure 1.7. When we discuss whether two such trees are behaviourally equivalent, it is intended that we refer to the roots of the trees. For instance, in Figure 1.7 asserting that P_2 and Q_2 are not bisimilar means that the roots of the two trees are non-bisimilar processes. □

Exercise 1.4.8 Reasoning as in Example 1.4.6, show that the processes P_2, Q_2 and R_2 of Figure 1.7 are pairwise non-bisimilar. □

Exercise 1.4.9 The same as Exercise 1.4.8, for the processes P_3, Q_3 and R_3 of Figure 1.7. □

Exercise 1.4.10 ($\hookrightarrow$) Find an LTS with only two states, and in a bisimulation relation with the states of following LTS:

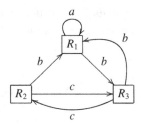

The next exercise involves processes with some non-trivial non-determinism, and may therefore be helpful (together with the following Exercise 1.4.12) for understanding the roles of the universal and existential quantifiers in the the definition of bisimulation.

Exercise 1.4.11 ($\hookrightarrow$) Consider the following LTSs:

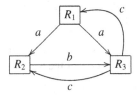
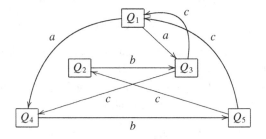

Show that R_1 and Q_1 are bisimilar. □

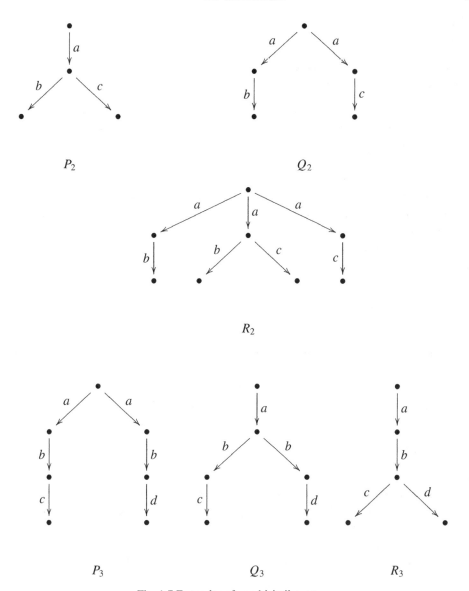

Fig. 1.7 Examples of non-bisimilar processes.

Exercise 1.4.12 ($\hookrightarrow$) Suppose the existential quantifiers in the definition of bisimulation were replaced by universal quantifiers. For instance, clause (1) would become:

- for all P' with $P \xrightarrow{\mu} P'$, and for all Q' such that $Q \xrightarrow{\mu} Q'$, we have $P' \mathcal{R} Q'$;

and similarly for clause (2). Would the process Q_2 of Figure 1.7 be bisimilar with itself? What do you think bisimilarity would become? □

Two features of the definition of bisimulation make its proof method practically interesting:

- the *locality* of the checks on the states;
- the lack of a *hierarchy* on the pairs of the bisimulation.

The checks are local because we only look at the immediate transitions that emanate from the states. An example of a behavioural equality that is non-local is trace equivalence (that we encountered when discussing automata). It is non-local because computing a sequence of transitions starting from a state s may require examining other states, different from s.

There is no hierarchy on the pairs of a bisimulation in that no temporal order on the checks is required: all pairs are on a par. As a consequence, bisimilarity can be effectively used to reason about infinite or circular objects. This is in sharp contrast with inductive techniques, that require a hierarchy, and that therefore are best suited for reasoning about finite objects. For instance, here is a definition of equality that is local but inherently inductive:

- $P = Q$ if, for all μ:
  - for all P' with $P \xrightarrow{\mu} P'$, there is Q' such that $Q \xrightarrow{\mu} Q'$ and $P' = Q'$;
  - the converse, on the transitions from Q.

This definition requires a hierarchy, as the checks on the pair (P, Q) must follow those on derivative pairs such as (P', Q'): the meaning of equal on (P, Q) requires having already established the meaning of equal on the derivatives. Hence the definition is ill-founded if the state space of the derivatives reachable from (P, Q) is infinite or includes loops. We shall find hierarchical characterisations of $\sim$, refining the idea above, in Section 2.10.2.

Exercise 1.4.13 (Recommended, $\hookrightarrow$)

(1) Show that the union of two bisimulations on a given LTS is also a bisimulation. (We require that the LTS is the same to ensure the consistency the two bisimulations: if a state appears in both bisimulations then the transitions assumed for it must be the same.) Generalise the statement to show that if $\{\mathcal{R}_i\}_i$ is a set of bisimulations on the LTS, then $\cup_i \mathcal{R}_i$ is also a bisimulation.
(2) Show that, in contrast, the intersection of two bisimulations need not be a bisimulation.

□

Some (very) basic properties of bisimilarity are exposed in Theorems 1.4.14 and 1.4.15. Their proofs are good examples of application of the bisimulation proof method.

Theorem 1.4.14

(1) $\sim$ *is an equivalence relation, i.e. the following holds:*
   (a) $P \sim P$ *(reflexivity);*
   (b) $P \sim Q$ *implies* $Q \sim P$ *(symmetry);*
   (c) $P \sim Q$ *and* $Q \sim R$ *imply* $P \sim R$ *(transitivity);*
(2) $\sim$ *itself is a bisimulation.*

Proof

(1) For reflexivity, one shows that the identity relation, that is the relation $\{(P, P) \mid P \text{ is a process}\}$, is a bisimulation.

For symmetry, one shows that if $\mathcal{R}$ is a bisimulation then so is its converse $\mathcal{R}^{-1}$; we let the reader prove this fact. Then if $P \sim Q$, by definition of $\sim$ there is a bisimulation $\mathcal{R}$ with $P \mathcal{R} Q$. We also have $Q \mathcal{R}^{-1} P$. By the previous fact, $\mathcal{R}^{-1}$ is a bisimulation. Hence $Q \sim P$.

For transitivity, one shows that if $\mathcal{R}_1$ and $\mathcal{R}_2$ are bisimulations, then so is their composition, that is the relation

$$\mathcal{R} \stackrel{\text{def}}{=} \{(P, R) \mid \text{there is } Q \text{ with } P \mathcal{R}_1 Q \text{ and } Q \mathcal{R}_2 R\}.$$

The proof is simple. Take $(P, Q) \in \mathcal{R}$. Suppose $P \stackrel{\mu}{\to} P'$ (the case when R makes the challenge is similar). Then, as $P \mathcal{R}_1 Q$ and $\mathcal{R}_1$ is a bisimulation, there is Q' with $Q \stackrel{\mu}{\to} Q'$ and $P' \mathcal{R}_1 Q'$. As $\mathcal{R}_2$ is a bisimulation too and $Q \mathcal{R}_2 R$, there must also be R' with $R \stackrel{\mu}{\to} R'$ and $Q' \mathcal{R}_2 R'$. We have thus found a transition from R matching the initial one from P; moreover the derivatives are in $\mathcal{R}$.

Having proved that the composition of bisimulations is again a bisimulation we can conclude the proof of transitivity. If $P \sim Q$ and $Q \sim R$, there must be bisimulations $\mathcal{R}_1$ and $\mathcal{R}_2$ with $P \mathcal{R}_1 Q$ and $Q \mathcal{R}_2 R$. The composition of $\mathcal{R}_1$ and $\mathcal{R}_2$ is again a bisimulation, and contains the pair (P, R). We can therefore conclude $P \sim R$.

(2) Follows from Exercise 1.4.13(1), as bisimilarity is the union of all bisimulations.

□

The second item of Theorem 1.4.14 brings us the impredicative flavour of the definition of bisimilarity: bisimilarity itself is a bisimulation and is therefore part of the union from which it is defined.[1] The item thus also gives us:

Theorem 1.4.15 $\sim$ *is the largest bisimulation, i.e., the largest relation $\sim$ on processes such that $P \sim Q$ implies, for all μ:*

(1) *for all P' with $P \stackrel{\mu}{\to} P'$, there is Q' such that $Q \stackrel{\mu}{\to} Q'$ and $P' \sim Q'$;*
(2) *for all Q' with $Q \stackrel{\mu}{\to} Q'$, there is P' such that $P \stackrel{\mu}{\to} P'$ and $P' \sim Q'$.* □

Bisimulation can also be defined on sequences of actions, but we then lose the benefits of the local checks.

Exercise 1.4.16 (Recommended, $\hookrightarrow$) Show that $\mathcal{R}$ is a bisimulation if and only if the following holds. Whenever $P \mathcal{R} Q$:

(1) for all P' and sequences s with $P \stackrel{s}{\to} P'$, there is Q' such that $Q \stackrel{s}{\to} Q'$ and $P' \mathcal{R} Q'$;
(2) the converse, on the actions from Q. □

---

[1] In logic, a definition is called *impredicative* when it involves quantification over a set containing the very object being defined.

Exercise 1.4.17 ($*$, Recommended, $\hookrightarrow$) **(Similarity)** A process relation $\mathcal{R}$ is a *simulation* if, whenever $P \mathrel{\mathcal{R}} Q$:

(1) for all P' and μ with $P \xrightarrow{\mu} P'$, there is Q' such that $Q \xrightarrow{\mu} Q'$ and $P' \mathrel{\mathcal{R}} Q'$.

Similarity, written $\leq$, is the union of all simulations; thus we say that Q *simulates* P if $P \leq Q$. The equivalence $\leq\geq$ induced by $\leq$ is called *simulation equivalence*; $P \leq\geq Q$ holds if both $P \leq Q$ and $Q \leq P$.

The difference with bisimulation is that in a simulation the converse of clause (1) is missing. Show that:

(1) $\mathcal{R}$ is a bisimulation iff $\mathcal{R}$ and $\mathcal{R}^{-1}$ are both simulations.
(2) If P is a process without transitions, then $P \leq Q$, for all Q.
(3) $Q_2 \leq P_2$, where P_2, Q_2 are the processes in Figure 1.7.
(4) Does the converse of the two points above hold?
(5) $\leq$ is reflexive and transitive.
(6) $\sim$ is strictly included in $\leq\geq$.
(7) $\leq\geq$ is strictly included in trace equivalence. (Hint: consider again P_2, Q_2 of Figure 1.7.)

$\square$

Exercise 1.4.18 ($*$, Recommended, $\hookrightarrow$) **(Bisimulation up-to $\sim$)** A process relation $\mathcal{R}$ is a *bisimulation up-to* $\sim$ if, whenever $P \mathrel{\mathcal{R}} Q$, for all μ we have:

(1) for all P' with $P \xrightarrow{\mu} P'$, there is Q' such that $Q \xrightarrow{\mu} Q'$ and $P' \sim\mathcal{R}\sim Q'$;
(2) the converse, on the transitions emanating from Q, i.e., for all Q' with $Q \xrightarrow{\mu} Q'$, there is P' such that $P \xrightarrow{\mu} P'$ and $P' \sim\mathcal{R}\sim Q'$.

(We recall that, following the notation for relational composition, $P' \sim\mathcal{R}\sim Q'$ holds if there are P'' and Q'' such that $P' \sim P''$, $P'' \mathrel{\mathcal{R}} Q''$, and $Q'' \sim Q'$.)

Show that if $\mathcal{R}$ is a bisimulation up-to $\sim$, then $\mathcal{R} \subseteq \sim$. (Hint: Prove that $\sim \mathcal{R} \sim$ is a bisimulation.)

$\square$

The result of Exercise 1.4.18 can be used to make the bisimulation proof method more powerful. It is in fact an example of the enhancements of the bisimulation proof method, called 'up-to techniques', discussed in [PS12].

1.4.1 Towards coinduction

The assertion of Theorem 1.4.15 could even be taken as the definition of $\sim$ (though we should first show that the largest relation mentioned in the statement does exist). It looks, however, like a circular definition. This seems strange: what kind of proof technique is it? Also, we claimed that we can prove $(P, Q) \in \sim$ by showing that $(P, Q) \in \mathcal{R}$ and $\mathcal{R}$ is a *bisimulation relation*, that is, a relation that satisfies the same clauses as $\sim$. This seems strange: what kind of proof technique is it?

There is a sharp contrast with the usual, familiar *inductive definitions* and *inductive proofs*. In the case of induction, there is always a basis, i.e., something to start from, and then, in the inductive part, one builds on top of what one has obtained so far. Indeed, the above definition of $\sim$, and its proof technique, are not inductive, but *coinductive*.

It is good to stop for a while, to get a grasp of the meaning of coinduction, and a feeling of the duality between induction and coinduction. This will be useful for relating the idea of bisimilarity to other concepts, and it will also allow us to derive a few results for bisimilarity. We do this in Chapter 2.

2

Coinduction and the duality with induction

After introducing bisimulation on processes in the previous chapter, we see here other examples of predicates and relations that are defined in a similar style, and proof techniques for them. This style is quite different with respect to that of ordinary inductive definitions and proofs. It is in fact the style of *coinduction*. Through the examples we will begin to build up some intuition about the difference between coinduction and induction. Then we will make these intuitions formal, using fixed-point theory.

Intuitively, a set A is defined *coinductively* if it is the *greatest* solution of an inequation of a certain form; then the *coinduction proof principle* just says that any set that is solution of the same inequation *is contained* in A. Dually, a set A is defined *inductively* if it is the *least* solution of an inequation of a certain form, and the *induction proof principle* then says that any other set that is solution to the same inequation *contains* A. As we will see, familiar inductive definitions and proofs can be formalised in this way.

An abstract formalisation of the meaning of coinduction is not necessary for applications. In the previous chapter, for instance, we have seen that bisimulation can be defined on processes without talking about fixed points. But the theory of fixed points allows us to understand what we are doing, and to understand the analogies among different worlds. It is also useful to re-use results: an example is the characterisation of bisimilarity via an inductive stratification that can be derived from a theorem of fixed-point theory; the same theorem underpins similar stratification results for other coinductive definitions.

The central ingredient for our explanation of induction and coinduction is the Fixed-point Theorem, which says that monotone functions in complete lattices have a least and a greatest fixed point. Inductive and coinductive sets will be special cases of such fixed points. The theorem also immediately gives us induction and coinduction proof principles. These schemata for induction and coinduction can be used to justify the definition of bisimulation and its proof method, as well as familiar inductive concepts such as mathematical induction and rule induction.

Other characterisations of inductive and coinductive sets are derived throughout the chapter: as limits of sequences of points obtained by repeatedly applying certain functions to the bottom or top elements of complete lattices; as sets defined by means of rules; as sets of elements with a well-founded or a non-well-founded proof; and finally characterisations

28

in terms of games. Different characterisations contribute to a better grasp of the concepts and may play a role on their own in applications.

In the chapter we discuss forms of induction and coinduction produced by monotone functions. A theory of induction and coinduction could also be developed for non-monotone functions, but it would be more complex. It is ignored in this book; see, however, Remarks 2.4.4 and 2.5.1.

We introduce examples of inductive and coinductive definitions in Section 2.1: finite and ω-traces of processes, convergence and divergence in the (call-by-name) λ-calculus, finite and infinite lists. Thus the duality between induction and coinduction begins to emerge; we comment on this in Section 2.2. We formalise the duality in Section 2.3, by means of the theory of fixed points in complete lattices. We can thus state, in Section 2.4, the meaning of inductively and coinductively defined sets and formulate the induction and coinduction proof principles. In Section 2.5, we show how a set of axioms and inference rules defines monotone functions on complete lattices. This allows us to derive inductive and coinductive interpretations for the rules, from fixed-point theory. Similarly we derive proof principles for the rules, called *rule induction* and *rule coinduction*. In Section 2.6, we go back to the examples considered earlier in the chapter (process traces, convergence and divergence in the λ-calculus, and lists). These examples had been presented in terms of rules, and only discussed informally. We can now revise the examples in the light of the formalisation of induction and coinduction for rules in the previous sections. In Section 2.7, first we show that, similarly to what we did for rule induction, we can use fixed-point theory to justify common inductive techniques such as *mathematical induction* (induction on the natural numbers), *structural induction* (induction on the structure of objects), *induction on derivation proofs* (induction on the proof tree with which some object is derived), *transition induction* (induction on the derivation of the transition of a process), *well-founded induction* (induction on a well-founded relation). Then we discuss, by means of examples, how induction and coinduction allow definitions of functions by recursion and corecursion. We conclude with examples of variants of the characterisations of least and greatest fixed points in the Fixed-point Theorem, with the purpose of obtaining enhancements of the basic induction and coinduction principles.

The Fixed-point Theorem in Section 2.3 talks about least and greatest fixed points of monotone functions, but does not tell us how to reach such fixed points. We show how to obtain, constructively, these fixed points in Section 2.8, via iterations over the natural and the ordinal numbers. For this we make extensive use of inductive principles introduced in the previous sections. We examine the meaning of the iterative constructions in the case of definitions by means of rules in Section 2.9.

In Section 2.10 we describe how the fixed-point theory in the earlier sections applies to bisimulation, the main coinductive object in the book. Thus we derive bisimilarity and the bisimulation proof methods as instances of a definition by coinduction and of its corresponding proof method. We also examine the iteration schemata for constructive characterisations of bisimilarity.

We conclude the chapter with two further perspectives on inductively and coinductively defined sets: in Section 2.11 we examine their duality from the point of view of the proof of the membership of an element in the set; and in Section 2.12 we present game-theoretic perspectives. In Sections 2.13 and 2.14 we discuss the meaning of the game-theoretic characterisation of bisimulation.

The chapter contains many exercises with solutions. We invite the reader novel to fixed-point theory to try them, or anyhow to consult the solutions.

2.1 Examples of induction and coinduction

We begin with some examples, described informally, in which we contrast induction with coinduction. We will continue the examples, with a formal treatment, in Section 2.6.

2.1.1 Finite traces and ω-traces on processes

As an example of an inductive definition, we consider a property akin to termination. For simplicity, we assume some finiteness condition on the LTS of the processes, such as image-finiteness. A *stopped process* cannot do any transitions (i.e., $P \xrightarrow{\mu}$ for all μ). A process P has *a finite trace*, written $P \downarrow$, if P has a finite sequence of transitions that lead to a stopped process as final derivative. Predicate $\downarrow$ has a natural inductive definition, using the following rules:

$$\frac{P \text{ stopped}}{P \downarrow} \qquad\qquad \frac{P \xrightarrow{\mu} P' \quad P' \downarrow}{P \downarrow}$$

When we say that $\downarrow$ is the predicate inductively defined by the rules, we mean that $P \downarrow$ holds if P is generated by the rules, in the usual inductive way: P can be derived from the rules in a finite number of steps. We can indeed obtain the set of all processes with a finite trace by means of the following construction. We start with the empty set $\emptyset$. Then we add to the set the conclusions of the the first rule of $\downarrow$, the axiom; these are the stopped processes. Then we continue with the second rule of $\downarrow$, the inference rule, by repeatedly adding to the set a process P if it has a transition $P \xrightarrow{\mu} P'$ to a process P' that is already in the set. If the LTS is finite-state, this iteration terminates and the final set is $\downarrow$. (We will prove in Section 2.9 that if the number of processes is infinite, the construction is still valid but $\downarrow$ is found as the limit of an infinite iteration.)

An equivalent formulation is to say that $\downarrow$ is the *smallest* set of processes that is *closed forward under the rules*; i.e., the smallest subset T of Pr (the processes) such that:

- all stopped processes are in T;
- if there is μ such that $P \xrightarrow{\mu} P'$ for some $P' \in T$, then also $P \in T$.

The closure is 'forward' because we follow the rules in the direction from the premises to the conclusion: whenever the premises of a rule are satisfied, then its conclusion must be satisfied too.

We will prove later that this formulation is equivalent to the above iterative construction. But we can already grasp something of it: it is not difficult to see that the set resulting from the iteration is closed forward under the rules, and that all processes in the set are necessary for the closure.

While the iterative presentation is useful for constructing the inductive set, the new formulation gives us a proof principle for $\lfloor$: given a predicate T on the processes, to prove that all processes in $\lfloor$ are also in T it suffices to show that T is closed forward under the above rules.

We will see that we obtain a proof principle of this kind whenever we have a set of rules and, moreover, it precisely gives us the familiar inductive proof method for sets generated by rules. For this, the examples with lists in Section 2.6.3, and with natural numbers in Section 2.7.1, should be most enlightening. Here is, however, an example with finite traces. Consider a partial function f, from processes to integers, that satisfies the following conditions:

$$f(P) = 0 \qquad\qquad\qquad \text{if } P \text{ is stopped,}$$
$$f(P) = \min\{f(P')+1 \mid P \xrightarrow{\mu} P' \text{ for some } P'$$
$$\text{and } f(P') \text{ is defined}\} \qquad \text{otherwise,}$$

with the understanding that f can have any value, or even be undefined, if the set on which the min is taken is empty (for instance f could be undefined on all processes of Figure 1.2). Suppose we wish to prove that f must be defined on processes with a finite trace, that is $\mathrm{dom}(\lfloor) \subseteq \mathrm{dom}(f)$, where dom indicates the domain of a function or predicate. For this, it suffices to show that the set $\mathrm{dom}(f)$ is closed forward under the rules defining $\lfloor$. This requires ensuring that $f(P)$ is defined whenever P is stopped; and that, if there are μ, P' with $P \xrightarrow{\mu} P'$ and $f(P')$ is defined, then also $f(P)$ is defined. Both requirements immediately follow from the definition of f. The reader familiar with induction will recognise this as a proof by *rule induction* (rule induction is formally introduced in Section 2.5).

Remark 2.1.1 A proof of the result above by *induction on the derivation proof of $P \lfloor$* would have been very similar. In this form of induction (discussed in Section 2.7.1), a property is proved to hold at all P such that $P \lfloor$ by reasoning on the shape of the proof with which $P \lfloor$ is derived from the rules. First, one has to check the property for the derivation proofs consisting of a single node, that is, when $P \lfloor$ is derived from the axiom; in our case this means checking that $f(P)$ is defined if P is stopped. Second, one considers any larger derivation proof, when the conclusion node is derived from the inference rule; one checks that the property holds at the conclusion under the assumption that the property holds at all internal nodes; in our case this means precisely checking that, when $P \xrightarrow{\mu} P'$, if we assume $f(P')$ defined, then also $f(P)$ is defined. $\qquad\qquad\Box$

In summary, the set inductively defined by the rules is the smallest set satisfying a certain forward closure. This formulation yields a proof principle that corresponds to the usual technique for reasoning inductively with rules. Moreover, the set can also be obtained as the limit of a certain increasing sequence produced by an iterative construction, or as the set of processes derivable from the rules with a finite proof.

We now turn our attention to coinductive definitions. As an example we consider a property akin to non-termination. Informally, given an action μ, a process P has an ω-*trace under* μ (more simply, an ω-trace, when μ is clear), written $P \upharpoonright_\mu$, if it is possible to observe an infinite sequence of μ-transitions starting from P. The set $\upharpoonright_\mu$ has a natural *coinductive* definition. We only need the following inference rule:

$$\frac{P \xrightarrow{\mu} P' \qquad P' \upharpoonright_\mu}{P \upharpoonright_\mu} \tag{$*$}$$

An object is in the set coinductively defined by a set of rules if there is a finite or infinite proof of that object using the rules. In the case of $\upharpoonright_\mu$ we have no axioms, so all valid proofs are infinite (as we shall see in Section 2.1.3, coinductive definitions can use axioms too, and then proofs may be finite). For instance, suppose that we have two processes P_1, P_2 with transitions $P_1 \xrightarrow{a} P_2$ and $P_2 \xrightarrow{a} P_1$. The following infinite proof shows that $P_1 \upharpoonright_a$ holds:

$$\frac{P_1 \xrightarrow{a} P_2 \qquad \frac{P_2 \xrightarrow{a} P_1 \qquad \frac{P_1 \xrightarrow{a} P_2 \qquad \frac{\vdots}{P_2 \upharpoonright_a}}{P_1 \upharpoonright_a}}{P_2 \upharpoonright_a}}{P_1 \upharpoonright_a}$$

If a process P is not in $\upharpoonright_\mu$ then an attempt of proof for P eventually reaches a point where the proof, still incomplete, cannot be further continued. For instance, if $Q_1 \xrightarrow{a} Q_2 \xrightarrow{a} Q_3$ and $Q_3 \not\xrightarrow{a}$ then a proof attempt for Q_1 is blocked on the third step:

$$\frac{Q_1 \xrightarrow{a} Q_2 \qquad \frac{Q_2 \xrightarrow{a} Q_3 \qquad \frac{??}{Q_3 \upharpoonright_a}}{Q_2 \upharpoonright_a}}{Q_1 \upharpoonright_a}$$

Thus if we wish to obtain, constructively, the set $\upharpoonright_\mu$ we can proceed as follows. We start with the set Pr of all processes. Then we repeatedly remove a process P from the set if P has no μ-transitions, or if all μ-transitions from P lead to derivatives that are not anymore in the set. If the LTS is finite-state, this decreasing iteration terminates and the final set is $\upharpoonright_\mu$. (Again, we will see in Section 2.9 that if the number of processes is infinite, the construction is still valid but $\upharpoonright_\mu$ is found as the limit of an infinite iteration, assuming image-finiteness; and if even image-finiteness is not guaranteed then the iteration has to be transfinite, that is, on the ordinals.)

Equivalently, $\lceil_\mu$ is the *largest* predicate on processes that is *closed backward under the rule* (∗); i.e., the largest subset T of processes such that if $P \in T$ then

- there is $P' \in T$ such that $P \xrightarrow{\mu} P'$.

The closure is 'backward' because the rules are used in the direction from the conclusion to the premises: we require that each element in the closure be the conclusion of a rule whose premises must also belong to the closure.

Here, too, we will prove later that these different formulations coincide. We can, however, already see that the set resulting from the iterative construction is closed backward, and that the closure is lost by adding more processes to the set.

The formulation with the closure gives us a proof principle: to prove that each process in a set T has an ω-trace under μ it suffices to show that T is closed backward under the rule above; this is the coinduction proof principle, for ω-traces. Thus, if we wish to prove that a specific process P has an ω-trace under μ we should find some subset T of Pr that is closed backward under the rule and with $P \in T$.

For instance, consider the processes P_1, P_2, P_3 and P_4 with the following transitions:

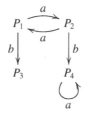

The set $T_1 \overset{\text{def}}{=} \{P_1, P_2\}$ is closed backward under the rules for $\lceil_a$, hence $P_1 \lceil_a$ and $P_2 \lceil_a$ hold. Other such sets are $T_2 = \{P_4\}$ and $T_1 \cup T_2$. Note that on the processes P_1 and P_2 both $\lfloor$ and $\lceil_a$ hold.

In summary, with coinduction the argument is dual to induction. Thus, the set coinductively defined by the rules is the largest set satisfying a certain backward closure or, equivalently, the limit of a certain decreasing sequence produced by an iterative construction, or as the set of processes derivable from the rules with a finite or infinite proof. And the backward closure yields a proof principle for coinduction – again the dual of the corresponding one for induction.

In the first example, the term 'closed forward' is to remind us that we are using the rules top-down, from the premises to the conclusion: if T is closed forward, then whenever the premises of a rule are satisfied by T, the resulting conclusion should be satisfied too. Dually, the term 'closed backward' emphasises that we use the rules bottom-up: if T is closed backward, then each element of T must match a conclusion of a rule in such a way that its premises are satisfied by T.

Note also that in the first example we look for a smallest set, whereas in the second we look for a largest set. And in the first example the iterative construction follows the rules in the forward direction starting with $\emptyset$, whereas in the second the iteration follows the rules backward and starting from Pr (the maximal set).

Of course, the existence of the smallest set closed forward, or the largest set closed backward, must be established. This will follow from the general framework of induction and coinduction that will be introduced later. One can, however, also prove the existence directly; for sets closed forward, showing that one such set exists (in the example, the set of all processes), and that the intersection of sets closed forward is again a set closed forward. One proceeds dually for sets closed backward: the empty set is closed backward, and the union of sets closed backward is again a set closed backward.

2.1.2 Reduction to a value and divergence in the λ-calculus

For readers familiar with the λ-calculus, a variant of the previous examples (and probably more enlightening) can be given using the relation of convergence and the predicate of divergence on the λ-terms. Readers unfamiliar with the λ-calculus may safely skip the example.

We recall that the set Λ of λ-terms is given by the following grammar (note: this is an inductive definition!):

$$e ::= x \mid \lambda x.e \mid e_1 \, e_2,$$

where, in $\lambda x.e$, the construct λx is a binder for the free occurrences of x in e, and x ranges over the set of variables. We omit the standard definitions of free and bound variables. The set Λ^0 of *closed λ-terms* is the subset of Λ whose elements have no free variables; $e\{e'/x\}$ is the term obtained from e by replacing its free occurrences of x with e'. We identify terms that are obtained one from the other with a renaming of bound variables (whereby a bound variable is replaced by a variable that is fresh, that is, it does not occur anywhere else in the term); for instance $\lambda x.x = \lambda y.y$, and $((\lambda x.x)(\lambda x.x))(\lambda y.y) = ((\lambda x.x)(\lambda y.y))(\lambda y.y)$. We call a term of the form $\lambda x.e$ an *abstraction* and one of the form $e_1 \, e_2$ an *application*.

The relation $\Downarrow \, \subseteq \Lambda^0 \times \Lambda^0$ (reduction to a value, or convergence) for the call-by-name λ-calculus, the simplest form of reduction in the λ-calculus, is defined with the following two rules:

$$\frac{}{\lambda x.e \Downarrow \lambda x.e} \qquad \frac{e_1 \Downarrow \lambda x.e_0 \qquad e_0\{e_2/x\} \Downarrow e'}{e_1 \, e_2 \Downarrow e'}$$

(The choice of x in the rules is irrelevant as bound variables can be renamed.) The pairs of terms we are interested in are those generated by these rules; this is an inductive definition. As in the example of finite traces of Section 2.1.1, so here the pairs we are interested in are those obtained with a finite proof from the rules. And the set of all such pairs is produced with an iterative construction that starts with the empty set similar to that described in Section 2.1.1.

Equivalently, $\Downarrow$ is the *smallest* relation on (closed) λ-terms that is *closed forward* under the rules; i.e., the smallest relation $\mathcal{S} \subseteq \Lambda^0 \times \Lambda^0$ such that

- $\lambda x.e \; \mathcal{S} \; \lambda x.e$ for all abstractions,
- if $e_1 \; \mathcal{S} \; \lambda x.e_0$ and $e_0\{e_2/x\} \; \mathcal{S} \; e'$ then also $e_1 \, e_2 \; \mathcal{S} \; e'$.

This immediately gives us a proof method for $\Downarrow$ (an example of the induction proof method): given a relation $\mathcal{R}$ on λ-terms, to prove that all pairs in $\Downarrow$ are in $\mathcal{R}$ it suffices to show that $\mathcal{R}$ is closed forward under the above rules. (What is the largest relation closed forward?)

In contrast, the predicate $\Uparrow \subseteq \Lambda^0$ (divergence), in call-by-name λ-calculus, is defined coinductively with the following two rules:

$$\frac{e_1 \Uparrow}{e_1 \, e_2 \Uparrow} \qquad\qquad \frac{e_1 \Downarrow \lambda x.e_0 \qquad e_0\{e_2/x\} \Uparrow}{e_1 \, e_2 \Uparrow}$$

As the processes with an infinite trace in Section 2.1.1, so here the divergent λ-terms are those with an infinite proof. And the set $\Uparrow$ is obtained, iteratively, starting from Λ^0 and then repeatedly removing elements from it that do not fit the rules.

Equivalently, $\Uparrow$ is the *largest* predicate on (closed) λ-terms that is *closed backward* under these rules; i.e., the largest subset T of Λ^0 such that if $e \in T$ then

- either ($e = e_1 \, e_2$ and $e_1 \in T$),
- or ($e = e_1 \, e_2$, $e_1 \Downarrow \lambda x.e_0$ and $e_0\{e_2/x\} \in T$).

Hence, to prove that a given term e is divergent it suffices to find $T \subseteq \Lambda^0$ that is closed backward and with $e \in T$ (an example of the coinduction proof method). (What is the smallest predicate closed backward?)

Exercise 2.1.2 ($\hookrightarrow$) Use induction, following the forward-closure argument, to show that if $e \Downarrow e'$ then e' is an abstraction, that is, it has the form $\lambda x.e_0$, for some e_0. $\qquad\square$

Example 2.1.3 We use the coinduction proof method to show that if a closed term e does not converge (that is, there is no e' with $e \Downarrow e'$) then $e \Uparrow$.

Let T be the set of non-converging terms; we show that it is closed backward with respect to the rules defining $\Uparrow$. Take a term $e \in T$. This term cannot be an abstraction, otherwise $e \Downarrow e$ would hold. Therefore e must be an application, say $e_1 \, e_2$, and then we distinguish two cases. One case is when $e_1 \in T$. In this case we are done, as we can match e against the first of the rules defining $\Uparrow$. The second case is when e_1 converges. By Exercise 2.1.2, e_1 is an abstraction, say $\lambda x.e_0$. Consider thus $e_0\{e_2/x\}$. If this term is in T, then we are done, matching e against the second of the rules defining $\Uparrow$; otherwise $e_0\{e_2/x\}$ converges and therefore also e converges (according to the second of the rules for $\Downarrow$), which contradicts the hypothesis $e \in T$. $\qquad\square$

Exercise 2.1.4 ($\hookrightarrow$) Show, using the forward-closure argument of induction, that if $e \Downarrow e'$ then $e \Uparrow$ does not hold. $\qquad\square$

Example 2.1.5 Let $e_1 \stackrel{\text{def}}{=} \lambda x.xx$ (application has precedence over abstraction, thus $\lambda x.xx$ is $\lambda x.(xx)$). We show that the term $e_1 \, e_1$ is divergent, using the coinduction proof method.

We take the set $T \stackrel{\text{def}}{=} \{e_1\ e_1\}$. We claim that T is closed backward under the rules for $\Uparrow$. This holds because we can match the only element in T against the conclusion of the second rule and then fulfill the premises, thus.

$$\frac{e_1 \Downarrow e_1 \qquad e_1\ e_1 \in T}{e_1\ e_1 \in T}$$

From the backward closure of T we deduce that $T \subseteq \Uparrow$. $\square$

Exercise 2.1.6 ($\hookrightarrow$) Let e_1 be as in Example 2.1.5, and $e_2 \stackrel{\text{def}}{=} \lambda x.xxx$. Show that the terms $e_2\ e_2$, $e_1\ e_2$ and $e_2\ e_1$ are all divergent, using the coinduction proof method, proceeding as in Example 2.1.5. $\square$

Exercise 2.1.7 Consider the call-by-value λ-calculus, as in [Pit12]. What are the rules for defining convergence and divergence there? Adapt Example 2.1.3 and Exercise 2.1.4 to call-by-value. $\square$

2.1.3 Lists over a set A

Let A be a set. The set of finite lists with elements from A is the set $\texttt{FinLists}_A$ inductively generated by the rules below, for $\mathcal{L} = \texttt{FinLists}_A$:

$$\frac{}{\texttt{nil} \in \mathcal{L}} \qquad\qquad \frac{s \in \mathcal{L} \qquad a \in A}{\langle a \rangle \bullet s \in \mathcal{L}}$$

Once more, the finite lists, as an inductive set, is the set of all objects that can be obtained with a finite proof from the rules. And it is also the smallest set closed forward under these rules, where T is closed forward if: $\texttt{nil} \in T$ and $s \in T$ implies $\langle a \rangle \bullet s \in T$, for each $a \in A$.

In contrast, the set of finite and infinite lists,[1] $\texttt{FinInfLists}_A$, is the set coinductively defined by the rules, for $\mathcal{L} = \texttt{FinInfLists}_A$; i.e., it is the set of all objects that can be obtained with a finite or infinite proof from the rules (a proof can be finite because the rules include an axiom; when an axiom is used, a branch of the proof is completed successfully, as no new subgoals are produced); the set of finite and infinite lists is also the largest set closed backward under the same rules.

Example 2.1.8 We show that the infinite list

$$s_1 \stackrel{\text{def}}{=} \langle a \rangle \bullet \langle b \rangle \bullet \langle a \rangle \bullet \langle b \rangle \bullet \cdots$$

is in the set coinductively defined by the two rules above, assuming $a, b \in A$. For this we take $T \stackrel{\text{def}}{=} \{s_1, s_2\}$, where

$$s_2 \stackrel{\text{def}}{=} \langle b \rangle \bullet \langle a \rangle \bullet \langle b \rangle \bullet \langle a \rangle \bullet \cdots$$

---

[1] In programming languages, infinite lists are often called *streams*.

and show that T is closed backward under the rules. Thus we have to check that each element of T can match the conclusion of a rule in such a way that its premises are satisfied. Let's begin with s_1; as $s_1 = \langle a \rangle \bullet s_2$, and $s_2 \in T$, we can match the second rule thus:

$$\frac{s_2 \in T \qquad a \in A}{\langle a \rangle \bullet s_2 \in T}$$

Similarly, with $s_2 = \langle b \rangle \bullet s_1$, since $s_1 \in T$, we match the same rule thus:

$$\frac{s_1 \in T \qquad b \in A}{\langle b \rangle \bullet s_1 \in T}$$

The reader may check that also $T \cup \{\texttt{nil}, \langle a \rangle \bullet \texttt{nil}\}$ is closed backward. $\qquad \square$

Other examples and exercises of coinductive reasoning with lists will be given in Section 2.6.4.

2.2 The duality

From the examples of the previous section, although informally treated, the pattern of the duality between induction and coinduction begins to emerge.

- An inductive definition tells us what the *constructors* are for generating the elements: this is the forward closure of the previous section.
- A coinductive definition tells us what the *destructors* are for decomposing the elements: this is the backward closure. The destructors show what we can *observe* of the elements. If we think of the elements as black boxes, then the destructors tell us what we can do with them; this is clear in the case of infinite lists, and also in the definition of bisimulation.

We discuss the pattern of the dualities in this section. Examining the dualities between the world of induction and the world of coinduction is useful for understanding the concepts. It also strengthens the importance of coinduction, if we accept induction as a fundamental mathematical tool.

In the examples of Section 2.1, the inductive and coinductive sets are defined by means of rules. In such cases:

- if the definition is inductive, we look for the *smallest* universe in which such rules live; this is the set of all objects that can be constructed in a finite number of steps following the rules in the *forward* direction;
- if the definition is coinductive, we look for the *largest* universe; this is the set of all objects that never produce a 'contradiction' (i.e., a blockage) following the rules in the *backward* direction;
- the inductive proof principle allows us to infer that the *inductive set* is included in a given set (i.e., has a given property) by proving that the property satisfies the *forward* closure;
- the coinductive proof principle allows us to infer that a given set is included in the *coinductive set* by proving that the given set satisfies the *backward* closure.

A set T being closed forward intuitively means that

> for each rule whose premises are satisfied in T
> there is an element of T
> such that the element is the conclusion of the rule.

In the backward closure for T, the order between the two quantified entities (those underlined) is swapped:

> for each element of T
> there is a rule whose premises are satisfied in T
> such that the element is the conclusion of the rule.

In the fixed-point theory of Section 2.3, the duality between forward and backward closure will be the duality between pre-fixed points and post-fixed points.

There is also a duality between the concepts of *congruence* and *bisimulation equivalence* (a bisimulation that is also an equivalence), as well as between the *identity* relation and *bisimilarity*. This is a duality on relations, and once more, it stems from the duality between forward and backward closures. In a language whose terms have a structure (i.e., they are constructed from a set of operators), a congruence is an equivalence relation that respects the structure (i.e., the relation is preserved by the operators of the language). If we consider the rules that formalise the notion of *syntactic equality* in the language, then a *congruence* is an equivalence relation that is closed forward under the rules, and the *identity relation* is the smallest such relation. For instance, in the λ-calculus the rules for syntactic equality are:

$$\frac{}{x = x} \qquad \frac{e_1 = e_2}{\lambda x.e_1 = \lambda x.e_2} \qquad \frac{e_1 = e_2 \qquad e_1' = e_2'}{e_1\, e_2 = e_1'\, e_2'}$$

where x is any variable. A relation $\mathcal{R}$ is closed forward under these rules if: $\mathcal{R}$ relates any variable with itself; whenever $\mathcal{R}$ relates two terms it also relates all abstractions derived from those terms; whenever $\mathcal{R}$ relates to pairs of terms, it also relates the application obtained from them.

In contrast, consider some rules that express the notion of *semantic equality* on the elements of a set by stipulating what are observables of such elements. A *bisimulation* is a relation that is closed backward under the rules (for bisimulation on processes, this will be proved in Section 2.10); and *bisimilarity* is the largest such relation.

The duality between the inductive definition of identity and the coinductive definition of bisimilarity is the duality between syntactic and semantic equalities; or, more broadly but tentatively, between *syntax* and *semantics*.

In the above reasoning on congruence, the equivalence requirement is not necessary. We can leave it aside, obtaining the duality between *bisimulations* and *substitutive relations* (a relation is substitutive if whenever two terms t and s are related, then a term t' must be related to any term s' obtained from t' by replacing occurrences of t with s).

Whenever we define bisimilarity on a term language, we can ask ourselves the question whether bisimilarity is a congruence. We will indeed do so in the language for processes in

Chapter 3. This inevitably leads us to proofs where inductive and coinductive techniques are intertwined. In certain languages, for instance higher-order languages, such proofs may be hard, and how to best combine induction and coinduction remains a research topic (see [Pit12]). What makes the combination delicate is that the rules on which congruence and bisimulation are defined – the rules for syntactic and semantic equality – are different.

The characterisations of least and greatest fixed points via iterative constructions evokes also a duality between semi-decidable and cosemi-decidable sets. A subset S of a set U is *semi-decidable* if there is an algorithm that enumerates all the members of S (or, equivalently, there is an algorithm that halts on the members of S with a positive answer, and does not halt, or halts with a negative answer, on elements in the complement of S); whereas S is *cosemi-decidable* if its complement set, $U - S$, is semi-decidable. Recall that in the iteration construction an inductive set is obtained from the empty set by progressively adding elements; when this procedure is computable, the resulting set is semi-decidable. Dually, a coinductive set is obtained from the top set by progressively removing elements (the elements of the complement set); under computability hypothesis, the coinductive set is therefore cosemi-decidable. While we are not aware of results that formally relate the duality between induction and coinduction to that between semi-decidable and cosemi-decidable sets, the relationship with semi-decidability and cosemi-decidability should be beared in mind when one considers algorithms for computing inductive or coinductive sets.

In the discussion after Example 1.4.4 we mentioned how bisimulations are often found by *enlarging* an initial candidate set, when the proof for the initial candidate could not be completed (because the backward closure fails). This *weakening of the candidate* is frequent with coinduction, and has a dual for induction: it is the *strengthening of the inductive assumption* (or *strengthening of the candidate*, to make the contrast with the terminology for coinduction). Anybody who has made inductive proofs has met it: one wishes to prove that the elements of an inductive set have a property, and starts with a candidate statement (i.e., trying to prove that the inductive set is included in a certain candidate set); then one realises that the proof cannot be completed (because the forward closure fails), and thereby make the statement of the induction stronger (i.e., one proves inclusion into a *smaller* set).

Table 2.1 gives a summary of the dualities. Some dualities mentioned in the table are useful but informal analogies, whereas others are precise mathematical dualities. Examples of informal dualities are those between constructors and observations, and between syntax and semantics; examples of mathematical dualities are those between least and greatest fixed points, between induction and coinduction, and between algebra and coalgebra.

A final remark on rules is worthwhile. The presentation in Section 2.1 of only examples of sets inductively and coinductively defined from rules is not limiting. As we shall see (Exercises 2.5.2 and 2.5.3), under very mild conditions all inductive and coinductive sets can be expressed in terms of rules; this also includes bisimilarity, though this may not be obvious at first sight.

In the next sections we use fixed-point theory to explain the meaning of induction and coinduction. We will thus be able to see why induction and coinduction are related to

Table 2.1 *The duality*

inductive definition	coinductive definition
induction proof principle	coinduction proof principle
constructors	observations
smallest universe	largest universe
'forward closure' in rules	'backward closure' in rules
congruence	bisimulation equivalence
substitutive relation	bisimulation
identity	bisimilarity
least fixed point	greatest fixed point
pre-fixed point	post-fixed point
algebra	coalgebra
syntax	semantics
semi-decidable set	cosemi-decidable set
strengthening of the candidate in proofs	weakening of the candidate in proofs

least and greatest fixed points, and prove the equivalence of the different formulations of inductively and coinductively defined sets discussed in the examples in Section 2.1: as sets of elements with finite and infinite proofs, as sets resulting from certain iterative constructions, and as smallest and largest sets satisfying a forward and backward closure. We will also show further formulations in terms of games. Most importantly, we will give a formal meaning to the induction and coinduction proof principles. We refer to [RJ12] for the explanation of induction and coinduction in terms of algebras and coalgebras.

2.3 Fixed points in complete lattices

In this section we recall a few important results of lattice theory that will then be used to explain induction and coinduction. A relation $\mathcal{R}$ is *antisymmetric* if $x \mathcal{R} y$ and $y \mathcal{R} x$ implies $x = y$.

Definition 2.3.1 (Poset) A *partially ordered set* (or *poset*) is a non-empty set equipped with a relation on its elements that is a partial order (that is, the relation is reflexive, antisymmetric and transitive). □

We usually indicate the relation in a poset by $\leq$. Here is a simple poset:

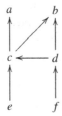

An arrow represents an inequality (thus $f \leq d$), and the other inequalities (such as $f \leq f$ or $f \leq a$) are derived from the reflexivity and transitivity axioms of a poset. The relation in a poset need not be total – there may be pairs of unrelated elements, such as (a, b) and (d, e) in the figure.

Other examples of posets are the sets of natural numbers and of real numbers, with the usual ordering relation on numbers. We can obtain a poset from the natural and real numbers in other ways. For instance, we can set the $\leq$ relation on the natural numbers as follows: $n \leq m$ if n divides m. The reader may check that the product $L_1 \times L_2$ of two posets L_1 and L_2 is a poset (the elements in this set are pairs (a_1, a_2) with $a_i \in L_i$, and $(a_1, a_2) \leq (a'_1, a'_2)$ holds in $L_1 \times L_2$ if $a_i \leq a'_i$ holds in L_i, for $i = 1, 2$); similarly if S is a set and L a poset, then the set of functions from S to L is a poset, where $f \leq g$ holds if for all $a \in S$ we have $f(a) \leq g(a)$. Further examples of posets will be given in the remainder of the chapter.

Example 2.3.2 A *preordered set* is a non-empty set equipped with a relation on its elements that is a preorder (i.e., reflexive and transitive). If L is such a set, and $\leq$ the relation, then we can define an equivalence relation $\bowtie$ on L thus:

$$x \bowtie y \text{ if } x \leq y \text{ and } y \leq x.$$

The equivalence classes of L under $\bowtie$ form the set

$$L/\bowtie \stackrel{\text{def}}{=} \{[x] \mid x \in L\}, \qquad \text{where } [x] \stackrel{\text{def}}{=} \{y \mid x \bowtie y\}.$$

(Note that if $x \bowtie y$ then $[x] = [y]$.) Then $L/\bowtie$ is a poset, with a relation $\leq'$ that stipulates $[x] \leq' [y]$ if $x \leq y$ in L. □

Exercise 2.3.3 ($\hookrightarrow$) Use Exercise 1.4.17 to define a poset from the similarity relation. □

When a set L with relation $\leq$ is a poset, we often simply say that L is a poset. If $x \leq y$ we sometimes say that x is *below* y, and y is *above* x. We also write $y \geq x$ when $x \leq y$ holds. We sometimes call the elements of a set *points*.

Turning a poset upside-down (that is, reversing the partial order relation) gives us another poset. Thus statements about a poset have a dual, in which each of the relations $\leq$ and $\geq$ is replaced by the other in the statement.

Definition 2.3.4 Let L be a poset. For a set $S \subseteq L$, a point $y \in L$ is an *upper bound of S* if $x \leq y$ for all points $x \in S$. The dual of an upper bound of S is a *lower bound of S*: a point $y \in L$ with $y \leq x$ for all $x \in S$. □

Definition 2.3.5 Let L be a poset. The *least* element of a subset $S \subseteq L$ is an element $y \in S$ that is a lower bound of S. The least upper bound of S (that is, an upper bound y with $y \leq z$ for all upper bounds z of S) is also called the *join* of S.

The dual of these concepts gives us the *greatest* element of S (an element of S that is an upper bound of S) and the *meet* of S (the greatest lower bound of S). □

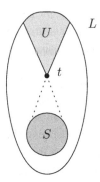

Fig. 2.1 Upper bounds and meet in poset.

In Figure 2.1, L is the poset, S a subset of L, U the set of upper bounds for S and t the least upper bound, or join, of S (the join t could also be an element of S; this would mean that S has a top element).

An element y of a subset S of a poset could have the property that no element $x \in S$ exists with $x \leq y$ without y being the least element of S (in the literature such elements are usually called *minimal*). Thus the least element of a subset S may not exist; if it exists, however, then it is unique, by the antisymmetry property. Similarly, a greatest element may not exist (an element y for which no element $x \in S$ exists with $y \leq x$ without y necessarily being the greatest element of S is usually called *maximal*).

Exercise 2.3.6 If L is a poset, call L^{op} the dual poset, obtained by reversing the relation on L (that is, $x \leq y$ in L^{op} if $y \leq x$ in L). Check that meets (respectively joins) in L corresponds to joins (respectively meets) in L^{op}.   □

Exercise 2.3.7 Let L be a poset. Show that, for all $x, y \in L$, we have $x = \cap\{x, y\}$ iff $x \leq y$ iff $y = \cup\{x, y\}$.   □

An *endofunction* on a set L is a function from L onto itself.

Definition 2.3.8 Let F be an endofunction on a poset L.

- F is *monotone* if $x \leq y$ implies $F(x) \leq F(y)$, for all x, y.
- An element x of the poset is a *pre-fixed point* of F if $F(x) \leq x$. Dually, a *post-fixed point* of F is an element x with $x \leq F(x)$.
- A *fixed point* of F is an element x that is both a pre-fixed point and a post-fixed point, that is, $F(x) = x$. In the set of fixed points of F, the least element and the greatest element are respectively called the *least fixed point* of F and the *greatest fixed point* of F.   □

We write $\cup S$ (or $\cup_{x \in S} S$) for the join of a subset S of a poset, and $\cap S$ (or $\cap_{x \in S} S$) for its meet. We also write $\mathrm{lfp}(F)$ and $\mathrm{gfp}(F)$ for the least and greatest fixed points of F.

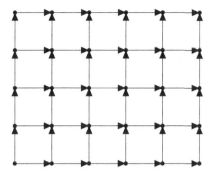

Fig. 2.2 A complete lattice.

Example 2.3.9 We take the poset of the (positive) natural numbers with $n \leq m$ if n divides m. If $S = \{4, 8, 16\}$ then $\{1, 2, 4\}$ is the set of lower bounds of S, and 4 is the least element in S and also its meet; 16 is the greatest element and also the join of S. If $S = \{2, 3, 4\}$ then 1 is the only lower bound and is also the meet; there is no least element, as 2 and 3 are both minimal; any multiple of 12 is an upper bound, 12 is the join, and there is no greatest element.

Consider then the endofunction F on the same poset where $F(n)$ is the sum of the factors of n that are different from n, with the exception of 1 that is mapped onto itself; thus $F(1) = 1$, $F(2) = 1$, $F(3) = 1$, $F(4) = 3$, $F(6) = 6$. Then $1, 2, 3, 6$ are examples of pre-fixed points, and 1, 6 examples of fixed points. □

Definition 2.3.10 (Complete lattice) A *complete lattice* is a poset with all joins (i.e., all the subsets of the poset have a join). □

The above implies that a complete lattice has also all meets; see Exercise 2.3.17. Further, taking the meet and the join of the empty set, it implies that there are bottom and top elements, i.e., a least and greatest element in the lattice. This because if $S = \emptyset$, then every element x of the lattice is both a lower bound and an upper bound of S, as $x \leq y$ and $x \geq y$ for all $y \in S$ is vacuously true; hence the meet of $\emptyset$ is an element that is below all elements of the lattice, and the join of $\emptyset$ is an element that is above all elements.

We indicate the bottom and top elements of a complete lattice by $\bot$ and $\top$, respectively.

Exercise 2.3.11 Derive the existence of the bottom and top elements for a lattice L using meet and join on the whole set L. □

Example 2.3.12 Figure 2.2 shows an example of a complete lattice. Two points x, y are in the relation $\leq$ if there is a path from x to y following the directional edges (a path may also be empty, hence $x \leq x$ holds for all x).

Some edges can be removed while remaining with a complete lattice; we should not, however, remove all the outgoing edges or all the ingoing edges of a node because such node would not be anymore related to the bottom node or to the top node. □

Example 2.3.13

- The set of all natural numbers i with $n \leq i < m$, for n, m given, is a complete lattice, with n and m as bottom and top elements.
- If S is a set, then $\wp(S)$, the *powerset* of S, is a complete lattice, ordering the elements of $\wp(S)$ by means of the set inclusion relation $\subseteq$. In this complete lattice, $\emptyset$ (the empty set) and S are the bottom and top elements; join is given by set union, and meet by set intersection. For instance, given S, take $T \stackrel{\text{def}}{=} \{T_1, \ldots, T_n\}$ where each T_i is a subset of S. Thus each T_i is an element of $\wp(S)$, and T a set of elements of $\wp(S)$; an upper bound of T is a set T' with $T_i \subseteq T'$ for all i; and $\cup_i T_i$ is the join of T. $\qquad\square$

The powerset constructions are the kind of complete lattice we mainly use in this chapter. This explains the union and intersection notations adopted for joins and meets.

Exercise 2.3.14 (Recommended, $\hookrightarrow$) Is the set of all natural numbers a complete lattice? Is it a lattice (that is, is a poset in which all *pairs* of elements have a join)? Can we add elements to the set of natural numbers so as to make it a complete lattice? $\qquad\square$

Exercise 2.3.15 ($\hookrightarrow$) Show that the set of all equivalence relations over a given set S is a complete lattice, where the ordering on relations is given by the usual relational inclusion. What is the bottom element of the complete lattice? And the top element? $\qquad\square$

Exercise 2.3.16 Suppose L is a complete lattice and $X, Y \subseteq L$. Show that if for each $x \in X$ there is $y \in Y$ with $x \leq y$ then $\cup X \leq \cup Y$; whereas if for each $x \in X$ there is $y \in Y$ with $y \leq x$ then $\cap Y \leq \cap X$. $\qquad\square$

Exercise 2.3.17 ($*, \hookrightarrow$) Show that in the definition of complete lattice the existence of all joins implies the existence of all meets. (As usual, the dual is also true, exchanging meets and joins in the definition of complete lattice.) $\qquad\square$

Remark 2.3.18 A lattice (as in Exercise 2.3.14) is complete if and only if every monotone endofunction on the lattice has a fixed point. Other characterisations of the difference between lattices and complete lattices exist, see books on lattice theory such as [DP02] for details. $\qquad\square$

Exercise 2.3.19 (Recommended, $\hookrightarrow$)

(1) Show that if F is a monotone endofunction on a complete lattice, and x and y are post-fixed points of F, then also $\cup\{x, y\}$ is a post-fixed point.
(2) Generalise the previous point to an arbitrary set S of post-fixed points: $\cup S$ is also a post-fixed point. Then dualise the result to pre-fixed points.
(3) Show that, in contrast, $\cap\{x, y\}$ need not be a post-fixed point. $\qquad\square$

For our developments in the book, the second part of the Fixed-point Theorem below, relating least and greatest fixed points to the sets of pre-fixed and post-fixed points, is most relevant. On complete lattices generated by the powerset construction, the statement becomes: if $F : \wp(X) \to \wp(X)$ is monotone, then

$$\mathtt{lfp}(F) = \bigcap\{S \mid F(S) \subseteq S\},$$

$$\mathtt{gfp}(F) = \bigcup\{S \mid S \subseteq F(S)\}.$$

Its proof is simpler than that of the Fixed-point Theorem.

Exercise 2.3.20 (Recommended, $\hookrightarrow$) Prove the above statement. (Hint: use Exercise 2.3.19(2).) $\quad\square$

Theorem 2.3.21 (Fixed-point Theorem) *On a complete lattice, a monotone endofunction has a complete lattice of fixed points. In particular the least fixed point of the function is the meet of all its pre-fixed points, and the greatest fixed point is the join of all the post-fixed points.* $\quad\square$

Thus the least fixed point is also the least pre-fixed point, and the greatest fixed point is also the greatest post-fixed point.

Exercise 2.3.22 ($\hookrightarrow$)(**Proof of the Fixed-point Theorem**) This exercise invites the reader to carry out a proof of the Fixed-point Theorem.

(1) Let L be the lattice, F the monotone endofunction and S the set of fixed points of L. Consider a subset $X \subseteq S$, and take the set Y of pre-fixed points that are also upper bounds of X:

$$Y \stackrel{\text{def}}{=} \{y \in L \mid F(y) \le y \text{ and, } \forall x \in X, x \le y\}.$$

Take now the meet z of Y (which exists because L is a complete lattice). Show that this is also the join of X in S. (Hint: this is similar to the proof of Exercise 2.3.17.)

(2) Using the previous result, complete the proof of the theorem. $\quad\square$

Exercise 2.3.23 Another equivalent formulation of the first part of the Fixed-point Theorem can be given in terms of pre-fixed points: the monotone endofunction has a complete lattice of pre-fixed points. Similarly for post-fixed points. Prove these assertions. (Hint: it is similar to the proof of the Fixed-point Theorem.) $\quad\square$

Remark 2.3.24 Exercise 2.3.20 actually shows that the existence of the least and greatest fixed points of a monotone function F can be guaranteed also in structures that are weaker than complete lattices, namely posets in which the sets of pre-fixed and post-fixed points of F have a meet and join, respectively. See the proof of the exercise in the Appendix. $\quad\square$

2.4 Inductively and coinductively defined sets

Definition 2.4.1 (Sets inductively and coinductively defined by F) For a complete lattice L whose points are sets (as in the complete lattices obtained by the powerset construction), and an endofunction F on L, the sets

$$F_{\text{ind}} \stackrel{\text{def}}{=} \bigcap \{x \mid F(x) \leq x\},$$

$$F_{\text{coind}} \stackrel{\text{def}}{=} \bigcup \{x \mid x \leq F(x)\}$$

(the meet of the pre-fixed points, and the join of the post-fixed points) are, respectively, the sets *inductively defined by F* and *coinductively defined by F.* □

Hence the following rules hold.

Corollary 2.4.2 (Induction and coinduction proof principles) *In the hypothesis of Definition 2.4.1, we have:*

$$\text{if } F(x) \leq x \text{ then } F_{\text{ind}} \leq x \qquad \text{(induction proof principle)};$$

$$\text{if } x \leq F(x) \text{ then } x \leq F_{\text{coind}} \qquad \text{(coinduction proof principle)}.$$

□

The above principles are also sometimes referred to as the *principle of induction* and *principle of coinduction*. By the Fixed-point Theorem, we know that, when F is monotone, F_{ind} is the least fixed point (and the least pre-fixed point) of F, and dually for F_{coind}. More generally, we know that the meet of pre-fixed points is itself a pre-fixed point, and dually so. We can thus re-state the principles as follows.

Corollary 2.4.3 (Induction and coinduction proof principles for monotone functions) *For a monotone endofunction F on a complete lattice, we have:*

$$\text{if } F(x) \leq x \text{ then } \mathtt{lfp}(F) \leq x;$$

$$\text{if } x \leq F(x) \text{ then } x \leq \mathtt{gfp}(F).$$

□

To understand the definitions of induction and coinduction given above, in Section 2.6 we revisit the examples from Section 2.1. These examples were expressed by means of rules: rules for generating the elements of an inductive set, or for 'observing' a coinductive element. So we first show in what sense a set of rules produces monotone operators on complete lattices.

Remark 2.4.4 (Non-monotone functions and other fixed points) It is possible to give coinductive and inductive definitions even for functions F that are not monotone. The basis in the study of non-monotone induction was set in the 1970s, in the works of, e.g., Aczel, Gandy, Moschovakis, Richter, and others, see [Acz77, Mos74]. An example of a form of bisimulation (on a higher-order functional language) that corresponds to a non-monotone function can be found in [SKS07b].

There are also situations where one is interested in fixed points other than the least or the greatest. In Computer Science, this happens for instance in finite model theory and in databases; scc, c.g. [GK03]. □

2.5 Definitions by means of rules

In this section we introduce rule induction and rule coinduction. They are among the most pervasive inductive and coinductive concepts in Computer Science. We show how to derive and justify them from the theory of fixed points.

Given a set X, a *ground rule on X* is a pair (S, x) with $S \subseteq X$ and $x \in X$. In the inductive (forward) reading, it intuitively says that from the premises S we can derive the conclusion x; in the coinductive (backward) reading, it says that x can be observed and thus reduced to the set S. A *set $\mathcal{R}$ of ground rules on X* is a subset of $\wp(X) \times X$; it allows us, inductively, to obtain elements of X from subsets of X or, coinductively, to reduce elements of X to subsets of X.

Note that what is usually called an inference rule corresponds, in the above terminology, to a set of ground rules, namely the set of all instances of the inference rule. As an example, consider the inference rule for $\Uparrow$:

$$\frac{e_1 \Uparrow}{e_1 \, e_2 \Uparrow}$$

on closed λ-terms (Λ^0) that we saw in Section 2.1.2. Here, e_1 and e_2 are metavariables: there is an implicit universal quantification on e_1 and e_2, which are supposed to be instantiated with concrete λ-terms in applications of the rule. The rule relates any closed term e_1 in the premise to any term of the form $e_1 \, e_2$ in the conclusion, where e_2 is also closed. We call a rule like this, which uses metavariables, *open*. Moving to ground rules, we have to take all concrete instances of the open rule. This yields the set of all pairs of the form $(\{e\}, e \, e')$, with $e, e' \in \Lambda^0$.

Similarly, the other open rule for $\Uparrow$, namely

$$\frac{e_1 \Downarrow \lambda x.e_0 \qquad e_0\{e_2/x\} \Uparrow}{e_1 \, e_2 \Uparrow},$$

when moving to ground rules becomes the set of all pairs of the form $(\{e\}, e_1 \, e_2)$, with $e, e_1, e_2 \in \Lambda^0$ and such that $e_1 \Downarrow \lambda x.e_0$ for some e_0 with $e_0\{e_2/x\} = e$.

Remark 2.5.1 Proceeding as above, the (open) inference rules employed for the inductive and coinductive definitions in the examples of Section 2.1 can be straightforwardly transformed into ground rules. Can we always transform the kind of inference rules commonly used to define inductive or coinductive sets into ground rules? The translation is immediate if, as in the examples of Section 2.1, the relation (or predicate) being defined is used in the premises of the inference rules in a 'first-order' manner. That is, the premises do not contain functions, or similar constructions, that manipulate the relation being defined. The translation may not be possible for rules in which the relation being defined appears in 'negative' (contravariant) position, for instance as input argument of a function. The reason is that such definitions may correspond to fixed points of non-monotone functions, whereas, as we shall see soon, ground rules yield monotone functions; we are thus beyond the fixed-point theory examined in this chapter. An example is the rule

$$\frac{f \in \mathcal{P} \to \mathcal{P} \qquad Q \in \mathcal{P}}{f\,\mathcal{P} \in \mathcal{P}}$$

(we are defining $\mathcal{P}$ while using it in contravariant position). Rules of this kind may be found in certain formalisations of the λ-calculus or in (the rule characterisation of) bisimulations for higher-order languages. See also Remark 2.4.4. □

A ground rule in which the first component is empty is called an *axiom*. In the remainder of the section we often omit the adjective 'ground'. We sometimes write a rule (S, x) as

$$\frac{x_1 \quad \cdots \quad x_n \quad \cdots}{x} \qquad \text{where } \{x_1, \ldots, x_n, \ldots\} = S.$$

A set $\mathcal{R}$ of rules on X yields a monotone endofunction $\Phi_{\mathcal{R}}$, called the *functional of $\mathcal{R}$* (or *rule functional*, when $\mathcal{R}$ is clear), on the complete lattice $\wp(X)$, where

$$\Phi_{\mathcal{R}}(T) = \{x \mid (T', x) \in \mathcal{R} \text{ for some } T' \subseteq T\}$$

(the set of conclusions derived from the subsets of T according to the rules in $\mathcal{R}$). We will see examples of this in Section 2.6.

Exercise 2.5.2 Show that $\Phi_{\mathcal{R}}$ above is indeed monotone. □

The relationship between rule functionals and monotone functions is in fact tight, as the following exercise shows.

Exercise 2.5.3 ($\hookrightarrow$) Show that every monotone operator on the complete lattice $\wp(X)$ can be expressed as the functional of some set of rules, and vice versa. Try then to obtain rules that are 'minimal', in that the number of the rules is as small as possible and, in each rule, the set of the premises is as small as possible. □

As the functional $\Phi_{\mathcal{R}}$ of a set of rules $\mathcal{R}$ is monotone, by the Fixed-point Theorem it has a least fixed point and a greatest fixed point, $\mathrm{lfp}(\Phi_{\mathcal{R}})$ and $\mathrm{gfp}(\Phi_{\mathcal{R}})$. They are obtained via the join and meet in Definition 2.4.1, and are indeed called the *sets inductively* and *coinductively defined by the rules*. Such definitions of sets are also referred to as *definitions by rule induction* and by *rule coinduction*.
We also get, from Corollary 2.4.3, induction and coinduction proof principles, respectively stating:

$$\text{if } \Phi_{\mathcal{R}}(T) \subseteq T \text{ then } \mathrm{lfp}(\Phi_{\mathcal{R}}) \subseteq T,$$
$$\text{if } T \subseteq \Phi_{\mathcal{R}}(T) \text{ then } T \subseteq \mathrm{gfp}(\Phi_{\mathcal{R}}).$$

It is useful to spell out concretely what all this means, beginning with the more familiar induction. A set T being a pre-fixed point of $\Phi_{\mathcal{R}}$ (i.e., the hypothesis $\Phi_{\mathcal{R}}(T) \subseteq T$) means that:

> *for all rules $(S, x) \in \mathcal{R}$, if $S \subseteq T$, then also $x \in T$.*

That is,

(i) the conclusion of each axiom is in T;
(ii) each rule whose premises are in T also has the conclusion in T.

This is precisely the 'forward' closure of Sections 2.1 and 2.2. Now, the Fixed-point Theorem tells us that the least fixed point is the least pre-fixed point: the set inductively defined by the rules is therefore the smallest set closed forward. The induction proof principle, in turn, says:

> *for a given T,*
> *if for all rules $(S, x) \in \mathcal{R}, S \subseteq T$ implies $x \in T$*
> *then* $\mathtt{lfp}(\Phi_{\mathcal{R}}) \subseteq T$. $\hspace{2cm}$ (2.1)

That is, if we have a property T, and we wish to prove that all elements in the set inductively defined by $\mathcal{R}$ have the property, we have to show that T is a pre-fixed point of $\Phi_{\mathcal{R}}$. Establishing (2.1) corresponds exactly to the familiar way of reasoning inductively on rules that the reader may have already met in textbooks or papers. The assumption '$S \subseteq T$' is the *inductive hypothesis*. The *base* of the induction is given by the axioms of $\mathcal{R}$, where the set S is empty.

In applications, sometimes T is taken to be a subset of $\mathtt{lfp}(\Phi_{\mathcal{R}})$, that is, a property on $\mathtt{lfp}(\Phi_{\mathcal{R}})$, and one is interested in proving $T = \mathtt{lfp}(\Phi_{\mathcal{R}})$. We thus use (2.1) to obtain $\mathtt{lfp}(\Phi_{\mathcal{R}}) \subseteq T$. In these cases, in the condition $S \subseteq T$ of (2.1), S ranges over the subsets of $\mathtt{lfp}(\Phi_{\mathcal{R}})$. We will use this variant of (2.1) in Section 2.6.3 to justify the familiar induction principle for lists.

In the case of coinduction, the hypothesis is that T is a post-fixed of $\Phi_{\mathcal{R}}$. This means that

> *for all $x \in T$, there is a rule $(S, x) \in \mathcal{R}$ with $S \subseteq T$.*

That is, each element of T is conclusion of a rule whose premises are satisfied in T. This is precisely the 'backward' closure of Sections 2.1 and 2.2. By the Fixed-point Theorem, the greatest fixed point is the greatest post-fixed point; therefore the set coinductively defined by the rules is the largest set closed backward. The coinduction proof principle reads thus:

> *for a given T,*
> *if for all $x \in T$ there is a rule $(S, x) \in \mathcal{R}$ with $S \subseteq T$,*
> *then* $T \subseteq \mathtt{gfp}(\Phi_{\mathcal{R}})$ $\hspace{2cm}$ (2.2)

In the literature, (2.1) and (2.2) are called the *principles of rule induction* and of *rule coinduction*.

Exercise 2.5.4 Let $\mathcal{R}$ be a set of ground rules, and suppose each rule has a non-empty premise. Show that $\mathtt{lfp}(\Phi_{\mathcal{R}}) = \emptyset$.   □

The above explanations rely on the characterisation of least and greatest fixed points in the Fixed-point Theorem. In the informal discussion of examples in Section 2.1, however, we mentioned two other formulations of the sets inductively and coinductively defined by means of rules. For induction, one formulation describes the elements of the set as those 'with a finite proof'; the other formulation describes the set as the result of an iterative construction that starts from the empty set. The two formulations for coinduction were similar. These formulations can be justified from two further characterisations of least and greatest fixed points. The first relies on the inductive and coinductive meaning of a derivation proof, and is studied in Section 2.11; the second relies on iterative schemata to reach least and greatest fixed points, and is studied in Section 2.8. Before doing this, we revisit the examples of Section 2.1, as well as other well-known examples of induction, in the light of the formal presentation of rules carried out in this section.

2.6 The examples, continued

In this section we show that the examples of induction and coinduction discussed in Section 2.1 are instances of the concepts of rule induction and rule coinduction introduced in Section 2.5.

2.6.1 Finite traces and ω-traces for processes as fixed points

We show how the predicates $\downarrow$ and $\uparrow_\mu$, from Section 2.1.1, are obtained for suitable sets of ground rules on the set *Pr* of all processes. In the case of $\downarrow$, the open rules given in Section 2.1.1 were:

$$\frac{P \text{ stopped}}{P \downarrow} \qquad\qquad \frac{P \xrightarrow{\mu} P' \qquad P' \downarrow}{P \downarrow}$$

These rules are open, in that P and P' are used as metavariables, therefore, as such, implicitly universally quantified. These open rules become the following set $\mathcal{R}_\downarrow$ of ground rules, where each rule is a pair of a subset of processes and a process (the first component is actually always either the empty set or a singleton):

$$\mathcal{R}_\downarrow \overset{\text{def}}{=} \{(\emptyset, P) \mid P \text{ is stopped}\}$$
$$\bigcup \{(\{P'\}, P) \mid P \xrightarrow{\mu} P' \text{ for some } \mu\}.$$

This yields the following functional, on the complete lattice $\wp(Pr)$:

$$\Phi_{\mathcal{R}_\downarrow}(T) \overset{\text{def}}{=} \{P \mid P \text{ is stopped, or there are } P', \mu \text{ with } P' \in T \text{ and } P \xrightarrow{\mu} P'\}.$$

The sets 'closed forward', in the terminology of Section 2.1.1, are the pre-fixed points of $\Phi_{\mathcal{R}_\downarrow}$. (In particular, in the case of the function f of Section 2.1.1, the proof that $\mathrm{dom}(\downarrow) \subseteq \mathrm{dom}(f)$ amounts to showing that $\mathrm{dom}(f)$ is such a pre-fixed point.) Thus the smallest set closed forward and the proof technique mentioned in Section 2.1.1 become examples of an inductively defined set and of the induction proof principle.

In the case of $\lceil_\mu$, in Section 2.1.1 we used the open rule

$$\frac{P \overset{\mu}{\to} P' \qquad P' \lceil_\mu}{P \lceil_\mu}$$

This becomes the set of ground rules

$$\mathcal{R}_{\lceil_\mu} \overset{\text{def}}{=} \{(\{P'\}, P) \mid P \overset{\mu}{\to} P'\},$$

which then yields the following functional:

$$\Phi_{\mathcal{R}_{\lceil_\mu}}(T) \overset{\text{def}}{=} \{P \mid \text{there is } P' \in T \text{ and } P \overset{\mu}{\to} P'\}.$$

Thus the sets 'closed backward' of Section 2.1 are the post-fixed points of $\Phi_{\mathcal{R}_{\lceil_\mu}}$, and the largest set closed backward is the greatest fixed point of $\Phi_{\mathcal{R}_{\lceil_\mu}}$. Similarly the proof technique for ω-traces is derived from the coinduction proof principle.

Exercise 2.6.1 Show that $\mathrm{gfp}(\Phi_{\mathcal{R}_\downarrow})$ is the set of all processes, and $\mathrm{lfp}(\Phi_{\mathcal{R}_{\lceil_\mu}})$ is the empty set. □

Exercise 2.6.2 ($\hookrightarrow$) Show that $P \in \mathrm{gfp}(\Phi_{\mathcal{R}_{\lceil_\mu}})$ if and only if there are processes P_i ($i \geq 0$) with $P_0 = P$ and such that, for each i, $P_i \overset{\mu}{\to} P_{i+1}$. □

The meaning of $\mathrm{lfp}(\Phi_{\mathcal{R}_\downarrow})$ is considered in Exercise 2.9.9.

2.6.2 Reduction to a value and divergence in the λ-calculus as fixed-points

Continuing Section 2.1.2, we show how convergence and divergence in the λ-calculus ($\Downarrow$ and $\Uparrow$) can be formulated as least and greatest fixed points of rule functionals. We only show the definition of the functionals, leaving the remaining details to the reader.

In the case of $\Downarrow$, the rules manipulate pairs of closed λ-terms, thus they act on the set $\Lambda^0 \times \Lambda^0$. The rule functional for $\Downarrow$, written $\Phi_\Downarrow$, is

$$\begin{aligned}
\Phi_\Downarrow(T) \overset{\text{def}}{=} \ & \{(e, e') \mid e = e' = \lambda x.e'', \text{ for some } e'' \in \Lambda \text{ and variable } x\} \\
& \cup \{(e, e') \mid \text{there are } e_1, e_2 \in \Lambda^0, e_0 \in \Lambda, \text{ and a variable } x \text{ with} \\
& \qquad e = e_1 \, e_2 \text{ and } (e_1, \lambda x.e_0) \in T \text{ and } (e_0\{e_2/x\}, e') \in T\}.
\end{aligned}$$

In the case of $\Uparrow$, the rules are on Λ^0. The rule functional for $\Uparrow$ is

$$\begin{aligned}
\Phi_\Uparrow(T) \overset{\text{def}}{=} \ & \{e_1 \, e_2 \mid e_1 \in T, \} \\
& \cup \{e_1 \, e_2 \mid \text{there is } e_0 \in \Lambda \text{ and a variable } x \text{ with} \\
& \qquad e_1 \Downarrow \lambda x.e_0 \text{ and } e_0\{e_2/x\} \in T\}.
\end{aligned}$$

2.6.3 Lists over a set A as fixed points

We now consider the rules for lists over a set A in Section 2.1.3. We can take X to be the set of all (finite and infinite) strings with elements from the alphabet $A \cup \{\text{nil}, \langle, \rangle, \bullet\}$. The ground rules are $(\emptyset, \text{nil})$ and, for each $s \in X$ and $a \in A$, the rule $(\{s\}, \langle a \rangle \bullet s)$. The corresponding rule functional $\Phi_{A\text{list}}$ is

$$\Phi_{A\text{list}}(T) \overset{\text{def}}{=} \{\text{nil}\} \cup \{\langle a \rangle \bullet s \mid a \in A, s \in T\}.$$

We indicate with FinLists_A the set of finite lists over A, that is, the set with elements of the form

$$\langle a_1 \rangle \bullet \langle a_2 \rangle \bullet \cdots \langle a_n \rangle \bullet \text{nil}$$

for some $n \geq 0$ (for $n = 0$ we get nil); and we indicate with FinInfLists_A the set of finite and infinite lists over A, that is, the set that adds to FinLists_A the infinite lists, of the form

$$\langle a_1 \rangle \bullet \langle a_2 \rangle \bullet \cdots \langle a_n \rangle \bullet \cdots$$

The reader may check that FinLists_A and FinInfLists_A are indeed fixed points of $\Phi_{A\text{list}}$. We defer proving that they are the least and the greatest fixed points to Exercise 2.9.11, after discussing continuity and cocontinuity.

Exercise 2.6.3 ($\hookrightarrow$) Suppose that A has more than one element. Does $\Phi_{A\text{list}}$ have other fixed points, besides FinLists_A and FinInfLists_A? (Hint: think about the infinite lists in which all elements are identical and what $\Phi_{A\text{list}}$ does on them.) □

From Corollary 2.4.3, we infer: suppose S is a property on FinLists_A, that is, a subset of FinLists_A; if $\Phi_{A\text{list}}(S) \subseteq S$ then $\text{FinLists}_A \subseteq S$ (hence $S = \text{FinLists}_A$). Proving $\Phi_{A\text{list}}(S) \subseteq S$ requires proving

- $\text{nil} \in S$;
- $s \in \text{FinLists}_A \cap S$ implies[2] $\langle a \rangle \bullet s \in S$, for all $a \in A$.

This is the familiar inductive proof technique for finite lists: to prove that a property on lists holds on all lists, prove that the property holds on the empty list, and assuming the property on a list s, prove that the property holds on $\langle a \rangle \bullet s$.

Exercise 2.6.4 ($\hookrightarrow$) Suppose we remove the first of the rules for lists in Section 2.1.3 (the axiom). What are the least and greatest fixed points of the resulting functional? □

Remark 2.6.5 In this section we have used the set X to 'bootstrap', via the powerset construction, thus assuming that X is already given. The choice of the specific X is not mandatory: any set in which the lists exist would do. This bootstrap essentially means that

---

[2] The condition $s \in \text{FinLists}_A \cap S$ could be simplified to $s \in S$, as we are assuming $S \subseteq \text{FinLists}_A$; it is so written to remind us that s is a finite list, and to make the analogy with the familiar inductive technique for lists clearer.

we have already a vague idea of the universe in which the objects of interest – in our case the lists – live, so that the goal becomes identifying the relevant portion of this universe.

An alternative would be to define lists taking the functional Φ_{Alist} on the universe of all sets. This would, however, take us beyond complete lattices and the fixed-point theory described in the present chapter – the universe of all sets is not a complete lattice because of paradoxes such as Russell's. Indeed, in this approach the natural mathematical tool to define `lfp` and `gfp` of Φ_{Alist} would be the algebra/coalgebra machinery explained in [RJ12], which generalises the theory of fixed points. ☐

2.6.4 Bisimulation on lists

An interesting issue is the proof of equality between lists. For finite lists, the problem is simple, because the proofs with which the lists are derived are finite: we can thus establish equalities by inspecting such proofs. Moreover, as finite lists are inductive objects, we can reason on them, for equality or other properties, using various inductive techniques, e.g., those discussed in Section 2.7.1. For instance, we can use induction on the depth of derivation proofs (the number of steps with which the finite lists are obtained).

These methods do not apply to infinite lists, and more generally to coinductively defined sets, in which derivation proofs can have infinite paths (i.e., generate a non-well-founded relation on nodes moving upward, from a node towards one of its children). We can still hope to employ inductive methods to prove equalities, since a list, be it finite or infinite, is uniquely identified by the sequence of elements from A it contains. Thus, writing s_n for the n-th element of a list s (and extracted from s in the expected way), on two infinite lists t and t' we have $t = t'$ when $t_n = t'_n$ for all n. We can then use mathematical induction on n to infer $t = t'$.[3] However, on coinductively defined sets, coinductive techniques are more natural and effective. In particular, we can prove equalities adapting the idea of bisimulation that we have earlier examined on LTSs. We show this for $FinInfLists_A$; the same idea applies to any data type coinductively defined via some rules.

The coinductive definition of a set tells us what can be observed of these elements. We can make this explicit in $FinInfLists_A$ defining an LTS on top of the lists. The domain of the LTS is the set $FinInfLists_A$, the labels are elements of A, and the transitions are given by the following rule:

$$\frac{}{\langle a \rangle \bullet s \xrightarrow{a} s} \tag{2.3}$$

The rule says that we can observe the head of a list and the result is its tail. As usual we write $\sim$ for the resulting bisimilarity, as by Definition 1.4.2. The next lemma shows that bisimilarity coincides with syntactic identity.

Lemma 2.6.6 *For $s, t \in FinInfLists_A$, it holds that $s = t$ if and only if $s \sim t$.*

---

[3] Sometimes this method may, however, be difficult to apply; for instance in programming languages with higher-order features, see [Fio93].

Proof Bisimilarity is reflexive, which proves the implication from left to right in the lemma. For the converse, one shows, by induction on n, that $s \sim t$ implies $s_n = t_n$ for all n; this means that the sequence of elements from A in the definitions of s and t are the same, that is, $s = t$. $\qquad\qquad\square$

The property stated in Lemma 2.6.6 is often referred to as *(strong) extensionality for* $FinInfLists_A$, to indicate that the identity relation is the maximal bisimulation on the set.

Of course it is not necessary to define an LTS from lists. We can directly define a kind of bisimulation on lists, as follows. A relation $\mathcal{R} \subseteq FinInfLists_A \times FinInfLists_A$ is a *list bisimulation* if whenever $(s, t) \in \mathcal{R}$ then

(1) $s = \texttt{nil}$ implies $t = \texttt{nil}$;
(2) $s = \langle a \rangle \bullet s'$ implies there is t' such that $t = \langle a \rangle \bullet t'$ and $(s', t') \in \mathcal{R}$.

Then we obtain *list bisimilarity* as the union of all list bisimulations.

To see how natural the bisimulation method on lists is, it may also be useful to consider the following characterisation of equality between lists, by means of rules (on X):

$$\frac{}{\texttt{nil} = \texttt{nil}} \qquad\qquad \frac{s_1 = s_2 \qquad a \in A}{\langle a \rangle \bullet s_1 = \langle a \rangle \bullet s_2}$$

The inductive interpretation of the rules gives us equality on $FinLists_A$, as the least fixed point of the corresponding rule functional. In contrast, the coinductive interpretation gives us equality on $FinInfLists_A$, and list bisimulation as associated proof technique. To see this, it suffices to note that the post-fixed points of the rule functional are precisely the list bisimulations; hence the greatest fixed point is list bisimilarity and, by Lemma 2.6.6, it is also the equality relation.

The exercises and example below show applications of the bisimulation method for lists.

Exercise 2.6.7 Let A be a set, and $map : (A \rightarrow A) \rightarrow (FinInfLists_A \rightarrow FinInfLists_A)$ be defined by the following equation:

$$map\ f\ \texttt{nil} \stackrel{\text{def}}{=} \texttt{nil},$$
$$map\ f\ \langle a \rangle \bullet s \stackrel{\text{def}}{=} \langle f(a) \rangle \bullet (map\ f\ s).$$

These equations are satisfied by the function G that, given a function f and a list, replaces each element a in the list with $f(a)$. Show the unicity of the function satisfying the equations: for any other function G' that satisfies the same equations, and for any function $f : A \rightarrow A$ and list $s \in FinInfLists_A$, it holds that $Gfs \sim G'fs$. $\qquad\square$

Remark 2.6.8 In Exercise 2.6.7, the definition of a function G satisfying the equations for map was sketchy. The argument can be refined as follows. We have already mentioned that a list on a set A is uniquely identified by the sequence of elements from A it contains. We can therefore associate a list s with a function, say $\bar{s}$, from natural numbers to A, that can be undefined on a suffix of the naturals (i.e., $\bar{s}(n)$ undefined and $m > n$ imply $\bar{s}(m)$ undefined). Call such functions *list functions on A*. Given a list function $\bar{s}$ and a function $f : A \rightarrow A$, the composition of f and $\bar{s}$ is another list function, $f \circ \bar{s}$, mapping n onto $f(\bar{s}(n))$. Now, the function G in Exercise 2.6.7 is the function that, on arguments f and s, returns the list associated with the list function $f \circ \bar{s}$.

Instead of identifying a list with a list function, we could identify a list with the set of all the prefixes of the list (a prefix-closed set of finite sequences of characters). These sets could then be manipulated using induction, since the sequences they contain are finite, so that G can be defined using recursion (see Section 2.7.2). This representation may be more convenient in the case of data types more sophisticated than lists (see, e.g., the representation of proof trees in Remark 2.11.1). $\qquad\square$

In the examples and exercises below we use other systems of equations that, as map, define functions onto $\mathtt{FinInfLists}_A$. These are functions defined by *corecursion* (discussed in Section 2.7.2). The proofs that such functions exist and are unique can be done as for map (Exercise 2.6.7 and Remark 2.6.8).

Moreover, to enhance readability, in the remainder of the section we avoid some brackets by adopting the following conventions. Expressions such as

$$\langle a \rangle \bullet \mathtt{map}\ f\ s$$

(a function symbol on the right of the append symbol '$\bullet$') read as $\langle a \rangle \bullet (\mathtt{map}\ f\ s)$; expressions such as

$$\mathtt{map}\ f\ \langle a \rangle \bullet s$$

(append underneath a function) read as $\mathtt{map}\ f\ (\langle a \rangle \bullet s)$; expressions such as

$$\mathtt{map}\ f\ g(a)$$

(a function application, $g(a)$, in the argument of another function, map) read as $\mathtt{map}\ f\ (g(a))$ (the two arguments required by the outermost function, map, are f and $g(a)$).

Example 2.6.9 Consider the function

$$\mathtt{iterate} : (A \rightarrow A) \rightarrow (A \rightarrow \mathtt{FinInfLists}_A)$$

defined by:

$$\mathtt{iterate}\ f\ a \stackrel{\mathrm{def}}{=} \langle a \rangle \bullet \mathtt{iterate}\ f\ f(a).$$

Thus $\mathtt{iterate}\ f\ a$ builds the infinite list

$$\langle a \rangle \bullet \langle f(a) \rangle \bullet \langle f(f(a)) \rangle \bullet \cdots$$

We show that, for all $a \in A$, we have

$$\text{map } f \text{ (iterate } f \; a) = \text{iterate } f \; f(a).$$

For this, we consider the relation

$$\mathcal{R} \overset{\text{def}}{=} \{(\text{map } f \text{ (iterate } f \; a), \text{iterate } f \; f(a)) \mid a \in A\}.$$

We prove that this is a bisimulation, using the LTS and the bisimulation for lists defined above, so that we can derive the final result from Lemma 2.6.6. Let $(P, Q) \in \mathcal{R}$, for

$$P \overset{\text{def}}{=} \text{map } f \text{ (iterate } f \; a),$$
$$Q \overset{\text{def}}{=} \text{iterate } f \; f(a).$$

Applying the definition of iterate, we have

$$Q = \langle f(a) \rangle \bullet \text{iterate } f \; f(f(a)),$$

hence (using the LTS rule (2.3) at page 53)

$$Q \xrightarrow{f(a)} \text{iterate } f \; f(f(a)) \overset{\text{def}}{=} Q'.$$

Similarly, using also the definition of map,

$$
\begin{aligned}
P &= \text{map } f \; \langle a \rangle \bullet (\text{iterate } f \; f(a)) \\
&= \langle f(a) \rangle \bullet \text{map } f \text{ (iterate } f \; f(a)) \\
&\xrightarrow{f(a)} \text{map } f \text{ (iterate } f \; f(a)) \\
&\overset{\text{def}}{=} P'.
\end{aligned}
$$

We have $P' \; \mathcal{R} \; Q'$, as $f(a) \in A$. Summarising, we have showed that P and Q have a single transition, with the same label, and with derivatives that are in $\mathcal{R}$. This concludes the proof that $\mathcal{R}$ is a bisimulation. □

The two exercises below are due to Pitts [Pit93]. They make use of proofs and definitions of functions by induction on the natural numbers. These are common concepts, and we assume that the reader has already some familiarity with them. Their justification from fixed-point theory is treated in Section 2.7.

Exercise 2.6.10 ($\hookrightarrow$) Let $+_1$ be the function that returns the successor of a natural number. Consider the infinite list nats of natural numbers, and the function from that takes a natural number and returns a list of natural numbers, recursively defined as follows:

$$\text{nats} \overset{\text{def}}{=} \langle 0 \rangle \bullet (\text{map } +_1 \text{ nats}),$$
$$\text{from}(n) \overset{\text{def}}{=} \langle n \rangle \bullet \text{from}(n+1).$$

Show that

$$\text{nats} = \text{from}(0).$$

(Hint: write $(\text{map} +_1)^n \text{nats}$, with $n \geq 0$, for

$$\underbrace{\text{map} +_1 \ (\text{map} +_1 \ (\ldots(\text{map} +_1 \ \text{nats})\ldots))}_{n \ \text{times}}.$$

That is, $(\text{map} +_1)$ is applied n times starting from nats, with $(\text{map} +_1)^0 \text{nats} = \text{nats}$. Show that

$$\mathcal{R} \stackrel{\text{def}}{=} \bigcup_n \{((\text{map} +_1)^n \text{nats}, \text{from}\,(n))\}$$

is a bisimulation, proceeding as in Example 2.6.9.) □

Exercise 2.6.11 $(*, \hookrightarrow)$ Consider the Fibonacci function f on natural numbers defined recursively thus:

$$f(0) \stackrel{\text{def}}{=} 0, \qquad f(1) \stackrel{\text{def}}{=} 1, \qquad f(n+1) \stackrel{\text{def}}{=} f(n) + f(n-1).$$

Let now fibs be the infinite list of natural numbers recursively defined thus:

$$\text{fibs} \stackrel{\text{def}}{=} \langle 0 \rangle \bullet \langle 1 \rangle \bullet \text{plus}\,(\text{fibs}, \text{tail}\,(\text{fibs})),$$

where plus adds componentwise the elements of two infinite lists, thus producing another infinite list, and tail takes a list, strips off its first element, and returns the remaining list. Proceed as in Example 2.6.9 and Exercise 2.6.10 to prove

$$\text{fibs} = \text{map}\, f\, \text{nats}$$

for nats defined as in Exercise 2.6.10. (Hint: use a property of $(\text{map} +_1)^n \text{nats}$ in the proof of Exercise 2.6.10, and try to develop $\text{plus}\,(\text{fibs}, \text{tail}\,(\text{fibs}))$ so as to find some recurring pattern.) □

2.7 Other induction and coinduction principles

In this section we consider other induction and coinduction principles, and show how to justify them from fixed-point theory. First, we consider a few induction principles that are common in Mathematics and Computer Science. Then we touch on definitions of functions by recursion and corecursion. Finally, we discuss examples of variants of the characterisations of least and greatest fixed points in the Fixed-point Theorem and their associated principles.

2.7.1 Common induction principles: mathematical induction, structural induction, and others

We have seen that the examples of induction and coinduction in Section 2.1 can be formally explained as definitions and proofs by rule induction and rule coinduction and these, in turn, can be derived as instances of the general schema for induction and coinduction that was set up using fixed-point theory. We consider here other examples of well-known inductive proof principles: mathematical induction, structural induction, induction on derivation proofs, transition induction, well-founded induction and transfinite induction. We show how to derive them from rule induction and the corresponding principle (2.1) in Section 2.5.

The goal of the section is to illustrate the relationship between these principles and the general concept of induction as defined in terms of fixed-point theory. We do this via rule induction, since we have already derived this from fixed-point theory. Two observations are worthwhile here. First, reducing all the principles to rule induction is not necessary: we could derive, for instance, well-founded induction directly from fixed-point theory, and reduce all the other principles to well-founded induction. Second, the soundness of the principles can also be proved directly, without appeal to fixed-point theory. An example of such a proof is given in Exercise 2.7.1.

We do not discuss the coinductive versions of these principles, which are not well-established; see, however, the comments at the end of the section.

Mathematical induction

Similarly to the example of finite lists, one can treat the best known example of inductive set: the natural numbers.

The rules on the set $\{0, 1, \ldots\}$ of natural numbers, or any other set containing the natural numbers, are:

$$\frac{}{0} \qquad \text{and} \qquad \frac{n}{n+1} \qquad \text{for all } n \geq 0.$$

The set inductively defined by these rules is indeed the set of natural numbers. And the principle of rule induction then says: if a property on the naturals holds at 0 and, whenever it holds at n, it also holds at $n + 1$, then the property is true for all naturals. We have thus obtained the natural numbers and the standard proof method by induction on the natural numbers, also called *mathematical induction*, from rule induction.

In a variant of mathematical induction, the inductive step uses the assumption that the property holds at all numbers less than or equal to n and requires proving the property at $n + 1$. This reasoning is useful when the proof for $n + 1$ makes use of several smaller integers. Such induction corresponds to a variant presentation of the natural numbers, where the rules are

$$\frac{}{0} \qquad \text{and} \qquad \frac{0 \quad 1 \quad \ldots \quad n}{n+1} \qquad \text{for all } n \geq 0.$$

These rules are the ground-rule translation of the following (open) inference rule, where S is a property on the natural numbers:

$$\frac{i \in S, \ \forall i < j}{j \in S}$$

This is the common rule with which mathematical induction is used.

Structural induction

The rules for lists, in Section 2.1.3, interpreted inductively, allow us to build up objects that have a structure, in the sense of being composed of simpler objects. Other examples of rules that produce structured objects are those of a grammar, such as that for λ-terms in Section 2.1.2 and that for CCS in Chapter 3. In these cases, the object obtained can be *atomic*, if derived from an axiom, or *composite*. A composite object is of the shape $f(t_1, \ldots, t_n)$, where the t_is are immediate subobjects, and f is the operator that puts them together and determines the final shape. The principle of *structural induction* says that, given a property on the objects produced by the rules, if

(i) the property holds at all atomic objects, and
(ii) for any composite object t, if the property holds of the immediate subobjects of t then it also holds at t,

then the property is true in the whole set inductively defined by the rules. That is, the reasoning in structural induction consists in proving that the act of building up complex structures from simpler ones preserves the property of interest. The peculiarity of structural induction is that the validity of the inductive steps relies on a syntactic check.

In the case of lists, the structural induction principle is the same as the proof principle derived in Section 2.6.3 following rule induction. Similarly, structural induction can be justified from rule induction in other cases.

Induction on derivation proofs

When playing with rules, one often finds results proved by induction on *derivation proofs*. In this case the reasoning focuses on the derivation trees with which the rules generate elements. The root of the tree is the element produced by the concluding rule in the derivation. The principle says that if a property holds at the atomic trees (those with only one node) and, for any other tree t, whenever the property holds at the immediate subtrees of t then it also holds at t, then the property holds for all derivation trees. A proof by induction on derivation proofs proceeds by a case analysis on the concluding rule of the derivation. One considers each rule (S, x) and proves that, if the derivation tree of each $s \in S$ has the desired property, then the whole derivation tree has it too. The case when S is empty corresponds to the basis of the induction.

The trees have a structure and therefore this form of induction is a special case of structural induction. One can also obtain it as a special form of rule induction, by defining appropriate rules that manipulate derivation trees.

If the derivation trees are finitely branching (each node has only finitely many children) then the height of a tree can be defined and an induction on derivation trees can be turned into a mathematical induction. In general, however, derivation trees need not be finitely branching.

Transition induction

In the book, beginning in Chapter 3, we will often consider transition relation on processes defined by means of rules. The corresponding induction on derivation proofs is called *transition induction*. It is frequently used in concurrency theory, hence the special name given to it.

Well-founded induction

Well-founded induction says that, given a relation $\mathcal{R}$ that is well-founded on a set X (recall that a relation is well-founded if it does not give rise to infinite descending chains) and a property T on X, to show that $X \subseteq T$ (the property T holds at all elements of X), it suffices to prove that, for all $x \in X$: if $y \in T$ for all y with $y \mathcal{R} x$, then also $x \in T$.

Mathematical induction is a special case of well-founded induction, where X is the set of natural numbers, and $\mathcal{R}$ is the predecessor relation. Another obvious special case is structural induction, where X is the set of all expressions and $\mathcal{R}$ is the 'immediate subexpression' relation (where $e \mathcal{R} f$ if e is an immediate subexpression of f). Well-founded induction is indeed the natural generalisation of mathematical induction to sets and, as such, it is frequent to find it in Mathematics and Computer Science. For instance, we can use it to prove a property reasoning on the lexicographical order of pairs of natural numbers (whereby $(n, m) < (n', m')$ if either $n < n'$ or $n = n'$ and $m < m'$), which is a well-founded relation. A nice application of this is proving that the algorithmic recursive definition of the Ackermann's function terminates.

We can derive well-founded induction from fixed-point theory in the same way as we did for rule induction. In fact, we can reduce well-founded induction to rule induction taking as rules, for each $x \in X$, the pair (S, x) where S is the set $\{y \mid y \mathcal{R} x\}$ and $\mathcal{R}$ the well-founded relation. The set inductively defined by the rules is precisely X (Exercise 2.7.2); that is, any set equipped with a well-founded relation is an inductive set.

Exercise 2.7.1 ($\hookrightarrow$) Prove the validity of well-founded induction directly: given a well-founded relation on a set X and a property T on X that satisfies the requirements of well-founded induction, assume that $y \notin T$ for some $y \in X$ and derive a contradiction. $\square$

Exercise 2.7.2 Prove formally the reduction of well-founded induction to rule induction, in particular that X is the set inductively defined by the rules given above. (Hint: you may find useful the initial observation in the proof of Exercise 2.7.1, in the Appendix.) $\square$

Transfinite induction

Transfinite induction is the extension of mathematical induction to ordinals (introduced in Section 0.5). Transfinite induction says that to prove that a property T on the ordinals holds at all ordinals, it suffices to prove, for all ordinals α: if $\beta \in T$ for all ordinals $\beta < \alpha$ then also $\alpha \in T$. In proofs, this is usually split into three cases, according to whether α is 0, a successor ordinal, or a limit ordinal. This means proving:

(i) $0 \in T$;
(ii) for each successor ordinal α, if $\alpha - 1 \in T$ then also $\alpha \in T$;
(iii) for each limit ordinal α, if $\beta \in T$ for all $\beta < \alpha$ then also $\alpha \in T$.

In a variant of transfinite induction, (ii) and (iii) are merged by requiring that for each ordinal α above 0, if $\beta \in T$ for all $\beta < \alpha$ then also $\alpha \in T$.

Transfinite induction acts on the ordinals, which form a proper class rather than a set. As such, we cannot derive it from the fixed-point theory presented. However, in practice, transfinite induction is used to reason on sets, in cases where mathematical induction is not sufficient because the set has 'too many' elements. We will see an example of this in Theorem 2.8.8. In these cases, in the transfinite induction each ordinal is associated with an element of the set. Then the $<$ relation on the ordinals yields a well-founded relation on the set, so that transfinite induction becomes a special case of well-founded induction on sets. Another possibility for justifying transfinite induction would be to lift the theory of induction to classes. While this is possible, we do not pursue it in the book, where we always work with sets.

Exercise 2.7.3 ($\hookrightarrow$) Let X be the set of all (finite and infinite) strings over the alphabet $\{a, b\}$, and consider the following rules:

$$(\emptyset, \epsilon) \qquad\qquad (\{s\}, a.s.b) \qquad\qquad (\{s_1, s_2\}, s_1.s_2)$$

where '.' is the concatenation of strings, ϵ is the empty string, and for all s we assume that: $\epsilon.s = s.\epsilon = s$; if s' is infinite then $s'.s = s'$. Let S be the set of strings inductively defined from such rules. What does the principle of rule induction say in this case? Prove that in any string in S the number of a symbols is equal to that of b symbols. What is S? And the set coinductively defined by the rules?

Suppose now we replace the rule $(\emptyset, \epsilon)$ with the rule $(\emptyset, a.b)$. Is there anything that changes in the previous answers? What if we also remove ϵ from X? $\qquad\square$

Exercise 2.7.4 (Reflexive and transitive closure) Consider an LTS with a special action τ (something we will study in Chapter 4). Define rules that produce, as least fixed point of the corresponding functional, the reflexive and transitive closure of $\xrightarrow{\tau}$ (i.e., prove that such least fixed point is the relation $\Longrightarrow$ of Definition 4.1.1, and is also the smallest relation that is reflexive, transitive, and contains $\xrightarrow{\tau}$). $\qquad\square$

Having seen all the above variants of induction, a question that naturally arises is: what is their counterpart for coinduction? A tentative answer for the case of structural induction is the following. In structural induction, we assume a property for simple terms, and we have to derive the same property for complex terms, where the relationship between 'simple term' and 'complex term' is *syntactical*. In coinduction, given a set of terms, we have to 'decompose' any such term or, more generally, we have to extract observations from it, possibly thus producing other terms in the set. When the validity of this step is justified by a *syntactic* argument, we could call the coinduction 'structural'. For instance, in the coinductive reading of the rules for finite and infinite lists, a list is decomposed into a head and a tail; in applications of the rules, a syntactic check ensures the occurrence of a decomposition step. A less trivial example of syntactic conditions in coinduction is the formalisation of corecursion (a coinductive concept discussed in the next section) in the theorem prover Coq; see [BC04].

2.7.2 Function definitions by recursion and corecursion

One often finds (total) functions defined by means of systems of equations. Such definitions may follow the schema of *recursion* or *corecursion*.

In a definition by *recursion* the domain of the function is an inductive set. One specifies the result of the function on a given argument by exploiting the results of the functions on smaller arguments. The meaning of 'smaller' depends on the nature of inductive set in the domain, analogously to the different forms of inductive proof and inductive definition discussed in earlier sections. For instance, in *well-founded recursion*, the domain is a set equipped with a well-founded relation and 'a smaller than b' means 'a in relation with b'; in *structural recursion*, the domain is a set whose elements have a structure, being built from atomic objects by means of appropriate constructors, and 'a smaller than b' means 'a is a subterm of b'. Well-founded recursion is the most interesting case, and entails structural recursion as a special case.

Examples on the well-founded set of the natural numbers are the Fibonacci function of Exercise 2.6.11, and the factorial function recursively defined thus:

$$f(0) \stackrel{\text{def}}{=} 1, \qquad f(n+1) \stackrel{\text{def}}{=} (n+1) \times f(n),$$

where $\times$ is multiplication.

Example 2.7.5 We sketch a proof of the existence and of the unicity of the the function satisfying the above equations for the factorial. We can establish existence by appealing to rule induction. Consider the following rules on pairs of natural numbers:

$$\frac{}{(0,1)} \qquad \qquad \frac{(n,m)}{(n+1,(n+1) \times m)}$$

where n, m are arbitrary natural numbers. Now, let G be the set of pairs of naturals inductively defined by these rules. One shows that G is the graph of a function, say g, whereby $g(n) = m$ if $(n,m) \in G$. For this, one has to check that G is

- single-valued, in that for all n, m, m' if both $(n,m) \in G$ and $(n,m') \in G$ then $m = m'$;
- total, in that for all n there is m with $(n,m) \in G$.

Both statements are proved by induction on n; the details are simple and are left to the reader. Having proved that G indeed yields a function, one checks that such a function satisfies the equations of the factorial.

Now, it remains to prove unicity: there is only one function satisfying the equations of the factorial. For this one uses mathematical induction to show that for any two functions h and h' on the natural numbers satisfying the equations, it holds that $h(n) = h'(n)$ for all n. Again, the details are straightforward. □

An example of structural recursion is the function f that defines the number of λ-abstractions in a λ-term:

$$f(x) \stackrel{\text{def}}{=} 0, \qquad f(\lambda x.e) \stackrel{\text{def}}{=} 1 + f(e), \qquad f(e\,e') \stackrel{\text{def}}{=} f(e) + f(e').$$

It is possible to define patterns of equations for well-founded recursion, and prove that whenever the patterns are respected the functions specified exist and are unique. The proof makes use of well-founded induction, both to prove that such functions exist and to prove their unicity, along the lines of the proof in the Example 2.7.5 of the factorial. The interested reader may find details in [Win93].

While a function defined by recursion acts on the elements of an inductive set, one defined by *corecursion* produces an element of a coinductive set. An equation for a corecursive function specifies the immediate observables of the element returned by the function; for instance, if the element is an infinite list, the equation must tell us what is the head of the list. Examples are the definitions of the functions map, iterate, nats, from and fibs from Section 2.6.4 (we can regard nats and fibs as functions with a singleton domain). We considered the existence and unicity of map in Exercise 2.6.7 and Remark 2.6.8, and pointed out that the other functions can be treated similarly. As in the case of recursion, so for corecursion one can produce general equation schemata, and prove that any system of equations satisfying the schemata defines a unique function (or unique functions, in case of mutually recursive equations); see for instance [BM96], for equations on non-well-founded sets.

2.7.3 Enhancements of the principles

The induction and coinduction principles in Corollary 2.4.3 have been derived as straight-forward corollaries of the Fixed-point Theorem. With a bit of work, we can also derive more powerful principles, which may sometimes be useful. Applications of induction and coinduction are about finding points that are above the least fixed point or below the greatest fixed point. The new principles are more powerful because they are derived from charac-terisations of least and greatest fixed points as meet and join of sets that are larger than the sets mentioned in the Fixed-point Theorem. As the sets in the characterisations have more points, the search for them in applications may be easier.

Below are some examples, in the case of coinduction, from [Len98]. These and other more sophisticated constructions will be the basis, in [PS12], for the study of enhancements of the bisimulation proof method. We sometimes use an infix notation for the join on two points.

Theorem 2.7.6 *Let F be a monotone endofunction on a complete lattice L, and y a post-fixed point of F (i.e., $y \leq F(y)$). Then*

$$\mathrm{gfp}(F) = \bigcup \{x \mid x \leq F(x \cup y)\}.$$

Proof Let $S_1 \stackrel{\text{def}}{=} \{x \mid x \leq F(x)\}$ be the set of all post-fixed points of F, and $S_2 \stackrel{\text{def}}{=} \{x \mid x \leq F(x \cup y)\}$. By the Fixed-point Theorem 2.3.21, $\mathrm{gfp}(F) = \cup S_1$. We show that $\cup S_1 = \cup S_2$. First, since by monotonicity of F for any points z_1, z_2, we have $F(z_1) \leq F(z_1 \cup z_2)$, any point $x \in S_1$ is also in S_2, which proves $\cup S_1 \leq \cup S_2$.

For the opposite, take $x \in S_2$. We show that $x \cup y \in S_1$. From the hypothesis $y \leq F(y)$ and using monotonicity as above, we derive $y \leq F(x \cup y)$; from $x \in S_2$ we know

$x \leq F(x \cup y)$. Thus $F(x \cup y)$ is an upper bound for both x and y, and we can conclude $x \cup y \leq F(x \cup y)$, that is, $x \cup y \in S_1$. Since this holds for all x in S_2, and $x \leq x \cup y$, we can conclude that $\bigcup S_1$ is an upper bound of S_2, therefore $\bigcup S_2 \leq \bigcup S_1$.   □

From the theorem we derive the *principle of coinduction up-to* $\cup$:

> *Let F be a monotone endofunction on a complete lattice,*
> *and suppose $y \leq F(y)$;*
> *then $x \leq F(x \cup y)$ implies $x \leq \mathrm{gfp}(F)$.*

The advantage of this principle is that it may be easier to prove $x \leq F(x \cup y)$, instead of $x \leq F(x)$ as by Corollary 2.4.3, since $F(x \cup y)$ is above $F(x)$ (on the lattices of powersets, $F(x \cup y)$ will be a set larger than $F(x)$). The most useful instance of Theorem 2.7.6 is when $y = \mathrm{gfp}(F)$ (it is the most useful because, $F(x \cup \mathrm{gfp}(F))$ is 'larger' than $F(x \cup y)$, for any post-fixed point y, i.e., we have $F(x \cup y) \leq F(x \cup \mathrm{gfp}(F))$). Thus the principle becomes:

> *If F is a monotone endofunction on a complete lattice,*
> *then $x \leq F(x \cup \mathrm{gfp}(F))$ implies $x \leq \mathrm{gfp}(F)$.*

We discuss the meaning of this, for bisimulation, in Exercise 2.10.7.

Exercise 2.7.7 ($\hookrightarrow$) Prove the following variant of Theorem 2.7.6. Let F be a monotone endofunction on a complete lattice L, and y a post-fixed point of F. Then

$$\mathrm{gfp}(F) = \bigcup \{x \mid x \leq F(x) \cup y\}.$$

(Hint: proceed as in the proof of Theorem 2.7.6; some more care is needed to establish $x \cup y \leq F(x \cup y)$.)   □

Theorem 2.7.8 *Let F be a monotone endofunction on a complete lattice L, and $\diamond$: $L \times L \to L$ an associative function such that:*

(1) *for all $x, y, x', y' \in L$, whenever both $x \leq F(x')$ and $y \leq F(y')$, then $x \diamond y \leq F(x' \diamond y')$;*

(2) *for all x with $x \leq F(x)$ we have both $x \leq x \diamond \mathrm{gfp}(F)$ and $x \leq \mathrm{gfp}(F) \diamond x$.*

Then

$$\mathrm{gfp}(F) = \bigcup \{x \mid x \leq F(\mathrm{gfp}(F) \diamond x \diamond \mathrm{gfp}(F))\}.$$

Proof We write gfp as an abbreviation for $\mathrm{gfp}(F)$, and we use the associativity of $\diamond$ without mentioning it. As in the proof of Theorem 2.7.6, it suffices to prove:

(i) $x \leq F(x)$ implies $x \leq F(\mathrm{gfp} \diamond x \diamond \mathrm{gfp})$; and
(ii) $x \leq F(\mathrm{gfp} \diamond x \diamond \mathrm{gfp})$ implies there is y with $x \leq y$ and $y \leq F(y)$.

Property (i) follows from assumptions (1) and (2), using $x \leq F(x)$ and $\mathrm{gfp} \leq F(\mathrm{gfp})$.

We now consider (ii). First, using the greatest fixed-point property of gfp and assumption (2), we note that $\mathrm{gfp} \leq \mathrm{gfp} \diamond \mathrm{gfp}$. Using assumption (1), we derive $\mathrm{gfp} \diamond \mathrm{gfp} \leq$

$F(\text{gfp} \diamond \text{gfp})$; thus $\text{gfp} \diamond \text{gfp}$ is a post-fixed point, and hence $\text{gfp} \diamond \text{gfp} \leq \text{gfp}$. We have therefore proved $\text{gfp} = \text{gfp} \diamond \text{gfp}$. We now prove (ii) taking $y \stackrel{\text{def}}{=} F(\text{gfp} \diamond x \diamond \text{gfp})$, for which $x \leq y$ holds by hypothesis. From $x \leq F(\text{gfp} \diamond x \diamond \text{gfp})$ and $\text{gfp} \leq F(\text{gfp})$, using assumption (1) twice, we derive $\text{gfp} \diamond x \diamond \text{gfp} \leq F(\text{gfp} \diamond \text{gfp} \diamond x \diamond \text{gfp} \diamond \text{gfp})$. Since $\text{gfp} = \text{gfp} \diamond \text{gfp}$, also $\text{gfp} \diamond x \diamond \text{gfp} \leq F(\text{gfp} \diamond x \diamond \text{gfp})$. Finally, by monotonicity of F, we conclude $F(\text{gfp} \diamond x \diamond \text{gfp}) \leq F(F(\text{gfp} \diamond x \diamond \text{gfp}))$.

□

From this theorem we derive the *principle of coinduction up-to* gfp:

> Let F be a monotone endofunction on a complete lattice L,
> and $\diamond : L \times L \to L$ an associative function
> for which the assumptions (1) and (2) of Theorem 2.7.8 hold;
> then $x \leq F(\text{gfp}(F) \diamond x \diamond \text{gfp}(F))$ implies $x \leq \text{gfp}(F)$.

We show in Exercise 2.10.8 that in the case of bisimilarity this principles precisely corresponds to the 'bisimulation up-to $\sim$' technique of Exercise 1.4.18.

Exercise 2.7.9 ($\hookrightarrow$) Show that Theorem 2.7.8 also holds when assumption (2) is replaced by

$$\text{gfp}(F) \leq \text{gfp}(F) \diamond \text{gfp}(F).$$

□

Of course the dual versions of the theorems and the principles, for induction, also hold. For instance, the dual of coinduction up-to $\cup$ is the *principle of induction up-to* $\cap$:

> Let F be a monotone endofunction on a complete lattice,
> and suppose $F(y) \leq y$;
> then $F(x \cap y) \leq x$ implies $\text{lfp}(F) \leq x$.

Exercise 2.7.10 ($\hookrightarrow$) Prove the principle of induction up to $\cap$ above. □

The (very simple) principles examined in this section are, by themselves, not extremely important: a proof that uses them can be turned into a proof that uses the original principles of Corollary 2.4.3 with a little extra effort. What this section is meant to suggest is the possibility of enhancing the induction and coinduction principles. In certain cases, notably with bisimulation, one can derive powerful principles. We do not pursue the topic here. The details are examined in [PS12], where a rich theory of enhancements of the bisimulation proof method is defined, with strong implications on concrete proofs of bisimilarity.

As a final remark, note that the principles in this section are all complete, in that they are derived from theorems that express characterisations of greatest and least fixed points. However, when looking for inductive and coinductive proof techniques, completeness is not mandatory. What we need are techniques for proving that points in the lattice are above the least fixed point or below the greatest fixed point. It may be quite acceptable that in certain cases the technique is not applicable.

2.8 Constructive proofs of the existence of least and greatest fixed points

The proof of the Fixed point Theorem 2.3.21 we have seen is not constructive (least fixed point and greatest fixed point of a function are obtained from the sets of its pre- and post-fixed points and we are not told how to find these). Theorems 2.8.5 and 2.8.8 give constructive proofs, by means of iterative schemata. Theorem 2.8.5 uses iteration over the natural numbers, but needs additional hypotheses on the function; Theorem 2.8.8 avoids the additional hypotheses by iterating over the ordinals. The main advantage of these iteration schemata is that they give us a means of approximating, and possibly even computing, least fixed points and greatest fixed points. The constructions are indeed at the heart of the algorithms used today for computing these fixed points, including those for checking bisimilarity, see [AIS12]. The iteration schemata also offer us an alternative way for reasoning about the fixed points. For instance, on greatest fixed point the schema is useful to prove that a point is not below the greatest fixed point (see for bisimilarity Examples 2.10.15 and 2.10.16).

The first iteration schema requires properties on functions – continuity and cocontinuity – that are stronger than monotonicity. We write $\bigcup_i \alpha_i$ as abbreviation for $\bigcup_i \{\alpha_i\}$, and $\bigcup_i F(\alpha_i)$ for $\bigcup_i \{F(\alpha_i)\}$; similarly for $\bigcap_i \alpha_i$ and $\bigcap_i F(\alpha_i)$.

Definition 2.8.1 (Continuity and cocontinuity) An endofunction F on a complete lattice is:[4]

- *continuous* if for all sequences $\alpha_0, \alpha_1, \ldots$ of increasing points in the lattice (i.e., $\alpha_i \leq \alpha_{i+1}$, for $i \geq 0$) we have $F(\bigcup_i \alpha_i) = \bigcup_i F(\alpha_i)$;
- *cocontinuous* if for all sequences $\alpha_0, \alpha_1, \ldots$ of decreasing points in the lattice (i.e., $\alpha_i \geq \alpha_{i+1}$, for $i \geq 0$) we have $F(\bigcap_i \alpha_i) = \bigcap_i F(\alpha_i)$. □

As a simple example, take the complete lattice made of the integers plus the points ω and $-\omega$, with the ordering $-\omega \leq n \leq \omega$ for all n. Now take a function F that maps an integer onto its successor, and the points ω and $-\omega$ onto themselves. For the increasing sequence $3, 4, 6$, we have $F(\cup\{3, 4, 6\}) = F(6) = 7$ and also $\cup\{F(3), F(4), F(6)\} = \cup\{4, 5, 7\} = 7$. For the increasing sequence of the positive integers, we have $F(\cup_i n_i) = F(\omega) = \omega = \cup_i n_{i+1} = \cup_i F(n_i)$. Dually, for the decreasing sequence of the negative integers, we have $F(\cap_i - n_i) = -\omega = \cap_i F(-n_i)$.

In the remainder of this section, we present the details for greatest fixed points and cocontinuity, as they are related to coinduction. The dual statements, using least fixed points and continuity, also hold.

Exercise 2.8.2 (Recommended, ↪) If F is cocontinuous (or continuous), then it is also monotone. (Hint: take $x \geq y$, and the sequence $x, y, y, y, \ldots$.) □

---

[4] In some textbooks, continuity is called *upper-continuity*, the dual property *lower-continuity*.

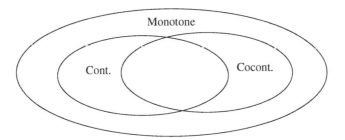

Fig. 2.3 Monotone, continuous and cocontinuous functions.

Exercise 2.8.3 (Recommended, ↪) Show that a function can be cocontinuous without being continuous, and conversely. □

Thus the relationship among the sets of monotone, continuous, and cocontinuous functions is as in Figure 2.3.

Exercise 2.8.4 (Recommended, ↪) Show that if F is monotone, then:

(1) for all sequences $\alpha_0, \alpha_1, \ldots$ of increasing points it holds that $F(\bigcup_i \alpha_i) \geq \bigcup_i F(\alpha_i)$;
(2) for all sequences $\alpha_0, \alpha_1, \ldots$ of decreasing points it holds that $F(\bigcap_i \alpha_i) \leq \bigcap_i F(\alpha_i)$.

□

For an endofunction F on a complete lattice, $F^n(x)$ indicates the n-th iteration of F starting from the point x:

$$F^0(x) \stackrel{\text{def}}{=} x,$$
$$F^{n+1}(x) \stackrel{\text{def}}{=} F(F^n(x)).$$

Then we set:

$$F^{\cup\omega}(x) \stackrel{\text{def}}{=} \bigcup_{n \geq 0} F^n(x),$$
$$F^{\cap\omega}(x) \stackrel{\text{def}}{=} \bigcap_{n \geq 0} F^n(x).$$

Theorem 2.8.5 (Continuity/Cocontinuity Theorem) *Let F be an endofunction on a complete lattice, in which $\bot$ and $\top$ are the bottom and top elements. If F is continuous, then*

$$\mathtt{lfp}(F) = F^{\cup\omega}(\bot);$$

if F is cocontinuous, then

$$\mathtt{gfp}(F) = F^{\cap\omega}(\top).$$

□

The sequence $F^0(\bot), F^1(\bot), \ldots$ is increasing, whereas $F^0(\top), F^1(\top), \ldots$ is decreasing. Least and greatest fixed points of F are the join and meet of the two sequences.

As in the book we are mainly interested in coinduction, we will sometimes refer to the second part of Theorem 2.8.5 as the 'Cocontinuity Theorem'. In the remainder of the section we focus on greatest fixed points; of course the dual statements for least fixed points also hold.

Exercise 2.8.6 (Recommended, $\hookrightarrow$) Prove Theorem 2.8.5. (Hint: referring to the second part, first show that $F^{\cap \omega}$ is a fixed point, exploiting the definition of cocontinuity; then show that it is the greatest fixed point, exploiting the definition of meet.) □

If F is not cocontinuous, and only monotone, we only have $\mathrm{gfp}(F) \le F^{\cap \omega}(\top)$. The converse need not hold, as the following example shows.

Example 2.8.7 Let L be the set of negative integers plus the elements $-\omega$ and $-(\omega+1)$, with the expected ordering $-n \ge -\omega \ge -(\omega+1)$, for all n. Let now F be the following function on L:

$$F(-n) = -(n+1),$$
$$F(-\omega) = -(\omega+1),$$
$$F(-(\omega+1)) = -(\omega+1).$$

The top and bottom elements are -1 and $-(\omega+1)$. The function F is monotone but not cocontinuous, and we have $F^{\cap \omega}(-1) = -\omega$ and $\mathrm{gfp}(F) = -(\omega+1)$. □

However, if it happens that $F^{\cap \omega}(\top)$ is a fixed point, then we are sure that it is indeed the greatest fixed point. Having only monotonicity, to reach the greatest fixed point using induction, we need to iterate over the transfinite ordinals.

Theorem 2.8.8 *Let F be a monotone endofunction on a complete lattice L, and define $F^\lambda(\top)$, where λ is an ordinal, as follows:*

$$F^0(\top) \overset{def}{=} \top,$$
$$F^\lambda(\top) \overset{def}{=} F(\textstyle\bigcap_{\beta < \lambda} F^\beta(\top)) \qquad \text{for } \lambda > 0.$$

Define also $F^\infty(\top) \overset{def}{=} \bigcap_\lambda F^\lambda(\top)$. Then $F^\infty(\top) = \mathrm{gfp}(F)$.

Proof In the proof, we abbreviate $\mathrm{gfp}(F)$ as gfp, and $F^\lambda(\top)$ as F^λ, for any λ. First, using transfinite induction, and exploiting the monotonicity of F, we derive

$$\mathrm{gfp} \le F^\lambda \qquad \text{for all } \lambda. \tag{2.4}$$

For $\lambda = 0$ we have $\mathrm{gfp} \le \top = F^0$ by definition of $\top$. For $\lambda > 0$, by induction we have $\mathrm{gfp} \le F^\beta$ for all $\beta < \lambda$. Thus gfp is a lower bound for $\{F^\beta\}_{\beta < \lambda}$ and therefore also $\mathrm{gfp} \le \bigcap_{\beta < \lambda} F^\beta$. By the fixed-point property of F and monotonicity of F,

$$\mathrm{gfp} = F(\mathrm{gfp}) \le F(\bigcap_{\beta < \lambda} F^\beta) = F^\lambda.$$

Secondly, we show that

$$\beta < \lambda \text{ implies } F^\beta \ge F^\lambda. \tag{2.5}$$

The assertion is straightforward if β or λ is 0. Otherwise $S_1 \stackrel{\text{def}}{=} \{F^{\beta'} \mid \beta' < \beta\}$ is a subset of $S_2 \stackrel{\text{def}}{=} \{F^{\lambda'} \mid \lambda' < \lambda\}$, hence $\bigcap S_1 \geq \bigcap S_2$. By monotonicity of F, $F(\bigcap S_1) \geq F(\bigcap S_2)$, which is to say $F^\beta \geq F^\lambda$.

Using the two points above, we can now prove that if $\beta < \lambda$ and $F^\beta = F^\lambda$, then $F^\beta = \text{gfp}$. Indeed, if $\beta < \lambda$, from (2.5) we have $F^\beta \geq F^{\beta+1} \geq F^\lambda$. And since $F^\beta = F^\lambda$, also $F^\beta = F^{\beta+1}$. However,

$$F^{\beta+1} = F(\bigcap_{\alpha < \beta+1} F^\alpha)$$

and, using (2.5), also

$$= F(F^\beta).$$

Thus F^β is a fixed point of F and then, by definition of greatest fixed point, $F^\beta \leq \text{gfp}$. This and (2.4) yield $F^\beta = \text{gfp}$.

Moreover, as L is a set, there must be an ordinal α with $F^\alpha = F^{\alpha+1}$. (If it were not the case, take the first ordinal α with cardinality strictly greater than that of L; by the previous points it would follow that F is injective on all the ordinals up to α, which is impossible by a cardinality argument.)

Summing up, there must be an ordinal on which F reaches a fixed point, and this fixed point must be the greatest fixed point. $\qquad\square$

As the ordinals are linearly ordered, and each ordinal is either the successor of another ordinal or the least upper bound of all its predecessors, the above definition can also be given thus:

$$F^0(\top) \stackrel{\text{def}}{=} \top,$$
$$F^{\lambda+1}(\top) \stackrel{\text{def}}{=} F(F^\lambda(\top)) \quad \text{for successor ordinals,}$$
$$F^\lambda(\top) \stackrel{\text{def}}{=} \bigcap_{\beta < \lambda} F^\beta(\top) \quad \text{for limit ordinals.}$$

Having separated successor and limit ordinals, the definition of F on a limit ordinal λ is simpler:

$$\bigcap_{\beta < \lambda} F^\beta(\top),$$

in place of $F(\bigcap_{\beta < \lambda} F^\beta(\top))$ as in Theorem 2.8.8. The latter value, $F(\bigcap_{\beta < \lambda} F^\beta(\top))$, is reached on the following successor ordinal $\lambda + 1$, so that the final value of $F^\infty(\top)$ does not change. On the naturals, the definitions of the F^n used in Theorem 2.8.5 coincides with those used in Theorem 2.8.8, which explains why the notation is the same.

The proof of Theorem 2.8.8 shows that there is an ordinal α of cardinality less than or equal to that of the lattice such that for all $\beta \geq \alpha$ the greatest fixed point of F is $F^\beta(\top)$. That is, at α the function reaches its greatest fixed point; on ordinals larger than α, of course, the function remains on such a fixed point. In other words, $F^\lambda(\top)$ returns the greatest fixed point of F for all sufficiently large ordinals λ. In the case when F is cocontinuous, the Cocontinuity Theorem 2.8.5 assures us that we can take α to be the first ordinal limit, ω (not counting 0 as an ordinal limit).

Exercise 2.8.9 generalises (the second part of) Theorem 2.8.5, for an arbitrary pre-fixed point in place of $\top$. It is a generalisation because the top element $\top$ of a complete lattice is a pre-fixed point of any function on the lattice, and, as a top element, it is above all post-fixed points of the lattice.

Exercise 2.8.9 ($\hookrightarrow$) Let F be a cocontinuous endofunction on a complete lattice L, and x a pre-fixed point of F, and let $F^n(x)$, $F^{\cap\omega}(x)$ be defined as above in Theorem 2.8.5. Show that:

(1) $F^0(x)$, $F^1(x)$, ... is a decreasing sequence, and $F^{\cap\omega}(x)$ is a fixed point of F;
(2) $F^{\cap\omega}(x)$ is the greatest fixed point of F that is below x;
(3) this fixed point is also the join of all post-fixed points of F that are below x, i.e.,

$$F^{\cap\omega}(x) = \bigcup\{y \mid y \leq x \text{ and } y \leq F(y)\}.$$

□

In Exercise 2.8.9 the use of sequences defined from F and starting on a pre-fixed point is necessary: if we take an arbitrary decreasing sequence $x_0, x_1, \ldots$, then its meet need not be a fixed point. For a counterexample, take x that is not a fixed point and the sequence constant to x. Similarly, the join of the post-fixed points below x need not be a fixed point, as is seen by taking a function for which $\bot$ is not a fixed point, and $x = \bot$.

Exercise 2.8.10 In the same manner as Exercise 2.8.9 is a generalisation of the Cocontinuity Theorem 2.8.5, state the corresponding generalisation of Theorem 2.8.8, and then prove it.   □

Exercise 2.8.11 State and prove the dual of Theorem 2.8.8, for least fixed points.   □

Remark 2.8.12

- Theorems 2.8.5 and 2.8.8, and the dual of the latter, just mention least and greatest fixed points. It is possible to give similar constructive proofs, using iteration schemata, of the full statement of the Fixed-point Theorem 2.3.21; see, e.g., [CC79].
- In Theorem 2.8.5 and 2.8.8, and related results, it is the existence of greatest lower bounds of decreasing sequences of points, and the dual property, that matter; the existence of arbitrary meets and joins is not needed. Thus the theorems also hold on structures that are weaker than complete lattices.   □

Exercise 2.8.13 ($*$, $\hookrightarrow$) Use Theorem 2.8.8 to show that if L is the complete lattice of binary relations on a given set A, and F is a monotone endofunction on L (that is, a function from relations on A to relations on A) and such that

(1) $\mathcal{I} \subseteq F(\mathcal{I})$ (where $\mathcal{I}$ is the identity relation),
(2) for all $\mathcal{R}, \mathcal{R}'$, $F(\mathcal{R})F(\mathcal{R}') \subseteq F(\mathcal{R}\mathcal{R}')$,
(3) for all $\mathcal{R}$, $(F(\mathcal{R}))^{-1} \subseteq F(\mathcal{R}^{-1})$,

then $\mathsf{gfp}(F)$ is an equivalence relation (we recall that for relations $\mathcal{S}_1$ and $\mathcal{S}_2$, we write $\mathcal{S}_1\mathcal{S}_2$ for their relational composition). □

We will see concrete examples of the computations produced by the iterative schemata in the following section (proofs of Exercises 2.9.8 and 2.9.11) and, for bisimilarity, in Section 2.10.2.

2.9 Continuity and cocontinuity, for rules

The functional given by a set of rules need not be continuous or cocontinuous. As an example, consider a rule

$$\frac{a_1 \quad \cdots \quad a_n \quad \cdots}{a}$$

and call ϕ the associated functional. Let $T_n = \{a_1, \ldots, a_n\}$. We have $a \in \phi(\bigcup_n T_n)$, but $a \notin \bigcup_n \phi(T_n)$, which proves that ϕ is not continuous. We can recover continuity and cocontinuity for rule functionals adding some conditions. Here the duality is less obvious, and needs some care. For continuity, the condition is that in each rule the set of premises is finite.

Definition 2.9.1 A set $\mathcal{R}$ of rules is *finite in the premises*, briefly FP, if for each rule $(S, x) \in \mathcal{R}$ the premise set S is finite. □

In the literature, rules with the property above are sometimes called *finitary*. The need for the FP condition comes out clearly in the proof of the following exercise.

Exercise 2.9.2 (Recommended, $\hookrightarrow$) Show that if the set of rules $\mathcal{R}$ is FP, then the rule functional $\Phi_\mathcal{R}$ is continuous; conclude that $\mathsf{lfp}(\Phi_\mathcal{R}) = \Phi_\mathcal{R}^{\bigcup\omega}(\emptyset)$. □

However, surprisingly at first sight, the statement of Exercise 2.9.2 does not hold for cocontinuity. As a counterexample, take $X = \{b\} \cup \{a_1, \ldots, a_n, \ldots\}$, and the set of rules $(\{a_i\}, b)$, for each i, and let Φ be the corresponding rule functional. Thus $\Phi(T) = \{b\}$ if there is i with $a_i \in T$, otherwise $\Phi(T) = \emptyset$. Consider now the sequence of decreasing sets $T_0, \ldots, T_n, \ldots$, where

$$T_i \overset{\text{def}}{=} \{a_j \mid j \geq i\}.$$

We have $\Phi(\bigcap_n T_n) = \emptyset$ (because $\bigcap_n T_n = \emptyset$), but $\bigcap_n \Phi(T_n) = \{b\}$.

To obtain cocontinuity we need some finiteness conditions on the conclusions of the rules (rather than on the premises as for continuity). The condition was violated in the previous example, where b is the conclusion of infinitely many rules.

Definition 2.9.3 A set of rules $\mathcal{R}$ is *finite in the conclusions*, briefly FC, if for each x, the set $\{S \mid (S, x) \in \mathcal{R}\}$ is finite (i.e., there is only a finite number of rules whose conclusion is x; note that, by contrast, each premise set S may itself be infinite). □

Theorem 2.9.4 *If a set of rules $\mathcal{R}$ is FC, then $\Phi_{\mathcal{R}}$ is cocontinuous.* □

Exercise 2.9.5 (Recommended, ↪) Prove Theorem 2.9.4. □

Corollary 2.9.6 *If a set of rules $\mathcal{R}$ on X is FC, then* $\mathtt{gfp}(\Phi_{\mathcal{R}}) = \Phi_{\mathcal{R}}^{\cap\omega}(X)$. □

Without FC, and therefore without cocontinuity, we have nevertheless $\mathtt{gfp}(\Phi_{\mathcal{R}}) \subseteq \Phi_{\mathcal{R}}^{\cap\omega}(X)$.

With the FP or FC hypothesis we are thus able to apply the Continuity/Cocontinuity Theorem 2.8.5. For FP and continuity, the theorem tells us that given some rules $\mathcal{R}$, the set inductively defined by $\mathcal{R}$ can be obtained as $\Phi_{\mathcal{R}}^{\cup\omega}(\emptyset)$, that is, as the limit of the increasing sequence of sets

$$\emptyset, \ \Phi_{\mathcal{R}}(\emptyset), \ \Phi_{\mathcal{R}}(\Phi_{\mathcal{R}}(\emptyset)), \ \Phi_{\mathcal{R}}(\Phi_{\mathcal{R}}(\Phi_{\mathcal{R}}(\emptyset))), \ldots.$$

This means that we construct the inductive set starting with the empty set, adding to it the conclusions of the axioms in $\mathcal{R}$ (i.e., $\Phi_{\mathcal{R}}(\emptyset)$), and then repeatedly adding elements following the inference rules in $\mathcal{R}$ in a 'forward' manner. This corresponds to the usual constructive way of interpreting inductively a bunch of rules, as discussed informally in the examples in Section 2.1. As usual, the case for coinductively defined sets is dual.

In the exercises below we examine the continuity and cocontinuity of some of the examples in Section 2.1, and use this, via the iteration schemata, to understand the inductive and coinductive sets obtained from the rules.

Exercise 2.9.7 (↪) Are the functionals $\Phi_{\mathcal{R}_1}$ and $\Phi_{\mathcal{R}_{1\mu}}$ of Section 2.6.1 continuous? Show that $\Phi_{\mathcal{R}_{1\mu}}$ is cocontinuous if the processes are image-finite. Show that, without image-finiteness, $\Phi_{\mathcal{R}_{1\mu}}$ need not be cocontinuous, and indeed it may be the case that $\mathtt{gfp}(\Phi_{\mathcal{R}_{1\mu}})$ is not $\Phi_{\mathcal{R}_{1\mu}}^{\cap\omega}(Pr)$, where Pr is the set of all processes. (Hint: use the process P of Example 2.10.11 with $\mu = a$.) □

Exercise 2.9.8 (Recommended, ↪) Continuing Exercise 2.9.7, show that:

(1) $P \in \Phi_{\mathcal{R}_1}^n(\emptyset)$, for $0 \leq n$, if and only if there are $0 \leq m \leq n$, processes $P_0, \ldots, P_m$, and actions $\mu_1, \ldots, \mu_m$ with $P = P_0$ and such that $P_0 \xrightarrow{\mu_1} P_1 \ldots \xrightarrow{\mu_m} P_m$ and P_m is stopped.
(2) $P \in \Phi_{\mathcal{R}_{1\mu}}^n(Pr)$, for $0 \leq n$, if and only if there are processes $P_0, \ldots, P_n$ with $P = P_0$ and such that $P_0 \xrightarrow{\mu} P_1 \cdots \xrightarrow{\mu} P_n$. □

Exercise 2.9.8 well shows the computation involved with the iteration approximants. With $\Phi_{\mathcal{R}_1}$, at step 0 we have the empty set; then at step 1 we add the stopped processes; at step 2 we add the processes that have a stopped derivative; and so on. At step n we have obtained all processes that reach a stopped process in at most n transitions. In applications in which the set of all processes is finite, the sequence $\{\Phi^n_{\mathcal{R}_\downarrow}(\emptyset)\}_n$ will not increase forever, and we are therefore sure that the set inductively defined by the rules will be obtained.

With $\Phi_{\mathcal{R}_{\uparrow\mu}}$, in contrast, at step 0 we have the set Pr of all processes; at step 1 we remove the processes that do not have a μ-derivative; at step 2 the processes that cannot perform two consecutive μ-transitions; and so on. Here too, if the set of processes is finite, the sequence will eventually produce the set coinductively defined by the rules.

Exercise 2.9.9 ($\hookrightarrow$) Continuing Exercise 2.9.8, show that $P \in \mathtt{lfp}(\Phi_{\mathcal{R}_\downarrow})$ if and only if there are $n \geq 0$, processes $P_0, \ldots, P_n$, and actions $\mu_1, \ldots, \mu_n$ with $P = P_0$ and such that $P_0 \xrightarrow{\mu_1} P_1 \cdots \xrightarrow{\mu_n} P_n$ and P_n is stopped. $\qquad\square$

Example 2.9.10 The rules defining $\Phi_{\mathtt{Alist}}$ in Section 2.6.3 are both FP and FC, hence $\Phi_{\mathtt{Alist}}$ is both continuous and cocontinuous. $\qquad\square$

Exercise 2.9.11 (Recommended, $\hookrightarrow$) Show that $\mathtt{lfp}(\Phi_{\mathtt{Alist}}) = \mathtt{FinLists}_A$, and $\mathtt{gfp}(\Phi_{\mathtt{Alist}}) = \mathtt{FinInfLists}_A$. $\qquad\square$

2.10 Bisimilarity as a fixed point

In this section we revise the example of bisimulation and bisimilarity, in the light of the fixed-point theory in earlier sections of the chapter. Precisely, we refer to Sections 2.3 and 2.4, where we set the meaning of coinductively defined set and of the coinduction proof principle, and to Section 2.8, where we derived constructive characterisations of greatest fixed points. We instantiate the concepts in those sections to the case of bisimulation.

2.10.1 The functional of bisimilarity

To see how bisimulation and its proof method fit the coinductive schema, consider the function $F_\sim : \wp(Pr \times Pr) \to \wp(Pr \times Pr)$ defined thus.

$F_\sim(\mathcal{R})$ is the set of all pairs (P, Q) such that:

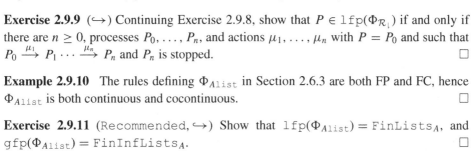

(1) for all P' with $P \xrightarrow{\mu} P'$, there is Q' such that $Q \xrightarrow{\mu} Q'$ and $P' \, \mathcal{R} \, Q'$;
(2) for all Q' with $Q \xrightarrow{\mu} Q'$, there is P' such that $P \xrightarrow{\mu} P'$ and $P' \, \mathcal{R} \, Q'$.

We call $F_\sim$ the *functional associated to bisimulation*, for it gives us precisely the clauses of a bisimulation.

Lemma 2.10.1 $\mathcal{R}$ *is a bisimulation iff* $\mathcal{R} \subseteq F_\sim(\mathcal{R})$. $\qquad\square$

Moreover, $F_\sim$ is monotone on the complete lattice of the relations on $Pr \times Pr$.

Lemma 2.10.2 $F_\sim$ *is monotone.* $\qquad\square$

Since the bisimulations are precisely the post-fixed points of the monotone functional $F_\sim$, from the Fixed-point Theorem 2.3.21 (or, better, Exercise 2.3.20), we infer:

Theorem 2.10.3

(1) $\sim$ *is the greatest fixed point of* $F_\sim$;
(2) $\sim$ *is the largest relation* $\mathcal{R}$ *such that* $\mathcal{R} \subseteq F_\sim(\mathcal{R})$; *thus* $\mathcal{R} \subseteq \sim$ *for all* $\mathcal{R}$ *with* $\mathcal{R} \subseteq$ $F_\sim(\mathcal{R})$. $\qquad\square$

For the functional $F_\sim$, the coinduction principle of Corollary 2.4.3 asserts that any bisimulation only relates pairs of bisimilar states.

Exercise 2.10.4 ($\hookrightarrow$)

(1) Show that if $\mathcal{R}$ is an equivalence relation on the processes of a given LTS, then also $F_\sim(\mathcal{R})$ is so;
(2) Use point (1) and Theorem 2.8.8 to conclude that $\sim$ is an equivalence relation;
(3) Prove that $\sim$ is an equivalence relation using Exercise 2.8.13. $\qquad\square$

Exercise 2.10.5 ($\hookrightarrow$) What does Exercise 2.3.19(1-2) say from the bisimulation point of view? $\qquad\square$

Exercise 2.10.6 ($\hookrightarrow$) In this exercise, assume for simplicity that the LTS is finitely branching (Definition 1.2.5). What is the least fixed point of $F_\sim$? What is the difference between least and greatest fixed points of $F_\sim$ on finite LTSs? $\qquad\square$

Exercise 2.10.7 ($\hookrightarrow$) What is the operational meaning of the principle of coinduction up-to $\cup$ (page 64) in the case of bisimulation? Write the corresponding bisimulation clauses. $\qquad\square$

Exercise 2.10.8 Show that the principle of coinduction up-to gfp (page 65), instantiated to the case of bisimulation, yields the 'bisimulation up-to $\sim$' technique of Exercise 1.4.18. $\qquad\square$

2.10.2 Approximants of bisimilarity

We can approximate, and even characterise, coinductively defined sets using the iteration schemata of Theorems 2.8.5 and 2.8.8. In this section we examine the operational meaning of these iterations, and related concepts, in the case of bisimilarity.

Definition 2.10.9 (Stratification of bisimilarity, on the natural numbers) Let Pr be the states of an LTS. We set:

- $\sim_0 \stackrel{\text{def}}{=} Pr \times Pr$;
- $P \sim_{n+1} Q$, for $n \geq 0$, if for all μ:

  (1) for all P' with $P \stackrel{\mu}{\rightarrow} P'$, there is Q' such that $Q \stackrel{\mu}{\rightarrow} Q'$ and $P' \sim_n Q'$;
  (2) the converse, i.e., for all Q' with $Q \stackrel{\mu}{\rightarrow} Q'$, there is P' such that $P \stackrel{\mu}{\rightarrow} P'$ and $P' \sim_n Q'$;

- $\sim_\omega \stackrel{\text{def}}{=} \bigcap_{n \geq 0} \sim_n$. $\qquad\square$

Exercise 2.10.10 (Recommended, ↪)

(1) Show that $\sim_0, \ldots, \sim_n, \ldots$ is a decreasing sequence of relations.
(2) Show that for all $0 \le n < \omega$, we have $\sim_n = F_{\sim}^n(Pr \times Pr)$, and $\sim_\omega = F_{\sim}^{\cap \omega}(Pr \times Pr)$, where $F_{\sim}^n$ and $F_{\sim}^{\cap \omega}$ are the iterations of $F_{\sim}$ following the definitions used in the Cocontinuity Theorem 2.8.5. □

The characterisation in the Cocontinuity Theorem 2.8.5 required cocontinuity. In general the functional of bisimilarity is not cocontinuous; and $\sim_\omega$ does not coincide with $\sim$, as the following example shows.

Example 2.10.11 Suppose $a \in Act$, and let a^0 be a state with no transitions, a^ω a state whose only transition is

$$a^\omega \xrightarrow{a} a^\omega,$$

and a^n, for $n \ge 1$, states with only transitions

$$a^n \xrightarrow{a} a^{n-1}.$$

Also, let P, Q be states with transitions

$$P \xrightarrow{a} a^n \qquad \text{for all } n \ge 0$$

and

$$Q \xrightarrow{a} a^n \qquad \text{for all } n \ge 0.$$
$$Q \xrightarrow{a} a^\omega$$

It is easy to prove, by induction on n, that $P \sim_n Q$ for all n, hence also $P \sim_\omega Q$. However, it holds that $P \not\sim Q$: the transition $Q \xrightarrow{a} a^\omega$ can only be matched by P with one of the transitions $P \xrightarrow{a} a^n$. But, for all n, we have $a^\omega \not\sim a^n$, as only from the former state $n + 1$ transitions are possible. □

Exercise 2.10.12 (↪) Use Example 2.10.11 to show formally that the function $F_{\sim}$ is not cocontinuous. □

We can obtain $\sim$ by iteration over the natural numbers if we add some finiteness hypothesis on the branching structure of the LTS. We begin with the finitely-branching condition, then, in exercises, we examine weaker conditions.

In Example 2.10.11, the LTS is not finitely-branching. It becomes so if we remove all transitions $P \xrightarrow{a} a^n$ and $Q \xrightarrow{a} a^n$, for all $n \ge m$, where m is any given number. The LTSs in Figures 1.1–1.5 are finitely-branching (as the LTS itself has only a finite number of states).

Theorem 2.10.13 *On finitely-branching LTSs, relations $\sim$ and $\sim_\omega$ coincide.*

Proof The inclusion $\sim \,\subseteq\, \sim_\omega$ is easy: one proves that $\sim \,\subseteq\, \sim_n$ for all n, using the fact that $\sim$ is a bisimulation (or, using the fact that $\sim$ is a fixed point of $F_\sim$, monotonicity of $F_\sim$, and $\sim_{n+1} = F_\sim(\sim_n)$; we can also directly derive it from Exercise 2.10.10(2) and fixed-point theory).

Now the converse. We show that the set

$$\mathcal{R} \overset{\text{def}}{=} \{(P, Q) \mid P \sim_\omega Q\}$$

is a bisimulation. Thus, take $(P, Q) \in \mathcal{R}$, and suppose $P \overset{\mu}{\to} P'$. We need a matching transition from Q. For all n, as $P \sim_{n+1} Q$, there is Q_n such that $Q \overset{\mu}{\to} Q_n$ and $P \sim_n Q_n$. However, as the LTS is finitely-branching, the set $\{Q_i \mid Q \overset{\mu}{\to} Q_i\}$ is finite. Therefore there is at least a Q_i for which $P' \sim_n Q_i$ holds for infinitely many n. As the relations $\sim_n$ are decreasing with n, $P' \sim_n Q_i$ holds for all n. Hence $P' \sim_\omega Q_i$ and therefore $(P', Q_i) \in \mathcal{R}$.
$\square$

Exercise 2.10.14 gives us another proof of Theorem 2.10.13, appealing to the cocontinuity of $F_\sim$ and Theorem 2.8.5 (see also Exercise 2.10.23). The proof technique used in the direct proof above is, however, a useful one to know.

Exercise 2.10.14 Check that under the finitely-branching hypothesis the functional $F_\sim$ is cocontinuous.
$\square$

The approximants of bisimilarity can be usefully employed to prove non-bisimilarity results. For some (very simple) examples, we revisit Example 1.4.6 and Exercise 1.4.9.

Example 2.10.15 (Continues Example 1.4.6) We show that the processes P_1 and Q_1 in Figure 1.4 are not bisimilar, via approximants. We have to find n such that $P_1 \not\sim_n Q_1$. We construct the relations $\sim_i$, starting from 0 and going up. For $i = 0$, we have $Pr \times Pr$. At $i = 1$ we have the pairs of states with the same labels in their immediate transitions: $(P_1, Q_1), (P_3, Q_2), (P_2, Q_3), (P_4, Q_3)$. Thus $i = 1$ is not sufficient, for (P_1, Q_1) is still present. However, $i = 2$ breaks the pair: the transition $P_1 \overset{a}{\to} P_2$ cannot be matched by Q_1, whose only transition is $Q_1 \overset{a}{\to} Q_2$ but P_2 and Q_2 are not related in $\sim_1$.
$\square$

Example 2.10.16 (Continues Exercise 1.4.9) In the approximant method it is sufficient to recall, at each step, the pairs of non-bisimilar processes discovered that are relevant for the final non-bisimilarity result. For instance, suppose we want to prove the inequality between the processes P_3 and Q_3 of Figure 1.7 that, for convenience, are reported below with names in all nodes:

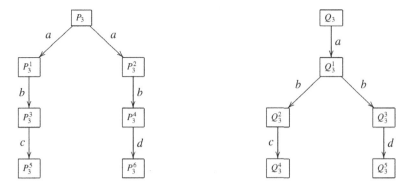

At $n = 0$ there is no non-bisimilar pair. At $n = 1$ we discover that $P_3^3 \nsim_1 Q_3^3$ and $P_3^4 \nsim_1 Q_3^2$, as their only transitions have different labels. At $n = 2$ we find $P_3^1 \nsim_2 Q_3^1$ and $P_3^2 \nsim_2 Q_3^1$; for instance, Q_3^1 has a transition $Q_3^1 \xrightarrow{b} Q_3^3$ that cannot be matched by $P_3^1 \xrightarrow{b} P_3^3$ because we already know that P_3^3 and Q_3^3 are different. Finally, and reasoning similarly, at $n = 3$ we obtain $P_3 \nsim_3 Q_3$. $\qquad\square$

Exercise 2.10.17 Use the approximant method to show that the processes P_4 and Q_4 of Figure 2.4 are not bisimilar. $\qquad\square$

Theorem 2.10.13 can be strengthened, requiring finiteness on single labels rather than on all transitions; that is, replacing 'finitely-branching' with 'image-finite'.

Exercise 2.10.18 Modify the proof of Theorem 2.10.13, if needed, so as to use the weaker hypothesis of image-finiteness. $\qquad\square$

The theorem can be further strengthened by requiring image-finiteness up-to $\sim$.

Definition 2.10.19 (Image-finiteness up-to $\sim$) An LTS is *image-finite up-to* $\sim$ if for each process P and action μ the following holds: there are finitely many processes $P_1, \ldots, P_n$ such that for all P' with $P \xrightarrow{\mu} P'$ there is P_i with $P' \sim P_i$. A process P is *image-finite up-to* $\sim$ if the LTS generated by P is image-finite up-to $\sim$. $\qquad\square$

Exercise 2.10.20 $(*, \hookrightarrow)$ Prove the variant of Theorem 2.10.13 on the set of processes that are image-finite up-to $\sim$ rather than finitely-branching. $\qquad\square$

In general, however, as by Theorem 2.8.8, in order to reach $\sim$ we need to replace the ω-iteration that defines $\sim_\omega$ with a transfinite iteration, using the ordinal numbers. At successor ordinals and at 0 the definition of $\sim_\lambda$ (for λ ordinal) is as in Definition 2.10.9; for limit ordinals we have:

$$\sim_\lambda \stackrel{\text{def}}{=} \bigcap_{\beta < \lambda} \sim_\beta \qquad\qquad \text{if } \lambda \text{ is a limit ordinal}$$

and then $\sim_\infty \stackrel{\text{def}}{=} \bigcap_\lambda \sim_\lambda$.

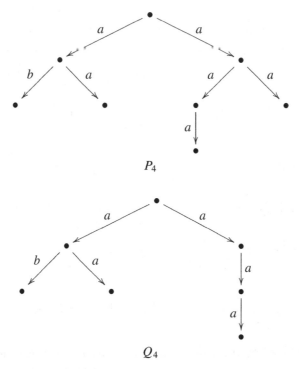

P_4

Q_4

Fig. 2.4 More non-bisimilar processes.

Theorem 2.10.21 *Relations* $\sim$ *and* $\sim_\infty$ *coincide.*

Proof The result follows from Theorem 2.8.8.   □

We have seen that every monotone function on the complete lattice $\wp(X)$ can be expressed as the rule functional of some set of rules on X (Exercise 2.5.3). Thus this also applies to $F_\sim$:

Exercise 2.10.22 (Recommended, $\hookrightarrow$) Instantiate the statement of Exercise 2.5.3 to the case of $F_\sim$, showing precisely what is a 'minimal' set of rules that has $F_\sim$ as its functional.
                                                                                □

Viewing $F_\sim$ as a rule functional, we can derive the cocontinuity of $F_\sim$ for finitely-branching LTSs as a special case of the more general theorem relating cocontinuity of rule functionals to the FC property, thus also deriving Theorem 2.10.13 from Corollary 2.9.6 (and, in turn, from the Cocontinuity Theorem 2.8.5). This is done in Exercise 2.10.23; the proof is simpler than directly deriving the cocontinuity of $F_\sim$ as done in Exercise 2.10.14.

Exercise 2.10.23 (Recommended, $\hookrightarrow$) Use Exercise 2.10.22 to show that finitely-branching of the LTS implies FC (and FP) of the rules for $F_\sim$ and therefore derive Theorem 2.10.13. Show also that image-finiteness does not imply FC.   □

Exercise 2.10.24 (Recommended, ↪) Define coinductively the set of processes in an LTS that are image-finite. What is the corresponding set of rules? □

Exercise 2.10.25 The same as Exercise 2.10.24, for the set of processes in an LTS that are image-finite up-to ~. □

Exercise 2.10.26 (↪) Analogously to what was done for ~ and $F_\sim$, define the functional for the similarity relation of Exercise 1.4.17 and prove the analogue of Theorem 2.10.3 and Exercise 2.10.23. □

2.11 Proofs of membership

A set of ground rules is used to derive elements, by composing the rules into proof trees. Then an element is derivable from the rules if there is a proof tree whose root is that element. We have seen examples of this throughout the chapter. Here is another one, in the case of lists of Section 2.6.3 where the ground rules are $(\emptyset, \texttt{nil})$ and $(\{s\}, \langle a \rangle \bullet s)$ for each $s \in X$ and $a \in A$. A proof tree that derives the list $\langle a \rangle \bullet \langle a \rangle \bullet \langle b \rangle \bullet \texttt{nil}$ is

$$\frac{\dfrac{\dfrac{\overline{\texttt{nil}}}{\langle b \rangle \bullet \texttt{nil}}}{\langle a \rangle \bullet \langle b \rangle \bullet \texttt{nil}}}{\langle a \rangle \bullet \langle a \rangle \bullet \langle b \rangle \bullet \texttt{nil}}$$

For the infinite list $\langle a \rangle \bullet \langle b \rangle \bullet \langle a \rangle \bullet \langle b \rangle \bullet \langle a \rangle \bullet \langle b \rangle \bullet \cdots$ the proof tree is infinite:

$$\frac{\dfrac{\dfrac{\cdots}{\langle a \rangle \bullet \langle b \rangle \bullet \langle a \rangle \bullet \langle b \rangle \bullet \cdots}}{\langle b \rangle \bullet \langle a \rangle \bullet \langle b \rangle \bullet \langle a \rangle \bullet \langle b \rangle \bullet \cdots}}{\langle a \rangle \bullet \langle b \rangle \bullet \langle a \rangle \bullet \langle b \rangle \bullet \langle a \rangle \bullet \langle b \rangle \bullet \cdots}$$

In the case of rules for lists, each node of a proof tree that is not a leaf has exactly one child. In general, however, a node can have several children, due to rules whose premises are sets with more than one element (e.g., the rules for bisimulation in Section 2.13).

The list $\langle a \rangle \bullet \langle a \rangle \bullet \langle b \rangle \bullet \texttt{nil}$ belongs both to the set inductively defined by the rules for list, and to the coinductive set. The infinite list $\langle a \rangle \bullet \langle b \rangle \bullet \langle a \rangle \bullet \langle b \rangle \bullet \cdots$, in contrast, only belongs to the coinductive set. There is, therefore, a difference between induction and coinduction on the meaning of 'correct' proof tree. This is what we look at in this section: we examine the duality between sets inductively and coinductively defined from a set of ground rules from the point of view of the proofs of the membership of an element in such sets. Thus we will justify the informal explanations of the examples of inductively and coinductively defined sets in Section 2.1 as the sets of elements with a finite proof, and with a finite or infinite proof. We will actually make the conditions on the derivation proofs more precise, using well-foundedness and non-well-foundedness. In the proofs of the results in the section, we assume that the rules are both FP and FC, as this makes some technicalities simpler.

The set of *trees over X* is the set of all trees, possibly infinite both in depth and in breadth, in which each node is labelled with an element from the set X and, moreover, the labels of the children of a node are pairwise distinct. If T is such a tree, then the *root* of T is the only node without a parent.

Remark 2.11.1 The definition of trees over X above is informal because we assume that the reader knows what a tree is. For a formal definition, we can take a tree over X to be a set of sequences of elements of X, namely all sequences obtained by picking up a node h in the tree and reading the sequence of labels in the path that goes from the root of the tree to h. Thus a tree over X is a set T of non-empty finite sequences of elements in X such that

(1) there is only one sequence of length one (corresponding to the root of the tree);
(2) if the sequence $x_1 \ldots x_{n+1}$ is in T then also $x_1 \ldots x_n$ is in T.

In this formulation, a sequence $x_1 \ldots x_n$ uniquely identifies a node of the tree; and the children of this node are identified by the set of sequences $\bigcup_x \{x_1 \ldots x_n x\}$.

In the remainder, in proofs we sometimes refer to this definition of a tree. □

For now, the form of trees allowed is very general: for instance, a node can have infinitely many children; and there can be paths of infinite length in the tree that start from the root of the tree and continue moving from a node to one of its children. However, we will see that the trees that we obtain for proofs of rules under the FP condition or for induction are more constrained. Below we usually omit reference to X, and simply call tree over X a *tree*.

A tree is *non-well-founded* if it has paths of infinite length; that is, the relation on the nodes that contains a pair of nodes (h, k) if k is the parent of h is non-well-founded (there are nodes h_i, for $i > 0$, with (h_{i+1}, h_i) in the relation, for each i). The tree is *well-founded* if the relation is well-founded; thus all the paths have a finite length. Referring to the definition of a tree in Remark 2.11.1, a tree T is non-well-founded if there is an infinite sequence $x_1 \ldots x_i \ldots$ whose prefixes (i.e., all finite sequences $x_1 \ldots x_i$, $i > 0$) are all in T. See Figures 2.5 and 2.6 for examples. In the tree (c) of Figure 2.5, the root of the tree has infinitely many children, one for each natural number, and the i-th child leads to a path with i nodes; each path is finite, but there are infinitely many of them, hence their length is not bounded.

Now, let $\mathcal{R}$ be a set of ground rules. A tree T is *a proof tree for $x \in X$ under $\mathcal{R}$* if x is the label of the root of T and, for each node h with label y, if S is the set of the labels of all children of h, then (S, y) is a rule in $\mathcal{R}$.

Theorem 2.11.2 $x \in \mathtt{lfp}(\Phi_{\mathcal{R}})$ *iff there is a well-founded proof tree for x under $\mathcal{R}$.* □

We discuss the proof of the theorem supposing that $\mathcal{R}$ is FP. This allows us to use continuity and therefore to apply the approximants of least fixed points over the natural numbers. The FP hypothesis may be dropped, by iterating over the ordinal numbers (the extension is easy, with some acquaintance of transfinite iteration).

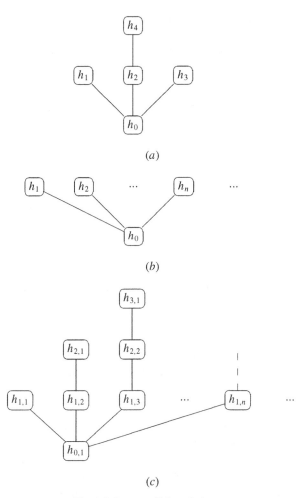

(a)

(b)

(c)

Fig. 2.5 Some well-founded trees.

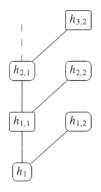

Fig. 2.6 A non-well-founded tree.

The FP hypothesis ensures us that each node has only finitely many children, and therefore a well-founded proof tree has a finite height, that is, there is a bound on the maximal length of paths in the tree [5] In other words, with FP a proof tree is well founded iff it is finite, in that it has a finite number of nodes. In the examples of Section 2.1, the rules are FP, which explains why in that section we referred to the inductive objects as those with a 'finite derivation proof'. Without FP, a well-founded proof tree need not have a finite height, as in the tree (c) of Figure 2.5; in Figure 2.5, only (a) is a tree of FP rules.

We recall that $\Phi_{\mathcal{R}}^n$ is the n-th iteration of the functional for the rules $\mathcal{R}$.

Lemma 2.11.3 $x \in \Phi_{\mathcal{R}}^n(\emptyset)$ *iff there is a proof tree for x under $\mathcal{R}$ whose height is less than or equal to n.* □

Exercise 2.11.4 ($\hookrightarrow$) Prove Theorem 2.11.2, assuming that the rules are FP. (Hint: use Lemma 2.11.3.) □

Theorem 2.11.2 shows that the set inductively defined by a set of rules has precisely all those elements that are obtained from well-founded proofs. We show below that, in contrast, the set coinductively defined has the elements obtained from the well-founded *and* the non-well-founded proofs.

Theorem 2.11.5 $x \in \mathtt{gfp}(\Phi_{\mathcal{R}})$ *iff there is a proof tree for x under $\mathcal{R}$.* □

Proof First, the direction from left to right. If $x \in \mathtt{gfp}(\Phi_{\mathcal{R}})$, then x belongs to some post-fixed point of $\Phi_{\mathcal{R}}$; that is, there is T with $x \in T$ and $T \subseteq \Phi_{\mathcal{R}}(T)$. Now, as $T \subseteq \Phi_{\mathcal{R}}(T)$, by definition of $\Phi_{\mathcal{R}}$, for each $y \in T$ there is at least one rule (S, y) in $\mathcal{R}$ with $S \subseteq T$; we pick one of these rules and call it R_y.

The proof tree for x is defined as follows. The root is x. The children of a node y in the tree are the nodes $y_1, \ldots, y_n$ that form the premise of the rule R_y chosen for y. Formally, the tree is defined as the set of all sequences of the form $x_1 \ldots x_n$ where $x_1 = x$ and for each $1 \leq i < n$, x_{i+1} is in the premises of the rule R_{x_i}.

Conversely, suppose that there is a proof tree for x. Let T be the set of all the (labels of) nodes in the tree. We show that T is a post-fixed point of $\Phi_{\mathcal{R}}$. For this, we have to show that any $y \in T$ is in $\Phi_{\mathcal{R}}(T)$. If $y \in T$ then there is a node in the tree that is labelled y. Let $\{y_1, \ldots, y_n\}$ be the set of the labels of the children of such node. By definition of proof tree, $(\{y_1, \ldots, y_n\}, y)$ is a rule in $\mathcal{R}$ and, by definition of T, we have $(\{y_1, \ldots, y_n\} \subseteq T$. Hence we also have $y \in \Phi_{\mathcal{R}}(T)$. □

Remark 2.11.6 The proof of Theorem 2.11.5 does not follow the schema of the analogous proof for least fixed points in Theorem 2.11.2, based on approximants. The problem is the implication from left to right. One could define a notion of approximant for a (possibly non-well-founded) proof tree: call *a proof tree for $x \in X$ under $\mathcal{R}$ up-to stage n ($n \geq 0$) a* tree in which x is the label of the root and the tree is 'correct' only up to level n (we check

---

[5] This is a consequence of König's Lemma. On trees, König's lemma says that if the number of nodes in a tree is infinite and each of them has only finitely many outgoing edges then the tree has an infinite path.

that the children of a node are the premises of a rule only for nodes whose distance from the root is at most n). Then we do have: $x \in \Phi_{\mathcal{R}}^n(X)$ iff there is a proof tree for x under $\mathcal{R}$ up-to stage n. However, combining the 'partially correct' trees resulting from these $\Phi_{\mathcal{R}}^n(X)$, for all n (partially correct because the parent/children relationship is checked only up to a certain level), into a single 'totally correct' tree is delicate because two partially correct trees might be be incompatible, in that they may result from the application of different rules. This may occur when more rules have the same conclusion; the root itself could be the conclusion of different rules, for instance.

The approximant scheme works well for least fixed points because the trees obtained at stage n are complete, and therefore also totally correct. On the other hand, the schema used in the proof of Theorem 2.11.5 would be more difficult for least fixed points because a least fixed point is obtained via an *intersection* operation (from the pre-fixed points), rather than an *union* (from the post-fixed points) as for a greatest fixed point. $\qquad\square$

When we progressively build a bisimulation starting from a given pair (P, Q), as in Example 1.4.4, we are essentially building a proof of $P \sim Q$, using the rules for $\sim$; the only difference is that we do not repeat the analysis of pairs that we have already encountered (the rules for $\sim$ are discussed in Exercise 2.10.22 and Section 2.13).

2.12 Game interpretations

We conclude this overview of induction and coinduction with game-theoretic characterisations of sets inductively and coinductively defined from rules. For this, we re-use some of the ideas in the 'proof-tree' presentation of Section 2.11.

Consider a set $\mathcal{R}$ of ground rules (on X). A *game in* $\mathcal{R}$ involves two players, which we indicate as V (the verifier) and R (the refuter), and an element $x_0 \in X$ with which a play of the game begins. V attempts to show that a proof tree for x_0 exists, while R attempts to show that there is no such proof. A play begins with V choosing a set S_0 such that x_0 can be derived from S_0, that is, $(S_0, x_0) \in \mathcal{R}$. Then R answers by picking up an element $x_1 \in S_0$, thus challenging V to continue with the proof on x_1. Now V has to find a set S_1 with $(S_1, x_1) \in \mathcal{R}$; then R picks $x_2 \in S_1$, and so on. Thus *a play for* $\mathcal{R}$ *and* x_0 is a sequence

$$x_0, S_0, \dots, x_n, S_n, \dots$$

which can be finite or infinite. If it is finite, then the play may end with some x_n (meaning that R made the last move) or with some S_n (V moved last).

In the definition of win of a play we have to distinguish induction from coinduction. We write $\mathcal{G}^{\text{ind}}(\mathcal{R}, x_0)$ for the inductive game, and $\mathcal{G}^{\text{coind}}(\mathcal{R}, x_0)$ for the coinductive game. In both games, when the play is finite, and one of the players is supposed to make a move but he/she is unable to do so, then the other player wins. This occurs if V's last move was the empty set $\emptyset$; V wins because R has no further element to throw in. The end of the game also occurs if R's last move was an element x that does not appear in conclusions of the rules $\mathcal{R}$, in which case R is the winner. The difference between induction and coinduction is in the interpretation of wins for infinite plays. In the inductive world an infinite play is a win for R. This because, as seen in Section 2.11, the proof of an element of an inductive set must be well-founded, and infinite plays represent non well founded paths in the proof tree. In contrast, in the coinductive world an infinite play is a win for V as here non-well-founded paths in proof trees are allowed.

Example 2.12.1 We have seen in Section 2.5 the rules that correspond to the divergence predicate $\Uparrow$ of the λ-calculus. Each rule is either of the form $(\{e\}, e\,e')$ with $e, e' \in \Lambda^0$, or of the form $(\{e\}, e_1\,e_2)$ with $e, e_1, e_2 \in \Lambda^0$ and with $e_1 \Downarrow \lambda x.e_0$ for some e_0 with $e_0\{e_2/x\} = e$. Call $\mathcal{R}$ this set of rules.

For $e_1 = \lambda x.xx$, the following is an infinite play for $e_1\,e_1$ in the game in $\mathcal{R}$:

$$e_1\,e_1,\ \{e_1\,e_1\},\ e_1\,e_1,\ \ldots.$$

And for $e_2 = \lambda x.xxx$, an infinite play for $e_2\,e_2$ is

$$e_2\,e_2,\ \{(e_2\,e_2)\,e_2\},\ (e_2\,e_2)\,e_2,\ \{e_2\,e_2\},\ \ldots.$$

Both plays, in the coinductive game, represent a win for V. A finite play for $e_2\,e_2$ is

$$e_2\,e_2,\ \{e_2\},\ e_2$$

and it is a win for R.   □

Example 2.12.2 Consider the rules $\mathcal{R}_{\downharpoonleft}$ for the finite-trace predicate $\downharpoonleft$ described in Section 2.6.1. Take then the process Ω_b^a with transitions $\Omega_b^a \xrightarrow{b} \Omega_b^a$ and $\Omega_b^a \xrightarrow{a} P$ and $\Omega_b^a \xrightarrow{a} Q$, where P, Q have no further transitions. A play for $\mathcal{R}_{\downharpoonleft}$ and Ω_b^a is

$$\Omega_b^a,\ \{\Omega_b^a\},\ \Omega_b^a,\ \ldots,$$

where V follows the b-transitions from Ω_b^a; another play is

$$\Omega_b^a,\ \{P\},\ P,\ \emptyset,$$

where V follows an a-transition. The latter play is a win for V. In the inductive game, the first play is a win for R.   □

Both in a game $\mathcal{G}^{\text{ind}}(\mathcal{R}, x_0)$ and in a game $\mathcal{G}^{\text{coind}}(\mathcal{R}, x_0)$, however, one of the two players has the possibility of carefully choosing his/her moves so to win all plays, irrespective of the other player's moves. We say that the winning player *has a winning strategy* in the game, that is, a systematic way of playing that will produce a win in every run of the game.

Definition 2.12.3 (Strategy) In a game $\mathcal{G}^{\text{ind}}(\mathcal{R}, x_0)$ or $\mathcal{G}^{\text{coind}}(\mathcal{R}, x_0)$, a *strategy for* V is a partial function that associates with each play

$$x_0, S_0, \ldots, x_n, S_n, x_{n+1}$$

a set S_{n+1}, with $(S_{n+1}, x_{n+1}) \in \mathcal{R}$, to be used for the next move for V; similarly, a *strategy for* R in $\mathcal{G}^{\text{ind}}(\mathcal{R}, x_0)$ or $\mathcal{G}^{\text{coind}}(\mathcal{R}, x_0)$ is a partial function that associates with each play

$$x_0, S_0, \ldots, x_n, S_n$$

an element $x_{n+1} \in S_n$. The strategy of a player is *winning* if that player wins every play in which he/she has followed the strategy. $\square$

The strategies we need for inductively and coinductively defined sets can actually be history-free, meaning that the move of a player is dictated only by the last move from the other player, as opposed to the entire play as we have defined above. Both presentations of the strategies can be useful. (In game theory, the move to history-free strategy is not always possible.)

Example 2.12.4 In Example 2.12.1, in some steps V has two possible moves, reflecting the two inference rules in the original definition of $\Uparrow$, whereas R at any time has only one possible move. The two infinite plays shown also implicitly describe winning strategies for V. In Example 2.12.2, at the beginning V has three possible moves. A winning strategy is obtained by selecting $\{P\}$; after this, the remaining moves for V and R are fixed, and result in the second play of the example. Another winning strategy for V is obtained by selecting $\{Q\}$ in the first move. $\square$

Theorem 2.12.5

(1) $x_0 \in \mathtt{lfp}(\Phi_{\mathcal{R}})$ *iff player* V *has a winning strategy in the game* $\mathcal{G}^{\text{ind}}(\mathcal{R}, x_0)$;
(2) $x_0 \in \mathtt{gfp}(\Phi_{\mathcal{R}})$ *iff player* V *has a winning strategy in the game* $\mathcal{G}^{\text{coind}}(\mathcal{R}, x_0)$.

Proof We examine (1), as (2) is similar. We appeal to Theorem 2.11.2 and to the representation of trees as sets of sequences in Remark 2.11.1. Consider all the plays

$$x_0, S_0, \ldots, x_n, S_n$$

that can be obtained following the winning strategy of V. Each such play gives us a sequence

$$x_0 \ldots x_n.$$

The set of all these sequences is a proof tree for x_0. It is easy to check that all conditions of a tree and a proof tree hold. Moreover, the tree is well-founded because an infinite path in the tree would yield an infinite play.

The converse is proved similarly, defining a winning strategy from a proof tree for x_0. $\square$

2.13 The bisimulation game

In Exercise 2.10.22 the reader has seen that the set of rules that correspond to the coinductive definition of bisimulation has all elements of the form

$$\frac{\mathrm{Der}(P, Q, f, g)}{(P, Q)}$$

where

- f is a function that maps a pair (μ, P') such that $P \xrightarrow{\mu} P'$ into a process Q' such that $Q \xrightarrow{\mu} Q'$, and conversely function g maps a pair (μ, Q') such that $Q \xrightarrow{\mu} Q'$ into a process P' such that $P \xrightarrow{\mu} P'$, and
- $\mathrm{Der}(P, Q, f, g)$ is the set of process pairs

$$\{(P', f(\mu, P')) \mid P \xrightarrow{\mu} P'\} \cup \{(g(\mu, Q'), Q') \mid Q \xrightarrow{\mu} Q'\}.$$

There may be several rules with the same conclusion: it suffices that the processes in the conclusion have non-determinism in their derivatives.

Call $\mathcal{R}$ the set of rules for bisimulation. In the game interpretation for $\mathcal{R}$, given a pair (P, Q), the verifier V essentially has to choose the functions f and g that determine the pairs $\mathrm{Der}(P, Q, f, g)$ needed in the premise. If no such f and g exist, then V cannot continue and R wins. If V's move succeeds, the refuter R then picks up one of the pairs in $\mathrm{Der}(P, Q, f, g)$ to continue the game. When $\mathrm{Der}(P, Q, f, g)$ is empty (which happens if both P and Q are stopped), R cannot continue and V wins. As the game is coinductive, an infinite play represents a win for V.

Example 2.13.1 Consider the processes P_1 and Q_1 of Figure 1.4. On the game for these processes, there are plays that R wins, and plays that V wins. An example of a play in which V wins is

$$(P_1, Q_1), \ \{(P_2, Q_2), (P_3, Q_2)\}, \ (P_3, Q_2), \ \{(P_4, Q_3)\}, \ (P_4, Q_3), \ \emptyset.$$

A play with a win for R is

$$(P_1, Q_1), \ \{(P_2, Q_2), (P_3, Q_2)\}, \ (P_2, Q_2).$$

R has a winning strategy, which consists in following the latter play, thereby always selecting, in the first move, the pair (P_2, Q_2). □

2.14 A simpler bisimulation game

In the game for bisimulation in Section 2.13, given a pair (P, Q), V has to exhibit all relevant derivatives $\mathrm{Der}(P, Q, f, g)$, from which R then selects a pair $(P', f(\mu, P'))$ or $(g(\mu, Q'), Q')$. We can formulate the game a bit differently, letting R move first: R first chooses a transition, say $P \xrightarrow{\mu} P'$ or $Q \xrightarrow{\mu} Q'$, and then V has to find a matching derivative, that is $f(\mu, P')$ or $g(\mu, Q')$. While equivalent to the previous formulation, the new one is somewhat simpler and gives us a more vivid and immediate understanding of the 'bisimulation game'. A play for (P_0, Q_0) in the new game is a finite or infinite sequence of pairs

$$(P_0, Q_0), (P_1, Q_1), \ldots, (P_i, Q_i), \ldots.$$

R tries to show that the processes P_0 and Q_0 of the initial pair are not equal, and conversely for V. When the game has reached a pair (P_i, Q_i), the following pair is determined thus: R makes the challenge by choosing either a transition $P_i \xrightarrow{\mu} P'$ or a transition $Q_i \xrightarrow{\mu} Q'$; then V has to answer, in the former case with a transition $Q_i \xrightarrow{\mu} Q'$, in the latter case with a transition $P_i \xrightarrow{\mu} P'$; the pair (P', Q') is $(i + 1)$th one of the play. As expected, if at some point V is unable to answer because there is no transition from the appropriate process with the required label, then R wins. If this situation never occurs, that is, either the play stops because there are no transitions from the processes in the current pair and therefore R cannot formulate a challenge, or the play is infinite, then V is the winner.

As usual, we can define the notion of strategy for R and V. A strategy for R specifies, for all possible current plays

$$(P_0, Q_0), (P_1, Q_1), \ldots, (P_i, Q_i),$$

which transition to choose as the next challenge. And a strategy for V specifies, for all possible current plays and all possible next challenges from R, the transition to pick up as an answer. (Again, the strategy can be history-free, i.e., based only on the last pair of the current play.) A strategy, for R or V, is winning if it leads to a win in all possible plays.

Exercise 2.14.1 (∗, Recommended, ↪) Show that $P \sim Q$ if and only if V has a winning strategy for (P, Q). (Hint: in one direction, define the appropriate bisimulation; in the other direction define a winning strategy, possibly also using the fact that the strategy can be history-free.) □

Exercise 2.14.2 (∗, Recommended, ↪) Show that $P \nsim Q$ if and only if R has a winning strategy for (P, Q). (Hint: use Exercise 2.14.1, and the stratification of bisimilarity over the ordinals in Section 2.10.2.) □

The game interpretation is not useful only to explain bisimulation, but also to reason about it, especially to prove non-bisimilarity results.

Example 2.14.3 We describe a winning strategy for the refuter R for the game on the processes P_3, Q_3 of Example 2.10.16. The initial transition chosen by R is $P_3 \xrightarrow{a} P_3^1$. The only answer for V can be via the transition $Q_3 \xrightarrow{a} Q_3^1$, and the resulting pair is (P_3^1, Q_3^1). Now R chooses the transition $Q_3^1 \xrightarrow{b} Q_3^3$, and V has only the transition $P_3^1 \xrightarrow{b} P_3^3$, resulting in the new pair (P_3^3, Q_3^3). Finally, R makes the challenge on the transition $Q_3^3 \xrightarrow{d} Q_3^5$, and V cannot answer. □

Exercise 2.14.4 Describe another winning strategy for R on the game of Example 2.14.3, where R initially chooses a move from Q_3. □

Exercise 2.14.5 Describe a winning strategy for R on the game for the processes P_4 and Q_4 of Figure 2.4. ☐

The reader may want to compare Example 2.14.3 with the solutions to Exercise 1.4.9 and Example 2.10.16, and similarly, the strategy in Exercise 2.14.5 with the solution of Exercise 2.10.17.

Example 2.14.6 (A winning strategy for V**)** We give a winning strategy for the verifier V on the game for the processes R_1 and Q_1 of Exercise 1.4.11. We define the strategy pair by pair, according to the current pair of a play.

(R_1, Q_1) There are only a-transitions emanating from these processes, and R has four possible choices, corresponding to the two transitions from R_1 and the two from Q_1, leading to one of the processes R_2, R_3, Q_3, Q_4. The verifier answers by making sure that the following pair in the play is (R_2, Q_4) or (R_3, Q_3).

(R_2, Q_4) R can choose $R_2 \xrightarrow{b} R_3$, and V answers using $Q_4 \xrightarrow{b} Q_5$. Conversely, if R chooses $Q_4 \xrightarrow{b} Q_5$ then V picks $R_2 \xrightarrow{b} R_3$. The next pair is (R_3, Q_5).

(R_3, Q_5) R has four possibilities of choice, along c-transitions. V makes sure that the next pair in the play is (R_2, Q_2) or (R_1, Q_1).

(R_2, Q_2) There is only one outgoing b-transition from each process. Regardless of R's choice, V can ensure that the next pair is (R_3, Q_3).

(R_3, Q_3) The reasoning is similar to that for (R_3, Q_5).

The reader may check that the pairs described also define a bisimulation. ☐

Exercise 2.14.7 Describe the analogue of the two game interpretations for bisimulation (Sections 2.13 and 2.14) for case of the similarity relation (Exercise 1.4.17). ☐

For more details on this game interpretation of bisimulation, see [Sti01, Tho93]. In the remainder of the book, we will not use the above game interpretations of bisimilarity. We will occasionally use the term 'bisimulation game', but simply to refer to the challenge–answer mechanism in the clauses of bisimulation (Definition 1.4.2).

3

Algebraic properties of bisimilarity

In this chapter we introduce some common process operators, which impose a structure on processes and bring in concepts from algebra. The operators we consider are inspired by those of the Calculus of Communicating Systems (CCS) [Mil89, AILS07], one of the most studied process calculi. Given a process calculus (or a language), one obtains an LTS by providing, for each operator, a set of inference rules that determine the possible transitions of the processes in the syntax-driven fashion of Plotkin's Structured Operational Semantics (SOS) [Plo04a, Plo04b]. We restrain from going into a thorough discussion on process calculi. We do present, however, nearly all the operators of CCS. What here, and in the following chapters, is called CCS is in fact very close to the standard presentation as in, e.g., [Mil89, AILS07]. The only technical differences are that we do not introduce the relabelling operator, and, for writing processes with an infinite behaviour, we use constant symbols instead of recursive process equations; each constant comes with its own transitions. These differences are discussed in Remark 3.5.8 and following exercises, and Remark 3.2.3.

The chapter offers a number of examples of the bisimulation proof method. The method is used to prove that bisimilarity is preserved by the operators considered (and that therefore it is a congruence in CCS), to prove some basic algebraic laws, and in various examples. Another important result is an axiomatisation of bisimilarity, that is, an algebraic characterisation of bisimilarity on the term algebra generated by the operators – roughly the processes with a finite behaviour. In the literature, axiomatisations of bisimilarity can be found for various sets of finite, or finite-state, processes. In general it is impossible to axiomatise fully-fledged languages, as these are Turing complete and bisimilarity is not even semi-decidable [AIS12].

The use of operators also allows us to see how to formalise the meaning of a construct via an LTS using inference rules in the SOS style. Indeed, besides the basic CCS operators, we will mention a few other operators, here and in the following chapters. We will also consider classes of operators, defined in terms of the format of the SOS rules describing their behaviour. One of the reasons is to show the robustness of the bisimilarity theory.

We introduce the basic CCS operators in Section 3.1. We define the CCS language, and some basic notations for it, in Section 3.2. In Section 3.3 we show some examples of equalities among CCS processes. In Section 3.4 we derive some important algebraic laws. In Section 3.5 we discuss the compositionality properties of bisimilarity. Finally, in Section 3.6 we present the algebraic characterisation of bisimilarity.

3.1 Basic process operators

Our main operator is parallel composition, which allows us to run two processes in parallel, and to make them interact. Following CCS, interaction for us is handshaking between two processes. In doing so, no value is exchanged: interaction is just synchronisation. This is very useful for simplification purposes, as value passing introduces additional and orthogonal concerns.

An interaction occurs when a process can perform an action a and another process, running in parallel, can perform the complementary action $\bar{a}$. We call a a *name*, and $\bar{a}$ a *coname*. The occurrence of the interaction is indicated by a transition labelled with the special action τ. We assume, for convenience in the presentation of the SOS rules, that $\bar{\bar{a}} = a$, and that τ is different from any name or coname. Thus in all the LTSs of this chapter the set of actions is $Act = Names \cup Conames \cup \{\tau\}$ where *Names* and *Conames* are the sets of names and conames, and the three sets (*Names*, *Conames*, $\{\tau\}$) are disjoint. We use $a, b, c, \ldots$ to range over the names. We can think of a name a as a communication port (or a channel), and of actions a and $\bar{a}$ as inputs and outputs on such a port. Hence a transition $P \xrightarrow{a} P'$ says that P is capable of offering an input at port a, and in doing so it evolves into P'; likewise for a transition $P \xrightarrow{\bar{a}} P'$, where P offers an output at a. A transition $P \xrightarrow{\tau} P'$ says that P can internally do some work and then become P'. This work can be an interaction between two subcomponents of P, as explained above. More generally, in the operational semantics of process calculi, τ represents a computation internal to a process, including a synchronisation between components, but also an evaluation step on an arithmetic expression, the access to a local memory, and so on. The work is 'internal' because the process does not require the intervention of the external environment. In contrast, an input (or output) transition is an offer towards the environment: the environment accepts it by contributing with the complementary action. We sometimes call input and output actions the *visible* actions.

Below we present the five operators we consider (nil, prefixing, parallel composition, choice, restriction) and, for each of them, its inference rules for transition. We then give examples of equalities that make use of such operators.

Nil

The first, and simplest, operator is nil, written **0**. It represents a terminated process, and therefore has no transitions.

Prefixing

Prefixing allows us to turn an action μ and a process P into a new process $\mu.P$ in which the action μ must be executed before any action from P. This imposes a temporal sequentialisation between μ and P. More complex forms of sequentialisation can be derived, see for instance Exercise 4.5.6. The inference rule for prefixing is actually an axiom, as the set of premises is empty:

$$\text{PRE} \quad \frac{}{\mu.P \xrightarrow{\mu} P}$$

For instance, the only transition for the process $a.b.\mathbf{0}$ is $a.b.\mathbf{0} \xrightarrow{a} b.\mathbf{0}$, and after this we have $b.\mathbf{0} \xrightarrow{b} \mathbf{0}$.

Parallel composition

We have already introduced the operator of parallel composition above. Its behaviour is described by three inference rules:

$$\text{PARL} \quad \frac{P_1 \xrightarrow{\mu} P_1'}{P_1 \mid P_2 \xrightarrow{\mu} P_1' \mid P_2}$$

$$\text{PARR} \quad \frac{P_2 \xrightarrow{\mu} P_2'}{P_1 \mid P_2 \xrightarrow{\mu} P_1 \mid P_2'}$$

$$\text{COM} \quad \frac{P_1 \xrightarrow{\mu} P_1' \qquad P_2 \xrightarrow{\bar{\mu}} P_2'}{P_1 \mid P_2 \xrightarrow{\tau} P_1' \mid P_2'}$$

Rules PARL and PARR show that a component can still perform its own transitions, so to interact with external processes, without affecting the parallel structure of the system. Rule COM shows that the two components can interact with each other, when they are capable of performing complementary actions. The notation convention for $\bar{\mu}$, namely $\bar{\bar{a}} = a$, allows us to avoid the symmetric rule. Because of PARL and PARR, the interaction in COM is not forced (but the addition of the operator of restriction can force it, see Exercise 3.3.4).

As an example, the process $P \stackrel{\text{def}}{=} (a.\mathbf{0} \mid b.\mathbf{0}) \mid \bar{a}.\mathbf{0}$ has the transitions

$$P \xrightarrow{a} (\mathbf{0} \mid b.\mathbf{0}) \mid \bar{a}.\mathbf{0}, \qquad P \xrightarrow{\tau} (\mathbf{0} \mid b.\mathbf{0}) \mid \mathbf{0},$$
$$P \xrightarrow{b} (a.\mathbf{0} \mid \mathbf{0}) \mid \bar{a}.\mathbf{0}, \qquad P \xrightarrow{\bar{a}} (a.\mathbf{0} \mid b.\mathbf{0}) \mid \mathbf{0}.$$

Choice

The binary operator choice (sometimes also called *sum*), written $+$, gives us an alternative between two behaviours. The process $P + Q$ can behave as P or as Q, depending on which of them performs the first transition. If P goes first, then Q is discarded, and conversely. This is expressed by the two inference rules for choice:

$$\text{SUML} \quad \frac{P_1 \xrightarrow{\mu} P_1'}{P_1 + P_2 \xrightarrow{\mu} P_1'}$$

$$\text{SUMR} \quad \frac{P_2 \xrightarrow{\mu} P_2'}{P_1 + P_2 \xrightarrow{\mu} P_2'}$$

As an example, the process $P \overset{\text{def}}{=} (\bar{a}.Q_1 \,|\, a.Q_2) + b.R$ has the transitions

$$P \overset{\tau}{\rightarrow} Q_1 \,|\, Q_2, \qquad\qquad P \overset{a}{\rightarrow} \bar{a}.Q_1 \,|\, Q_2,$$
$$P \overset{\bar{a}}{\rightarrow} Q_1 \,|\, a.Q_2, \qquad\qquad P \overset{b}{\rightarrow} R.$$

Restriction

Restricting a port a in a process P, written $va\ P$, makes a private to P, hiding the port to the external environment. The construct v binds a, with scope P, much in the same way as the construct λ of the λ-calculus binds name x with scope M in the term $\lambda x.M$. There is one inference rule for restriction:

$$\text{RES} \quad \frac{P \overset{\mu}{\rightarrow} P'}{va\ P \overset{\mu}{\rightarrow} va\ P'} \quad \mu \notin \{a, \bar{a}\}$$

The rule shows that v blocks any action that involves the restricted port, and has no effect on the other actions. For instance, $P \overset{\text{def}}{=} va\ ((a.Q_1 \,|\, \bar{a}.Q_2) + b.R)$ has transitions

$$P \overset{\tau}{\rightarrow} va\ (Q_1 \,|\, Q_2) \qquad \text{and} \qquad P \overset{b}{\rightarrow} va\ R.$$

The notation we use for restriction is borrowed from the π-calculus; in the CCS literature a restriction $va\ P$ is often written $P\backslash a$.

Exercise 3.1.1

(1) Which transitions can the process $P \overset{\text{def}}{=} va\ ((a.0 + b.0)\,|\,\bar{a}.0)$ make?
(2) Find a process Q in which there is no parallel composition and restriction and with $P \sim Q$. $\square$

3.2 CCS

In summary, the CCS languages we use have a set of actions $Act = Names \cup Conames \cup \{\tau\}$, and a set of processes Pr given by this grammar:

$$P ::= P_1 \,\big|\, P_2 \ \big|\ P_1 + P_2 \ \big|\ \mu.P \ \big|\ va\ P \ \big|\ 0 \ \big|\ K,$$

where K is a *constant*. Each constant K has a behaviour specified by a set of transitions of the form $K \overset{\mu}{\rightarrow} P$. The set of all constants is $Cons$, and the set of all transitions for the constants in $Cons$ is $\mathcal{T}_{Cons} \subseteq Cons \times Act \times Pr$. The transitions for the processes in Pr are determined by $\mathcal{T}_{Cons}$ plus the inferences rules for the operators in Section 3.1. Such a process language is called CCS($Act, Cons, \mathcal{T}_{Cons}$), but we always abbreviate it as CCS, since either the specific sets of actions and constants are not important, or anyhow there are no risks of ambiguities.

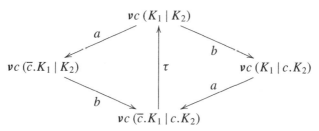

Fig. 3.1 An infinite behaviour, using constants.

Example 3.2.1 Figure 3.1 shows the LTS for the process $vc\,(K_1 \mid K_2)$, where K_1 and K_2 are the constants with the transitions

$$K_1 \xrightarrow{a} \overline{c}.K_1,$$
$$K_2 \xrightarrow{b} c.K_2.$$

$\square$

The language obtained with the empty set of constants is *finCCS*. All processes in *finCCS* are finite: they cannot perform an infinite sequence of transitions.

We assign choice the lowest syntactic precedence among the operators; prefixing has the highest. For instance, $b.P + c.R$ is $(b.P) + (c.R)$, and $a.b.P \mid c.Q + a.c.R$ is $((a.b.P) \mid c.Q) + (a.c.R)$. We shall see that both parallel composition and choice are associative. Therefore we write compositions and choices involving multiple processes as $P_1 \mid \cdots \mid P_n$ and $P_1 + \cdots + P_n$, respectively, forgetting that the operators are binary. Further, we sometimes abbreviate $P_1 \mid \cdots \mid P_n$ as $\Pi_{1 \leq i \leq n} P_i$, and $P_1 + \cdots + P_n$ as $\Sigma_{1 \leq i \leq n} P_i$, and $va_1 \ldots va_n\,P$ as $va_1 \ldots a_n\,P$ or $(va_1 \ldots a_n\,)P$. We usually omit a trailing $\mathbf{0}$, for instance abbreviating $a.\mathbf{0} + b.\mathbf{0}$ as $a + b$.

Assumption 3.2.2 In all CCS languages, we assume that, for any process P, the set $\{a \mid a \text{ or } \overline{a} \text{ is in } \text{sort}(P)\}$ is strictly included in the set of the names; that is, no process uses all available names. (We recall, from Definition 1.2.7, that $\text{sort}(P)$ is the set of actions that P and its multi-step derivatives can perform.) $\square$

The above assumption, which from a practical point of view is quite reasonable, allows us, when manipulating processes, to be always capable of picking fresh names. This can be formally achieved, for instance, by requiring that the set of transitions is countable whereas the set of actions is uncountable; or that the former is finite, whereas the latter is infinite; or also that the former is a set whereas the latter is a proper class (these conditions are achieved by placing analogous conditions on the set of constant transitions). The availability of fresh names is useful in Theorems 4.4.12 and 7.3.9.

Remark 3.2.3 (Recursive definitions) We briefly explain how infinite processes can be defined by means of recursive process definitions, instead of constants with predefined transitions. Basically, rather than saying that there is a symbol K with transitions $K \xrightarrow{\mu_i}$

P_i, for $1 \leq i \leq n$, one defines K via the equation $K \stackrel{\text{def}}{=} \mu_1.P_1 + \cdots + \mu_n.P_n$. The initial prefixes in the body of the definition are the actions that can be immediately performed. This form of recursive definition, where the body is a head standard form (Definition 3.4.7), is usually called *guarded*. One can be more general, and allow recursive definitions $K \stackrel{\text{def}}{=} P$ where P is an arbitrary process. In both cases, one adds among the transition rules of the calculus the following one

$$\frac{P \stackrel{\mu}{\rightarrow} P'}{K \stackrel{\mu}{\rightarrow} P'} \text{ if } K \stackrel{\text{def}}{=} P$$

The two methods of dealing with constants – defining their transitions or setting up equations – are equivalent. The reader may check this, assuming for simplicity that the set of constants is finite, and that each constant has only finitely many transitions. □

3.3 Examples of equalities

Example 3.3.1 We write Ω_μ for the constant whose only transition is

$$\Omega_\mu \stackrel{\mu}{\rightarrow} \Omega_\mu.$$

Thus Ω_μ perpetually performs the action μ. Having two, or more, copies of Ω_μ has no visible effect, that is, for all $n \geq 1$, we have

$$\underbrace{\Omega_\mu \mid \ldots \mid \Omega_\mu}_{n \text{ times}} \sim \Omega_\mu.$$

The result is proved, showing that for each $n \geq 1$ the relation

$$\{(\underbrace{\Omega_\mu \mid \ldots \mid \Omega_\mu}_{n \text{ times}}, \Omega_\mu)\}$$

is a bisimulation. □

Exercise 3.3.2 Show that $\mu \mid \Omega_\mu \sim \Omega_\mu$, for Ω_μ as in Example 3.3.1. □

Example 3.3.3 Show that

- $a.P \mid b.Q \sim a.(P \mid b.Q) + b.(a.P \mid Q)$;
- $a.P \mid \bar{a}.Q \sim a.(P \mid \bar{a}.Q) + \bar{a}.(a.P \mid Q) + \tau.(P \mid Q)$. □

Exercise 3.3.4 Show that $\nu a\,(a.P \mid \bar{a}.Q) \sim \tau.\nu a\,(P \mid Q)$. The restriction forces an interaction between the two parallel components. □

Example 3.3.5 Semaphores are widely used, for instance in operating systems, to protect access to resources. An example of resource is a critical region, that is, a piece of code that manipulates program variables that are shared among several threads. Semaphores can be used to ensure that at most one thread at a time is executing the region and can therefore manipulate the shared variables. For this, *binary* semaphores are needed. In general, an n-ary semaphore can be used to guarantee that at most n processes (or threads) have concurrent access to a resource. A semaphore provides two operations, usually called p and v. The former is invoked in order to obtain access to the resource, the latter to signal the completion of the activity on the resource. (These operations are called p and v after Edsger Dijkstra, who introduced semaphores in the 60s, and named the operations using the initials of Dutch expressions for 'try-and-decrease' and 'increase'.) With an LTS, the behaviour of a binary semaphore is described by constants K_2^0 and K_2^1 with transitions

$$K_2^0 \xrightarrow{p} K_2^1 \qquad \text{and} \qquad K_2^1 \xrightarrow{v} K_2^0,$$

where K_2^0 is the initial state, and K_2^1 an auxiliary state indicating that one instance of the resource is active. A 3-ary semaphore is then described by constants K_3^0, K_3^1, and K_3^2 with the following transitions:

$$K_3^0 \xrightarrow{p} K_3^1 \qquad\qquad K_3^1 \xrightarrow{p} K_3^2$$
$$K_3^2 \xrightarrow{v} K_3^1 \qquad\qquad K_3^1 \xrightarrow{v} K_3^0$$

where again the superscript indicates the number of resources presently active. We obtain a 3-ary semaphore by composing two binary semaphores:

$$K_2^0 \mid K_2^0 \sim K_3^0.$$

A bisimulation that proves the equality is

$$\mathcal{R} \stackrel{\text{def}}{=} \{(K_2^0 \mid K_2^0, K_3^0), (K_2^1 \mid K_2^0, K_3^1), (K_2^0 \mid K_2^1, K_3^1), (K_2^1 \mid K_2^1, K_3^2)\}.$$

We let the reader check that $\mathcal{R}$ is indeed a bisimulation.

More generally, we can describe the behaviour of an n-ary semaphore by constants K_n^j, for $0 \le j < n$, with transitions

$$K_n^0 \xrightarrow{p} K_n^1, \qquad\qquad K_n^{n-1} \xrightarrow{v} K_n^{n-2}$$

and, for $0 < j < n-1$,

$$K_n^j \xrightarrow{p} K_n^{j+1}, \qquad\qquad K_n^j \xrightarrow{v} K_n^{j-1}.$$

For $n, m \ge 2$ and $u \ge 3$, we have: if $n + m = u + 1$ then $K_n^0 \mid K_m^0 \sim K_u^0$. To prove this, one takes, for each such n, m, u, the relation containing all pairs

$$(K_n^j \mid K_m^i, K_u^r)$$

with $0 \le j < n, 0 \le i < m, 0 \le r < u$, and $i + j = r$. Then one shows that such a relation is a bisimulation. We let the reader fill in the missing details. □

Exercise 3.3.6 Prove that $vc\ (K_1 \mid K_2) \sim H$, where K_1, K_2 are defined as in Exercise 3.2.1, and constant H has transitions $H \xrightarrow{a} b.\tau.H$ and $H \xrightarrow{b} a.\tau.H$. □

Exercise 3.3.7 Prove the following equalities:

- $va\ (c.a.P\,|\,\overline{a}.Q) \sim c.\tau.va\ (P\,|\,Q),$
- $vc\ (a.(c\,|\,\overline{c}) + b.c.d) \sim a.\tau + b.$ □

3.4 Some algebraic laws

As the language of processes now has some structure, we can examine the algebraic theory of bisimilarity. We begin with some basic laws for the operators. Parallel composition satisfies the laws of a commutative monoid, with $\mathbf{0}$ being the neutral element.

Lemma 3.4.1 (Parallel composition)

$$P\,|\,Q \sim Q\,|\,P,$$
$$P\,|\,(Q\,|\,R) \sim (P\,|\,Q)\,|\,R,$$
$$P\,|\,\mathbf{0} \sim P.$$

Proof Each law is proved by exhibiting a suitable bisimulation. For instance, in the case of commutativity, the bisimulation is the set of all pairs of the form

$$(P\,|\,Q, Q\,|\,P).$$

To see that this is a bisimulation, suppose $P\,|\,Q \overset{\mu}{\rightarrow} R$. This transition may have been obtained using one of the three rules: PARL, PARR or COM. We consider the first case, and leave the others as exercises to the reader.

Thus suppose there is P' such that $P \overset{\mu}{\rightarrow} P'$ and $R = P'\,|\,Q$. Then, using PARR, also $Q\,|\,P \overset{\mu}{\rightarrow} Q\,|\,P'$. This is sufficient, because $P'\,|\,Q$ and $Q\,|\,P'$ are related.

The case when $Q\,|\,P$ moves first is similar.   □

The same monoidal laws hold for choice, which, in addition, is also idempotent.

Lemma 3.4.2 (Sum)

$$P + Q \sim Q + P,$$
$$P + (Q + R) \sim (P + Q) + R,$$
$$P + \mathbf{0} \sim P,$$
$$P + P \sim P.$$

Proof Commutativity is proved using the relation

$$\mathcal{R} \overset{\text{def}}{=} \mathcal{I} \cup \left(\bigcup_{P,Q} \{(P + Q, Q + P)\} \right),$$

where $\mathcal{I}$ is the identity relation, and proving that $\mathcal{R}$ is a bisimulation. The checks for the pairs in $\mathcal{I}$ are straightforward.

For a pair $(P + Q, Q + P)$, suppose $P + Q \overset{\mu}{\rightarrow} R$ (the case when $Q + P$ moves first is similar). This transition must have been derived using rule SUML or SUMR. In the former case, $R = P'$ for some P' with $P \overset{\mu}{\rightarrow} P'$. Using SUMR, also $Q + P \overset{\mu}{\rightarrow} P'$, and we are done because $(P', P') \in \mathcal{I}$. In the latter case, rules SUML and SUMR are used in the opposite order.

The remaining laws are proved similarly. □

Exercise 3.4.3 ($\hookrightarrow$)

(1) Show that parallel composition is not idempotent.
(2) Give an example of a process P with $P \nsim \mathbf{0}$ and for which $P \mid P \sim P$ nevertheless holds. Can P be a *finCCS* process? □

Next we consider restriction (other laws for restriction, which are about its binder properties, are in Lemma 3.6.9).

Lemma 3.4.4 (Restriction)

$$va \; vb \; P \sim vb \; va \; P,$$
$$va \; (\mu.P) \sim \begin{cases} \mathbf{0} & \text{if } \mu = a \text{ or } \mu = \bar{a}, \\ \mu.va \; P & \text{otherwise}, \end{cases}$$
$$va \; (P + Q) \sim va \; P + va \; Q,$$
$$va \; \mathbf{0} \sim \mathbf{0}.$$

□

Exercise 3.4.5 Fill the remaining details of Lemmas 3.4.1, 3.4.2 and 3.4.4. □

Exercise 3.4.6 ($\hookrightarrow$) Is law $va \; (P \mid Q) \sim (va \; P) \mid (va \; Q)$ valid? Explain why. □

The equalities of Example 3.3.3 are instances of the *Expansion Lemma*, which establishes an important connection among the operators of parallel composition, sum and prefixing. In concurrency theory, expanding, or unfolding, a process is a fundamental analytical technique. Expanding a process involves transforming it into an equivalent summation in which all of its capabilities for action are explicit. By iterating the procedure, the behaviour of the process can be calculated to any desired depth.

Definition 3.4.7 (Head standard form) A process of the form $\Sigma_{i \in I} \mu_i . P_i$ is in *head standard form* (note that I can also be empty, in which case we have the process $\mathbf{0}$). □

Lemma 3.4.8 (Expansion Lemma) *If $P \stackrel{def}{=} \Sigma_i \mu_i . P_i$ and $P' \stackrel{def}{=} \Sigma_j \mu'_j . P'_j$, then*

$$P \mid P' \sim \Sigma_i \mu_i . (P_i \mid P') + \Sigma_j \mu'_j . (P \mid P'_j) + \Sigma_{\mu_i \; \text{opp} \; \mu'_j} \tau.(P_i \mid P'_j),$$

where μ_i opp μ'_j holds if they are complementary actions, that is, either $\mu_i = \bar{a}$ and $\mu'_j = a$, or the converse. □

Exercise 3.4.9 (Recommended, $\hookrightarrow$) Prove Lemma 3.4.8. □

The Expansion Lemma allows us to rewrite a composition of processes in head standard form into a new head standard form whose summands represent the possible immediate transitions of the parallel composition. The summands stem either from transitions of one of the components or from interactions between the two components. This reflects the two kinds of inference rule for the operator of parallel composition, one given by PARL and PARR, the other by COM.

Exercise 3.4.10 (Recommended, $\hookrightarrow$) Is law $\mu.(P + Q) \sim \mu.P + \mu.Q$ valid? What about $(P + Q) \,|\, R \sim (P \,|\, R) + (Q \,|\, R)$? □

Corollary 3.4.11 *Suppose $\{P \xrightarrow{\mu_i} P_i\}_i$ is the set of transitions emanating from P. Then*

(1) $P \sim \Sigma_i \mu_i.P_i$;

(2) *if $\{P' \xrightarrow{\mu'_j} P'_j\}_j$ is the set of transitions emanating from P', we have*

$$P \,|\, P' \sim \Sigma_i \mu_i.(P_i \,|\, P') + \Sigma_j \mu'_j.(P \,|\, P'_j) + \Sigma_{\mu_i \text{ opp } \mu'_j} \tau.(P_i \,|\, P'_j).$$

Proof (1) is easy; (2) follows from (1) and Lemma 3.4.8. □

Exercise 3.4.12 Refine Corollary 3.4.11(2) by adding some restrictions on top; i.e., describe the head normal form for a process of the form $\nu a_1 \ldots a_n \, (P \,|\, P')$. □

3.5 Compositionality properties

We show that bisimilarity is preserved by all process constructs. This allows us to replace, in any process expression, a subterm with a bisimilar one. An equivalence relation with this property is called a *congruence*. A proof of congruence of bisimilarity involves both inductive and coinductive arguments, as the syntax of the processes and of the contexts is defined inductively, whereas bisimilarity is defined coinductively.

Lemma 3.5.1 *If $P \sim Q$ then for all R, μ, and a:*

(1) $P \,|\, R \sim Q \,|\, R$;
(2) $P + R \sim Q + R$;
(3) $\nu a \, P \sim \nu a \, Q$;
(4) $\mu.P \sim \mu.Q$.

Proof We only show the proof of (1); the other cases are easy and left to the reader. We show that

$$\mathcal{R} \overset{\text{def}}{=} \{(P \,|\, R, Q \,|\, R) \,|\, P \sim Q\}$$

is a bisimulation. Suppose $P \,|\, R \xrightarrow{\mu} S$; there are three possibilities to consider, depending on whether the transition has been derived using rule PARL, PARR or COM.

PARL Then $P \xrightarrow{\mu} P'$ and $S = P' \mid R$. Since $P \sim Q$ there is Q' with $Q \xrightarrow{\mu} Q'$ and $P' \sim$
Q'. Therefore, again using PARL, $Q \mid R \xrightarrow{\mu} Q' \mid R$ and we have $(P' \mid R, Q' \mid R) \in \mathcal{R}$.

PARR Then $R \xrightarrow{\mu} R'$ and $S = P \mid R'$. We also have $Q \mid R \xrightarrow{\mu} Q \mid R'$ and $(P \mid R', Q \mid R') \in$
$\mathcal{R}$.

COM Then $\mu = \tau$ and for some λ, $P \xrightarrow{\lambda} P'$, $R \xrightarrow{\bar{\lambda}} R'$ and $S = P' \mid R'$. From $P \sim Q$ we
deduce $Q \xrightarrow{\lambda} Q'$, for some Q' with $P' \sim Q'$. Thus again applying COM, $Q \mid R \xrightarrow{\tau} Q' \mid R'$
and $(P' \mid R', Q' \mid R') \in \mathcal{R}$.

The reasoning when $Q \mid R$ moves first is similar. □

A *context* is a process expression with a single occurrence of a hole $[\cdot]$ in it, as a subexpression. An example is $\nu a\, (b.[\cdot] \mid P)$. We use C to range over contexts, and write $C[P]$ for the process obtained by replacing the hole of C with process P; similarly, if C' is another context then $C[C']$ is the context in which C' has replaced the hole of C.

Theorem 3.5.2 (Congruence) *In CCS, $\sim$ is a congruence relation.*

Proof We know that $\sim$ is an equivalence relation from Theorem 1.4.14. It remains to show that $P \sim Q$ implies $C[P] \sim C[Q]$, for all process contexts C. This is done using induction on the structure of C. The base case of the induction is given by the hypothesis $P \sim Q$, the inductive case by Lemma 3.5.1. □

Exercise 3.5.3 Prove, algebraically, $\nu b \left(a.(b \mid c) + \tau.(b \mid \bar{b}.c) \right) \sim \tau.\tau.c + a.c$. □

Remark 3.5.4 (Transformations on the body of recursive definitions) Theorem 3.5.2 allows us to modify subterms of process subexpressions. However, it does not allow us to manipulate the body of constants. For instance, suppose we have constants K and H with transitions

$$K \xrightarrow{c} c.(a.a.K + b.K),$$
$$H \xrightarrow{c} c.(b.H + a.a.H).$$

We may want to prove $H \sim K$ by appealing to the commutativity of sum and Theorem 3.5.2. This can be done, but it requires a few more technicalities (e.g., introducing process expressions with free variables and bisimilarity on them) that go beyond the scope of this book. We refer the interested reader to [Mil89, chapter 4]. □

Bisimilarity is in fact extremely robust as far as being preserved by the operators of a language. In fact it is generally recognised that a 'good' operator should preserve bisimilarity. A number of formats of operators have been studied, where a format is roughly a specification of the form that the transition rules of an operator should follow, and compositionality results for bisimilarity in these formats have been established. Below is an example of format and corresponding preservation result. More examples can be found in Section 5.12.

Example 3.5.5 (De Simone format)   We consider a language whose terms (the processes) are generated by some grammar (i.e., the language is the term algebra for a certain signature). The transition relation for the terms is defined structurally, in the SOS style, assigning a set of transition rules to each symbol in the grammar. Suppose that all the transition rules follow the format below, called the *De Simone format*. (It is a simplified version of the format introduced by De Simone [DS85], the main restriction being that only one action at a time is observable.) We can then prove that $\sim$ is a congruence. In the rule below, X_r (for $1 \leq r \leq n$), and Y_j (for $j \in J$), are metavariables which are instantiated with processes when the rule is applied.

A transition rule is in *De Simone format* if it has the form

$$\frac{X_j \xrightarrow{\mu_j} Y_j \ (j \in J)}{f(X_1, \ldots, X_n) \xrightarrow{\mu} T}$$

where

(1) f is an operator symbol in the language, of arity n;
(2) $J \subseteq \{1, \ldots, n\}$;
(3) $X_r \ (1 \leq r \leq n)$, and $Y_j \ (j \in J)$ are distinct variables;
(4) T is a term of the language possibly containing the variables $X'_1, \ldots, X'_n$, where for $r \in \{1, \ldots, n\}$ we have $X'_r = Y_r$ if $r \in J$ and $X'_r = X_r$ otherwise; moreover each X'_i occurs at most once in T.

For instance, the CCS rule PARL would be written thus, maintaining the infix notation for parallel composition:

$$\frac{X_1 \xrightarrow{\mu} Y_1}{X_1 \mid X_2 \xrightarrow{\mu} Y_1 \mid X_2}$$

Indeed, all the rules for the CCS operators, in Section 3.1, follow the format. (The rule for restriction we presented has a side condition, which is not mentioned in the format above; it can be avoided using a set of rules, one for each restricted name and for each label.)

To prove that if all the operators of the language have transition rules in the De Simone format then bisimilarity is a congruence, we take the relation

$$\mathcal{R} \stackrel{\text{def}}{=} \{(C[P], C[Q]) \mid C \text{ is a context of the language and } P \sim Q\} \cup \mathcal{I},$$

where $\mathcal{I}$ is the identity relation, and show that $\mathcal{R}$ is a bisimulation. Consider a pair $(C[P], C[Q])$ and a transition $C[P] \xrightarrow{\mu} P_1$ (the case of a move from $C[Q]$ is similar). One finds a matching transition from $C[Q]$ proceeding by induction on the structure of C. The base of the induction is when $C = [\cdot]$, and can be dealt with using the hypothesis $P \sim Q$. In the inductive case, C is of the form $f(R_1, \ldots, R_{i-1}, C', R_{i+1}, \ldots, R_m)$, where C' is another context. For simplicity of presentation (the extension to the general case is straightforward, only notationally more complex, and we leave it to the reader) we assume that $m = 1$ and that the rule applied for the transition of $C[P]$ is as follows:

$$\frac{C'[P] \xrightarrow{\mu'} P'}{f(C'[P]) \xrightarrow{\mu} D[P']}$$

where $D[P']$ is P_1, and D is some context. (The case when P' is not used in P_1 is easier, and is dealt with using the fact that $\mathcal{I} \subseteq \mathcal{R}$; we also omit the simple case in which the rule has no premises.) Here we make use of the linearity on the occurrences of variables in condition (4) of the De Simone format, ensuring that P' is not duplicated in the final derivative (see, however, Exercise 3.5.6). Exploiting the inductive assumption, $C'[Q] \xrightarrow{\mu'} Q'$ and either

(i) $(P', Q') \in \mathcal{I}$, or
(ii) there is a context D' and processes P'', Q'', with $P'' \sim Q''$ and $P' = D'[P'']$, $Q' = D'[Q'']$.

In both cases, we infer $f(C'[Q]) \xrightarrow{\mu} D[Q']$. In (i), we also have $(D[P'], D[Q']) \in \mathcal{I}$ and we are done. In (ii), we have $D[P'] = D[D'[P'']]$ and $D[Q'] = D[D'[Q'']]$. We can thus conclude that the derivatives of $C[P]$ and $C[Q]$ are in $\mathcal{R}$, using the context $D[D']$. □

Exercise 3.5.6 $(*, \hookrightarrow)$ Extend the result in Example 3.5.5 to the case in which, in condition (4) of the De Simone format, the restriction that each variable X'_i may occur at most once in T is dropped. (Hint: you need to work with polyadic contexts.) □

Example 3.5.7 (A specification and an implementation of a counter, from [AILS07])
We specify a counter using constants Counter_n, for $n \geq 0$, with transitions

$$\text{Counter}_0 \xrightarrow{\text{up}} \text{Counter}_1$$

and, for $n > 0$,

$$\text{Counter}_n \xrightarrow{\text{up}} \text{Counter}_{n+1}, \qquad\qquad \text{Counter}_n \xrightarrow{\text{down}} \text{Counter}_{n-1}.$$

The initial state is Counter_0. We reach the state Counter_n if the number of up actions performed exceeds by n the number of downs. In particular, the number of ups is always greater than, or equal to, the number of downs. Consider now an implementation of the counter in term of a constant C with transition

$$C \xrightarrow{\text{up}} C \,|\, \text{down}.\mathbf{0}.$$

It holds that $\text{Counter}_0 \sim C$. This can be proved using the relation

$$\mathcal{R} \stackrel{\text{def}}{=} \{(C \,|\, \Pi_1^n \text{ down}.\mathbf{0}, \text{Counter}_n) \,|\, n \geq 0\},$$

showing that $\mathcal{R}$ is a bisimulation up-to $\sim$, and then appealing to the soundness of this technique (Exercise 1.4.18).

Take a pair $(C \,|\, \Pi_1^n \text{ down}.\mathbf{0}, \text{Counter}_n)$ in $\mathcal{R}$. Suppose $C \,|\, \Pi_1^n \text{ down}.\mathbf{0} \xrightarrow{\mu} P$. We find P' and Q such that $P \sim P'$, $\text{Counter}_n \xrightarrow{\mu} Q$, and $P' \mathcal{R} Q$ (this is sufficient for the schema of the 'up-to $\sim$' technique, because $\sim$ is reflexive, and therefore $Q \sim Q$). By inspecting the inference rules for parallel composition, we find that μ can only be either up or down.

$\mu = $ up. Then the transition from $C \mid \Pi_1^n$ down.0 originates from C, which performs the transition $C \xrightarrow{\text{up}} C \mid$ down.0, and $P = C \mid \Pi_1^{n+1}$ down.0. Process Counter$_n$ can answer with the transition Counter$_n \xrightarrow{\text{up}}$ Counter$_{n+1}$. For $P = P'$ and $Q = $ Counter$_{n+1}$, this closes the diagram.

$\mu = $ down. It must be $n > 0$. The action must originate from one of the down.0 components of Π_1^n down.0, which has made the transition down.$0 \xrightarrow{\text{down}} 0$. Therefore $P = C \mid \Pi_1^n P_i$, where exactly one P_i is 0 and all the others are down.0. Applying the third law of Lemma 3.4.1, and using the compositionality of $\sim$, we have $P \sim C \mid \Pi_1^{n-1}$ down.0. Process Counter$_n$ can answer with the transition Counter$_n \xrightarrow{\text{down}}$ Counter$_{n-1}$. This closes the diagram, for $P' \stackrel{\text{def}}{=} C \mid \Pi_1^{n-1}$ down.0 and $Q \stackrel{\text{def}}{=}$ Counter$_{n-1}$, as $P' \mathcal{R} Q$.

The case when Counter$_n$ moves first and $C \mid \Pi_1^n$ down.0 has to answer is similar. □

Remark 3.5.8 (Relabelling) The only CCS operator so far neglected is *relabelling*. It is less elegant and fundamental than other operators, and indeed it is omitted in developments of CCS such as the π-calculus. In [Mil89] relabelling is written $P[f]$, where the function $f :$ $Act \rightarrow Act$ is the *relabelling function*. The effect is that of renaming the actions performed by P according to f. A relabelling function should respect the name/coname ties, i.e., $f(\overline{a}) = \overline{f(a)}$, and should not alter internal moves, i.e., $f(\tau) = \tau$. The transition rule for relabelling is

$$\frac{P \xrightarrow{\mu} P'}{P[f] \xrightarrow{f(\mu)} P'[f]}$$

□

Exercise 3.5.9 Show that $\sim$ is preserved by relabelling. □

Exercise 3.5.10 ($\hookrightarrow$)

(1) Show that $(P + Q)[f] \sim (P[f]) + (Q[f])$.
(2) Is it true that $(P \mid Q)[f] \sim (P[f]) \mid (Q[f])$? If not, formulate conditions on f so that the property holds. (Hint: consider the process P in Exercise 3.5.11.)
(3) Same question as in the point above for $(va\ P)[f] \sim va\ (P[f])$. □

Exercise 3.5.11 ($\hookrightarrow$)

(1) Relabelling looks like a substitution, but they are not the same. For instance, consider the processes $P \stackrel{\text{def}}{=} a \mid \overline{b}$, and the relabelling function that sends b into a and is the identity on all other names. Show that $P[f]$ is not bisimilar with the process $a \mid \overline{a}$ obtained by replacing b with a in P.

(2) Continue by showing that bisimilarity is not preserved by substitution of names. For this, exhibit two processes in *finCCS* and that do not use restriction that are bisimilar but become different when a name substitution is applied to them (a name substitution is a function σ from names to names that replaces each occurrence of a name a in a process with $\sigma(a)$ and each occurrence of the coname $\overline{a}$ with $\overline{\sigma(a)}$). ☐

The fact that bisimilarity is not preserved by name substitutions, as indicated in Exercise 3.5.11, becomes important in calculi such as the π-calculus whose semantics involve name substitutions, see [SW01].

Exercise 3.5.12 (Recommended, $\hookrightarrow$) Consider the operator $P \parallel Q$ defined as follows:

$$P \parallel Q \stackrel{\text{def}}{=} \nu a_1 \dots a_n (P \mid Q),$$

where

$$\{a_1, \dots, a_n\} = \{a \mid a \text{ or } \overline{a} \text{ is both in sort}(P) \text{ and in sort}(Q)\} .$$

Show that $\parallel$ is commutative but not associative. ☐

3.6 Algebraic characterisation

In general, bisimilarity in process calculi is undecidable, indeed not even semi-decidable if the calculi are Turing complete. In certain cases, however, decidability holds. In these cases it may be possible to give algebraic characterisations of bisimilarity, in the form of *axiomatisations*. We examine below *finCCS*, where the set of sequences of actions that each process can execute is finite. More sophisticated examples of process calculi where bisimilarity is decidable are discussed in [AIS12]. See [Mil89] for an axiomatisation of finite-state processes (recall that 'finite' is different from 'finite-state').

By an axiomatisation of an equivalence on a set of terms, we mean some axioms that, together with the rules of equational reasoning, suffice for proving all and only the equations among the terms that are valid for the given equivalence. The rules of equational reasoning are reflexivity, symmetry, transitivity and substitutivity rules that make it possible to replace any subterm of a process by an equivalent term. (A *proof system* achieves the same goal, but may have, in addition to axioms and some of the rules of equational reasoning, other inference rules.)

Axiomatisations (and proof systems) are of interest for two main reasons. The first is simply that axioms and rules contributing to completeness are often useful for reasoning on terms. A good example of this is the Expansion Lemma. The second reason is that axiomatisations are often good for contrasting equivalences: light can be shed on the differences between equivalences by isolating small collections of axioms and rules that distinguish them. We will see this in the following chapters, discussing other behavioural equivalences.

Summation S1	$P + 0 = P$
S2	$P + Q = Q + P$
S3	$P + (Q + R) = (P + Q) + R$
S4	$P + P = P$

. . . .

Restriction R1		$va\ 0 = 0$
R2	if $\mu \in \{a, \overline{a}\}$	$va\ \mu.P = 0$
R3	if $\mu \notin \{a, \overline{a}\}$	$va\ \mu.P = \mu.va\ P$
R4		$va\ (P + Q) = va\ P + va\ Q$

. . . .

Expansion E

For $P \overset{\text{def}}{=} \sum_{0 \le i \le n} \mu_i.P_i$ and $P' \overset{\text{def}}{=} \sum_{0 \le j \le m} \mu'_j.P'_j$ infer:

$P \mid P' = \Sigma_{0 \le i \le n}\mu_i.(P_i \mid P') + \Sigma_{0 \le j \le m}\mu'_j.(P \mid P'_j) + \Sigma_{\mu_i \text{ opp } \mu'_j}\tau.(P_i \mid P'_j)$

where $\mu_i \text{ opp } \mu'_j$ holds if they are complementary actions, that is, either $\mu_i = \overline{a}$ and $\mu'_j = a$, or the converse.

Fig. 3.2 The axiom system $\mathcal{SB}$.

We write $P \in finCCS$ to mean that P is a process of $finCCS$. We call the axiom system in Figure 3.2 $\mathcal{SB}$, and write $\mathcal{SB} \vdash P = Q$ if we can derive $P = Q$ from the axioms in $\mathcal{SB}$ plus the laws of equational reasoning. The axioms can be partitioned into three groups: the axioms of a commutative abelian monoid for choice; axioms about the commutativity properties of restriction with respect to nil, prefixing and choice (in certain cases commutativity fails and produces nil, in the case of choice it becomes a distributivity law); and the Expansion law. We already considered these laws in Lemmas 3.4.2, 3.4.4 and 3.4.8. We wish to prove the following algebraic characterisation of strong bisimilarity in $finCCS$.

Theorem 3.6.1 *For P, $Q \in finCCS$, we have $P \sim Q$ iff $\mathcal{SB} \vdash P = Q$.*

The proof of the theorem rewrites the processes from $finCCS$ into a special form, called *full standard form*, using the laws of $\mathcal{SB}$. We first treat such rewriting, and prove it correct, and then present the proof of Theorem 3.6.1.

Remark 3.6.2 (Axiom schema, finite axiomatisations and prime processes) The Expansion in system $\mathcal{SB}$ is not an axiom, but an axiom schema. It is an abbreviation for countably infinite axioms (one for each possible value of n and m, and for each choice of initial prefixes). Hence the axiomatisation is not finite. Jan Bergstra and Jan Willem Klop [BK84] have obtained a finite axiomatisation by introducing two auxiliary operators, called *left merge* (see Exercise 4.4.4) and *communication merge*. Faron Moller [Mol90a, Mol90b] has proved that bisimilarity is indeed not finitely axiomatisable without introducing such auxiliary operators. Moller's results are based on beautiful unique decomposition properties of processes as parallel compositions of prime processes up to $\sim$, where a process P is *prime* if $P \not\sim \mathbf{0}$ and $P \sim P_1 \mid P_2$ implies $P_1 \sim \mathbf{0}$ or $P_2 \sim \mathbf{0}$. The first such decomposition result is in [MM93]; scc also [Mol89, Chr93, LvO05]. These decompositions are also exploited in proofs of decidability of bisimilarity in various languages (e.g., [CHM93, HJ99]), and are simpler and and sharper than the corresponding results for most of the behavioural equivalences other than bisimilarity.

The results on axiomatisations have in turn inspired Aceto *et al.* [ABV94], who have produced general algorithms for the generation of (finite) axiomatisations for bisimilarity in process calculi. The axioms are based on the format of the SOS rules of the operators in the calculus, and require the presence of the choice operator.

Strictly speaking, also laws **R2** and **R3** are not purely algebraic, as they have side conditions. In a pure axiomatisation they would be replaced by a set of axioms, one for each choice of names a and prefix μ. $\qquad\qquad\square$

Definition 3.6.3 A process $P \in finCCS$ is in *full standard form* if P and all its subterms are in head standard form. If P is in full standard form, then the *depth* of P is the maximal number of nested prefixes in P. $\qquad\qquad\square$

Lemma 3.6.4 *If $P, Q \in finCCS$ are in full standard form, then $S\mathcal{B} \vdash P \mid Q = R$, for some R in full standard form.*

Proof The result is proved using the Expansion schema and reasoning by induction on the sum of the depths of P and Q. Essentially, it is a matter of repeatedly applying Expansion so as to push the parallel composition to smaller and smaller depths until it disappears when applied to $\mathbf{0}$ components. $\qquad\qquad\square$

Lemma 3.6.5 *If $P \in finCCS$ is in full standard form, then $S\mathcal{B} \vdash \nu a\, P = Q$, for some Q in full standard form.*

Proof It is similar to Lemma 3.6.4, using induction on the depth of P, but this time applying the laws for restriction so as to push the restriction at a inside the structure of P (laws **R3** and **R4**) until it disappears, because either the $\mathbf{0}$ process (law **R1**) or a prefix at a (law **R2**) are met. We may also need **S1** to clean up $\mathbf{0}$ summands. $\qquad\qquad\square$

Lemma 3.6.6 *If $P \in finCCS$, then $S\mathcal{B} \vdash P = Q$, for some Q in full standard form.*

Proof We essentially have to remove all occurrences of parallel composition and restriction from P. We proceed by structural induction on P. The interesting cases are when P is of the form $P_1 \mid P_2$ or $\nu a\, P'$, and for this we use Lemmas 3.6.4 and 3.6.5 plus the inductive hypothesis. When P is of the form $P_1 + P_2$ law **S1** may be needed. $\qquad\qquad\square$

Exercise 3.6.7 Complete the proof of Lemma 3.6.6. $\qquad\qquad\square$

We are now ready to prove the correctness of the axiomatisation.

Proof (of Theorem 3.6.1) The soundness of SB (direction from right to left of the theorem) follows from the validity of each axiom in SB and the congruence of $\sim$ (Lemmas 3.4.2, 3.4.4, 3.4.8 and Theorem 3.5.2).

For the completeness, by Lemma 3.6.6 we can assume that P, Q are full standard forms. We then proceed by induction on the sum of the number of prefixes in P and Q. (We could also use induction on the sum of the depths, or structural induction.) If this sum is 0, then $P = Q = 0$, and the lemma holds because reflexivity is part of the laws for equational reasoning.

Otherwise, we first show that each summand $\mu.P'$ of P is provably equal to some summand $\mu.Q'$ of Q, and conversely. Then we can conclude $SB \vdash P = Q$ using the laws for sum to handle duplicates (law **S4**), and to rearrange summands (laws **S2** and **S3**).

So, suppose $\mu.P'$ is a summand of P. We therefore have $P \xrightarrow{\mu} P'$. As $P \sim Q$, there is Q' such that $Q \xrightarrow{\mu} Q'$ with $P' \sim Q'$. Since Q is a full standard form, $\mu.Q'$ is a summand of Q. Furthermore, as P' and Q' have fewer prefixes than P and Q, by induction $SB \vdash P' = Q'$, hence also (by equational reasoning) $SB \vdash \mu.P' = \mu.Q'$. $\qquad\square$

We conclude the section with some further laws for the restriction operator. While these laws are not needed in the axiomatisation of *finCCS*, they are often useful for manipulating scope and bound names of restrictions. The laws have some conditions, mentioning free and bound names of processes, which we first introduce.

As in *finCCS* there are no constants, the syntax of the processes, precisely their prefixes, determines the actions they can perform. We can then define, by structural induction, the set $fn(P)$ of *free names* in a process P:

$$
\begin{aligned}
fn(\mathbf{0}) &= \emptyset, \\
fn(P \mid Q) = fn(P + Q) \;&= fn(P) \cup fn(Q), \\
fn(a.P) = fn(\bar{a}.P) \;&= \{a\} \cup fn(P), \\
fn(\tau.P) &= fn(P), \\
fn(\nu a\ P) &= fn(P) - \{a\}.
\end{aligned}
$$

Thus a name a is free in a process P if a appears in a prefix of P that is not underneath a restriction at a. A name a is *bound* in P if a restriction νa appears in P. The set of bound names of P is $bn(P)$. For instance, if $P = c.\nu a\ \nu b\ (a \mid \bar{b} \mid d)$ then $fn(P) = \{c, d\}$ and $bn(P) = \{a, b\}$, and for $Q = a.\nu a\ (a \mid b)$, we have $fn(Q) = \{a, b\}$ and $bn(Q) = \{a\}$.

Lemma 3.6.8 *If $P \in finCCS$ and $P \xrightarrow{\mu} P'$, then $fn(P') \subseteq fn(P)$; further, if $\mu \in \{a, \bar{a}\}$ then $a \in fn(P)$.* $\qquad\square$

Hence the sort of a processes is included in its free names. We write $\{b/a\}$ for the name substitution (as by Exercise 3.5.11) that sends a into b and is the identity elsewhere. Thus $P\{b/a\}$ is the process obtained from P by replacing each occurrence of a in P with b.

Lemma 3.6.9 (Further laws for restriction, in *fin*CCS**)**

$$va\ P \sim P \qquad\qquad\qquad if\ a \notin \mathrm{fn}(P),$$
$$va\ (P\,|\,Q) \sim (va\ P)\,|\,Q \quad\ if\ a \notin \mathrm{fn}(Q),$$
$$va\ P \sim vb\ (P\{^b\!/a\}) \quad if\ b \notin (\mathrm{fn}(P) \cup \mathrm{bn}(P)).$$

☐

The first and second laws show that a restriction does not affect a process in which the restricted name is not used (note that law **R1** is an instance of the first law, and so is $va\ va\ P \sim va\ P$). The third law, often called the α-conversion law, shows that a restricted name may be replaced by another name, provided this is *fresh* so as not to modify the bindings in the process.

Exercise 3.6.10 Prove Lemma 3.6.9. ☐

Exercise 3.6.11 Show that the side conditions in the laws of Lemma 3.6.9 are necessary.

☐

Remark 3.6.12 As constants have a behaviour but not a syntax, defining the free names of a process that may contain constants requires some care. Also, the third law of Lemma 3.6.9 needs to be refined to make sure that the substitution is propagated, and modifies, the behaviour of the constants. See, for instance, the definition of sort of a process in [Mil89]. ☐

4

Processes with internal activities

In Section 3.1, defining CCS, we obtained LTSs in which the set of actions includes the special symbol τ, representing internal activity. Internal activity is not directly observable (also because we are not assuming time-related attributes for actions). It is then desirable that the behavioural equality for the processes be insensitive to the number of τ-actions they perform. As an example consider the CCS process $P \overset{\text{def}}{=} va\,(b.\bar{a} \mid a.c)$. We have

$$P \sim b.\tau.c$$

and therefore, when we regard τ as internal, we would also like to consider P equal to $b.c$. This does not hold for the bisimilarity $\sim$, which is deficient in this respect as it treats internal action and visible actions equally.

For an analogy with ordinary sequential programming languages, consider the two programs

$$\texttt{print(5)} \quad \text{and} \quad \texttt{if true then print(5) else skip.} \quad (4.1)$$

The first program immediately performs the printing action. The second does so after evaluation of the conditional, an act that represents some internal activity. Indeed, we can describe the behaviours of those programs with the following transitions:[1]

$$\texttt{if true then print(5) else skip} \overset{\tau}{\to} \texttt{print(5)}$$

$$\texttt{print(5)} \xrightarrow{\text{print(5)}} \mathbf{0}$$

where $\mathbf{0}$ indicates the successful termination of the evaluation of a program. Thus the two programs have different transitions and are not equal according to the definition of bisimilarity. This is disturbing, because the observable behaviour of the two programs is the same: in both cases only the printing action is visible. For another example, consider the λ-calculus terms

$$(\lambda x.x)3 \quad \text{and} \quad 3.$$

---

[1] In sequential languages, such an operational semantics is often called 'small-step', as opposed to the 'big-step' in which only the final value produced by the programs is represented; moreover the relation $\overset{\tau}{\to}$ is often written $\longrightarrow$.

The first returns the value 3 after the reduction step

$$(\lambda x.x)3 \xrightarrow{\tau} 3$$

in which the initial λ term – the identity function – is consumed. Semantically, we wish to identify the two terms. But again, only the first term has an internal transition, and therefore the two terms are distinguished in behavioural equalities that treat all actions equally.

In this chapter we see how to modify the definition of bisimilarity in order to to give a more satisfactory account of internal activity. The resulting forms of bisimulation are called *weak*. The most studied and used is *weak bisimilarity*.

In Section 4.1 we introduce weak LTSs and weak transitions. We present weak bisimilarity, and its basic properties, in Section 4.2. We discuss its treatment of divergence in Section 4.3. As weak bisimilarity is not preserved by the choice operator, in Section 4.4 we refine the bisimilarity so to obtain a full congruence over CCS. In Section 4.5 we show an algebraic characterisation of such a congruence, on finite CCS. We then discuss a few variations of weak bisimilarity. The first variation, in Section 4.6, removes the challenge on τ-moves; it is, however, mainly presented as a curiosity, due to a number of problems both in applications and in the theory. The second, in Section 4.7 makes bisimilarity divergence-sensitive. The third, in Section 4.8, changes the weak transition used to answer a challenge, so as to obtain a bisimulation relation that is a full congruence. The fourth, in Section 4.9, actually comprises three sub-variations; they modify the requirements on weak transitions so as to have bisimilarities that respect more closely the branching structure of the LTSs.

The variations examined in Sections 4.6–4.9 are in fact orthogonal to each other. They can also be combined, resulting in several possibilities (see, e.g., Exercise 4.9.14). Further, most versions, including the bisimulation game on τ-moves, are not preserved by the choice operator and we have therefore also the corresponding induced congruences. We will use the adjective 'rooted' to identify these congruences, as they differ in the requirement on the initial step, i.e., on the root of the computation tree associated with the behaviour of a process.

4.1 Weak LTSs and weak transitions

We call an LTS in which a special action τ represents internal activity *weak*. Correspondingly, we sometimes call the ordinary LTSs *strong*.

To abstract away from internal actions, a key ingredient is the *weak transition* relations, $\Longrightarrow$ and $\overset{\mu}{\Longrightarrow}$. We write $P \Longrightarrow Q$ to mean that P can evolve to Q by performing some number, possibly zero, of internal actions; and $P \overset{\mu}{\Longrightarrow} Q$ to mean that P can become Q as a result of an evolution that includes an action μ, and that may involve any number of internal actions before and after μ. The relation $\overset{\tau}{\Longrightarrow}$ is different from $\Longrightarrow$, as the former indicates that at least one τ action has been performed. Again, we sometimes call the 'single' transitions $\overset{\mu}{\longrightarrow}$ *strong*, to distinguish them from the weak ones.

Definition 4.1.1 (Weak transitions)

- Relation $\Longrightarrow$ is the reflexive and transitive closure of $\overset{\tau}{\to}$. That is, $P \Longrightarrow P'$ holds if there is $n \geq 0$ and processes $P_1, \ldots, P_n$ with $P_n = P'$ such that $P \overset{\tau}{\to} P_1 \cdots \overset{\tau}{\to} P_n$. Further, we say that n is a *weight* of $P \Longrightarrow P'$. (It can be $n = 0$, hence $P \Longrightarrow P$ holds for all processes P.)
- For all $\mu \in Act$, relation $\overset{\mu}{\Longrightarrow}$ is the composition of the relations $\Longrightarrow$, $\overset{\mu}{\to}$, and $\Longrightarrow$; that is, $P \overset{\mu}{\Longrightarrow} P'$ holds if there are P_1, P_2 such that $P \Longrightarrow P_1 \overset{\mu}{\to} P_2 \Longrightarrow P'$.

We extend the transition relations to finite sequences of actions as in the strong case:

- $P \overset{\epsilon}{\Longrightarrow} P'$ (where ϵ is the empty sequence) holds if $P \Longrightarrow P'$;
- $P \overset{\mu s}{\Longrightarrow} P'$ holds if there is P'' such that $P \overset{\mu}{\Longrightarrow} P''$ and $P'' \overset{s}{\Longrightarrow} P'$. $\qquad\square$

On the meaning of $\Longrightarrow$, see also Exercise 2.7.4. There may be several weights for a transition $P \Longrightarrow P'$. For instance, if $P = \tau.\mathbf{0} + \tau.\tau.\mathbf{0}$ then $P \Longrightarrow \mathbf{0}$ can be derived in two ways, with weights 1 and 2. The *minimum* weight for a transition is the least weight for that transition. Note that the largest weight for a transition need not exist. For instance, on the process Ω_τ of Exercise 4.3.2, the transition $\Omega_\tau \Longrightarrow \Omega_\tau$ can be given weight n for each $n \geq 0$.

An example of a weak LTS is the one obtained from CCS. Indeed we will often use CCS to write processes in examples. We will also use it to study the algebraic properties of the weak behavioural relations.

Example 4.1.2 If $Q \overset{\text{def}}{=} \tau.a.\tau.b$, then $Q \overset{\tau}{\Longrightarrow} a.\tau.b$; we also have $Q \overset{a}{\Longrightarrow} \tau.b$ and $Q \overset{a}{\Longrightarrow} b$. Similarly, for $P \overset{\text{def}}{=} \overline{a}.c.d \mid a.b.\overline{c}$ we have $P \overset{b}{\Longrightarrow} c.d \mid \overline{c}$ and $P \overset{b}{\Longrightarrow} d \mid \mathbf{0}$. $\qquad\square$

Definition 4.1.3 An LTS is *image-finite under weak transitions* if for each μ the relation $\overset{\mu}{\Longrightarrow}$ is image-finite. $\qquad\square$

Exercise 4.1.4 ($\hookrightarrow$) Suppose that each constant in CCS has only finitely many (strong) transitions. Show that all CCS processes are image-finite but not necessarily image-finite under weak transitions. $\qquad\square$

4.2 Weak bisimulation

We define *weak bisimulation* and *weak bisimilarity* on top of the weak transitions. The original bisimulation and bisimilarity of Definition 1.4.2 will be sometimes called *strong*.

We use ℓ to range over the visible actions; i.e., $P \overset{\ell}{\to} P'$ means that $P \overset{\mu}{\to} P'$ for some $\mu \neq \tau$.

Definition 4.2.1 (Weak bisimilarity) A process relation $\mathcal{R}$ is a *weak bisimulation* if, whenever $P \mathcal{R} Q$, we have:

(1) for all P' and ℓ with $P \overset{\ell}{\Rightarrow} P'$ there is Q' such that $Q \overset{\ell}{\Rightarrow} Q'$ and $P' \mathcal{R} Q'$;
(2) for all P' with $P \overset{\tau}{\Rightarrow} P'$, there is Q' such that $Q \Longrightarrow Q'$ and $P' \mathcal{R} Q'$;
(3) the converse of (1) and (2), on the actions from Q (i.e., the roles of P and Q are reversed).

P and Q are *weakly bisimilar*, written $P \approx Q$, if $P \mathcal{R} Q$ for some weak bisimulation $\mathcal{R}$. □

Weak bisimilarity is the relation obtained by playing the bisimulation game on the graph whose arrows are given by $\Longrightarrow$ and the $\overset{\mu}{\Rightarrow}$ relations. The only difference between strong bisimilarity and weak bisimilarity is what counts as a move in the bisimulation game. It is the special treatment accorded to τ transitions in defining the relations $\Longrightarrow$ and $\overset{\mu}{\Rightarrow}$ that makes abstraction from internal action possible using the weak equivalence.

Note the use of relation $\Longrightarrow$, in place of $\overset{\tau}{\Rightarrow}$, for the answer from process Q in clause (2). The use of $\overset{\tau}{\Rightarrow}$ would have given *dynamic bisimilarity*; see Definition 4.8.1 and following results, such as Exercise 4.8.3, for explanations.

Exercise 4.2.2 Show that $\approx$ is an equivalence relation. (Hint: proceed as for the analogous result for strong bisimilarity, Lemma 1.4.14.) □

Example 4.2.3 We have:

(1) $\tau.a \approx a$;
(2) $va\,(b.\bar{a} \,|\, a.c) \approx b.c$.

To prove (1), we use the relation

$$\mathcal{R} \overset{\text{def}}{=} \{(\tau.a, a), (a, a), (\mathbf{0}, \mathbf{0})\}$$

and show that this is a weak bisimulation. Consider the pair $(\tau.a, a)$. The process $\tau.a$ has the two weak transitions $\tau.a \overset{\tau}{\Rightarrow} a$ and $\tau.a \overset{a}{\Rightarrow} \mathbf{0}$. The former is matched by $a \Longrightarrow a$, as $a \mathcal{R} a$, and the latter by $a \overset{a}{\Rightarrow} \mathbf{0}$, as $\mathbf{0} \mathcal{R} \mathbf{0}$. Conversely, there is only one possible move for a, namely $a \overset{a}{\Rightarrow} \mathbf{0}$, and $\tau.a$ can answer thus: $\tau.a \overset{a}{\Rightarrow} \mathbf{0}$. The bisimulation game for the other pairs in $\mathcal{R}$ is easy, as they are identity pairs.
For (2), we can show that the relation

$$\mathcal{R} \overset{\text{def}}{=} \{(va\,(b.\bar{a} \,|\, a.c), b.c), (va\,(\bar{a} \,|\, a.c), c), (va\,(\mathbf{0} \,|\, c), c), (va\,(\mathbf{0} \,|\, \mathbf{0}), \mathbf{0})\}$$

is a weak bisimulation. We only show the details for the first pair, calling $P \overset{\text{def}}{=} va\,(b.\bar{a} \,|\, a.c)$ and $Q \overset{\text{def}}{=} b.c$. There are two weak transitions emanating from P, namely $P \overset{b}{\Rightarrow} va\,(\bar{a} \,|\, a.c)$ and $P \overset{b}{\Rightarrow} va\,(\mathbf{0} \,|\, c)$. The process Q can answer both of them with $Q \overset{b}{\Rightarrow} c$, as $va\,(\bar{a} \,|\, a.c) \mathcal{R} c$ and $va\,(\mathbf{0} \,|\, c) \mathcal{R} c$. Conversely, $Q \overset{b}{\Rightarrow} c$ is the only weak labelled transition from Q, and P can answer in two ways as above. □

Exercise 4.2.4 (Recommended, ↪) Suppose that $P \Longrightarrow\approx Q$ and $Q \Longrightarrow\approx P$. Conclude that $P \approx Q$. □

Exercise 4.2.5 ($\hookrightarrow$) Suppose that $P \Longrightarrow R$ and $R \Longrightarrow Q$ with $P \approx Q$. Conclude that $P \approx R \approx Q$. $\qquad\square$

Having introduced weak bisimilarity with the declared purpose of 'ignoring' τ-transitions, it may be surprising to find clause (2) in Definition 4.2.1, as this expresses a demand that only involves τ transitions. Indeed, τ moves cannot be completely disregarded in defining a weak equivalence because they can pre-empt other actions. To see this, consider the processes $P \stackrel{\text{def}}{=} \tau.a.0 + \tau.b.0$ and $Q \stackrel{\text{def}}{=} a.0 + b.0$. They would become bisimilar without clause (2). This is disturbing. Think of the processes as machines, in which a and b are buttons that customers of the machines can press. The machine P has a form of internal non-determinism: it can freely evolve into $a.0$ or $b.0$. In either case, only one of the two buttons is available. In contrast, both buttons remain available in the second machine, and the customer can indeed choose the button to press. We thus reject the equality between the two machines, for the same reason that we did so with the two vending machines of Figure 1.5. A more technical reason for requiring clause (2) is that bisimilarity would not otherwise be preserved by fundamental process operators such as parallel composition: see the discussion in Section 4.6 and Exercise 4.6.2(3).

Exercise 4.2.6 (Recommended, $\hookrightarrow$) Are the processes $\tau.0 + \tau.\bar{a}.0$ and $\bar{a}.0$ weakly bisimilar? $\qquad\square$

Exercise 4.2.7 ($\hookrightarrow$) Can clause (2) be removed in the case of deterministic processes? $\quad\square$

Remark 4.2.8 In presence of internal transitions, we prefer weak bisimilarity to strong bisimilarity as a behavioural equality. However, even when the goal is weak bisimilarity, examining strong bisimilarity first has benefits. Strong bisimilarity is mathematically simpler, and can thus represent a useful stepping-stone on the route to the weak equivalence. Also, strong bisimulation can be helpful when working with weak bisimilarity, because strong bisimilarity implies weak bisimilarity and many useful equalities can be established using strong bisimilarity, and because the strong equivalence is often useful as auxiliary relation in proof techniques (see [PS12], or just Exercise 4.2.15). Finally, the differences between the strong and weak equivalences correspond to subtle points in the theory of the weak equivalence. $\qquad\square$

In contrast with strong bisimulation, the definition of weak bisimulation uses two different clauses (plus their converse) and transition relations of two different shapes. We can, however, compact the definition by introducing a variant of the weak transitions. We set:

$$\stackrel{\hat{\mu}}{\Longrightarrow} \stackrel{\text{def}}{=} \begin{cases} \stackrel{\mu}{\Longrightarrow} & \text{if } \mu \neq \tau \\ \Longrightarrow & \text{otherwise.} \end{cases}$$

Lemma 4.2.9 *A process relation $\mathcal{R}$ is a weak bisimulation if and only if $P \mathcal{R} Q$ implies:*

(1) *whenever $P \stackrel{\hat{\mu}}{\Longrightarrow} P'$, there is Q' such that $Q \stackrel{\hat{\mu}}{\Longrightarrow} Q'$ and $P' \mathcal{R} Q'$;*
(2) *the converse, on the actions from Q.* $\qquad\square$

Using the clause of the lemma above, weak bisimulation becomes a strong bisimulation played on different transition relations. Thus, we inherit the properties of strong bisimilarity on LTSs; for instance the equivalence property, the fixed-point characterisation and the game characterisation.

We cannot, however, completely blur the distinction between strong and weak bisimilarity, and strong and weak transitions. First, we usually need strong transitions to express the behaviour of process operators in the SOS style. Second, when establishing weak bisimilarities between concrete processes, one prefers another characterisation of weak bisimulation, where both strong and weak transitions appear. The problem with the clauses of Definition 4.2.1 (and similarly for Lemma 4.2.9) is the appearance of the weak transitions $\stackrel{\mu}{\Longrightarrow}$ and $\Longrightarrow$ on the challenger side, which may engender a lot of work in proofs because there are more $\Longrightarrow$ and $\stackrel{\mu}{\Longrightarrow}$ transitions than $\stackrel{\mu}{\rightarrow}$ transitions. For instance, take the process K with a transition $K \stackrel{\tau}{\rightarrow} a \mid K$. For all n, we have

$$K \Longrightarrow \underbrace{(a \mid \ldots \mid a)}_{n} \mid K$$

and all these transitions have to be taken into account in the bisimulation game, when we consider clause (2) of Definition 4.2.1 and K is the challenger process. Even more significantly, the appearance of weak transitions on the challenger's side can make a proof of weak bisimulation rather awkward, as it might need an induction argument on the minimum weight of a weak transition of the challenger. To see an example, the reader may try the proof that weak bisimilarity is preserved by CCS parallel composition. All is not lost, however, for by virtue of the recursive nature of bisimulation, the same relation is obtained if in the bisimulation game the challenger's moves are restricted to only single transitions:

Lemma 4.2.10 *A process relation $\mathcal{R}$ is a weak bisimulation if and only if $P \mathcal{R} Q$ implies:*

(1) *whenever $P \stackrel{\mu}{\rightarrow} P'$, there is Q' such that $Q \stackrel{\widehat{\mu}}{\Longrightarrow} Q'$ and $P' \mathcal{R} Q'$;*
(2) *the converse of (1) on the transitions from Q.*

Proof We sketch the proof. Let us call a relation that satisfies the clauses of the lemma sw-bisimulation. Since $\stackrel{\mu}{\rightarrow} \subseteq \stackrel{\mu}{\Longrightarrow}$, every weak bisimulation is also an sw-bisimulation. For the converse, first one shows that if $\mathcal{R}$ is an sw-bisimulation and $P \mathcal{R} Q$, then whenever $P \Longrightarrow P'$ there is Q' such that $Q \Longrightarrow Q'$ and $P' \mathcal{R} Q'$. For this, one proceeds by induction on the minimum weight of the transition $P \Longrightarrow P'$. If the weight is 0 there is nothing to prove; in the inductive case, one uses the definition of sw-bisimulation.

Then the previous result is generalised to the case of transitions $P \stackrel{\mu}{\Longrightarrow} P'$, using the definition $\stackrel{\mu}{\Longrightarrow}$ as the relation composition $\Longrightarrow \stackrel{\mu}{\rightarrow} \Longrightarrow$. □

A more profound difference between strong and weak bisimilarity in process languages is that whereas the $\stackrel{\mu}{\rightarrow}$ relations are usually image-finite, this is often not true of $\Longrightarrow$ and hence of the $\stackrel{\mu}{\Longrightarrow}$ relations. For instance, this happens in calculi such as CCS (unless they contain some infinitary operators like infinite choice or unguarded recursive definitions, in which case even the $\xrightarrow{\mu}$ relations are not image-finite), see Exercise 4.1.4. This fact has important consequences: most notably we lose the cocontinuity of the functional of bisimilarity, and therefore we lose the possibility of characterising bisimilarity via the approximants on the natural numbers.

Exercise 4.2.11 ($\hookrightarrow$) Transport weak bisimilarity into the schema of coinduction discussed in Chapter 2. Thus, give characterisations of weak bisimilarity in terms of fixed points over complete lattices, akin to Theorem 2.10.3 for strong bisimilarity. What is the functional for weak bisimilarity? Similarly, derive the two game interpretations for weak bisimilarity (akin to the two interpretations for strong bisimilarity, in Sections 2.13 and 2.14). $\square$

Exercise 4.2.12 ($\hookrightarrow$) Here is another characterisation of weak bisimulation, where we play with sequences of actions as we did for strong bisimulation in Exercise 1.4.16. The result is thus theoretical more than practical, as the bisimulation checks required become rather heavy. We write $\widehat{s}$ for the sequence obtained from s by deleting every τ (for instance, $\widehat{\tau a \tau} = a$). Show that $\mathcal{R}$ is a weak bisimulation if and only if whenever $P \; \mathcal{R} \; Q$:

(1) for all P' and sequences s with $P \xRightarrow{s} P'$, there is Q' such that $Q \xRightarrow{\widehat{s}} Q'$ and $P' \; \mathcal{R} \; Q'$;
(2) the converse, on the actions from Q.

$\square$

Exercise 4.2.13 ($\hookrightarrow$) Let $\mathcal{L}$ be an LTS. Consider the LTS $\mathcal{L}'$ that has the same set of states as $\mathcal{L}$, and all transitions of $\mathcal{L}$ plus those defined by the following rules:

$$\frac{}{P \xrightarrow{\tau} P} \qquad\qquad \frac{P \xrightarrow{\tau} P' \qquad P' \xrightarrow{\mu} P'' \qquad P'' \xrightarrow{\tau} P'''}{P \xrightarrow{\mu} P'''}$$

Show that two processes P and Q are weakly bisimilar in $\mathcal{L}$ if and only if they are strongly bisimilar in $\mathcal{L}'$. $\square$

The 'bisimulation up-to' technique for strong bisimilarity examined in Exercise 1.4.18 cannot be directly generalised to the weak case. The experience from the strong case would suggest the following definition.

Definition 4.2.14 A process relation $\mathcal{R}$ is a *candidate weak bisimulation up-to* $\approx$ if, whenever $P \; \mathcal{R} \; Q$, for all μ we have:

(1) for all P' with $P \xrightarrow{\mu} P'$, there is Q' such that $Q \xRightarrow{\widehat{\mu}} Q'$ and $P' \approx \mathcal{R} \approx Q'$;
(2) the converse, on the transitions emanating from Q. $\square$

However, it is not true in general that, if $\mathcal{R}$ is a candidate weak bisimulation up-to $\approx$, then $\mathcal{R} \subseteq \approx$. A counterexample is given by $\mathcal{R} \overset{\text{def}}{=} \{(\tau.a.\mathbf{0}, \mathbf{0})\}$. It satisfies the clauses of

Definition 4.2.14, as shown by the following diagram chasing:

$$
\begin{array}{ccc}
\tau.a.0 & \mathcal{R} & 0 \\
\downarrow & & \Downarrow \\
a.0 \approx \tau.a.0 & \mathcal{R} & 0 \approx 0
\end{array}
$$

A solution is to replace the first occurrence of weak bisimilarity in the definition with strong bisimilarity.

Exercise 4.2.15 ($*$, $\hookrightarrow$) A process relation $\mathcal{R}$ is a *weak bisimulation up-to* $\approx$ if, whenever $P \mathcal{R} Q$, for all μ we have:

(1) for all P' with $P \xrightarrow{\mu} P'$, there is Q' such that $Q \xRightarrow{\widehat{\mu}} Q'$ and $P' \sim\mathcal{R}\approx Q'$;
(2) the converse, on the transitions emanating from Q.

Show that if $\mathcal{R}$ is a bisimulation up-to $\approx$, then $\mathcal{R} \subseteq \approx$. (Hint: prove that $\approx \mathcal{R} \approx$ is a weak bisimulation.) $\qquad\square$

Other solutions, and other enhancements of the proof method for weak bisimilarity, are deferred to [PS12].

4.3 Divergence

Definition 4.3.1 (Divergence)

- A process P *diverges* (or is *divergent*), written $P \Uparrow$, if – using the terminology in Section 2.1.1 – it has an ω-trace under τ. That is, divergence is the largest predicate $\Uparrow$ on processes such that $P \in \Uparrow$ implies $P \xrightarrow{\tau} P'$ for some $P' \in \Uparrow$.
- An LTS is *divergence-free* if no processes of the LTS diverge. $\qquad\square$

For the above coinductive definition, we have assumed that the reader has acquired sufficient familiarity with coinductive definitions to accept a definition directly in terms of 'the largest predicate (or relation) such that ...'. As pointed out in Section 2.1.2, this requires that such a largest relation exists. One might prefer a more plain definition, first introducing a notion of divergent set, as a set S of processes such that $P \in S$ implies $P \xrightarrow{\tau} P'$ for some $P' \in S$. Then $\Uparrow$ is the union of all divergent sets, and one can prove that $\Uparrow$ is indeed the largest divergent set.

Exercise 4.3.2 (Recommended, $\hookrightarrow$) Let Ω_τ be the 'purely divergent' process whose only transition is

$$
\Omega_\tau \xrightarrow{\tau} \Omega_\tau.
$$

- Show that $a \mid \Omega_\tau \approx a.0$ (the LTSs of these processes are shown in Figure 4.1).
- Generalise the previous result by showing that $P \mid \Omega_\tau \approx P$, for all P. $\qquad\square$

$$\Omega_\tau^a \stackrel{\text{def}}{=} a \mid \Omega_\tau \qquad\qquad P_a \stackrel{\text{def}}{=} a.\mathbf{0}$$

Fig. 4.1 Example of weak bisimilarity with divergence.

Fig. 4.2 Another example of weak bisimilarity with divergence.

The equalities in Exercise 4.3.2 may look surprising at first sight. In the first equality, for instance, the process $a \mid \Omega_\tau$ can diverge – it has a complete run that is only made of internal work. Furthermore, the divergence is persistent, that is, it remains even after the action a has been consumed. In contrast, the other process, $a.\mathbf{0}$, can never diverge. Here is another example of a similar situation.

Exercise 4.3.3 Show that the three states marked $\star$ in Figure 4.2 are all weakly bisimilar.

$\square$

Weak bisimilarity is indeed insensitive to τ-cycles (loops consisting only of τ-transitions). This aspect of weak bisimilarity can be justified. First, referring again to Exercise 4.3.2, the two components of the parallel composition $a \mid \Omega_\tau$ could be running on different machines, therefore the existence of a τ-cycle in a process does not prevent the execution of the other process. Second, even if the two components were running on the same machine, or the same processor, under a *fair* implementation of parallel composition, the right component cannot always prevail. Hence eventually the action a on the left-hand side will be executed (provided that the environment accepts the interaction at a, of course). More generally, if a process has a τ-cycle but with the possibility of escaping the cycle, then weak bisimilarity assumes that indeed the process will eventually escape: it will execute the loop an arbitrary but finite number of times. This property is sometimes called 'fair abstraction from divergence' (it is often mentioned in the literature in connection to the validity of Koomen's fair abstraction rule, see the discussion by Baeten, Bergstra and Klop [BBK87a]). The property is clearly expressed also by the equality in Exercise 4.3.5. Third, we introduced weak bisimilarity to abstract from internal work. The equality indeed abstracts from any finite amounts of internal work; as a consequence of this, however, in some cases, it also abstracts from infinite amounts (i.e., divergences).

Exercise 4.3.4 ($\hookrightarrow$) A τ-cycle cannot always be removed. Show that $a + \Omega_\tau \not\approx a + \mathbf{0}$. How should Ω_τ be replaced so to obtain a *finCCS* process weakly bisimilar with $a + \Omega_\tau$? $\quad\square$

There are variants of weak bisimilarity that treat divergence as a special event and where therefore the equalities of Exercises 4.3.2 and 4.3.3 fail; see Section 4.7. However, the theory becomes somewhat more cumbersome. Other forms of behavioural equality that are not coinductive, such as testing equivalence or failure equivalence, are naturally sensitive to divergence; see Chapter 5.

Exercise 4.3.5 Consider the constant K_P with transitions

$$K_P \xrightarrow{\tau} K_P \text{ and } K_P \xrightarrow{\tau} P.$$

Show that $K_P \approx \tau.P$. $\quad\square$

Exercise 4.3.6 ($\hookrightarrow$) **(Busy-waiting)** This example is about the implementation of choice using busy-waiting. The specification is

$$P \stackrel{\text{def}}{=} \texttt{init}.(b + c),$$

where `init` is some initialisation activity. The busy-waiting implementation is

$$BW \stackrel{\text{def}}{=} \boldsymbol{\nu}\, \texttt{timeout}\, (\Omega_{\texttt{timeout}} \,|\, (\texttt{init}.B + \texttt{init}.C)),$$

where B and C are the constants with the transitions

$$B \xrightarrow{b} \mathbf{0} \qquad B \xrightarrow{\overline{\texttt{timeout}}} C,$$
$$C \xrightarrow{c} \mathbf{0} \qquad C \xrightarrow{\overline{\texttt{timeout}}} B$$

and `timeout` indicates the occurrence of a timeout. The constant $\Omega_{\texttt{timeout}}$ (defined as in Example 3.3.1) and the restriction on `timeout` hide the timeout action from the outside.
Prove that $P \approx BW$. $\quad\square$

Exercise 4.3.6 intends suggesting that 'forgetting' divergences can be useful in practice. For instance, consider a protocol designed to operate on a lossy communication medium so to tolerate message losses. The system composed by the protocol and the medium would probably exhibit an infinite internal computation in which every message sent is lost by the medium and then retransmitted. In practice, however, such a behaviour is unlikely to occur. If the lossy medium is indeed capable of delivering some messages, then it will certainly deliver some of the messages that it is supposed to carry, so that the divergence never actually occurs. Proofs of protocol correctness that exploit these aspects may be found in [BK86, Bri99, LM92].

4.4 Rooted weak bisimilarity

In this and in the next section we discuss the basic algebraic properties of weak bisimilarity, over CCS. The properties are similar to those of the strong equivalence. However, a striking difference is that weak bisimilarity is not preserved by the choice operator. As a remedy to this, we first introduce a simple refinement of the bisimilarity, called *rooted weak bisimilarity*. (In some papers and textbooks, weak bisimilarity and rooted weak bisimilarity are respectively called *observational equivalence* and *observational congruence*, or else *observation equivalence* and *observation congruence*.)

Lemma 4.4.1 $\approx$ *is preserved by the operators of parallel composition, restriction and prefixing.*

Proof We only treat parallel composition, the other operators are simple and the proof is similar to the corresponding one for strong bisimilarity. We take

$$\mathcal{R} \stackrel{\text{def}}{=} \{(P_1 \mid Q, P_2 \mid Q) \mid P_1 \approx P_2\}$$

and show that $\mathcal{R}$ is a weak bisimulation exploiting the characterisation in Lemma 4.2.10. Suppose $P_1 \mid Q \stackrel{\mu}{\rightarrow} R_1$ (the case of action from $P_2 \mid Q$ is similar). There are three cases to consider, depending on the last rule used to infer the transition.

PARL Then $R_1 = P_1' \mid Q$, for some P_1' with $P_1 \stackrel{\mu}{\rightarrow} P_1'$. As $P_1 \approx P_2$, there is P_2' such that $P_2 \stackrel{\widehat{\mu}}{\Rightarrow} P_2'$ and $P_1' \approx P_2'$. Hence also $P_2 \mid Q \stackrel{\widehat{\mu}}{\Rightarrow} P_2' \mid Q$ and $P_1' \mid Q \mathcal{R} P_2' \mid Q$.

PARR Then $R_1 = P_1 \mid Q'$, for some Q' with $Q \stackrel{\mu}{\rightarrow} Q'$. We also have $P_2 \mid Q \stackrel{\mu}{\rightarrow} P_2 \mid Q'$, hence $P_2 \mid Q \stackrel{\widehat{\mu}}{\Rightarrow} P_2 \mid Q'$, and $P_1 \mid Q' \mathcal{R} P_2 \mid Q'$.

COM Then $\mu = \tau$, $P_1 \stackrel{\ell}{\rightarrow} P_1'$, $Q \stackrel{\overline{\ell}}{\rightarrow} Q'$, for some ℓ, and $R_1 = P_1' \mid Q'$. There is P_2' such that $P_2 \stackrel{\ell}{\Rightarrow} P_2'$ and $P_1' \approx P_2'$. Hence also $P_2 \mid Q \stackrel{\tau}{\Rightarrow} P_2' \mid Q'$, and $P_1' \mid Q' \mathcal{R} P_2' \mid Q'$.

$\square$

Exercise 4.4.2 Show that weak bisimilarity is preserved by the relabeling operator of Remark 3.5.8. $\square$

In contrast, $\approx$ is not preserved by the operator of sum, the reason for this being the pre-emption caused by the τ-actions. For instance, we have $\tau.a \approx a$, but $\tau.a + b \not\approx a + b$.

The problems caused by this negative result are, however, rather limited. First, in practice one normally uses guarded forms of summation, of the kind $\mu_1.P_1 + \cdots + \mu_n.P_n$, and for these sums we have the following preservation result.

Lemma 4.4.3 *If $P \approx Q$ then $\mu.P + R \approx \mu.Q + R$, for all R and μ.* $\square$

Exercise 4.4.4 ($\hookrightarrow$) Consider the *left merge* operator $\parallel$ [BK84], defined in terms of parallel composition with the following SOS rule:

$$\frac{P_1 \xrightarrow{\mu} P_1'}{P_1 \parallel P_2 \xrightarrow{\mu} P_1' \mid P_2}$$

Show that weak bisimilarity is not preserved by this operator. $\square$

Second, even with general summation we can avoid the congruence problem with a simple modification of the bisimulation clause on the first step.

Definition 4.4.5 (Rooted weak bisimilarity) Two processes P and Q are *rooted weakly bisimilar*, written $P \approx^c Q$, if for all μ we have:

(1) for all P' with $P \xrightarrow{\mu} P'$ there is Q' such that $Q \xRightarrow{\mu} Q'$ and $P' \approx Q'$;
(2) the converse, on the actions from Q. $\square$

With $\approx^c$, in the first step, we require a transition $\xrightarrow{\tau}$ to be matched by $\xRightarrow{\tau}$, rather than by $\Longrightarrow$ as for $\approx$. However, after the initial step, the bisimulation game continues as with $\approx$.

Exercise 4.4.6 Show that:

(1) $\tau.a \not\approx^c a$;
(2) $P \mid \tau.Q \approx^c \tau.(P \mid Q)$. $\square$

Lemma 4.4.7 $\sim \,\subseteq\, \approx^c \,\subseteq\, \approx$. $\square$

Exercise 4.4.8 Give examples to illustrate that the above inclusions are strict. $\square$

Exercise 4.4.9 (Recommended, $\hookrightarrow$) Show that $\approx^c$ is preserved by the sum operator. Continue by showing that $\approx^c$ is a congruence relation in CCS. Show that $\approx^c$ is also preserved by the left merge operator of Exercise 4.4.4. $\square$

Exercise 4.4.10 $P \approx Q$ iff $\tau.P \approx^c \tau.Q$. $\square$

Exercise 4.4.11 ($*$, Recommended, $\hookrightarrow$) $P \approx Q$ iff ($P \approx^c Q$, or $P \approx^c \tau.Q$, or $\tau.P \approx^c Q$). $\square$

Theorem 4.4.12 $P \approx^c Q$ *if and only if, for all contexts,* $C[P] \approx C[Q]$.

Proof The implication from left to right follows from Exercise 4.4.9 and $\approx^c \,\subseteq\, \approx$.

It is sufficient to prove the opposite implication for contexts of the form $[\cdot] + R$. Thus suppose for all R we have $P + R \approx Q + R$. We wish to derive $P \approx^c Q$. Take $a \notin (\mathrm{sort}(P) \cup \mathrm{sort}(Q))$, and suppose $P \xrightarrow{\mu} P'$. We also have $P + a \xrightarrow{\mu} P'$, and $Q + a$ can match it, as $P + a \approx Q + a$. As $\mu \neq a$, there are two possibilities for such a matching transition:

- $\mu = \tau$ and the transition is $Q + a \Longrightarrow Q + a$;
- the transition originates from Q, that is, there is Q' such that $Q \xRightarrow{\mu} Q'$ and $P' \approx Q'$.

T1 (1st τ-law) $\mu.\tau.P = \mu.P$
T2 (2nd τ-law) $P + \tau.P = \tau.P$
T3 (3rd ι-law) $\mu.(\Gamma + \iota.Q) = \mu.(P + \iota.Q) + \mu.Q$

Fig. 4.3 The τ-laws.

The first case is not possible, because $Q + a$ has an a-transition that P' does not have. We conclude that the second case must be true. We have thus obtained clause (1) of the definition of $\approx^c$; clause (2) is similar.   □

In the proof of the above theorem we make use of Assumption 3.2.2 that the set of actions is large enough (as we need $\text{sort}(P) \cup \text{sort}(Q) \neq Act$). The assumption can actually be removed [Gla05], but it allows us a (much) simpler proof.

We call a process P *stable* if P cannot perform a τ-transition.

Exercise 4.4.13 ($\hookrightarrow$) Show that on the set of processes that are not stable weak bisimilarity does not imply rooted weak bisimilarity.   □

4.5 Axiomatisation

We present an algebraic characterisation of $\approx^c$ over *finCCS*. (We are forced to consider $\approx^c$ rather than $\approx$, because the rules for equational reasoning require the relation to be a congruence.) The difference between the strong and weak congruences is captured by three simple axioms, the τ-*laws*, shown in Figure 4.3. The first and second law express absorption properties of τ-prefixes and processes. It is tempting to replace them with the simpler law $\tau.P = P$ but, as already noted (e.g., in Exercise 4.4.6(1)), this law is not valid for $\approx^c$. The third law shows that, under a prefix, a process reachable via τs can be brought up at the outermost level so to make explicit that possibility of evolution via a weak transition. We call the system obtained by adding the τ-laws to the system $\mathcal{SB}$ for strong bisimilarity in Figure 3.2 $\mathcal{WB}$.

Lemma 4.5.1 (τ laws) *The τ laws in Figure 4.3 are valid when $=$ is interpreted to be $\approx^c$ (and hence also for $\approx$).*

Proof The laws are proved following the definition of $\approx^c$, and using the facts that $\approx$ is reflexive and $\tau.P \approx P$.   □

Exercise 4.5.2 Show that $\mathcal{WB} \vdash P + \tau.(P + Q) = \tau.(P + Q)$.   □

Theorem 4.5.3 *For $P, Q \in finCCS$, we have $P \approx^c Q$ iff $\mathcal{WB} \vdash P = Q$.*

Proof As usual, soundness of system $\mathcal{WB}$ is established by showing that the axioms in $\mathcal{WB}$ and the laws for equational reasoning are valid for $\approx^c$. For the axioms of $\mathcal{WB}$ that come from the system $\mathcal{SB}$, this follows from the soundness of $\mathcal{SB}$ for $\sim$ and the inclusion

$\sim \, \subseteq \, \approx^c$. The remaining τ-laws are proved valid in Lemma 4.5.1, and equational reasoning in Exercise 4.4.9.

The difficult part is the completeness of $\mathcal{WB}$. We sketch the proof. Thus suppose $P \approx^c Q$; we wish to conclude that also $\mathcal{WB} \vdash P = Q$ holds. First, since the axioms in $\mathcal{WB}$ include those in $\mathcal{SB}$, proceeding as in the proof of Theorem 3.6.1 we can rewrite P and Q into full standard forms (where only the operators nil, choice and prefixing may appear). So there are full standard forms P' and Q' such that $\mathcal{WB} \vdash P = P'$ and $\mathcal{WB} \vdash Q = Q'$.

The second step consists of saturating the full standard forms so obtained; that is, we add summands that represent all weak transitions the processes can perform. Precisely, say that a process R is *saturated* if

$$R = \sum_{0 \leq i \leq m} \mu_i . R_i, \qquad \text{where:}$$

- each R_i is saturated;
- whenever $R \overset{\mu}{\Longrightarrow} R'$ there is i such that $\mu_i = \mu$ and $R_i = R'$.

We transform a process S in full standard form into a saturated process, proceeding by induction on the structure of S. Here the crucial axioms are the second and third τ-laws. We only report two examples, which should be enlightening enough, leaving the details of the transformation to the reader. If the process is $S = a.(b.\mathbf{0} + \tau.\mathbf{0})$, which is not saturated because the transition $S \overset{a}{\Longrightarrow} \mathbf{0}$ has not a corresponding summand, then using the third τ-law we have

$$\mathcal{WB} \vdash S = S + a.\mathbf{0},$$

resulting in a saturated process. And if $S = \tau.a.\mathbf{0}$, which is not saturated because of the transition $S \overset{a}{\Longrightarrow} \mathbf{0}$, then using the second τ-law we have

$$\mathcal{WB} \vdash S = S + a.\mathbf{0}.$$

In general, the saturated form so obtained can be rather long, because of the 'copying' axioms (second and third τ-laws, and **S4**), which may be applied several times, in the expanding direction.

So far we have obtained saturated forms P'' and Q'' such that $\mathcal{WB} \vdash P = P''$ and $\mathcal{WB} \vdash Q = Q''$. The final step consists of deriving $\mathcal{WB} \vdash P'' = Q''$. This is done proceeding on the sum of the depths of P'' and Q'' (we recall that the depth of a process is the maximal number of nested prefixes in its syntax). In the base case the sum is 0, and we have $P'' = Q'' = \mathbf{0}$; the result is then immediate. In the inductive case, one shows that for each summand $\mu.P'''$ of P'' there is a summand of Q'' that is provably equal to $\mu.P'''$, using the property that P'' and Q'' are saturated. A little care is needed in applying the induction hypothesis because $\approx^c$ is defined in terms of $\approx$: after the first transitions the derivative processes are related by $\approx$, and not necessarily $\approx^c$. This problem is overcome by applying the result of Exercise 4.4.11 and the first τ-law.

One then proves the converse, on the summands of Q'', and concludes $\mathcal{WB} \vdash P'' = Q''$ using the axioms for sum to handle duplicates.   □

Exercise 4.5.4 Complete the details of the proof above.   □

Remark 4.5.5 In the proof of Theorem 4.5.3 we can apply Exercise 4.4.11 because, following the result in the direction from left to right, the sum of the depths of the two processes increases at most by one and this is sufficient to make use of the inductive assumption. In contrast, we cannot appeal to Exercise 4.4.10 as this would increase the sum of the depths by two. Deng [Den07] shows how to modify the proof schema so as to use (a 'syntactic version' of) Exercise 4.4.10. This makes the proof a bit more involved but gives us a strategy that can be useful with behavioural equivalences in which Exercise 4.4.11 fails; see Remark 4.9.12.   □

Exercise 4.5.6 ($*, \hookrightarrow$) **(Process sequentialisation)**

(1) Let $P \stackrel{\text{def}}{=} a.b \mid \overline{c}$, and Q be any process. Suppose we want to start Q only when P is terminated (i.e., all its prefixes have been consumed). We can achieve this by using some fresh name d as a trigger for Q, activated by the components of P. Thus P becomes $P' \stackrel{\text{def}}{=} a.b.\overline{d} \mid \overline{c}.\overline{d}$. Show that

$$vd\,(P' \mid d.d.Q) \approx^c a.(b.\overline{c}.Q + \overline{c}.b.Q) + \overline{c}.a.b.Q.$$

(2) Guided by the above example, write down an encoding that transforms any *finCCS* process P (for simplicity, assume also that P does not use the choice operator) into a process $[\![P]\!]_d$, where d is a name fresh for P, such that $[\![P]\!]_d$ behaves exactly as P but emits an output at d when P is terminated. Using this encoding, the sequential composition between two processes P and Q can be written as follows:

$$P; Q \stackrel{\text{def}}{=} vd\,([\![P]\!]_d \mid d.Q), \qquad \text{where } d \notin \text{fn}(P, Q).$$

It can now be amusing to verify some properties of sequential composition. For instance, prove, algebraically:

$$a.0; P \approx^c a.P,$$
$$0; P \approx^c \tau.P.$$

More interesting properties of sequential composition are the following ones:

$$(P; Q); R \approx^c P; (Q; R),$$
$$P; 0 \approx^c P.$$

Their proof is, however, rather complex; a sketch may be found in Appendix A.   □

The reader who, at this stage, does not yet feel comfortable with weak bisimilarity may want to try other (and larger) examples. For instance, the examples in [AILS07, Section 3.4], and the Scheduler and Alternating Bit Protocol examples in [Mil89, Sections 5.4–5.5

and 6.3–6.4]. To understand them, the reader should just bear in mind the different notation for restriction (there written $P \backslash L$, where L is the set of restricted names), the use of recursive constant equations instead of constants with predefined transitions (as by Remark 3.2.3; there are also parametrised recursive equations, with the expected meaning for the parameters), and the use of the relabelling operator (Remark 3.5.8). Further, the two examples in [Mil89] make use of the restricted parallel composition operator ‖ of Exercise 3.5.12, of the weak bisimulation up-to $\approx$ technique of Exercise 4.2.15, and use the symbol $=$ in place of $\approx^c$.

4.6 On the bisimulation game for internal moves

We have seen a number of characterisations of $\approx$, where we played with the way strong transitions are combined into weak transitions. In this and the following sections of the chapter we present a few more variations. The resulting relations are, however, all different from each other and from $\approx$ (and from its congruence $\approx^c$). Whenever possible, the definitions will follow the style of Lemma 4.2.10, mixing strong and weak transitions, for reasons of efficiency.

First, we consider a form of bisimulation that completely ignores τ-actions: there is no bisimulation game on τ-actions (clause (2) of Definition 4.2.1 and its converse; we cannot follow Lemma 4.2.10 here).

Definition 4.6.1 A process relation $\mathcal{R}$ is a $\approx_\tau$-*bisimulation* if whenever $P \, \mathcal{R} \, Q$:

(1) for all P' and ℓ with $P \stackrel{\ell}{\Rightarrow} P'$ there is Q' such that $Q \stackrel{\ell}{\Rightarrow} Q'$ and $P' \, \mathcal{R} \, Q'$;
(2) the converse of (1) on the actions from Q.

Then $\approx_\tau$-*bisimilarity*, written $\approx_\tau$, is the union of all $\approx_\tau$-bisimulations. □

Such a $\approx_\tau$-bisimilarity is the one proposed for weak LTSs in [HM85], under a different name.

Exercise 4.6.2 ($\hookrightarrow$)

(1) Show that $\approx_\tau$ is preserved by the operators of restriction and sum.
(2) Show that $\tau.a + b \approx_\tau a + b$.
(3) Show that $\approx_\tau$ is not preserved by prefixing and parallel composition. (Hint: you might find the processes at point (2) useful). □

One can argue that $\approx_\tau$ is less natural than $\approx$ because of equalities such as those in Exercises 4.6.2(2) (see also the discussion after Exercise 4.2.5). But the killing argument against $\approx_\tau$ is the problem with parallel composition in Exercise 4.6.2(3). Parallel composition is a fundamental operator, one that imposes a precise structure on a system as a set of components running concurrently – the system could even be distributed and the components running on different machines. A behavioural equivalence that is not preserved by parallel composition is not acceptable, as we lose the possibility of compositional reasoning on such structures.

Exercise 4.6.3 $(*, \hookrightarrow)$ Show that the congruence induced by $\approx_\tau$ on CCS (the largest congruence contained in $\approx_\tau$) is $\approx^c$.   □

Exercise 4.6.4 Write $P \stackrel{\mu}{\Rightarrow}_s P'$ if $P \stackrel{\mu}{\Rightarrow} P'$ and P' is stable. Discuss whether we improve the problems of $\approx_\tau$ if the bisimulation clauses become as follows, at least on LTSs that do not contain divergent states:

- for all P' and ℓ with $P \stackrel{\ell}{\Rightarrow}_s P'$ there is Q' such that $Q \stackrel{\ell}{\Rightarrow}_s Q'$ and $P' \mathcal{R} Q'$,

and the converse, on the actions from Q. (Hint: you may show that the processes $c.(\tau.a + b)$ and $c.a$ become equivalent, and that the bisimilarity is still not preserved by parallel composition.)

                                                                                                        □

4.7 Bisimulation with divergence

We have justified in Section 4.3 the property that weak bisimilarity is insensitive to divergence. It is nevertheless technically possible to take divergence into account. In this section we sketch this solution.

A process that diverges is treated as a process whose behaviour is not fully specified; thus bisimilarity becomes a preorder, rather than an equivalence. Intuitively, P and Q bisimilar now means that they have the same behaviour except that P may diverge where Q accepts an action. The main modification is therefore in clause (3) of Definition 4.2.1 (or clause (2) of Lemma 4.2.10), where the bisimulation game is required only if P is not divergent, in which case, furthermore, Q should not be divergent either.

There are, however, two forms of divergence predicate that one may use. The first is the predicate $\Uparrow$ of Definition 4.3.1. The second is a family of predicates $\Uparrow_\mu$, for $\mu \in Act$, detecting whether a process may diverge before or after the action μ. Formally:

$$P \Uparrow_\mu \stackrel{\text{def}}{=} P \Uparrow \text{ or (there is } P' \text{ with } P \stackrel{\mu}{\Rightarrow} P' \text{ and } P' \Uparrow).$$

Now, within the standard schema of weak bisimilarity, as by Definition 4.2.1 or Lemma 4.2.10, it is recommended that one use the predicates $\Uparrow_\mu$. We defer comments on this to after the definition.

Definition 4.7.1 (Prebisimilarity with divergence) A process relation $\mathcal{R}$ is a *prebisimulation with divergence* if, whenever $P \mathcal{R} Q$, for each μ we have:

(1) for all P' with $P \stackrel{\mu}{\to} P'$ there is Q' such that $Q \stackrel{\widehat{\mu}}{\Rightarrow} Q'$ and $P' \mathcal{R} Q'$;
(2) if not $P \Uparrow_\mu$, then
    (a) also not $Q \Uparrow_\mu$, and
    (b) for all Q' with $Q \stackrel{\mu}{\to} Q'$ there is P' such that $P \stackrel{\widehat{\mu}}{\Rightarrow} P'$ and $P' \mathcal{R} Q'$.

Prebisimilarity with divergence, written $\leq_\Uparrow$, is the union of all prebisimulations with divergence.

Exercise 4.7.2 (∗) Show that $\leq_\Uparrow$:

(1) is a preorder;
(2) is preserved by the operators of prefixing and restriction. The enterprising reader may also try the proof for parallel composition. This, however, requires some work: the difficult part is to show that, when $P \leq_\Uparrow Q$, if not $P \mid R \Uparrow_\mu$ then also not $Q \mid R \Uparrow_\mu$, for any R. Details may be found in [Wal90]. ☐

As usual, $\leq_\Uparrow$ is not preserved by the choice operator. We can re-use counterexamples for $\approx$, as $\approx$ and $\leq_\Uparrow$ coincide on non-divergent processes. For instance, $\tau.\mathbf{0} \leq_\Uparrow \mathbf{0}$ but not $\tau.\mathbf{0} + a.\mathbf{0} \leq_\Uparrow \mathbf{0} + a.\mathbf{0}$. We refer to [Wal90] for the rooted version of $\leq_\Uparrow$, whose definition is not entirely standard.

Exercise 4.7.3 ($\hookrightarrow$) Show that

(1) if $P \Uparrow$ then for all Q we have $P \leq_\Uparrow P + Q$;
(2) $\Omega_\tau \leq_\Uparrow P$, for all P; is the same true for $\mathbf{0}$ in place of Ω_τ?
(3) $a.(b + \Omega_\tau) \leq_\Uparrow a.(b + \Omega_\tau) + a.\Omega_\tau$;
(4) if $P \Uparrow$, and $P \leq_\Uparrow Q$, and there is no P' such that ($P \overset{\tau}{\Rightarrow} P'$ and not $P' \Uparrow$), then for all R, we have $P \leq_\Uparrow Q + R$. Show also that the last condition, on the derivatives P', is necessary. ☐

The reason for using the predicates $\Uparrow_\mu$ instead of $\Uparrow$ in Definition 4.7.1 has to do with the appearance of weak transitions $\overset{\widehat{\mu}}{\Rightarrow}$ in the bisimulation game. Recall that $\overset{\mu}{\Rightarrow}$ stands for $\Longrightarrow \overset{\mu}{\rightarrow} \Longrightarrow$; the second $\Longrightarrow$ means that we can explore the behaviour of the process after the action μ arbitrarily down along internal moves. If divergence matters, it is then reasonable and natural to be able to detect also the existence of infinite paths of internal moves after the μ action. Indeed, if in Definition 4.7.1 we replaced the predicates $\Uparrow_\mu$ with the single predicate $\Uparrow$, the resulting preorder, say $\leq_\Uparrow'$, would have a rather complex algebraic theory; it would also be a mathematically deficient preorder, lacking properties such as continuity [Wal90, Abr87] (see also [AH92]). It is easy to see that $\leq_\Uparrow' \subseteq \leq_\Uparrow$. To see that the containment is strict, consider the terms $P \overset{\text{def}}{=} a.\Omega_\tau^b$ (for Ω_τ^b as in Figure 4.1) and $Q \overset{\text{def}}{=} P + a.\Omega_\tau$. We have $P \leq_\Uparrow Q$ but not $P \leq_\Uparrow' Q$. See [Wal90] for more details on $\leq_\Uparrow$. The preorder also appears in [HP80, Sti87].

If we wish to use the single divergence predicate $\Uparrow$, then in the bisimulation game we should only use weak transitions of the form $\Longrightarrow \overset{\mu}{\rightarrow}$ or $\Longrightarrow$ (that is, the process immediately stops after a visible action). This means adopting the 'delay' style of bisimulation, as by Lemma 4.9.6; see Exercise 4.9.14. This preorder appears in [Mil81, Abr87, Wal90].

4.8 Dynamic bisimulation

We have seen that $\approx$ is a bisimulation but not a full congruence in CCS (due to the presence of the sum operator), whereas $\approx^c$ has the desired congruence properties but is not a bisimulation (as it is defined in terms of another relation, $\approx$). The variation of weak bisimulation in this section combines the ideas in the definitions of $\approx$ and $\approx^c$ to obtain a relation that is at the same time a bisimulation and a congruence.

Definition 4.8.1 (Dynamic bisimilarity) A process relation $\mathcal{R}$ is a *dynamic bisimulation* if, whenever $P \mathcal{R} Q$, for all μ we have:

(1) for all P' with $P \xrightarrow{\mu} P'$, there is Q' such that $Q \xRightarrow{\mu} Q'$ and $P' \mathcal{R} Q'$;
(2) the converse of (1) on the actions from Q.

Dynamic bisimilarity, written $\approx_{\mathrm{dyn}}$, is the union of all dynamic bisimulations. ☐

The above form of bisimulation first appears in [HM85, Appendix C1]. It has been studied, and named dynamic bisimilarity, by Montanari and Sassone [MS92].

Exercise 4.8.2 Show that dynamic bisimilarity is a congruence in CCS. ☐

In dynamic bisimilarity we lose, however, some desirable equalities, such as $\mu.\tau.P = \mu.P$.

Exercise 4.8.3 Show that the equalities of Example 4.2.3 and the first τ-law (**T1**) fail for dynamic bisimilarity. ☐

Exercise 4.8.4 Show that the second and third τ-laws remain valid for dynamic bisimilarity. ☐

Exercise 4.8.5 ($\hookrightarrow$) Are the following laws valid for dynamic bisimilarity?

(1) $P = \tau.P$;
(2) $\tau.(P \mid Q) = P \mid \tau.Q$. ☐

4.9 Branching bisimulation, η-bisimulation and delay bisimulation

In the weak-bisimulation game, a process Q, in answering a challenge from another process P, may perform an arbitrary number of τ-transitions. Nothing is required of the intermediate states attained along the sequence. Referring to Figure 4.4, the only relations required are (1) and (4), involving the initial states P, Q and final states P' and Q'. It may indeed happen that some of the intermediate states are behaviourally different with respect to the initial or final states. For instance, consider the weakly bisimilar processes in Figure 4.5, and the move $P \xrightarrow{b} \mathbf{0}$. Process Q answers with the transition sequence $Q \xrightarrow{\tau} \xrightarrow{b} \mathbf{0}$; the intermediate state, $b.\mathbf{0}$, is unrelated to both Q and $\mathbf{0}$. In the variations of weak bisimulation

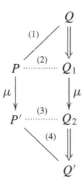

Fig. 4.4 The bisimulation game in $\approx$, $\approx_d$, $\approx_\eta$ and $\approx_{br}$.

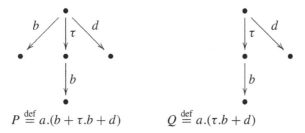

Fig. 4.5 Processes in $\approx$ and $\approx_d$, but not in $\approx_\eta$ or $\approx_{br}$.

in this section all, or parts of, the moves that abstract from τ-actions are not allowed to change the bisimilarity class of a process.

We begin with *branching bisimulation*. It has been proposed by van Glabbeek and Weijland [GW96, Gla01b]. Their motivating argument is that a bisimulation semantics, while remaining coarser than graph isomorphism, should faithfully respect the branching structure in the graph of an LTS, so to precisely take into account *when* a process has a choice point among different possible future behaviours. On the basis of examples such as that of Figure 4.5 discussed above, van Glabbeek and Weijland argue that weak bisimilarity is not fully 'branching time'. (In concurrency, the term 'branching time semantics' is used in opposition to 'linear time' semantics, where the meaning of a process is determined by its possible runs, or partial runs.) Branching bisimulation is then put forward as a remedy for this. Referring to Figure 4.4, branching bisimulation also imposes the relations (2) and (3). This is sufficient to guarantee that also all possible intermediate states between Q and Q_1 are equivalent to each other, and similarly for the states between Q_2 and Q'.

Definition 4.9.1 (Branching bisimilarity) A process relation $\mathcal{R}$ is a *branching bisimulation* if whenever $P \mathcal{R} Q$, for all μ we have:

(1) for all P' with $P \xrightarrow{\mu} P'$, either

    (a) $\mu = \tau$ and $P' \mathcal{R} Q$, or

    (b) there are Q', Q_1, Q_2 such that $Q \Longrightarrow Q_1$, $Q_1 \xrightarrow{\mu} Q_2$, and $Q_2 \Longrightarrow Q'$ with $P \mathcal{R} Q_1$, $P' \mathcal{R} Q_2$, and $P' \mathcal{R} Q'$;

(2) the converse of (1) on the actions from Q.

Branching bisimilarity, written $\approx_{br}$, is the union of all branching bisimulations. $\qquad\square$

The following lemma explains why, in Definition 4.9.1, the states between Q and Q_1, and those between Q_2 and Q', may be ignored: they are all equivalent.

Lemma 4.9.2 (Stuttering Lemma for $\approx_{br}$) *Suppose $P_i \xrightarrow{\tau} P_{i+1}$, for $0 \le i < n$, and $P_0 \approx_{br} P_n$. Then also $P_i \approx_{br} P_j$, for all $0 \le i, j \le n$.*

Proof Suppose $\{P_i\}_i$ as in the assertion, and take

$$\mathcal{R} \stackrel{\text{def}}{=} \{(P_0, P_i) \mid 0 < i \le n\} \cup \approx_{br}.$$

We show that $\mathcal{R}$ is a branching bisimulation. Consider a pair (P_0, P_i). If $P_i \xrightarrow{\mu} P_i'$ then P_0 can answer with the transition $P_0 \Longrightarrow P_i \xrightarrow{\mu} P_i'$, as $\approx_{br}$ is reflexive and therefore we have $P_i \mathcal{R} P_i$ and $P_i' \mathcal{R} P_i'$.

Consider now a move from P_0, $P_0 \xrightarrow{\mu} P_0'$. To find a matching transition from P_i, we first examine the matching transition from P_n, which must exist because $P_0 \approx_{br} P_n$ by hypothesis. There are two cases:

(i) $\mu = \tau$ and $P_0' \approx_{br} P_n$, or

(ii) there are P_n', P_n'', P_n''' with $P_n \Longrightarrow P_n' \xrightarrow{\mu} P_n'' \Longrightarrow P_n'''$ and $P_0 \approx_{br} P_n'$, $P_0' \approx_{br} P_n''$, and $P_0' \approx_{br} P_n'''$.

In case (i), as $i < n$, we can take $P_i \Longrightarrow P_{n-1} \xrightarrow{\tau} P_n$ as the matching transition, for $P_0 \mathcal{R} P_{n-1}$ and $P_0' \mathcal{R} P_n$.

In case (ii), we can conclude that also $P_i \Longrightarrow P_n' \xrightarrow{\mu} P_n'' \Longrightarrow P_n'''$ and we are done. $\quad\square$

Exercise 4.9.3 ($\hookrightarrow$) State and prove the branching bisimilarity version of Exercise 4.2.4. Then show that Lemma 4.9.2 is an immediate consequence of it. $\qquad\square$

Branching bisimilarity has a pleasant axiomatisation [Gla93b, GW96], briefly discussed at the end of this section, and logical characterisation [DV95], and is resistant to certain refinements of actions [DD91, GW96] (while weak bisimilarity is not), and has efficient checking algorithms (see [AIS12]). On the other hand, proofs of properties of branching bisimilarity (as well as η and delay bisimilarities) can sometimes require more work than the corresponding proofs for weak bisimilarity because the definition of the latter is simpler. Examples of this are the transitivity property (see [Bas96]; the composition of two branching bisimulations need not be a branching bisimulation), and the Stuttering Lemma 4.9.2 (its proof for weak bisimilarity, in Exercise 4.2.5, is simpler).

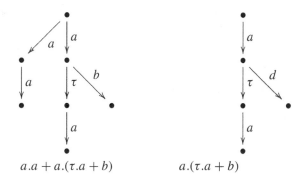

$$a.a + a.(\tau.a + b) \qquad\qquad a.(\tau.a + b)$$

Fig. 4.6 Processes in $\approx$ and $\approx_\eta$, but not in $\approx_d$ or $\approx_{br}$.

Referring again to Figure 4.4, one may also impose, besides (1) and (4), only the relation (2), or only the relation (3). The resulting bisimulations are called *η-bisimulation* and *delay bisimulation*.

Definition 4.9.4 (η-bisimilarity, delay bisimilarity)   *η-bisimulation* and *η-bisimilarity* (written $\approx_\eta$) are defined as branching bisimulation and branching bisimilarity, in Definition 4.9.1, except that the requirement $P'\ \mathcal{R}\ Q_2$ is omitted.

Delay bisimulation and *delay bisimilarity* (written $\approx_d$) are defined as branching bisimulation and branching bisimilarity, in Definition 4.9.1, except that the requirement $P\ \mathcal{R}\ Q_1$ is omitted.   □

The processes in Figure 4.5 are in the relation $\approx_d$, but not in $\approx_\eta$. On the other hand, the processes of Figure 4.6 are in the relation $\approx_\eta$, but not in $\approx_d$. Both pairs of processes in Figure 4.5 and in Figure 4.6 are in $\approx$; none of the pairs is in $\approx_{br}$. The relationship among these four bisimilarities is as follows, an arrow indicating a strict inclusion:

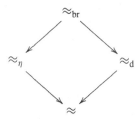

The name η for $\approx_\eta$ was coined in [BvG87], where η is a constant used for abstraction similarly to τ. A form of delay bisimulation, though divergence-sensitive, first appears in [Mil81] (under a different name, observation equivalence, which later, in the CCS community, became the predominant name for weak bisimilarity). The name 'delay' is first used in [Wei89], where delay bisimulation stems from a study of translations of asynchronous into synchronous calculi.

While η-bisimilarity appears to have a limited practical interest, delay bisimilarity may have a definite appeal, particularly on languages with exchange of values. To see why, we first have to make a simplification to its definition. The simplification is possible both for delay and for branching bisimulation, and makes use of the Stuttering Lemma 4.9.2 and its delay-bisimulation variant. In the definition of branching bisimulation, the transition $Q_2 \Longrightarrow Q'$ can be eliminated.

Lemma 4.9.5 $\approx_{\mathrm{br}}$ *is the largest relation $\mathcal{R}$ such that whenever $P \; \mathcal{R} \; Q$, for all μ we have:*

(1) *for all P' with $P \xrightarrow{\mu} P'$, either*

    (a) $\mu = \tau$ *and $P' \; \mathcal{R} \; Q$, or*

    (b) *there are Q', Q_1 such that $Q \Longrightarrow Q_1$ and $Q_1 \xrightarrow{\mu} Q'$ with $P \; \mathcal{R} \; Q_1$ and $P' \; \mathcal{R} \; Q'$;*

(2) *the converse of (1) on the actions from Q.* □

The same can be made for delay bisimulation.

Lemma 4.9.6 $\approx_{\mathrm{d}}$ *is the largest relation $\mathcal{R}$ such that $P \; \mathcal{R} \; Q$ implies:*

(1) *for all P' with $P \xrightarrow{\tau} P'$ there is Q' such that $Q \Longrightarrow Q'$ and $P' \; \mathcal{R} \; Q'$;*

(2) *for all P' and ℓ with $P \xrightarrow{\ell} P'$, there is Q' such that $Q \Longrightarrow \xrightarrow{\ell} Q'$ and $P' \; \mathcal{R} \; Q'$;*

(3) *the converse of (1) and (2), on the actions from Q.* □

In the presentation of delay bisimulation in Lemma 4.9.6, the only difference with weak bisimulation is on visible actions: abstraction from τ-actions is only permitted *before* the visible action. In other words, in delay bisimulation we do not continue the evaluation of a process when an intervention of the outside environment occurs. In higher-order calculi, such as the λ-calculi of [Pit12], bisimulation is often presented in this style (for instance, the applicative bisimulation in [Pit12] is a form of delay bisimulation). One might argue, more generally, that delay bisimulation is reasonable in languages in which interaction involves the exchange of values. If a process is expecting to receive a value in an interaction, then in general we cannot continue with the evaluation of the process until the value is actually received and substitutes the appropriate placeholder in the continuation. Delay bisimulation fits well with a semantics in which the act of 'allowing an interaction' is separated from the act of 'receiving and substituting a value'; the delay style may even be necessary to ensure important properties of the bisimulation such as transitivity, see 'late bisimilarity' in [San96, SW01].

Exercise 4.9.7 Define a fixed-point characterisation of branching bisimilarity, akin to the one in Theorem 2.10.3; prove also the analogue of Lemma 2.10.1. □

Exercise 4.9.8 Show that, in CCS, branching, η and delay bisimilarity have the same congruence properties as weak bisimilarity. □

As usual, to obtain equivalences that are preserved by the choice operator we must add a 'root condition'. Recall that in the case of weak bisimilarity the root condition for a pair (P, Q) means that the first challenge transition, say $P \xrightarrow{\mu} P'$, must be answered by a composite weak transition of the form $Q \Longrightarrow \xrightarrow{\mu} \Longrightarrow Q'$, with derivatives P' and Q' that are weakly bisimilar. The possibility for Q of making τ-transitions both before and after the μ-transition comes from the lack of conditions (2) and (3) in the bisimulation game as depicted in Figure 4.4. One or both possibilities of transitions are lost when (2) or (3) are included. Thus, using $<>$ to range over $\{\approx, \approx_\eta, \approx_d, \approx_{br}\}$, the rooted equivalence is written $<>^c$ and is defined thus:

- $P <>^c Q$ if for all μ and P' with $P \xrightarrow{\mu} P'$ there is Q' such that $(\star <>)$ and $P' <> Q'$
  (plus the converse, on the actions from Q)

where $(\star <>)$ is, depending on how $<>$ is instantiated:

$$
\begin{aligned}
(\star \approx) \quad & Q \Longrightarrow \xrightarrow{\mu} \Longrightarrow Q', \\
(\star \approx_\eta) \quad & Q \xrightarrow{\mu} \Longrightarrow Q', \\
(\star \approx_d) \quad & Q \Longrightarrow \xrightarrow{\mu} Q', \\
(\star \approx_{br}) \quad & Q \xrightarrow{\mu} Q'.
\end{aligned}
$$

In particular, in case of rooted branching bisimilarity, the answer to the first challenge is 'strong'.

Exercise 4.9.9 Show that in each case the rooted equivalence $<>^c$ is indeed the largest CCS congruence included in the equivalence $<>$, assuming, as usual, that fresh names are always available. (For $\approx^c$ and $\approx$ this was already done in Theorem 4.4.12.) □

A uniform approach to defining the 'root condition' in behavioural equivalences is proposed in [GW96], but it best applies to processes whose LTS is acyclic or, at least, LTSs in which the root does not have ingoing transitions.

A major interest of the rooted relations is that, being congruence, they can be axiomatised on *fin*CCS. We have seen the axiomatisation of $\approx$ in Section 4.5. We briefly discuss the others here. As usual, axiomatisations are an enlightening means of understanding the relationships among equivalences, their differences, and the meaning itself of the equivalences.

Exercise 4.9.10 ($\hookrightarrow$) Show that:

(1) the first τ-law, **T1**, remains valid for $\approx^c_{br}$, hence also for $\approx^c_\eta$ and $\approx^c_d$;
(2) the second τ-law, **T2**, is valid for $\approx_{br}$, hence also for $\approx_\eta$, but not for $\approx^c_\eta$, hence also not for $\approx^c_{br}$;
(3) the third τ-law, **T3**, is not valid for $\approx_d$, and hence also not for $\approx_{br}$. □

The following axiom, which first appeared in [BvG87], weakens the τ-law **T2**, and is a key axiom in the axiomatisations of $\approx^c_\eta$ and $\approx^c_{br}$:

$$\mathbf{B} \qquad \mu.(\tau.(P + Q) + P) = \mu.(P + Q).$$

Exercise 4.9.11 ($\hookrightarrow$) Show that, with the help of the axioms for strong bisimilarity, **B** subsumes **T1**, and can be derived from **T1** and **T2**. □

The following table summarises the axioms to be added to those for strong bisimilarity so as to obtain axiomatisations for the four rooted relations in *finCCS*. An entry X means that the axiom is not valid for that equivalence, ok means the axiom is valid, and (ok) means that the axiom is valid but is redundant in the axiom system. In certain languages, in the axiomatisation of rooted branching bisimilarity the axiom **B** can be simplified and replaced by **T1** alone [Gla93b, GW96]. We refer to [GW96, Gla93b, Den07] for proofs and more details.

	T1	**T2**	**T3**	**B**
$\approx^c$	ok	ok	ok	(ok)
$\approx_\eta^c$	(ok)	X	ok	ok
$\approx_d^c$	ok	ok	X	(ok)
$\approx_{br}^c$	(ok)	X	X	ok

Remark 4.9.12 The proofs of the axiomatisations for $\approx_\eta^c$ and $\approx_{br}^c$ are more involved than that for $\approx^c$ discussed in Section 4.5. This is partly due to the extra checks in the definitions of these relations but, more importantly, it is caused by the failure of the analogue of Exercise 4.4.11, which plays a key role in the proof for $\approx^c$. In contrast, the result remains valid for delay bisimilarity and its congruence $\approx_d^c$; indeed the proof of the axiomatisation for $\approx_d^c$ is similar to that for $\approx^c$. See also Exercise 4.9.13 and Remark 4.5.5. In presence of special operators, e.g., forms of iteration, the stronger demands of branching bisimilarity can, however, make algebraic reasoning simpler; see for instance [AvGFI96]. $\square$

Exercise 4.9.13 Show that the result in Exercise 4.4.11 remains valid for delay bisimilarity and its congruence, whereas it fails for branching and η bisimilarities and their congruences. (Hint: consider the processes $a + \tau.(a + b)$ and $a + b$.) $\square$

Exercise 4.9.14 Define a divergence-sensitive version of delay bisimilarity, using the ideas at the end of Section 4.7. Show that it is a preorder. $\square$

5

Other approaches to behavioural equivalences

In the first part of this chapter we present (yet) another characterisation of bisimilarity, namely bisimilarity as a *testing equivalence*. In a testing scenario two processes are *equivalent* if no experiment can distinguish them. An experiment on a process is set up by defining a *test*, that is, intuitively, a pattern of demands on the process (e.g., the ability of performing a certain sequence of actions, or the inability of performing certain actions). Depending on how the process behaves when such a test is conducted, the observer emits a verdict about the success or failure of the experiment. The experiments are means of understanding how the processes react to stimuli from the environment. A testing scenario has two important parameters.

(1) How are observations about the behaviour of a process gathered? In other words, what can the observer conducting the experiment do on a process? For instance, is he/she allowed to observe the inability of a process to perform certain actions? Is he/she allowed to observe whether a process can immediately perform two distinct actions? Is he/she allowed to make a copy of a process? These decisions are embodied in the language for the tests.

(2) How is the success or the failure of an experiment determined?

The choice for these parameters has an impact on the distinctions that can be made on the processes. We will set up a testing scenario whose induced equivalence is precisely bisimilarity. Weakenings of the scenario, where the control of the observer over the processes is reduced, may, however, lead to coarser equivalences. Some of them have arguably a natural justification; examples that we will consider are *may*, *must* and *testing equivalences*. We will also touch on *refusal* and *failure equivalences*. The testing theme thus becomes an excuse for pointing out the existence of several possible notions of behavioural equivalence for processes. Comparing different equivalences within the same framework, in our case the testing framework, is useful for understanding them and their discriminating power.

Another reason for defining a testing scenario for bisimilarity is investigating its constructivity, or effectiveness. Indeed, while it is hard to dispute that bisimilar processes should be considered semantically equal (particularly in the case of strong bisimilarity), one may wonder whether bisimilarity actually makes too many distinctions. A testing characterisation is informative, by revealing the form of tests that are needed to distinguish all and only the non-bisimilar processes.

Failure equivalence, while the same as testing equivalence under certain assumptions, stems from an approach different from that of testing. Roughly, the idea is that two processes should be different only if they can be distinguished by finite linear observations, where deadlock is included among the observables. The observations made on processes consist of a trace and a set of actions that cannot be performed after that trace.[1] Failure equivalence was indeed developed, in the language CSP (Communicating Sequential Processes, [Hoa85]), as a refinement of trace equivalence that respects deadlock. We will also see that, by requiring compositionality of the same property with respect to classes of operators larger than those given by the CCS or CSP operators, we can obtain equivalences finer than the original failure equivalence. And if the class is large enough we end up with bisimilarity. This characterisation of bisimilarity in terms of traces and deadlock is close in spirit, if not in the technicalities, to that in terms of tests. We will briefly discuss also a variant of failure equivalence, *ready equivalence*.

A class of operators can be formalised in terms of constraints on the *format* of the SOS rules that specify the behaviour of the operators. We will see that, no matter how large the class of operators is, bisimilarity cannot be broken: the bisimilarity between two processes is maintained when the processes are placed inside a context built out of the operators allowed. This property, which fails for the other equivalences discussed, confirms to us that bisimilarity is very robust and is the finest extensional equivalence one can impose on processes.

In summary, the main objectives of this chapter are:

- to present the testing framework;
- to show the characterisation of bisimilarity in this framework;
- to introduce a few well-established non-coinductive behavioural equivalences and preorders and to contrast them with the coinductive ones;
- to discuss the consequences on behavioural equivalences of variations of the classes of 'acceptable' process operators when the only observables are traces and deadlock.

In Section 5.1 we set the basis of a testing scenario. In Section 5.2 we specialise the scenario so as to obtain a characterisation of (strong) bisimilarity. In Section 5.3 we consider weak bisimilarity. In Section 5.4 we motivate the move to less powerful test languages, giving rise to the may, must and testing equivalences and preorders. We define them in Section 5.5, illustrate them with examples in Section 5.6, present alternative characterisations, useful for proofs, in Section 5.7, and adapt them to weak LTSs in Section 5.8. In Sections 5.9–5.11 we introduce refusal, failure and ready equivalences. In Section 5.12 we compare the discriminating power produced by classes of operators, following some of the best known formats of SOS rules. All behavioural equivalences in the chapter explain the parallelism between two independent processes as the interleaving of their actions.

---

[1] In retrospective, one may even see the observations made in failure equivalence as special kinds of test. But the motivations for failure equivalence are better understood differently, following the way it was discovered and developed.

In Section 5.13 we briefly comment on non-interleaving equivalences. We conclude the chapter, in Section 5.14, with a discussion on the variety of behavioural equivalences and models that we find in concurrency theory.

Assumption 5.0.1 In this chapter we assume that the LTSs are *image-finite*. □

Assumption 5.0.1 is both to simplify the presentation and to have sharper results. Also, in some cases there are different ways of extending the behavioural equivalences and preorders to infinitely branching processes, to account for, e.g., infinite traces or divergences. Such details would take us beyond the scope of the book. Image-finiteness is actually necessary in the characterisation of bisimilarity via tests in Corollary 5.2.18 or via completed traces in Section 5.12, as the proofs make use of the inductive stratification of bisimilarity (Theorem 2.10.13 and Exercise 2.10.18).

5.1 A testing scenario

An experiment is the application of a test on a process. To define a testing scenario we have to specify what the possible tests are and how the outcomes of the experiments are obtained.

A particular run of a test on a process can lead to success or not. We use $\top$ for success, and $\bot$ for lack of success; $\bot$ may indicate an explicit failure in the test, or may indicate that the run never reached a success. However, because of non-determinism, different runs of the same test on a process may produce different results: the process may react in different ways to interactions proposed by the environment. Therefore the result of all possible runs is a non-empty subset of $\{\top, \bot\}$.

Now, if we write $\mathcal{O}(T, P)$ for the set of all the results of running test T on process P (the *outcomes of the experiment*), then we can deem two processes P and Q *behaviourally equivalent* if

$$\mathcal{O}(T, P) = \mathcal{O}(T, Q), \text{ for all tests } T. \tag{$*$}$$

The function $\mathcal{O}$ may be defined denotationally or operationally. To distinguish them, we will write $\mathcal{O}_{\text{den}}$ for the former, and $\mathcal{O}_{\text{op}}$ for the latter. The denotational definition is typically given by structural induction, following the grammar of the tests.

The operational definition describes the run of a test on a process in a step-by-step fashion. For this, one first gives a grammar that specifies the possible states along the run of a test on a process, and then presents rules of a reduction relation $\longrightarrow$ among these states. We call the states *configurations*.

Definition 5.1.1 A *run of a test T on a process P* is a (possibly infinite) sequence of configurations $E_0, E_1, \ldots$, where E_0 is $\langle T, P \rangle$ (the *initial* configuration), and $E_i \longrightarrow E_{i+1}$ for each $i \geq 0$, meaning that E_i has evolved in one step into E_{i+1}. Further, the sequence is maximal, in the sense that if it is finite then the last element, say E_k, has no further possible reductions. □

The configuration $\langle T, P \rangle$ indicates the application of a test T to a process P; the initial configuration of a run should have such a form. The grammar for configurations is also required to have the symbols $\top$ and $\bot$, whose appearance in a run indicates, respectively, success and explicit failure. Depending on the testing scenario, the grammar of configurations may, however, have other productions. Configurations $\top$ and $\bot$ should be final, i.e., they cannot evolve further.

On configurations, $\Longrightarrow$ is the reflexive and transitive closure of $\longrightarrow$, and $\Uparrow$ the usual divergence predicate (the largest predicate $\Uparrow$ such that $E \Uparrow$ implies there is E' with $E \longrightarrow E'$ and $E'\Uparrow$). The set of the results of runs of an initial configuration $\langle T, P \rangle$ is written $\mathcal{O}_{\mathrm{op}}(\langle T, P \rangle)$. For proofs, it is, however, convenient to define the results of running a generic configuration E:[2]

$$\mathcal{O}_{\mathrm{op}}(E) \overset{\mathrm{def}}{=} \quad \{\top \text{ if } E \Longrightarrow \top\}$$
$$\cup \{\bot \text{ if } E \Longrightarrow \bot\}$$
$$\cup \{\bot \text{ if } E \Uparrow\}.$$

Thus, a run is successful only if it reaches the successful configuration; otherwise (case of a finite run that reaches $\bot$, or of an infinite run) it is considered unsuccessful. Success must arise in a finite amount of time (the run is finite), and by exploring only a finite part of the behaviour of the tested process (i.e., finitely many transitions). This is in accordance with the meaning of computability in the theory of computable functions. It is needed for the effectiveness of the testing scenario – the tests should be computable.

Of course, when both the denotational and the operational definitions of outcomes of an experiment are given, they should coincide, i.e., $\mathcal{O}_{\mathrm{den}}(T, P) = \mathcal{O}_{\mathrm{op}}(\langle T, P \rangle)$. Often, the denotational definition has the benefit of being simpler and more concise. The operational definition, however, may be more useful for understanding how the tests can be implemented.

We shall see that in certain approaches the language for the tests is different with respect to that of processes, whereas in other approaches the tests are a subset of the processes (possibly with the exception of special success signals that may only appear in the tests).

The testing approach to behavioural equivalence was developed by De Nicola and Hennessy [DH84, Hen88]. The characterisation of bisimilarity through tests in the next section is due to Abramsky [Abr87].

5.2 Bisimulation via testing

We define a testing scenario for bisimilarity, following the schema in Section 5.1. The language for the tests is the following:

$$T ::= \mathrm{SUCC} \mid \mathrm{FAIL} \mid \mu \,.\, T \mid \widetilde{\mu} \,.\, T \mid T_1 \wedge T_2 \mid T_1 \vee T_2 \mid \forall T \mid \exists T,$$

---

[2] Thus $\mathcal{O}_{\mathrm{op}}$ is formally a function on a single argument, a configuration, in contrast with $\mathcal{O}_{\mathrm{den}}$ that takes two arguments. The argument of $\mathcal{O}_{\mathrm{op}}$ is a configuration and is often, but not always, a pair (see the grammar for configurations in Definition 5.2.10).

where $\mu \in Act$ (the set of actions of the tested processes). The test constructs can be classified into four groups.

(1) The *trace* constructs comprise the first three productions in the grammar. SUCC and FAIL are the primitive tests; all processes pass SUCC, and fail on FAIL. A process passes the test $\mu . T$ if it can perform the action μ and the derivative then passes the rest of the test T.
(2) The *refusal* construct, $\widetilde{\mu} . T$, is used to check whether a process is unable to perform the action μ. On processes with μ-transitions, test $\widetilde{\mu} . T$ is the same as test $\mu . T$.
(3) The *copying* constructs, $\wedge$ and $\vee$, allow us to make conjunctions and disjunctions of tests. For instance, a process passes $T_1 \wedge T_2$ if it passes both T_1 and T_2. This implies the ability of making two copies of the process, on each of which the subtests T_1 and T_2 are run.
(4) The *global testing* constructs, $\forall$ and $\exists$, allow us to check the results of all possible runs of some subtests. A process passes $\forall T$ if all runs of T on the process are successful. And $\exists T$ is the dual: a process passes it if there is at least one successful run for the subtest T.

As far as the control required on the processes is concerned, the global testing constructs $\forall$ and $\exists$ are the most demanding ones. They amount to being able to make as many copies as needed of the original process and its derivatives, so as to follow all non-deterministic executions of the test. This could be achieved, for instance, if we have complete control over the scheduler in the operating system of the machine that is executing the tests on the processes, and we have enough memory to store all copies and all data structures needed.

Remark 5.2.1 A test like $\mu . \mathrm{SUCC}$ is the requirement, on a process P, that it should perform an action μ. We could thus view $\mu . \mathrm{SUCC}$ as an attempt of interacting with P along μ. Accordingly, if we took the CCS viewpoint and syntax for interaction, the test should be better written as $\overline{\mu} . \mathrm{SUCC}$, where $\overline{\mu}$ is the co-action of μ. We have not done so because we do not wish to bind ourselves to a specific process language, but rather remain in the general setting of LTSs. In other words, one should simply think of a test $\mu . \mathrm{SUCC}$ as a means for detecting whether a given process can produce an action μ. $\qquad\square$

We define the outcomes of an experiment first denotationally and then operationally. The former is presented in Table 5.1, as a function $\mathcal{O}_{\mathrm{den}}$ inductively defined on the structure of the test applied. We explain the notation used. We recall that $\wp(S)$ is the powerset of the set S, and S^n is the product of n copies of S.

Notation 5.2.2

- Given a function $f : S^n \to S$, its *pointwise extension* $f^\star : (\wp(S))^n \to \wp(S)$ (for $n \geq 1$) is defined as

$$f^\star(X_1, \ldots, X_n) = \{f(x_1, \ldots, x_n) \mid x_i \in X_i \text{ for } 1 \leq i \leq n\}$$

(the result of all possible applications of f to tuples of elements of $X_1, \ldots, X_n$).

Table 5.1 *Denotational definition of the outcomes of an experiment*

$$\mathcal{O}_{\text{den}}(\text{SUCC}, P) = \{\top\}$$

$$\mathcal{O}_{\text{den}}(\text{FAIL}, P) = \{\bot\}$$

$$\mathcal{O}_{\text{den}}(\mu.T, P) = \begin{cases} \{\bot\} & \text{if } P \text{ ref}(\mu) \\ \bigcup_{\{P' \mid P \xrightarrow{\mu} P'\}} \mathcal{O}_{\text{den}}(T, P') & \text{otherwise} \end{cases}$$

$$\mathcal{O}_{\text{den}}(\tilde{\mu}.T, P) = \begin{cases} \{\top\} & \text{if } P \text{ ref}(\mu) \\ \bigcup_{\{P' \mid P \xrightarrow{\mu} P'\}} \mathcal{O}_{\text{den}}(T, P') & \text{otherwise} \end{cases}$$

$$\mathcal{O}_{\text{den}}(T_1 \wedge T_2, P) = \mathcal{O}_{\text{den}}(T_1, P) \wedge^* \mathcal{O}_{\text{den}}(T_2, P)$$

$$\mathcal{O}_{\text{den}}(T_1 \vee T_2, P) = \mathcal{O}_{\text{den}}(T_1, P) \vee^* \mathcal{O}_{\text{den}}(T_2, P)$$

$$\mathcal{O}_{\text{den}}(\forall T, P) = \begin{cases} \{\top\} & \text{if } \bot \notin \mathcal{O}_{\text{den}}(T, P) \\ \{\bot\} & \text{otherwise} \end{cases}$$

$$\mathcal{O}_{\text{den}}(\exists T, P) = \begin{cases} \{\top\} & \text{if } \top \in \mathcal{O}_{\text{den}}(T, P) \\ \{\bot\} & \text{otherwise} \end{cases}$$

- $P \text{ ref}(\mu)$ (pronounced 'P refuses μ') holds if P cannot perform a μ-transition, i.e., $P \xnrightarrow{\mu}$. (On weak LTSs, the meaning of $P \text{ ref}(\mu)$ will be more subtle, which explains why we introduce a special notation for it.) □

In particular, $\wedge^*$ and $\vee^*$ are the pointwise extensions to powersets of the binary operators $\wedge$ and $\vee$ on $\{\top, \bot\}$; as $\wedge$ and $\vee$, so $\wedge^*$ and $\vee^*$ will be written in infix notation. For instance, $\{\top, \bot\} \wedge^* \{\top, \bot\}$ is $\{\top, \bot\}$, and $\{\top, \bot\} \vee^* \{\top\}$ is $\{\top\}$.

Exercise 5.2.3 (Recommended, $\hookrightarrow$) Every test T has an *inverse*, $\overline{T}$, defined thus:

$$\overline{\text{SUCC}} \stackrel{\text{def}}{=} \text{FAIL}, \qquad\qquad \overline{\text{FAIL}} \stackrel{\text{def}}{=} \text{SUCC},$$
$$\overline{\mu.T} \stackrel{\text{def}}{=} \tilde{\mu}.\overline{T}, \qquad\qquad \overline{\tilde{\mu}.T} \stackrel{\text{def}}{=} \mu.\overline{T},$$
$$\overline{T_1 \wedge T_2} \stackrel{\text{def}}{=} \overline{T_1} \vee \overline{T_2}, \qquad\qquad \overline{T_1 \vee T_2} \stackrel{\text{def}}{=} \overline{T_1} \wedge \overline{T_2},$$
$$\overline{\forall T} \stackrel{\text{def}}{=} \exists \overline{T}, \qquad\qquad \overline{\exists T} \stackrel{\text{def}}{=} \forall \overline{T}.$$

Show that for each T we have:

- $\top \in \mathcal{O}_{\text{den}}(T, P)$ iff $\bot \in \mathcal{O}_{\text{den}}(\overline{T}, P)$;
- $\bot \in \mathcal{O}_{\text{den}}(T, P)$ iff $\top \in \mathcal{O}_{\text{den}}(\overline{T}, P)$.

□

Here are some examples.

Example 5.2.4 Let P_2 and Q_2 be the non-bisimilar processes of Figure 1.7. For $T_1 \overset{\text{def}}{=}$ $a \cdot (b \, .\text{SUCC} \wedge c \, . \text{SUCC})$, we have $\mathcal{O}_{\text{den}}(T_1, P_2) = \{\top\}$ and $\mathcal{O}_{\text{den}}(T_1, Q_2) = \{\bot\}$. □

Exercise 5.2.5 (↪) The two tests SUCC and $\mu \, . \, T$ allow us to build traces of tests of the form $\mu_1 . \ldots . \mu_n \, . \text{SUCC}$, which allow us to check whether a process may, or may not, perform given sequences of actions. With such tests we can also observe some of the branching structure of terms. Show that the tests indeed are sufficient to distinguish the processes P_2 and Q_2 of Figure 1.7. □

Example 5.2.6 An example of a test that distinguishes the processes P_1 and Q_1 of Figure 1.4 is $T_3 \overset{\text{def}}{=} a \, . \, b \, .\text{SUCC}$. We have $\mathcal{O}_{\text{den}}(T_3, P_1) = \{\bot, \top\}$ and $\mathcal{O}_{\text{den}}(T_3, Q_1) = \{\top\}$. Another example is $T_4 = a \, . \, \widetilde{b} \, .\text{FAIL}$; we have $\mathcal{O}_{\text{den}}(T_4, P_1) = \{\bot, \top\}$ and $\mathcal{O}_{\text{den}}(T_4, Q_1) = \{\bot\}$. □

Example 5.2.7 An example of a test that distinguishes P_3 and Q_3 in Figure 1.7 is $T \overset{\text{def}}{=} \exists a \, . \forall b \, . c \, . \text{SUCC}$. We have $\mathcal{O}_{\text{den}}(T, P_3) = \{\top\}$ and $\mathcal{O}_{\text{den}}(T, Q_3) = \{\bot\}$. □

Exercise 5.2.8 (↪) Define other tests that distinguish between P_3 and Q_3 of Example 5.2.7. □

Exercise 5.2.9 (↪) Define tests that distinguish between P_4 and Q_4 in Figure 2.4. □

We now complete the definition in Section 5.1 of the function $\mathcal{O}_{\text{op}}$, which describes the outcomes of an experiment operationally, with the grammar and the reduction relation $\longrightarrow$ for the configurations.

Definition 5.2.10 (Grammar of configurations)

$$E ::= \top \mid \bot \mid \langle T, P \rangle \mid E_1 \wedge E_2 \mid E_1 \vee E_2 \mid \forall E \mid \exists E.$$

□

Configurations $\top$, $\bot$, and $\langle T, P \rangle$ are the base productions in a grammar for configurations, as explained in Section 5.1. The operators on configurations, $\wedge, \vee, \forall$ and $\exists$, mimic the corresponding operators on tests by allowing us to combine the results of subruns. (These symbols are thus overloaded, operating on both tests and configurations; in each case the context of use will allow us to make the distinction.) The reduction relation on configurations is inductively defined by the rules of Table 5.2, where:

- $E^{\rightarrow}$ is the set of derivatives of E, that is

$$\{E' \mid E \longrightarrow E'\}$$

(it is easy to check that, since the processes are image-finite, for each E the set $E^{\rightarrow}$ is finite);

Table 5.2 *Rules for the evaluation of a configuration*

$$\langle \text{SUCC}, P \rangle \longrightarrow \top \qquad\qquad \langle \text{FAIL}, P \rangle \longrightarrow \bot$$

$$\frac{P \xrightarrow{\mu} P'}{\langle \mu . T, P \rangle \longrightarrow \langle T, P \rangle} \qquad\qquad \frac{P \; \text{ref}(\mu)}{\langle \mu . T, P \rangle \longrightarrow \bot}$$

$$\frac{P \xrightarrow{\mu} P'}{\langle \widetilde{\mu} . T, P \rangle \longrightarrow \langle T, P \rangle} \qquad\qquad \frac{P \; \text{ref}(\mu)}{\langle \widetilde{\mu} . T, P \rangle \longrightarrow \top}$$

$$\langle T_1 \wedge T_2, P \rangle \longrightarrow \langle T_1, P \rangle \wedge \langle T_2, P \rangle \qquad \frac{E_1 \longrightarrow E_1' \qquad E_2 \longrightarrow E_2'}{E_1 \wedge E_2 \longrightarrow E_1' \wedge E_2'}$$

$$\top \wedge E \longrightarrow E \qquad\qquad E \wedge \top \longrightarrow E$$

$$\bot \wedge E \longrightarrow \bot \qquad\qquad E \wedge \bot \longrightarrow \bot$$

$$\langle T_1 \vee T_2, P \rangle \longrightarrow \langle T_1, P \rangle \vee \langle T_2, P \rangle \qquad \frac{E_1 \longrightarrow E_1' \qquad E_2 \longrightarrow E_2'}{E_1 \vee E_2 \longrightarrow E_1' \vee E_2'}$$

$$\top \vee E \longrightarrow \top \qquad\qquad E \vee \top \longrightarrow \top$$

$$\bot \vee E \longrightarrow E \qquad\qquad E \vee \bot \longrightarrow E$$

$$\langle \forall T, P \rangle \longrightarrow \forall \langle T, P \rangle \qquad\qquad \forall \top \longrightarrow \top$$

$$\forall \bot \longrightarrow \bot \qquad\qquad \frac{E^{\rightarrow} = \{E_1, \dots, E_n\}}{\forall E \longrightarrow \bigwedge_{i=1}^{n} \forall E_i}$$

$$\langle \exists T, P \rangle \longrightarrow \exists \langle T, P \rangle \qquad\qquad \exists \top \longrightarrow \top$$

$$\exists \bot \longrightarrow \bot \qquad\qquad \frac{E^{\rightarrow} = \{E_1, \dots, E_n\}}{\exists E \longrightarrow \bigvee_{i=1}^{n} \exists E_i}$$

- $\bigwedge_{i=1}^{n} E_i$ is an abbreviation for

$$E_1 \wedge (E_2 \wedge (\dots \wedge E_n)\dots)$$

and similarly for $\bigvee_{i=1}^{n} E_i$.

In the table we have grouped rules that concern the same operator (on tests or on configurations). We comment on some of the rules. In an experiment $\langle \mu . T, P \rangle$, if P cannot perform a μ-action then $\bot$ is reported immediately. Otherwise, the experiment continues as $\langle T, P' \rangle$, where P' is a μ-derivative of P. The rules for the refusal test $\widetilde{\mu} . T$ are similar.

In an experiment $\langle T_1 \wedge T_2, P \rangle$, two copies of P are made, so to apply separately each subtest T_i to P. The same is done in $\langle T_1 \vee T_2, P \rangle$. The remaining rules for $\wedge$ and $\vee$ are the expected ones for boolean connectors. In the inference rules for $\wedge$ and $\vee$, the subconfigurations are required to evolve simultaneously; however, we could just as well have required interleaved evolutions.

An experiment $\langle \forall T, P \rangle$ first evolves into $\forall \langle T, P \rangle$. Then each possible continuations of $\langle T, P \rangle$ is considered (the set $\langle T, P \rangle^{\rightarrow}$), and the construction is iterated on such continuations, combining the results conjunctively. This means following all possible runs of $\langle T, P \rangle$, at an arbitrary depth; only if *all* runs are successful the final result will be $\top$. The case of $\langle \exists T, P \rangle$ is dual: $\top$ is returned if *at least one* run is successful.

There are no rules for the configurations $\top$ and $\bot$, and these are indeed the only possible final configurations in a run.

Exercise 5.2.11 Show that for all tests T and processes P, any run of T on P is finite. □

In the proofs of the results in the remainder of this section we will not use the finiteness property of Exercise 5.2.11, so that proofs are easier to adapt to cases in which runs may be infinite, for instance when we take into account the internal moves of the processes in Section 5.3.

We first prove that the operational and denotational definitions of outcomes coincide (Theorem 5.2.14); then we show that they characterise bisimilarity (Corollary 5.2.18).

Lemma 5.2.12

(1) *If* $\top \in \mathcal{O}_{\mathrm{op}}(\forall E)$ *then* $\{\top\} = \mathcal{O}_{\mathrm{op}}(E)$.
(2) *If* $\bot \in \mathcal{O}_{\mathrm{op}}(\forall E)$ *then* $\bot \in \mathcal{O}_{\mathrm{op}}(E)$.

Proof

(1) We proceed by induction on the number of steps in a run from $\forall E$ that produces $\top$. If this number is 1 then it must be $E = \top$ and the assertion is trivial. Otherwise, let $E^{\rightarrow} = \{E_1, \ldots, E_n\}$; we have

$$\forall E \longrightarrow \bigwedge_{i=1}^{n} \forall E_i$$

and, for each i, it must be $\top \in \mathcal{O}_{\mathrm{op}}(\forall E_i)$; moreover, $\top$ is produced in fewer steps. We can therefore apply induction and infer that $\{\top\} = \mathcal{O}_{\mathrm{op}}(E_i)$, for each i, from which it follows that also $\{\top\} = \mathcal{O}_{\mathrm{op}}(E)$ holds.

(2) If $\bot \in \mathcal{O}_{\mathrm{op}}(\forall E)$, then either there is an infinite run from $\forall E$ or there is a finite run that ends with $\bot$. In the former case, following the operational rules of $\forall$ we construct also an infinite run for E; in the latter case, proceeding similarly, we construct a run for E that ends with $\bot$.

□

Corollary 5.2.13 $\mathcal{O}_{\mathrm{op}}(\forall E)$ *is either* $\{\top\}$ *or* $\{\bot\}$, *for each* E. □

Theorem 5.2.14 $\mathcal{O}_{\mathrm{den}}(T, P) = \mathcal{O}_{\mathrm{op}}(\langle T, P \rangle)$.

Proof We proceed by induction on the structure of T. The base case is when T is SUCC or FAIL, and is trivial. Below we consider the cases of the induction.

$T = \forall T'$ This is the most interesting case (together with its analogue, $T = \exists T'$). Suppose $\top \in \mathcal{O}_{op}(\langle \forall T', P \rangle)$. Since $\langle \forall T', P \rangle \longrightarrow \forall \langle T', P \rangle$, this holds if $\top \in \mathcal{O}_{op}(\forall \langle T', P \rangle)$. By Lemma 5.2.12(1), $\{\top\} = \mathcal{O}_{op}(\langle T', P \rangle)$. By induction, also $\{\top\} = \mathcal{O}_{den}(T', P)$; by the definition of $\mathcal{O}_{den}$, we conclude $\{\top\} = \mathcal{O}_{den}(\forall T', P)$.

Suppose now $\bot \in \mathcal{O}_{op}(\langle \forall T', P \rangle)$. We reason similarly; we have $\bot \in \mathcal{O}_{op}(\forall \langle T', P \rangle)$ and then, by Lemma 5.2.12(2), $\bot \in \mathcal{O}_{op}(\langle T', P \rangle)$. By induction, $\bot \in \mathcal{O}_{den}(T', P)$, hence also $\bot \in \mathcal{O}_{den}(\forall T', P)$.

The proofs that $\top \in \mathcal{O}_{op}(\langle \forall T', P \rangle)$ implies $\{\top\} = \mathcal{O}_{den}(\forall T', P)$ and $\bot \in \mathcal{O}_{op}(\langle \forall T', P \rangle)$ implies $\bot \in \mathcal{O}_{den}(\forall T', P)$ conclude the case since, by definition of $\mathcal{O}_{den}$, it cannot be $\{\top, \bot\} = \mathcal{O}_{den}(\forall T, P)$.

$T = \exists T'$ This case is similar to the previous one (requiring also the analogue of Lemma 5.2.12, with $\exists$ in place of $\forall$).

$T = \mu . T'$ We have $\top \in \mathcal{O}_{op}(\langle T, P \rangle)$ iff there is P' such that $P \xrightarrow{\mu} P'$ and $\top \in \mathcal{O}_{op}(\langle T', P' \rangle)$. By induction, $\top \in \mathcal{O}_{den}(T', P')$ and therefore, since $P \xrightarrow{\mu} P'$ holds, also $\top \in \mathcal{O}_{den}(\mu . T, P)$.

On the other hand, $\bot \in \mathcal{O}_{op}(\langle T, P \rangle)$ if either $P \operatorname{ref}(\mu)$ or $P \xrightarrow{\mu} P'$ and $\bot \in \mathcal{O}_{op}(\langle T', P' \rangle)$. In both cases, we derive $\bot \in \mathcal{O}_{den}(T, P)$ (in the latter case, proceeding as above).

We can reverse the steps, hence also $\mathcal{O}_{den}(T, P) \subseteq \mathcal{O}_{op}(\langle T, P \rangle)$.

$T = \tilde{\mu} . T'$ This is similar to the previous case.

$T = T_1 \wedge T_2$ or $T = T_1 \vee T_2$ We leave these cases as an exercise to the reader.

$\square$

If we use the denotational interpretation of tests, as in Table 5.1, then the language of tests reminds us of the formulas of a logic. Indeed, the proof below that the equivalence induced by the tests is bisimilarity reminds us of the proof of the modal characterisation of bisimilarity in terms of the Hennessy–Milner logic (see [Sti12]).

Lemma 5.2.15 *Suppose $P \not\sim_n Q$. Then there is a test T such that $\mathcal{O}_{den}(T, P) = \{\top\}$ whereas $\mathcal{O}_{den}(T, Q) = \{\bot\}$.*

Proof By induction on n. For $n = 0$ there is nothing to prove. In the inductive case, we assume the assertion for n. If $P \not\sim_{n+1} Q$ then either there is a move from P that Q cannot match, or the converse. Suppose the former holds, for a transition $P \xrightarrow{\mu} P'$. This means that

(1) either Q has no μ-derivatives,

(2) or Q has μ-derivatives $Q_1, \ldots, Q_n$ (there are only finitely many of them because the LTS is image-finite), and $P' \not\sim_n Q_i$, for all i.

If (1) holds, then the lemma is proved using the test $\mu . \text{SUCC}$. If (2) holds, then by induction there are tests T_i such that $\mathcal{O}_{den}(T_i, P') = \{\top\}$ whereas $\mathcal{O}_{den}(T_i, Q_i) = \{\bot\}$, for each i.

Then take the test $T = \exists \mu . (\bigwedge_i T_i)$. The reader may check that with such a T the lemma holds.

Finally, if $P \not\sim_{n+1} Q$ because a move $Q \xrightarrow{\mu} Q'$ cannot be matched by P, then, reasoning as above, we find a test T such that $\mathcal{O}_{\text{den}}(T, Q) = \{\top\}$ whereas $\mathcal{O}_{\text{den}}(T, P) = \{\bot\}$. The lemma is thus proved using the inverse test $\overline{T}$ (Exercise 5.2.3). □

Lemma 5.2.15 shows that there is a subset of the tests that allows us to separate all processes that are not bisimilar. Note that the proof uses all the operators in the test language; some of them are, however, implicit in the construction for the inverse tests. It now remains to check that the tests do not allow one to go beyond bisimilarity.

We write $P \simeq_{\text{test}} Q$ if P and Q cannot be distinguished by the tests, i.e., $\mathcal{O}_{\text{den}}(T, P) = \mathcal{O}_{\text{den}}(T, Q)$ for each T.

Lemma 5.2.16 $P \sim Q$ *implies* $P \simeq_{\text{test}} Q$.

Proof The proof is by induction on the structure of a test T; we leave the details to the reader. □

It is actually possible to prove something more general than Lemma 5.2.16, using a larger language of tests; that is, enriching the grammar of the tests with other operators, provided that these tests are semantically defined, in the sense that they do not allow us to inspect the syntax of the processes. An instance of this is Exercise 5.2.17. This kind of result is similar to those about the compositionality of bisimilarity with respect to classes of operators (Example 3.5.5 and Section 5.12).

Exercise 5.2.17 (From [Abr87]) Let f be a function from n non-empty subsets of $\{\top, \bot\}$ to $\{\top, \bot\}$, and T_f the n-ary operator on tests whose outcomes are so defined:

$$\mathcal{O}_{\text{den}}(T_f(T_1, \ldots, T_n), P) \stackrel{\text{def}}{=} f(\mathcal{O}_{\text{den}}(T_1, P), \ldots, \mathcal{O}_{\text{den}}(T_n, P)).$$

Show that the addition of T_f among the operators of the test language does not affect Lemma 5.2.16. □

Using the two previous lemmas and Exercise 2.10.18, we derive:

Corollary 5.2.18 *Relations $\sim$ and $\simeq_{\text{test}}$ coincide.* □

Remark 5.2.19 We exploited the image-finiteness Assumption 5.0.1 for LTSs in Lemma 5.2.15, Corollary 5.2.18, and in Table 5.2 to guarantee that $E^{\rightarrow}$ is finite. □

Lemma 5.2.15 can also be derived using the translation $[\![.]\!]$ below of the formulas of the Hennessy–Milner logic into the tests, and then exploiting the modal characterisation of bisimilarity. The reader is referred to [Sti12] for the Hennessy–Milner logic and related results. We use F to range over the modal formulas.

$$[\![\text{true}]\!] = \text{SUCC}, \qquad\qquad [\![\text{false}]\!] = \text{FAIL},$$
$$[\![F_1 \wedge F_2]\!] = [\![F_1]\!] \wedge [\![F_2]\!], \qquad [\![F_1 \vee F_2]\!] = [\![F_1]\!] \vee [\![F_2]\!],$$
$$[\![[\mu]F]\!] = \forall \tilde{\mu} \,.\, [\![F]\!], \qquad\qquad [\![\langle \mu \rangle F]\!] = \exists \mu \,.\, [\![F]\!].$$

The logic is mapped onto a subset of the tests that, when applied to a process, only produce one outcome.

Exercise 5.2.20   Show that for each formula F of the Hennessy–Milner logic, and for each P, we have (again, see [Sti12] for the definition of satisfaction, $\models$, in the logic):

(1) $P \models F$ iff $\mathcal{O}_{\text{den}}([\![F]\!], P) = \{\top\}$;
(2) $P \not\models F$ iff $\mathcal{O}_{\text{den}}([\![F]\!], P) = \{\bot\}$.

(Hint: proceed by induction on the structure of F.)   □

Remark 5.2.21 (Bisimilarity and similarity via probabilistic testing)   The testing scenario set up to characterise bisimilarity requires a tight control from the observer over the tested processes. In particular, one is allowed (i) to make copies of the processes at any stage of the run of an experiment (via the copying constructs), and (ii) to enumerate all possible non-deterministic transitions of a process (via the global testing constructs). The latter, which may be seen as a special option of the copying facility, is by far the strongest demand. It also appears in [Mil81] and referred to as the ability of 'controlling the weather condition'. The simple copying feature of (i), in contrast, is more realistic. It can be realised, for instance, using a standard core dump procedure.

Larsen and Skou [LS91] have showed that bisimilarity can also be obtained by retaining (i) but forbidding (ii) and using, instead, probabilities. Intuitively, an observer can, with arbitrary degree of confidence, assume that all non-deterministic transitions of a process have been examined by repeating an experiment often enough. Thus one can distinguish non-bisimilar processes with probability arbitrarily close to 1.

The discriminating power of probabilistic testers can be surprising. For instance, Deng, van Glabbeek, Hennessy and Morgan [DvGHM08] have shown that probabilistic testers can even give some of the power of the copying constructs (i). They use *probabilistic LTSs* (which are richer than the LTSs in [LS91]), and the testing framework of the testing preorder examined in Sections 5.4 to 5.8. Under conditions of image-finiteness, they are able to recover forms of similarity (similarity itself and failure similarity) – thus something weaker than bisimilarity but still coinductive and substantially finer than the testing preorder.   □

5.3 Tests for weak bisimilarities

The testing characterisation of bisimilarity presented in Section 5.2 can be adapted to *weak LTSs*, which have a special action τ representing internal activity, and *weak bisimilarities*. However, certain variants of weak bisimilarity may be difficult to recover while remaining strict on the requirement of effectiveness for the testing scenario. We do not show the details, but a few comments are mandatory.

Some obvious additions are the production $\tau.T$ to the grammar for the tests, and rules for allowing internal moves into Table 5.2, such as

$$\frac{}{\langle \tau.T, P \rangle \longrightarrow \langle T, P \rangle} \qquad \frac{P \overset{\tau}{\rightarrow} P'}{\langle \mu.T, P \rangle \longrightarrow \langle \mu.T, P' \rangle}$$

As a consequence, runs of configurations may now be infinite. Moreover, in the same table the occurrences of μ should be replaced by ℓ to indicate a visible action. Some modifications are also needed in the denotational definition of outcomes in Table 5.1. A major issue, however, is guaranteeing that the tests be ascertained effectively. For instance, consider the predicate P ref(ℓ). Its use in Section 5.2 has a simple experimental interpretation as 'I tried to push the button ℓ of the machine P and the machine refused'. The interpretation breaks down if, in the definition of P ref(ℓ), we simply replace the strong predicate $\overset{\ell}{\nrightarrow}$ with its weak counterpart $\overset{\ell}{\nRightarrow}$ (the negation of $\overset{\ell}{\Rightarrow}$). The reason is that a process could be capable of both performing the action ℓ, and avoiding it by silently evolving into a derivative in which ℓ is no longer available. An example is the CCS process $\tau.\mathbf{0} + \ell.\mathbf{0}$. Another tricky situation is illustrated by the process Ω_τ^a of Figure 4.1. Regardless of how it may internally evolve, Ω_τ^a is always capable of performing the action a. But Ω_τ^a can also continuously avoid a by performing τ moves. We are never sure that an action ℓ (for any $\ell \neq a$) will be refused: as the machine continues to perform internal work we can hope that ℓ will be accepted at some later stage. Thus it is natural to have $\perp$ as the only possible result of running the test $\widetilde{\ell}$. FAIL on Ω_τ^a (this test returns success only on the processes where ref(ℓ) holds). Similarly, the divergence of Ω_τ^a produces an infinite run, and hence a $\perp$ result, with the test a. SUCC. All this is troublesome for weak bisimilarity, for Ω_τ^a is weakly bisimilar with $a.\mathbf{0}$ (the process P_a in Figure 4.1) on which the tests $\widetilde{\ell}$. FAIL, for $\ell \neq a$, and a. SUCC always succeed. We would need some fairness assumption to avoid the divergence of Ω_τ^a in a run, ensure that the action a is eventually taken, and therefore obtain only success with the tests $\widetilde{\ell}$. FAIL and a. SUCC.

The forms of weak bisimilarity obtained by means of tests in [Abr87] take process divergences into account, along the lines of Definition 4.7.1, mainly to better address the problems mentioned above. For instance, in [Abr87] P ref(ℓ) holds if both $P \overset{\tau}{\nrightarrow}$ and $P \overset{\ell}{\nrightarrow}$; and in the denotational interpretation we have

$$\mathcal{O}_{\text{den}}(\ell.T, P) = S_1 \cup S_2 \cup S_3,$$

where

$$S_1 = \bigcup_{\{P' \mid P \overset{\ell}{\Rightarrow} P'\}} \mathcal{O}_{\text{den}}(T, P'),$$

$$S_2 = \begin{cases} \{\perp\} & \text{if } P \Longrightarrow P' \text{ and } P' \text{ ref}(\ell) \\ \emptyset & \text{otherwise,} \end{cases}$$

$$S_3 = \begin{cases} \{\perp\} & \text{if } P \Uparrow \\ \emptyset & \text{otherwise.} \end{cases}$$

A similar definition is given for the clause $\mathcal{O}_{\text{den}}(\widetilde{\ell}.T, P)$. Thus the divergent process Ω_τ^a above does not pass the test $\widetilde{\ell}$. FAIL, for any ℓ; indeed, the divergence-sensitive bisimilarity of Definition 4.7.1 does not consider Ω_τ^a equal to P_a (only $\Omega_\tau^a \leq_\Uparrow P_a$ holds).

A further limitation for weak bisimilarities is the image finiteness Assumption 5.0.1, which, when applied to weak LTSs and the relations $\overset{\mu}{\Longrightarrow}$, becomes more demanding.

5.4 Processes as testers

We have pointed out that one may consider the testing scenario for bisimilarity as unrealistic, especially for distributed systems. Another possible criticism is that the operators of the test language look like logical connectors more than process connectors (indeed, we have seen in Exercise 5.2.20 that they allow for a simple interpretation of the formulas of the Hennessy–Milner logic).

A natural alternative is a scenario in which the testers are just processes, with a behaviour given – as any other process – by some LTS. Thus performing a test amounts to observing the interactions between the tester and the tested processes. We need, however, a device to recognize success in an experiment. For this we assume the existence of a special action ω, indicating success, which may be used only by the tester processes. Aside from the special action ω, the sets of tester and tested processes could be the same (i.e., the two sets become equal by a renaming of ω). This, however, is not mandatory. Indeed, from the point of view of checking the behavioural equivalences obtained, it may be useful to reduce the set of testers as much as possible. In general the choice of the set of testers affects the discriminating power of the experiments, that is, the differences among the tested processes that may be observed. For instance, two processes might not be distinguishable by a given set of testers but they might become distinguishable in suitable extensions of the set.

We now set up, formally, this testing scenario; we only present the operational definitions of outcomes, following the schema in Section 5.1. The interested reader may consult [DH84, Hen88] for a denotational approach.

Let $\mathcal{L}_1 \overset{\text{def}}{=} (Pr_1, Act, \longrightarrow)$, with $\omega \notin Act$, be an LTS (the LTS of the tested processes, as usual ranged over by P, Q) and $\mathcal{L}_2 \overset{\text{def}}{=} (Pr_2, Act \cup \{\omega\}, \longrightarrow)$ another LTS (the LTS of the tester processes, ranged over by T). We do not need special operators on configurations, whose grammar has only the base productions:

$$E ::= \langle T, P \rangle \mid \top \mid \bot$$

for $T \in Pr_2$ and $P \in Pr_1$. The reduction relation $\longrightarrow$ on configurations is defined by the following three rules:

$$\frac{T \overset{\mu}{\rightarrow} T' \qquad P \overset{\mu}{\rightarrow} P'}{\langle T, P \rangle \longrightarrow \langle T', P' \rangle}$$

$$\frac{T \overset{\omega}{\rightarrow} T'}{\langle T, P \rangle \longrightarrow \top}$$

$$\frac{\text{if no other rule is applicable}}{\langle T, P \rangle \longrightarrow \bot}$$

In the first rule, tester and process evolve simultaneously. This is so because we are on strong LTSs – all actions are observable; in the Section 5.8, in the presence of silent transitions, independent transitions will be allowed. We write $P \asymp_{\text{test}} Q$ for the behavioural equivalence so obtained, i.e., $\mathcal{O}_{\text{op}}(\langle T, P \rangle) = \mathcal{O}_{\text{op}}(\langle T, Q \rangle)$ for all tests T.

Before giving examples of equalities and inequalities under $\asymp_{\text{test}}$ we present a refinement of the testing scenario that allows us to decompose the relation $\asymp_{\text{test}}$ into more elementary ones.

5.5 Testing preorders

The testing approach of Section 5.4 may be used not only to introduce behavioural *equiv-alences*, but also behavioural *preorders* (process relations that are reflexive and transitive). In this case we replace (∗) (in Section 5.1) as follows. Fixed a preorder $\leq$ on the non-empty subsets of $\{\top, \bot\}$, two processes P and Q are in the induced behavioural preorder if

$$\text{for all tests } T, \text{ we have } \mathcal{O}(T, P) \leq \mathcal{O}(T, Q). \qquad (**)$$

Intuitively, this means that the experiments on Q are 'at least as successful as those on P'. Preorders may be regarded as more primitive than equivalences, since a preorder $\leq$ generates an equivalence $\simeq$ in a natural way, where $\simeq$ is $(\leq \cap \geq)$. The preorder $\leq$, however, gives us more information than the equivalence $\simeq$, as two points may be related in $\leq$ without being related in $\simeq$. Also, a preorder may be sometimes more handy than an equivalence, for instance when comparing a specification and an implementation of a system. Indeed, often a specification has more non-determinism than an implementation, thus moving to an implementation involves a kind of deterministic reduction of the specified behaviour.

But what should $\leq$ mean in (∗∗)? Presumably we wish to have $\{\bot\} \leq \{\top, \bot\} \leq \{\top\}$: an experiment that always succeeds is better than one that may also fail, which in turn is better than one that always fails. However, we may also wish to have $\{\top\} \leq \{\top, \bot\}$, because in both experiments a success *may* be produced. Or else, we may wish to have $\{\top, \bot\} \leq \{\bot\}$, if we consider the possibility of failure of an experiment as disastrous. Thus three possible interpretations of $\leq$ emerge. They precisely correspond to the three possible ways to construct a *powerdomain* from a given domain. In our case, the domain to start from is the following two-point lattice, denoted $\emptyset$:

where the vertical line represents the partial order. Success is better than failure, hence the ordering given. The three powerdomains that we obtain may be depicted thus:

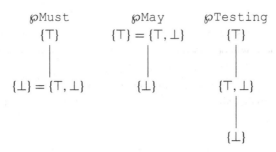

In ℘Must a process passing a test means that the test on the process *must* produce a success (i.e., no run can ever fail); in ℘May a process passing a test means that the test on the process *may* produce a success (i.e., at least a run does so); and ℘Testing allows us a more refined interpretation.

Remark 5.5.1 (Powerdomains) *Powerdomains* are to domains what powersets are to sets; they are the 'computable powersets'. Powerdomains were introduced by Plotkin [Plo76] as a tool to give denotation to non-deterministic programs, which have a set of possible results. Very roughly, given a partial order $(D, \leq)$ (more precisely, special partial orders called domains), we obtain a powerdomain by first taking the set $\overline{D}$ of all finite non-empty subsets of D; then lifting the order $\leq$ on D to $\overline{D}$; finally, making a certain completion (called *ideal* completion) on the resulting structure. There are, however, three ways of making the lifting required in the second step. The interpretations, and the resulting powerdomains, are called *upper*, *lower* and *convex* (they are also sometimes called, respectively, Smyth, Hoare and Plotkin powerdomains). In the upper interpretation, $X \leq Y$ (for subsets X, Y of D) if for all $y \in Y$ there is $x \in X$ with $x \leq y$; in the lower, $X \leq Y$ if for all $x \in X$ there is $y \in Y$ with $x \leq y$; and the convex is the conjunction of the previous two. Intuitively, in the upper interpretation, when comparing X and Y only their minimal elements matter; in the lower, only their maximal elements matter; and in the convex, both minimal and maximal elements matter. When powerdomains are used for the semantics of a non-deterministic program, in the upper powerdomain only the worst results produced by the program are retained and, dually, for the lower powerdomain; in the convex both the best and the worst results are retained.

In the case of the two-point lattice $\mathbb{O}$ above (which is also one of the simplest examples of a domain), ℘Must is the upper powerdomain, ℘May is the lower powerdomain, and ℘Testing is the convex one. The simplicity of $\mathbb{O}$ has allowed us to avoid the details of the construction of the powerdomain and to directly depict the resulting orderings on the subsets of $\mathbb{O}$. □

Remark 5.5.2 In the testing scenario for bisimilarity we used the powerdomain ℘Testing. This was necessary. If the outcomes of experiments were elements of the lattices ℘May or ℘Must, where there are only two elements, then the definitions of $\mathcal{O}_{den}(\forall T, P)$ and $\mathcal{O}_{den}(\exists T, P)$ in Table 5.1 would collapse. We needed both these operators to characterise bisimilarity. □

The *must may* and *testing* preorders, respectively written $\leq_{\text{must}}$, $\leq_{\text{may}}$ and $\leq_{\text{test}}$, are obtained from (∗∗) by interpreting the $\leq$ preorder symbol in the corresponding powerdomain $\wp\text{Must}$, $\wp\text{May}$, $\wp\text{Testing}$. We write $\simeq_{\text{must}}$, $\simeq_{\text{may}}$ and $\simeq_{\text{test}}$ for the induced must, may and testing equivalences.

Remark 5.5.3 We have:

(1) $P \leq_{\text{test}} Q$ iff $(P \leq_{\text{may}} Q$ and $P \leq_{\text{must}} Q)$;
(2) $P \simeq_{\text{test}} Q$ iff $(P \simeq_{\text{may}} Q$ and $P \simeq_{\text{must}} Q)$;
(3) $P \simeq_{\text{test}} Q$ iff $P \asymp_{\text{test}} Q$. $\qquad\qquad\qquad\qquad\qquad\qquad\qquad\qquad\qquad\qquad$ □

We have thus obtained the equivalence $\asymp_{\text{test}}$ of the previous section from a preorder, and we have broken down this preorder into two more primitive ones. These two preorders, $\leq_{\text{may}}$ and $\leq_{\text{must}}$, are in turn interesting on their own, as we will see better in the following sections.

Remark 5.5.4 (Preorders for bisimilarity) There is no natural way of obtaining bisimilarity from a preorder. This incidentally explains why it may be hard to give denotational semantics of processes based on bisimilarity – the mathematical constructions traditionally used in denotational semantics are based on preorders (more precisely, partial orders). One may hope to obtain bisimilarity from the *similarity* preorder of Exercise 1.4.17, or some of its refinements of Chapter 6, but their induced equivalences are different from bisimilarity.

For instance, if we applied the preorder definition (∗∗) to the testing scenario for bisimilarity in Section 5.2, since every test has an inverse (Exercise 5.2.3) the preorder would coincide with its induced equivalence. (Recall also from Remark 5.5.2 that for bisimilarity we must have the powerdomain $\wp\text{Testing}$.)

The main preorders used for bisimilarity in the literature are forms of bisimulation with divergence of the kind described in Section 4.7 and that either treat divergent processes as 'undefined' processes, which are below any other process in the preorder, or explicitly add a special 'undefined' process. $\qquad\qquad\qquad\qquad\qquad\qquad\qquad\qquad\qquad\qquad\qquad\qquad$ □

Definition 5.5.5 A process P *may pass* a test T if $\top \in \mathcal{O}_{\text{op}}(\langle T, P \rangle)$; and P *must pass* T if $\{\top\} = \mathcal{O}_{\text{op}}(\langle T, P \rangle)$. $\qquad\qquad\qquad\qquad\qquad\qquad\qquad\qquad\qquad\qquad\qquad$ □

Then $P \leq_{\text{may}} Q$ holds if P may pass T implies Q may pass T, for all tests T; similarly for $P \leq_{\text{must}} Q$.

5.6 Examples

The examples below illustrate the differences between the may, must and testing relations. When two processes are not related, we provide a test that distinguishes them. The proofs for the related processes are more tedious; they will become easier with the techniques in Section 5.7, and are therefore deferred to Exercise 5.7.5. The examples also illustrate the differences with bisimilarity.

Assumption 5.6.1 For the examples and results in this section, and up to Section 5.8, we assume that the LTS $\mathcal{L}_1$ and $\mathcal{L}_2$ for tester and tested processes are arbitrary (image-finite) LTSs with labels from the sets of actions $Act \cup \{\omega\}$ and Act. □

Example 5.6.2 The table below compares the three processes P_3, Q_3 and R_3 of Figure 1.7 on the may, must and testing relations, and on bisimilarity (an ok means that the processes of the column are in the relation of the row, a X means they are not).

	P_3, R_3	P_3, Q_3	Q_3, R_3
$\simeq_{\text{may}}$	ok	ok	ok
$\leq_{\text{must}}$	ok	ok	ok
$\simeq_{\text{must}}$	X	ok	X
$\simeq_{\text{test}}$	X	ok	X
$\sim$	X	X	X

As the processes are related by $\simeq_{\text{may}}$ they are also related by $\leq_{\text{may}}$. We have already considered the non-bisimilarity among the three processes in Exercise 1.4.9. We have $R_3 \not\simeq_{\text{must}} P_3$ because only the former must pass the test $a.b.c.\omega$, and similarly for $R_3 \not\simeq_{\text{must}} Q_3$. See Exercise 5.7.5 for the proof of the ok results. □

Example 5.6.3 Consider the processes P_2, Q_2 and R_2 of Figure 1.7. We saw in Exercise 1.4.8 that they are all distinguished by bisimilarity. We have $P_2 \simeq_{\text{may}} Q_2 \simeq_{\text{test}} R_2$; however $P_2 \not\leq_{\text{must}} Q_2$, as only the former must pass the test $a.b.\omega$. The other relationships follow from Fact 5.5.3. □

Example 5.6.4 Let

$$P \stackrel{\text{def}}{=} a.b + a.c + a.(c + d),$$
$$Q \stackrel{\text{def}}{=} a.b + a.(c + d).$$

We have $P \simeq_{\text{may}} Q$ and $P \leq_{\text{must}} Q$; however $Q \not\leq_{\text{must}} P$ because Q must pass the test $a.(b.\omega + d.\omega)$ whereas with P there is a run that fails. □

Example 5.6.5 Let

$$P \stackrel{\text{def}}{=} a.b + a.c,$$
$$Q \stackrel{\text{def}}{=} a.b.$$

We have $Q \leq_{\text{may}} P$ but $P \not\leq_{\text{may}} Q$ because only P may pass the test $a.c.\omega$. With $\leq_{\text{must}}$, the relationship is inverted: $Q \not\leq_{\text{must}} P$ (as only Q must pass $a.b.\omega$), and $P \leq_{\text{must}} Q$ (Exercise 5.7.5). □

5.7 Characterisations of the may, must and testing relations

In the testing approach it may be simple to prove that two processes are not equivalent: one needs to find *one* test that distinguishes the two processes, though of course finding it may require ingenuity. But it is in general long and tedious to prove that two processes are equivalent following the definition, as one needs to consider all possible tests and all possible results of such tests. However, in some cases alternative characterisations of the equivalences and preorders can be derived that are easier to work with. They use special enriched forms of traces, i.e., sequences of actions that the processes can take. We touch on this topic below.

We recall that s ranges over sequences of actions, ϵ is the empty sequence, and μs is the sequence obtained from s by adding μ on top.

Definition 5.7.1 Let s be a sequence of actions. Then:

- $s \in \text{Traces}(P)$ if $P \xrightarrow{s}$;
- $P \text{ after } s \stackrel{\text{def}}{=} \{P' \mid P \xrightarrow{s} P'\}$.

If A is a finite (possibly empty) set of actions, then:

- $P \text{ must } A$ holds if there are P' and $\mu \in A$ such that $P \xrightarrow{\mu} P'$.
- $P \text{ after } s \text{ must } A$ holds if $P' \text{ must } A$ for all $P' \in (P \text{ after } s)$. $\qquad\square$

If A is empty, then $P \text{ must } A$ is false, for all P. If P cannot perform the sequence of actions s, then $P \text{ after } s$ is empty and therefore $P \text{ after } s \text{ must } A$ holds for all A.

Definition 5.7.2 We set:

- $P \leq'_{\text{may}} Q$ if $\text{Traces}(P) \subseteq \text{Traces}(Q)$;
- $P \leq'_{\text{must}} Q$ if for all sequences s and finite sets of actions A, if $P \text{ after } s \text{ must } A$ then also $Q \text{ after } s \text{ must } A$.

The preorder $\leq'_{\text{may}}$ is *trace inclusion*, and its induced equivalence is *trace equivalence*. $\quad\square$

The preorder $\leq'_{\text{must}}$ is harder to check than $\leq'_{\text{may}}$: the latter involves a quantification on traces, the former involves a double quantification, on traces and sets of actions.

Theorem 5.7.3

(1) *the preorders $\leq_{\text{may}}$ and $\leq'_{\text{may}}$ coincide;*
(2) *the preorders $\leq_{\text{must}}$ and $\leq'_{\text{must}}$ coincide.* $\qquad\square$

We refer to [DH84, De87] for the proof of the theorem. (The proof is actually not very difficult; an enterprising reader might try it.)

It is easy to check that $P \text{ after } s \text{ must } \emptyset$ iff $s \notin \text{Traces}(P)$. From this, and Theorem 5.7.3, it follows that $P \leq_{\text{must}} Q$ implies $Q \leq_{\text{may}} P$ (in accordance with, say, Example 5.6.5), hence also:

Corollary 5.7.4 *The equivalences $\simeq_{must}$ and $\simeq_{test}$ coincide.* □

The difference between the must and testing equivalences only shows up on weak LTSs, more precisely on LTSs in which a divergence predicate may be defined on processes. See Section 5.8.

Exercise 5.7.5 (Recommended, ↪) Using the characterisation Theorem 5.7.3, prove the relations and the non-relations of Examples 5.6.2–5.6.5. □

Exercise 5.7.6 (Recommended, ↪) We have discussed in Exercise 3.4.10 the law $a.(P + Q) = a.P + a.Q$ under bisimilarity. Is it valid under $\simeq_{may}$? And under $\simeq_{must}$? What about $a.P + a.Q \leq_{must} a.(P + Q)$? □

Exercise 5.7.7 (*, ↪) Show that $P \leq_{must} Q$ holds iff for all s and Q' such that $Q \xrightarrow{s} Q'$ there is P' with $P \xrightarrow{s} P'$ and readies(P') ⊆ readies(Q') (Definition 5.11.1 says what readies is). □

On deterministic processes, bisimilarity coincides with trace equivalence.

Exercise 5.7.8 Show that for deterministic processes P, Q it holds that $P \sim Q$ iff $P \simeq_{may} Q$. □

5.8 Testing in weak LTSs

Of course, on weak LTSs, in the reduction relation on configurations we need rules to allow tester and tested processes to evolve silently and independently:

$$\frac{T \xrightarrow{\tau} T'}{\langle T, P \rangle \longrightarrow \langle T', P \rangle} \qquad\qquad \frac{P \xrightarrow{\tau} P'}{\langle T, P \rangle \longrightarrow \langle T, P' \rangle}$$

We recall from Section 5.1 that an infinite run produces ⊥ as a result. In the examples below for weak LTSs, we use CCS processes including some constants for expressing divergent behaviours in the tested processes (for testers, *finCCS* is sufficient).

Example 5.8.1 Let

$$P \stackrel{\text{def}}{=} \tau.a.0 + \tau.b.0,$$
$$Q \stackrel{\text{def}}{=} a.0.$$

It is easy to see that $Q \not\leq_{must} P$. We show that $P \leq_{must} Q$. Suppose P must pass a test T. Since $\langle T, P \rangle \longrightarrow \langle T, a.0 \rangle$, it must be $\mathcal{O}_{op}(\langle T, a.0 \rangle) = \{\top\}$, i.e., also Q must pass the test. In the may preorder, the converse relationship holds: $Q \leq_{may} P$, and $P \not\leq_{may} Q$. □

The distinction between the may and must relations, and consequently also the distinction between these and the testing relations, becomes significant in presence of *divergence*. While in the $\leq_{must}$ preorder a divergence is catastrophic, the $\leq_{may}$ preorder is insensitive to it.

Exercise 5.8.2 (Recommended, $\hookrightarrow$)

(1) Show that the equality

$$P + \Omega_\tau = \Omega_\tau$$

(where Ω_τ is defined in Exercise 4.3.2) holds for $\simeq_{must}$ for any P, whereas it does not hold for $\simeq_{may}$.

(2) Conversely, show that

$$P + \Omega_\tau = P$$

holds for $\simeq_{may}$ but not for $\simeq_{must}$. $\qquad\square$

Similarly to the first equality in the exercise, while $\Omega_\tau + a.0 \simeq_{must} \Omega_\tau + b.0$, the two processes are unrelated in the $\leq_{may}$ preorder.

The treatment of divergence also sets apart testing equivalence and weak bisimilarity. Consider for instance the processes Ω_τ^a and P_a of Figure 4.1. The difference between them is that only the former can produce an infinite sequence of τ-transitions. The two processes are weakly bisimilar, but not testing equivalent.

Exercise 5.8.3 Show that Ω_τ^a and P_a are not testing equivalent. $\qquad\square$

The supporters of testing equivalence use examples like this to argue against bisimulation because it is insensitive to divergence. The supporters of bisimulation would reply that the example shows that testing is not 'fair'. In $a|\Omega_\tau$ the divergence occurs when the right-hand side of the parallel composition always prevails on the other side. An implementation of the parallel composition that followed this schema could be blamed as unfair. See also the discussion on divergence in Section 4.3 and Exercise 5.8.5.

Divergence is also the reason why testing equivalence is not strictly included in weak bisimilarity. Notions of *fair testing*, also called *should testing*, have been proposed [NC95, RV07]; then bisimilarity is indeed strictly included in testing. Fair testing is based on a modified definition of success: the run of an experiment is successful if either the run itself has produced the success event, or at any point the run could have been continued so that success is produced later. Formally, the must preorder $\leq_{must}$ is replaced by the *fair must* preorder $\leq_{must}^F$ defined as follows. Say that P *must fairly pass* the test T if whenever $\langle T, P \rangle \Longrightarrow E$, then $E \Longrightarrow \top$ (that is, either E is $\top$ or E can reach $\top$ after some steps). Then $P \leq_{must}^F Q$ holds if, for all T, whenever P must fairly pass T then also Q must fairly pass T (compare this with Definition 5.5.5).

In weak LTSs, Theorem 5.7.3 continues to hold, provided that the definitions of $\leq_{may}'$ and $\leq_{must}'$ are made 'weak', and a check for divergences is introduced. Precisely, the modifications to Definitions 5.7.1 and 5.7.2 are as follows:

- s should be a sequence of visible actions, and similarly A a set of visible actions;
- relations $\xrightarrow{s}$ and $\xrightarrow{\mu}$ should be replaced by their weak counterparts $\xRightarrow{s}$ and $\xRightarrow{\mu}$.

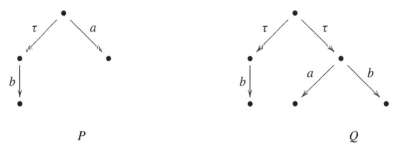

Fig. 5.1 Two testing equivalent weak LTSs.

- in the definition of $P \leq'_{\text{must}} Q$ the requirement $P \Downarrow s$ implies $Q \Downarrow s$ is added, where s is a sequence of visible actions, and a predicate $\Downarrow s$ holds of processes that never go through a divergent state while performing the sequence s; the predicates are defined inductively on the length of s:
  - $R \Downarrow \epsilon$ if not $R \Uparrow$ (where $\Uparrow$ indicates divergence);
  - $R \Downarrow \ell s$ if not $R \Uparrow$ and for all R' such that $R \overset{\ell}{\Rightarrow} R'$ also $R' \Downarrow s$.

Note that $R \Downarrow \ell s$ may hold even if $\{R' \mid R \overset{\ell}{\Rightarrow} R'\}$ is empty.

Exercise 5.8.4 ($\hookrightarrow$) Use the above weak version of Theorem 5.7.3 to prove that, on weak LTSs, strong bisimilarity implies testing equivalence, weak bisimilarity implies may equivalence and, if the LTSs are divergence-free, weak bisimilarity implies testing equivalence. □

Exercise 5.8.5 ($\hookrightarrow$) Show that the equality between the processes P and BW of Exercise 4.3.6 holds for $\simeq_{\text{may}}$ but not for $\simeq_{\text{must}}$ and $\simeq_{\text{test}}$. □

Exercise 5.8.6 ($\hookrightarrow$) Show that the processes in Figure 5.1 are testing equivalent. Show that the process would remain must equivalent if we replaced the label a in P with c. □

Remark 5.8.7 (Internal vs external non-determinism) The process

$$\tau.P_1 + \tau.P_2$$

internally decides whether to continue as P_1 or P_2. This choice is called *internal non-determinism*. In contrast,

$$a.Q_1 + b.Q_2$$

has *external non-determinism*: the choice is resolved following what the user proposes. If the user requests an a, then the process will oblige and become Q_1; whereas if b is requested then the continuation will be Q_2. In Figure 5.1, the process Q initially has an internal non-determinism and then, on the right-hand branch, an external one; the non-determinism in P, in contrast, is hybrid.

The possibility of hybrid non-determinism in the sum operator of CCS causes the congruence problems for weak bisimilarities, as well as for most of the behavioural equivalences and preorders in the literature. For instance, $\tau.a$ and a are weakly bisimilar and testing equivalent, but $\tau.a + b$ and $a + b$ are neither weakly bisimilar nor testing equivalent.

In *finCCS*, under testing equivalence it is possible to remove all forms of hybrid non-determinism, using some simple algebraic manipulations in which the main axiom employed is

$$P + \tau.Q = \tau.(P + Q) + \tau.Q, \qquad (5.1)$$

an instance of which is the equality between the processes of Figure 5.1 (Exercise 5.8.6).

The same property does not hold for (weak) bisimilarity. We can remove the hybrid non-determinism in $\tau.(a + b) + a$, since we have

$$\tau.(a + b) + a \approx a + b.$$

This transformation is an instance of the equality $\tau.(P + Q) + P \approx P + Q$, which relies on the presence of the same process both underneath and outside the τ. Other kinds of hybrid non-determinism may not be removed; an example is $\tau.a + b$. □

Exercise 5.8.8 (∗, ↪)

(1) Show that using axiom (5.1) of Remark 5.8.7, plus the monoidal axioms for sum and equational reasoning, all hybrid non-determinism in the process $a.c + \tau + b.d$ can be removed.

(2) Generalise the result above to any term in *finCCS*; you may find you need other laws. (Hint: prove the result first for processes in *full standard form*, as by Definition 3.6.3.) □

Exercise 5.8.9
Another interesting axiom of testing equivalence is $\mu.P + \mu.Q = \mu.(\tau.P + \tau.Q)$. The axiom makes it explicit that the choice between P and Q is internal to the process, as the initial actions offered to the outside are the same. Show the validity of the axiom. □

Exercise 5.8.10 (↪)
Show the validity of the law

$$(P \oplus Q) \oplus R = P \oplus (Q \oplus R)$$

for testing equivalence, where $\oplus$ is the *internal choice* operator, defined by the SOS rules:

$$\frac{}{P \oplus Q \xrightarrow{\tau} P} \qquad\qquad \frac{}{P \oplus Q \xrightarrow{\tau} Q}$$

As by Remark 5.8.7, in CCS internal choice is a derived operator and defined thus:

$$P \oplus Q \stackrel{\mathrm{def}}{=} \tau.P + \tau.Q.$$

Show that internal choice can also be written in CCS without the choice operator. □

Exercise 5.8.11 Continuing with the internal choice of Exercise 5.8.10, show that the equalities $\mu.P + \mu.Q = \mu.P \oplus \mu.Q = \mu.(P \oplus Q)$ (we assume that prefixing has precedence over $\oplus$, in the same way it has over $+$) holds for testing equivalence. □

5.9 Refusal equivalence

Refusal equivalence was introduced by Phillips [Phi87]. We discuss it here only informally.

The basic approach in refusal equivalence is the same as in testing equivalence, but now testers are more powerful: an observer is also allowed to see whether a process is *unable* to perform a certain action, and then can continue accordingly. This capability of testers is expressed by prefixes $\vec{\mu} . T$, where μ is an action in the alphabet of the tested processes, and transitions of the form $T \xrightarrow{\vec{\mu}} T'$. The reduction relation for configurations includes now the rule

$$\frac{T \xrightarrow{\vec{\mu}} T' \qquad P \; \texttt{ref}(\mu)}{\langle T, P \rangle \longrightarrow \langle T', P \rangle}$$

In the rule, the tester notices that the tested process is unable to perform the action μ and the run continues. For instance, if $T \stackrel{\text{def}}{=} \vec{\mu} . \omega$, then a run for $\langle T, P \rangle$ is successful only if P refuses μ. And a run for $\langle a.\vec{b}.\omega, P \rangle$ may lead to success only if P has an a-transition after which there is no b transition, as for $P = a.\mathbf{0}$ or $P = a.\mathbf{0} + a.b.\mathbf{0}$. However, with the former process the only result of a run is $\top$, whereas with the latter the result can be $\top$ or $\bot$. (The construct $\vec{\mu} . T$ is similar, but not the same, as the refusal construct $\tilde{\mu} . T$ used in the characterisation of bisimilarity; compare the rule above with the two rules for $\tilde{\mu} . T$ in Table 5.2.)

To see why the above capability makes the tests more powerful, consider the processes P_4 and Q_4 of Figure 2.4. They are testing equivalent but not bisimilar. They are also different for refusal equivalence. A test that distinguishes them is $T \stackrel{\text{def}}{=} a . \vec{b} . a . \vec{a} . \omega$. This test is successful on processes that have an a-transition, after which they have no b-transitions but have however another a-transition not followed by a third a-transition. P_4 exhibits such a behaviour (following the rightmost path in its tree), whereas Q_4 does not. Refusal equivalence is in fact strictly between testing equivalence and bisimilarity. The difference with bisimilarity is showed by the processes P_3 and Q_3 of Figure 1.7: they are equal for testing equivalence but not for bisimilarity, and remain equal for refusal equivalence.

Remark 5.9.1 What is most prominently missing in the testing scenario for refusal equivalence (or for testing equivalence) with respect to that for bisimilarity is a form of test that allows us to make copies of the state of a process *during* its execution. This is clear in the processes P_3 and Q_3 of Figure 1.7. They are different because in the latter after an a action both the sequence bc and the sequence bd are possible. To observe this, we would need to make two copies of the state of the processes after the initial a action. □

5.9.1 Weak LTSs

On weak LTSs, a tester may observe that a process refuses an action only if the process is *stable* (i.e., it cannot perform τ-actions). This sensitiveness to τ-actions allows us to separate the processes P and Q of Figure 5.1, which are also different for bisimilarity but are equal for testing equivalence. They are, for instance, distinguished by the test $\bar{c}.a.\omega$, as only Q may pass the test. (The test is satisfied by processes that have a stable derivative with an a transition.)

With τ-actions, another difference between testing and refusal equivalences is that the latter distinguishes a divergent run from a run that explicitly produces a failure. Thus in refusal equivalence the possible results for a run are three (success, failure, unsettled), rather than two as in testing equivalence. Indeed, in the refusal scenario, a tester process can perform, besides the special success action ω, also a special *failure action*, which determines the failure of a run. In both testing and refusal equivalence, however, a divergent run counts, and this breaks the inclusion in weak bisimilarity.

5.10 Failure equivalence

Refusal equivalence has also been inspired by *failure equivalence*. This equivalence, introduced by Brookes, Hoare and Roscoe [BHR84], has been, historically, one of the first forms of behavioural equivalence proposed for process languages, and it has quickly become the predominant behavioural equivalence in the community that uses concurrency languages based on CSP. On processes without divergences, failure equivalence coincides with testing equivalence. The ideas that led to the introduction of the two equivalences are, however, rather different.

Failure equivalence adopts the viewpoint that processes should be considered different only if they can be distinguished by some finite sequence of events. A natural candidate for such a behavioural equivalence would have been *trace equivalence*. Trace equivalence adequately accounts for a number of useful properties of processes, such as 'process P will have an a-transition', or 'process P may take a b-transition after performing an a-transition'. In presence of non-determinism, however, trace equivalence, as noted in Section 1.3.2, is not suited to reasoning about deadlock. A possible solution is to take into account the maximal sequences of actions that the processes can perform. We recall that a process P is *stopped* if there is no μ such that $P \xrightarrow{\mu}$.

Definition 5.10.1 A *complete trace* for a process P is a maximal sequence of actions that P may perform, that is, either an infinite sequence, or a finite sequence s such that there is P' stopped with $P \xrightarrow{s} P'$. Processes P and Q are *complete trace equivalent* if they have the same sets of complete traces. $\qquad\square$

For instance, the process $a.b + c$ has ab and c as complete traces, but not a because after performing a further transitions are possible.

Remark 5.10.2 In (standard) trace equivalence, infinite sequences are not taken into account. One can define an infinitary variant of it, where also infinite traces matter. On image-finite processes, the two versions of trace equivalence coincide, essentially as a consequence of König's Lemma; the crux of the proof is to show that if if all prefixes of a given infinite trace are in the traces of a process, then also that infinite trace can be executed by the process; see [Gla01a, proposition 2.4]. □

Complete trace equivalence is included in trace equivalence. The inclusion is strict. The trace equivalent processes P_1 and Q_1 of Figure 1.4 are not complete trace equivalent, since only the former has a as a complete trace.

The main problem of complete trace equivalence is compositionality with respect to many important operators, such as CCS restriction, or CSP synchronous parallel composition. For instance, the processes P_2 and Q_2 of Figure 1.7 have the same complete traces, but $\nu b\, P_2$ and $\nu b\, Q_2$ have not (only the latter has a).

The solution adopted by Hoare and his CSP coworkers is to adopt a finer refinement of trace equivalence, in which one is allowed to observe, at the end of a trace, a set of actions that are refused. A pair of a trace and a refusal is called a *failure*.

Definition 5.10.3 A *failure* is a pair (s, A), where s is a finite sequence of actions and A a set of actions. The failure (s, A) belongs to process P if, for some P':

- $P \xrightarrow{s} P'$;
- $P' \xrightarrow{\mu}\!\!\!\!/\,$, for all $\mu \in A$.

Two processes P and Q are *failure equivalent* if they have the same sets of failures. □

For instance, the process $Q_3 \stackrel{\text{def}}{=} a.(b.c + b.d)$ of Figure 1.7 has the following failures:

- (ϵ, A) for all A with $a \notin A$;
- (a, A) for all A with $b \notin A$;
- (ab, A) for all A with $\{c, d\} \not\subseteq A$;
- (abc, A) and (abd, A), for all A.

Exercise 5.10.4 Show that:

- the process P_3 of Figure 1.7 has the same set of failures as Q_3 above;
- the processes P_2 and Q_2 of Figure 1.7, as well as P_2 and R_2, are not failure equivalent.

□

A failure (s, A) for a process indicates the possibility of a deadlock if the environment, after allowing the trace s, only allows actions from A. (In the original proposal of failures [BHR84], the refusal set A had to be finite, insisting on the finiteness of an environment that, at any time, 'realistically can only perform a finite number of events'. In later papers, this finitary condition is dropped, as it seemed unnatural for processes with an infinite sort, see e.g., [BR84].)

Exercise 5.10.5 Show that processes P_1 and Q_1 of Figure 1.4 are not failure equivalent.

□

Theorem 5.10.6 *On (strong) LTSs, failure equivalence coincides with testing equivalence.*

□

The above result follows from the characterisation of testing in Theorem 5.7.3, for we have: P after s must A if and only if (s, A) is not a failure for P.

5.10.1 Weak LTSs

On weak LTSs, only refusals of stable processes are taken into account in failure equivalence. That is, in Definition 5.10.3, besides using the weak transition $P \overset{s}{\Rightarrow} P'$, we also require that P' is stable. This is natural in failure equivalence, where deadlock is observable, because a process that can perform a τ-transition is not deadlocked. In addition, failure equivalence considers divergence as a catastrophic condition, somewhat alike to must testing. Thus failure identifies all divergent processes, such as $a|\Omega_\tau$ (Figure 4.1) and Ω_τ. Technically, a divergent process is considered to have all possible failures. The motivation is that processes that might diverge are 'incorrect' and therefore it does no further harm to identify them all. As indicated by the equality between $a \mid \Omega_\tau$ and Ω_τ, some interesting information on the behaviour of processes is, however, thus lost. Variations of failure have been proposed with a more subtle treatment of divergence, see, e.g., [BR84, BKO87, OH86]. For instance, [BR84] takes into account, besides failures, also the divergence set of a process, that is, the set of traces that lead to a divergent state.

The characterisation of Theorem 5.10.6 in terms of testing equivalence remains true, provided that no states in the LTSs are divergent.

5.11 Ready equivalence

A variant of failure semantics is *ready equivalence* [OH86], in which one observes, after a trace, the maximal set of accepted actions.

Definition 5.11.1 The *ready set* of a process P, written $\text{readies}(P)$, is $\{\mu \mid P \overset{\mu}{\rightarrow}\}$. Then (s, A) is a *ready pair* for P if there is P' such that $P \overset{s}{\rightarrow} P'$ and A is the ready set for P'. Two processes are *ready equivalent* if they have the same sets of ready pairs.   □

Ready equivalence implies failure equivalence: the failure set of a process is derivable from its ready set. The inclusion is strict, as ready sets are *maximal* sets.

Exercise 5.11.2 (Recommended, ↪) Show that the processes Q_2 and R_2 of Figure 1.7 are failure, but not ready, equivalent.   □

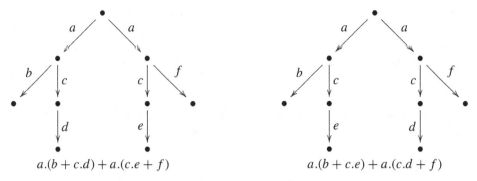

$$a.(b + c.d) + a.(c.e + f) \qquad\qquad a.(b + c.e) + a.(c.d + f)$$

Fig. 5.2 Ready, but not refusal, equivalent processes.

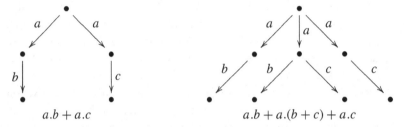

$$a.b + a.c \qquad\qquad a.b + a.(b + c) + a.c$$

Fig. 5.3 Refusal, but not ready, equivalent processes.

Testing equivalence coincides with failure equivalence. However, the two refinements of these that we have discussed, refusal equivalence and ready equivalence, are incomparable; see the two exercises below.

Exercise 5.11.3 ($\hookrightarrow$) (From [Gla01a])

(1) Show that the processes in Figure 5.2 are ready equivalent but not refusal equivalent.
(2) The processes Q_2 and R_2 of Figure 1.7, which for convenience are reported in Figure 5.3, are refusal equivalent but not ready equivalent. Show that the processes are not ready equivalent. Given a test of the form $\alpha_1.\alpha_2 \ldots .\alpha_n.\omega$, where each α_i is either an ordinary action μ or a refusal $\bar{\mu}$, show that the process on the right passes the test iff the process on the left does so.

5.12 Equivalences induced by SOS formats

We have presented failure equivalence as an improvement of complete trace equivalence that avoids its compositionality problems. There is actually a tight relationship between the two equivalences, at least in languages with CCS or CSP-like operators, which we explain below.

However, even failure may not be compositional in the presence of operators that go beyond CCS or CSP. An example, relevant for applications, is given by *priority* operators, as first formalised in [BBK87b]. A priority operator assumes a strict (i.e., irreflexive) partial order on the set of actions: actions higher in the ordering have a higher priority than those lower in the ordering. When applied to a process P, the operator removes all transitions emanating from P that are dominated by another transition, in the sense that the label of the latter is higher than that of the former in the ordering. This behaviour is expressed by the following SOS rule, where f is the priority operator and $<$ the ordering:

$$\frac{P \xrightarrow{\mu} P' \qquad (P \xnrightarrow{\mu'}, \text{for all } \mu' \text{ with } \mu < \mu')}{f(P) \xrightarrow{\mu} f(P')}$$

As a counterexample to compositionality of failure equivalence, consider the processes

$$P \stackrel{\text{def}}{=} a.b + a.(c+d),$$
$$Q \stackrel{\text{def}}{=} a.b + a.(c+d) + a.(b+c),$$

and suppose the partial order is $b < c < d$. Then P and Q are failure equivalent; but $f(P)$ and $f(Q)$ are not even trace equivalent, as the former has the traces ab and ad, whereas the latter has also ac. (Indeed, the counterexample shows that also trace equivalence is not preserved by priorities.)

Exercise 5.12.1 Show that bisimilarity is preserved by the priority operator above; that is, prove that if $P \approx Q$ then also $f(P) \approx f(Q)$. ☐

One may consider the congruence induced by complete traces (which essentially amounts to considering the coarsest congruence sensitive to deadlock) for classes of operators, where a class is defined in terms of the format for the SOS rules defining the operational behaviour of the operators. A number of formats have been studied in the literature. Some of the best known are the *De Simone* [DS85], *GSOS* [BIM95], *tyft/tyxt* [GV92] and *ntyft/ntyxt* [Gro91, Gro93, BG96] formats. We first describe the formats and then comment on the induced congruences. As the formats become more generous (by allowing more operators), the induced congruences become finer. The remainder of the section offers an informal discussion on the main formats and their induced congruences; the interested reader should follow the references for more comprehensive accounts.

We have described (a slightly simplified version of) the De Simone format in Example 3.5.5. The format is sufficient to define the rules of the CCS and CSP operators. The *GSOS format* goes beyond the structured rules needed for CCS and CSP – and captured in the De Simone format – mainly in two aspects. The first is the use of negative premises, which gives the possibility of performing a certain activity based on the *absence* of other activities. Negative premises are needed for defining priority operators of the kind described above [AI08]. The second additional aspect of GSOS is the possibility of copying the argument of an operator: a variable in the left-hand side of the conclusion may appear more than once in the right-hand side of the conclusion or in the left-hand side of a premise.

From a testing perspective, the contexts obtained from operators in the GSOS format allow us to observe the traces and the refusals of processes, and to make copies of processes at any moment; in contrast, referring to the terminology used for testing in Section 5.2, the global testing capability is absent.

With some simplifications, a rule in the GSOS format is as follows:

$$\{X_i \xrightarrow{\mu_{ij}} Y_{ij} \mid 1 \leq i \leq r, 1 \leq j \leq m_i\} \cup \{X_i \xrightarrow{\lambda_{ik}} \mid 1 \leq i \leq r, 1 \leq k \leq n_i\}$$
$$\overline{f(X_1, \ldots, X_r) \xrightarrow{\mu} T}$$

for some $n_i, m_i \geq 0$, where the variables are all distinct, and T is a term of the language possibly containing the variables $\{X_i, Y_{ij} \mid 1 \leq i \leq r, 1 \leq j \leq m_i\}$, and r is the arity of the operator f. GSOS is carefully crafted so to produce only finitely-branching LTSs.

With respect to the GSOS format, the most novel feature of the *tyft/tyxt format* is the presence of operators that have a *lookahead*. Technically, this means that the rule may have two premises with a variable in the target of one being present in the source of the other premise, as in the following rule:

$$\frac{X \xrightarrow{\tau} Y \qquad Y \xrightarrow{\mu} Z}{X \xrightarrow{\mu} Z}$$

Rules like this can be used to reduce weak bisimilarity to strong bisimilarity, by mimicking the absorption of τ-moves in weak bisimilarity, as done in Exercise 4.2.13. Lookahead also can be useful when one wants to describe a system at different levels of abstraction, and then express that an action on a certain level can be decomposed by several smaller actions at a lower level.

In the tyft/tyxt format, all rules are either in tyft or in tyxt format. A rule in the *tyft format* is as follows:

$$\frac{\{T_i \xrightarrow{\mu_i} Y_i \mid i \in I\}}{f(X_1, \ldots, X_r) \xrightarrow{\mu} T}$$

where the variables X_i, Y_i are all distinct (meaning that for all distinct $i, i' \in I$ and distinct j, j' with $1 \leq j, j' \leq r$ we have $Y_i \neq X_j, Y_i \neq Y_{i'}$ and $X_j \neq X_{j'}$), I is a (possibly infinite) set of indices, T, T_i are arbitrary terms, and r is the arity of the operator f. The *tyxt format* is the same except that the source of the conclusion is a variable distinct from all variables that appear in the target of the premises. The LTSs produced by the tyft/tyxt rules need not be finitely branching.

The lookaheads of the tyft/tyxt format essentially allow us to test whether a process will have certain actions in the future; one can even see whether a certain tree of actions occurs in the future. This represents a kind of global testing capability. However, lookaheads do not directly allow us to see negative information such as the absence of certain actions. As a consequence, the congruence induced by complete traces on the tyft/tyxt format remains below bisimilarity.

The addition of negative premises, as in the *ntyft/ntyxt format*, removes the gap, and allows us to recover bisimilarity. The combination of copying, lookahead and negative premises is quite powerful, and essentially allows one to define contexts that give us the discriminating power of the formulas of the Hennessy–Milner logic, somewhat similarly to the testing characterisation of bisimulation in Section 5.2 (although one does not explicitly have operators for global testing here). A rule in the ntyft/ntyxt format is as in the tyft/tyxt format, except that it may contain negative premises, in the following form:

$$\{T_j \xrightarrow{\lambda_j} \mid j \in J\},$$

where J is a (possibly infinite) set of indices, and T_j is an arbitrary term. Due to the sophisticated forms of negative premise allowed, some consistency conditions are added to guarantee the well-definiteness of the LTS produced by a set of rules, as discussed in Remark 5.12.2.

Remark 5.12.2 (Rules with negative premises) The use of negative premises in rules and rule formats requires some care. When rules have only positive premises, the meaning of 'transitions produced by the rules' is clear: these are all the transitions that can be derived with a well-founded proof, using the rules as inference rules, in the usual inductive way. Equivalently, the set is the least fixed point of a functional, as we did in Section 2.5 (where the functional is defined from all ground instances of the rules). If there are negative premises, however, the functional need not be monotone and therefore a least fixed point need not exist. This happens, for instance, with the following (self-contradictory) rule, where f and f' are constants (any term could be used in place of f'):

$$\frac{f \xrightarrow{a}}{f \xrightarrow{a} f'}$$

The issue of negative premises in LTS rules is related to that of negation in logic programming, and solutions to the latter problem can often be tailored to the former. An example of solution is that of *local stratification*, proposed for logic programming by Przymusinski [Prz88], and transported onto LTSs by Groote [Gro93]. The solution consists of assigning a weight to all possible process transitions in such a way that in all ground instances of a rule, the weight of the conclusion is greater than, or equal to, that of the positive premises and strictly greater than that of all transitions that deny a negative premise. Intuitively, this means that the validity of the transitions can be established in a step-by-step manner, following the weights. At weight 0 one obtains the transitions that are provable in the usual way, via rules that do not employ negative premises. Then at weight α one obtains the transitions whose negative premises can be resolved by the transitions already available at smaller weights. Thus, the weight of a transition is related to the maximal nesting of rules with negative premises that appear in the proof of the transition. □

Table 5.3 *Congruences for traces and complete traces*

format	traces	complete traces
De Simone	trace equivalence	failure equivalence
GSOS	ready simulation equivalence	ready simulation equivalence
tyft/tyxt	simulation equivalence	2-nested simulation equivalence
ntyft/ntyxt	bisimilarity	bisimilarity

As GSOS, so tyft/tyxt extends the De Simone format. However, GSOS and tyft/tyxt are incomparable, mainly due to the presence of negative premises in the former and of lookaheads in the latter. The ntyft/ntyxt subsumes both the GSOS and the tyft/tyxt format.

Table 5.3, from [Gro91, Gro93], summarises the results about the congruence induced by the contexts resulting from these formats with respect to trace equivalence (second column) and complete trace equivalence (third column). More precisely, two processes P and Q are in the congruence induced by trace equivalence (respectively complete trace equivalent) on a format $\mathcal{F}$ if, for all languages whose operators have transition rules that respect the format $\mathcal{F}$, and for all contexts C in the language, the terms $C[P]$ and $C[Q]$ are trace equivalent (respectively complete trace equivalence). It is assumed that the processes P and Q being 'tested' under the formats are finitely-branching. In the table, ready simulation equivalence and two-nested simulation equivalence are refinements of simulation equivalence presented in Chapter 6.

That complete traces produce failure equivalence on the De Simone format essentially follows from results in [DS85] and in [BKO88]; see also [Mai87] for CCS and CSP. (A direct proof is not very hard, in fact.) For the other results, as well as for more details on formats and associated theory, see [Gro91, GV92, Gro93, AFV01, Gla93c, MRG07]. Both in tyft/tyxt and in ntyft/ntyxt, the use of lookahead allows us to define some bizarre operators, rather far from the kind of operators one finds in practical concurrent systems or languages. Because of this, the significance of the congruence results for these formats (in particular, the possibility of recovering bisimilarity) has sometimes been questioned. Note that bisimilarity is the only behavioural equivalence among those discussed in this and other chapters that is compositional with respect to all formats. Indeed, compositionality of bisimilarity is often taken as a 'sanity requirement' for a rule format.

On weak LTSs, the theory of formats is more difficult; more variations are possible and therefore, overall, the results produced are less sharp and elegant. There is often a tension between the elegance of the definition of a format and the simplicity of the congruence induced by that format. In addition, there are the usual extra issues with weak equivalences, such as their sensitiveness to divergence and the congruence problems with operators like choice. For instance, Ulidowski's *ISOS format* [Uli92], proposed as a weak version of the GSOS format, yields a congruence that is similar, but not identical, to the 'natural' weak version of ready simulation equivalence (Section 6.4). The interested reader may consult [Uli92, AFV01, MRG07].

We have discussed congruences induced by complete traces. Indeed, the coarsest congruence that preserves traces and deadlock is usually considered to be also the coarsest useful form of behavioural equivalence. One may nevertheless consider other forms of contextual equivalences, using different notions of basic observables. For instance, Boreale, De Nicola and Pugliese [BDP99b] consider contextual equivalences defined on top of may and must predicates akin to the may and must success signals of testing equivalence, and show that, in CCS, well-known testing-like relations can be recovered.

5.13 Non-interleaving equivalences

All behavioural equivalences we have considered reduce parallelism to interleaving, in that

$$a.\mathbf{0} \mid b.\mathbf{0} \qquad \text{and} \qquad a.b.\mathbf{0} + b.a.\mathbf{0} \tag{5.2}$$

are considered equal. We have not discussed equivalences that reject the above equality, called non-interleaving (or true-concurrency) equivalences; the interested reader may consult, for instance, [Gla90, BPS01].

Some of these equivalences take into account the causal dependencies in the transitions performed. For instance, the two transitions

$$a.b.\mathbf{0} + b.a.\mathbf{0} \xrightarrow{a} \xrightarrow{b} \mathbf{0}$$

are causality related, as they emanate from the sequence of prefixes $a.b.\mathbf{0}$ in which the firing of the first prefix is necessary for that of the second. In contrast, there is no causality among the prefixes of $a.\mathbf{0} \mid b.\mathbf{0}$, and accordingly causality-based non-interleaving equivalences reject the equality (5.2). Other non-interleaving equivalences reject (5.2) because of the different degree of parallelism in the processes: the first process exhibit some parallelism, whereas the second process is purely sequential.

It is possible to formulate also some non-interleaving equivalences coinductively, for instance as forms of bisimulation in which transitions are enriched with information about their dependencies; see [Cas01] for a survey.

5.14 Varieties in concurrency

We have begun with a characterisation of bisimilarity in terms of computable tests. We noted that this requires considerable control over the processes being executed. This has been a motivation for discussing coarser forms of behavioural equivalences and preorders. We have first examined testing equivalence (and the associated may and must relations), which has an appealing interpretation as indistinguishability under experiments in which the tests applied to the processes are themselves processes. We have then considered testers with the additional capability of observing, and reacting to, refusals of processes, and noticed that the induced equivalence, refusal equivalence, is finer than testing equivalence. Finally, we have focused on the property of deadlock-sensitiveness. This has led to failure equivalence, via complete traces, and then to ready equivalence. We have, however, observed that other equivalences, including bisimilarity, may be derived in this way, insisting on the requirement of compositionality and varying the set of process operators. The relationship among the equivalences considered in this and other chapters is summarised in Figure 6.2.

The study of behavioural equivalences is a major topic in concurrency theory, with a long history. Van Glabbeek lists more than 50 forms of behavioural equivalences (and preorders) for strong LTSs [Gla01a], and many more for weak LTSs [Gla93a]. For applications, the choice of behavioural equivalence may depend on:

(1) the desired level of abstraction;
(2) the process language used and the environment in which the processes should operate;
(3) the techniques for reasoning available;
(4) the tools available, and the efficiency that they guarantee.

In (1), for instance, one should take into account which properties of processes are considered relevant. The coarsest semantics that respects the properties will be particularly appealing. In (2), if the processes are parts of an algebraic language, then the equivalence should be preserved by the operators of the language. If, however, the environment for the processes is not precisely known, or if the process language may be subject to extensions or modifications, then the equivalence should have robust compositionality properties.

Bisimilarity is the finest among the equivalences examined. Hence there may be systems that we wish to prove equal but they are not bisimilar. Bisimilarity is, however, very robust: it is preserved by a very large class of operators. It is therefore always a safe choice, regardless of the intended applications. A possible strategy is to try a verification under bisimulation semantics first, and only if this fails – and the reasons for the failure are not compelling enough – move to a coarser equivalence. On this line of reasoning, an even safer choice would be graphs isomorphism. However, as argued in Section 1.3.1, graph isomorphism is far too fine: a specification and an implementation of a system, for instance, would rarely yield isomorphic graphs.

Looking for equivalences coarser than bisimilarity, an alternative to dropping coinduction altogether is to weaken the game constraints imposed by bisimilarity. We discuss this alternative in Chapter 6, taking refinements, or variants, of simulation equivalence and also weakening the bisimulation game on internal moves. The resulting coinductive relations sometimes maintain reasonably efficient decision algorithms, see [AIS12].

The efficiency of its verification algorithms is indeed a major strength of bisimilarity. Other advantages are its elegant coinductive definition and its solid mathematical roots. See [AIS12] and [RJ12]. The benefits may be more significant on processes with subtle or sophisticated mechanisms of interaction. A striking example is given by higher-order process languages, in which processes may be exchanged or may move, as in the Higher-Order π-calculus. As pointed out in Section 7.1.2, various forms of bisimulation have been proposed and studied in these languages but, for reasons that have to do with the presence of processes within actions, the meaning of equality between traces remains rather unclear. All the characterisations of non-coinductive equivalences without a universal quantification on contexts (or something similar) that we have seen in this chapter make appeal to forms of trace equality. As a consequence, proving that two higher-order processes are, say, testing equivalent, will require, roughly, following the definition of testing and going through a tedious universal quantification on tests.

It is sometimes possible to define transformations on LTSs so as to reduce an equivalence $\simeq$ to another one $\simeq'$. That is, two processes are related by $\simeq$ in the original LTS if and only if the transformed processes are related by $\simeq'$ in the final LTS. In this way some equivalences may be reduced to bisimilarity. It is thus possible, for instance, to exploit the efficient algorithms for bisimilarity also for other equivalences. A good example of this is Cleveland and Hennessy [CH93], for testing equivalence. On finite-state processes, as testing equivalence is PSPACE-complete, while bisimilarity is of polynomial complexity, the transformation of the former into the latter in principle is heavy; in practice, however, the transformation is rather efficient, and is indeed a standard method for computing testing equivalence on processes in tools (see [AIS12]). For another example of transformation, from weak to strong bisimilarity, see Exercise 4.2.13.

Today, after more than 25 years of process calculi and behavioural equivalences, we can say that bisimulation (in its strong and weak forms) remains by far the most popular behavioural equivalence for languages that follow the CCS tradition, whereas failure equivalence plays this role for the languages on the CSP tradition. Discussing other behavioural equivalences, as we have done in this chapter and in Sections 4.7–4.9 and will be done in Chapter 6, is, however, important, both to the better understanding of the equivalences themselves, and because other equivalences may indeed occasionally be useful.

Varieties are common in concurrency, and we find them not only in behavioural equivalences, but also in process calculi (the CCS language of Section 3.1 is one of the most studied, but many others have been proposed), and even in models for the behaviour of the processes. Again, we used LTSs because they are very common, but one may also use Petri Nets, Event Structures, I/O automata, and so on.

6

Refinements of simulation

The simulation equivalence of Exercise 1.4.17 drops the symmetry of the bisimulation game: the challenge transitions may only be launched by one of the processes in the pairs. We have seen that simulation equivalence is strictly coarser than bisimilarity. Unfortunately, it does not respect deadlock. In this section we discuss a few refinements of simulation equivalence without this drawback. They are coinductively defined, much like bisimilarity, while being coarser than bisimilarity. Thus they can allow us to use coinduction in situations where bisimilarity may be over-discriminating. Another possible advantage of a simulation-like relation is that it naturally yields a preorder (with all the advantages mentioned in Section 5.5). With respect to simulation-based relations, however, bisimilarity remains mathematically more robust and natural. The most interesting refinements we examine are represented by *ready similarity* and *coupled similarity*.

We begin in Section 6.1 with complete simulation, and continue in Section 6.2 with ready simulation. They are to simulation what complete trace equivalence and failure (or ready) equivalence are to trace equivalence. In Section 6.3 we discuss two-nested simulation equivalence. In Section 6.4 we consider the weak versions of the relations in the previous sections. In Section 6.5 we present coupled similarity, which aims at relaxing the bisimulation requirements on the internal actions of processes. Finally, in Section 6.6, we summarise the various equivalences discussed in this and previous chapters.

6.1 Complete simulation

The arguments about the deadlock-insensitivity of trace equivalence in Section 1.3.2, such as the equality between the processes in Figure 1.4, apply to simulation equivalence too. We discussed possible solutions for trace equivalence in Section 5.10. We can apply similar solutions to simulation equivalence. Thus, first, as in complete trace equivalence, we add the observation of deadlock.

Definition 6.1.1 (Complete similarity) A simulation $\mathcal{R}$ is a *complete simulation* if whenever $P \mathcal{R} Q$:

- if P is stopped, then also Q is stopped.

Complete similarity, written $\leq_{comp}$, is the union of all complete simulations. Two processes P and Q are *complete simulation equivalent*, written $P \sim_{comp} Q$, if both $P \leq_{comp} Q$ and $Q \leq_{comp} P$ hold. □

Exercise 6.1.2 Show that processes P_2 and R_2 of Figure 1.7 are complete simulation equivalent. □

Like complete trace equivalence, complete simulation equivalence has compositionality problems.

Exercise 6.1.3 Show that equality between the processes P_2 and R_2 in Exercise 6.1.2 is broken by the restriction operator; i.e., $\mathit{vb}\ P_2 \not\sim_{comp} \mathit{vb}\ Q_2$. □

Exercise 6.1.4 Show that complete simulation equivalence implies complete trace equivalence. □

To see that complete simulation equivalence does not imply failure equivalence, or any equivalence finer than it, we can use the processes P_2 and R_2 of Figure 1.7 (Exercises 6.1.2 and 5.10.4). Note that P_2 and R_2 are also complete simulation equivalent with the following process:

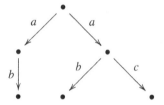

Again, this process is different from P_2 and R_2 under failure equivalence or any finer semantics. On the other hand, recall that refusal, failure and ready equivalences equate the processes P_3 and Q_3 of Figure 1.7. These processes are not simulation, or complete simulation, equivalent.

6.2 Ready simulation

Continuing the analogy with traces, we can improve complete simulation equivalence by moving to *failure similarity* and making visible the refusal sets of related states. This is the same as observing the *maximal* refusal sets of related states, and, going to the complement sets, it is also the same as observing their ready sets (Definition 5.11.1). Thus, the distinction between failure and ready equivalences of trace-based semantics disappears on simulation-based semantics, as the extra observations are made on single states, rather than on states reached after a certain trace.

Definition 6.2.1 (Ready similarity) A simulation $\mathcal{R}$ is a *ready simulation* if whenever $P\ \mathcal{R}\ Q$, it also holds that $\mathtt{readies}(P) = \mathtt{readies}(Q)$. *Ready similarity*, written $\leq_{rs}$, is the union of all ready simulations. Two processes P and Q are *ready simulation equivalent*, written $P \sim_{rs} Q$, if both $P \leq_{rs} Q$ and $Q \leq_{rs} P$ hold. ☐

Ready simulation equivalence was introduced by Bloom, Istrail and Meyer [BIM95] as the congruence induced by complete trace equivalence on the class of operators definable in the GSOS format (Section 5.12). The authors argue that GSOS is the 'largest reasonable format' that generalises CCS, and conclude that ready simulation equivalence is the finest equivalence that 'makes computationally meaningful distinctions'. Relational formulation were first given, independently, by Larsen and Skou [LS91] (who call it *2/3 bisimilarity*), and van Glabbeek [Gla91]; see also [AV93].

Exercise 6.2.2 Show that a simulation $\mathcal{R}$ is a ready simulation if and only if $P \mathcal{R} Q$ implies, for all μ:

• if there is Q' such that $Q \xrightarrow{\mu} Q'$ then there is P' such that $P \xrightarrow{\mu} P'$. ☐

Example 6.2.3 We have $a.b \leq_{rs} a.b + a.c$. Indeed, for any process P and Q, we have $\mu.P \leq_{rs} \mu.P + \mu.Q$, which is false for bisimilarity. ☐

The inequality $\mu.P \leq_{rs} \mu.P + \mu.Q$ expresses precisely the difference from bisimilarity on *finCCS*: indeed, together with the axioms for bisimilarity, the inequality yields a sound and complete inequational axiom system for ready similarity on *finCCS* [Blo89].

Exercise 6.2.4 Show that ready simulation equivalence is included in ready equivalence. ☐

Exercise 6.2.5 Show that the processes below are ready simulation equivalent but not bisimilar.

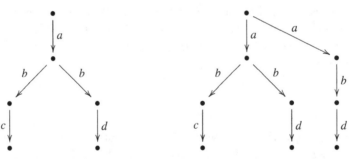

☐

Thus ready simulation equivalence is strictly coarser than bisimilarity. This property can sometimes be useful, as the following example shows.

Example 6.2.6 We show two *lossy delay links*, from [BIM95], that are ready simulation equivalent but not bisimilar. A lossy two-stage link repeatedly accepts an input v (from a set V of possible inputs), waits a time unit (action d below), and produces as output either the value v itself or the special signal z to indicate that v has been lost. The constants K_1

and K_2 below represent two lossy delay links, written in CCS. The first, K_1, receives inputs correctly but may lose them during the delay, and has thus a transition

$$K_1 \xrightarrow{v} d.\overline{v}.K_1 + d.z.K_1$$

for each $v \in V$. The second, K_2, may also lose the input during the reception step and has therefore an additional transition, for each v:

$$K_2 \xrightarrow{v} d.\overline{v}.K_2 + d.z.K_2,$$
$$K_2 \xrightarrow{v} d.z.K_2.$$

Under ready similarity the two lossy links are equal, and could therefore be used interchangeably in any system. In contrast, with bisimilarity they are different and therefore using one in place of the other in a system could be observable. □

Exercise 6.2.7 (Recommended, ↪) Prove formally the equalities (for ready simulation equivalence) and inequalities (for bisimilarity) in Example 6.2.6. □

6.3 Two-nested simulation equivalence

The final refinement of simulation equivalence that we present was obtained by Groote and Vaandrager [GV92] as the congruence induced by complete trace equivalence on the class of operators definable in the tyft/tyxt format.

Definition 6.3.1 (Two-nested simulation equivalence) A *two-nested simulation* is a simulation contained in simulation equivalence. *Two-nested similarity*, written $\leq_{2n}$, is the union of all two-nested simulations. Two processes P and Q are *two-nested simulation equivalent*, written $P \sim_{2n} Q$, if both $P \leq_{2n} Q$ and $Q \leq_{2n} P$ hold. □

In practice the interest of two-nested simulation equivalence is very limited, as the differences with ready simulation equivalence and bisimilarity are rather artificial. Moreover, proving that two processes are two-nested simulation equivalent can be tedious as, besides exhibiting two simulations, one may have to prove separately some simulation equivalence results. For instance, consider the processes $P \overset{\text{def}}{=} a.(b.c + b)$ and $Q \overset{\text{def}}{=} P + a.b.c$ whose behaviour is reported below:

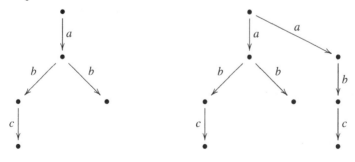

We can prove that P and Q are simulation equivalent using the two simulations $\mathcal{R} \stackrel{\text{def}}{=}$
$\{(P, Q)\} \cup \mathcal{I}$ and $\mathcal{S} \stackrel{\text{def}}{=} \mathcal{R}^{-1} \cup \{(b.c, b.c + b)\}$. This is not sufficient to establish that P and
Q are also two-nested simulation equivalent. We do have $\mathcal{R} \subseteq \mathcal{S}^{-1}$, and therefore all pairs
in $\mathcal{R}$ are also in simulation equivalence. However, $\mathcal{S}$ has an extra pair, $(b.c, b.c + b)$, and
one has to prove separately that this pair is in simulation equivalence too (though in this
simple example it is easy).

A two-nested simulation is also a ready simulation, since two processes that are simulation equivalent must also have the same ready sets.

Exercise 6.3.2 ($\hookrightarrow$)

(1) Complete the proof that the processes P and Q above are two-nested simulation
equivalent. Show that they are not bisimilar.
(2) Show that the processes of Exercise 6.2.5 are not two-nested simulation equivalent.

$\square$

One can actually define n-nested simulation equivalence, for all natural numbers n,
proceeding by induction as follows (one could even go further, using the ordinals rather
than the naturals), where Pr is the set of all processes:

- $\leq_{0n} = \sim_{0n} \stackrel{\text{def}}{=} Pr \times Pr$;
- $P \leq_{n+1n} Q$ if there is a simulation $\mathcal{R} \subseteq \sim_{nn}$ with $P \mathcal{R} Q$;
- $P \sim_{n+1n} Q$ if ($P \leq_{n+1n} Q$ and $Q \leq_{n+1n} P$).

The relations $\sim_{0n}, \sim_{1n}, \ldots$ form a decreasing sequence of relations with respect to set
containment.

Exercise 6.3.3 ($\hookrightarrow$) Show that $P \leq_{n+1n} Q$ iff there is a simulation $\mathcal{R} \subseteq (\leq_{nn})^{-1}$ with
$P \mathcal{R} Q$. $\square$

Exercise 6.3.4 ($*, \hookrightarrow$)

(1) Show that the processes P and Q of Exercise 6.3.2(1) are not three-nested simulation
equivalent. Are they in a three-nested similarity relation?
(2) Show that $a.Q$ and $a.P + a.Q$ are three-nested simulation equivalent but not four-
nested simulation equivalent. $\square$

Exercise 6.3.5 ($\hookrightarrow$) Consider the processes $P \stackrel{\text{def}}{=} a.(a.(b + c) + a.b)$ and $Q \stackrel{\text{def}}{=} P +$
$a.a.(b + c)$. Draw their behaviour. Are they two-nested simulation equivalent? Are they
three-nested simulation equivalent? Are they bisimilar? $\square$

On image-finite transition systems, the intersection, on all n, of the $\sim_{nn}$ relations
coincides with bisimilarity.

Exercise 6.3.6 ($\hookrightarrow$) Prove the claim above. $\square$

As in other forms of stratification results for bisimilarity, the image-finiteness condition is necessary, see [GV92].

On the algebraic side, a negative result holds for the equivalences $\sim_{n\,n}$ (as well as for the preorders $\leq_{n\,n}$), $n \geq 2$, in sharp contrast with most of the behavioural relations studied in the literature: the relations cannot be finitely axiomatised (that is, no finite set of axioms captures all and only the valid process relations), even on the very simple language of finite trees (essentially, the sublanguage of CCS comprising the operators nil, prefixing and choice) [AFvGI04]. On finite trees, bisimilarity is axiomatised with the axioms **S1–S4** of Figure 3.2.

6.4 Weak simulations

Weak simulation is to simulation what weak bisimulation is to bisimulation. As expected, the process answering a challenge transition uses a weak transition.

Definition 6.4.1 (Weak simulation) *Weak simulation* is defined by replacing the strong transition $Q \xrightarrow{\mu} Q'$ with the weak transition $Q \xLongrightarrow{\widehat{\mu}} Q'$ in Exercise 1.4.17. The union of all weak simulations (and also the largest weak simulation) is *weak similarity*. Two processes P and Q are *weakly simulation equivalent*, written $P \approx_{\mathrm{se}} Q$, if there are simulations $\mathcal{R}_1$ and $\mathcal{R}_2$ with $P\,\mathcal{R}_1\,Q$ and $Q\,\mathcal{R}_2\,P$. $\square$

Exercise 6.4.2 Show that in Definition 6.4.1:

(1) when μ is τ we can take $Q \xLongrightarrow{\widehat{\mu}} Q'$ to be $Q \Longrightarrow Q'$;
(2) we can take μ to range over visible actions only, replacing the challenge transition $P \xrightarrow{\mu} P'$ with $P \xLongrightarrow{\ell} P'$.

Neither (1) nor (2) affects the resulting weak similarity. $\square$

Exercise 6.4.3 ($\hookrightarrow$) In CCS, is weak similarity a precongruence (that is, a preorder preserved by the operators of the language)? Is weak simulation equivalence a congruence? $\square$

Both in the strong and the weak case, simulation equivalence strictly includes bisimilarity, and is insensitive to deadlock. The proofs that we saw for the strong case can be transported onto the weak one.

We only highlight modifications to be made to the refinements of similarity in the previous Sections 6.1–6.3 so as to adapt them to weak semantics. First, in each definition, 'simulation' should mean 'weak simulation'. There is nothing else to modify in the definition of *weak two-nested similarity*. If we wish to maintain τ-actions invisible and, similarly, maintain the ordering among the equivalences (Figure 6.2) then, in *weak complete similarity* a *stopped* process should be one that will never perform visible actions (i.e., a process

P for which there is no ℓ and *P'* with $P \overset{\ell}{\Rightarrow} P'$). And in *weak ready similarity*, the ready set of a process *P* should be $\{\ell \mid P \overset{\ell}{\Rightarrow}\}$.

Exercise 6.4.4 ($\hookrightarrow$) Show that the modifications of Exercise 6.4.2 do not apply to the complete, ready and two-nested variants of weak simulation equivalence. $\quad\square$

Exercise 6.4.5 ($\hookrightarrow$) Show that weak complete similarity is not preserved by the choice operator. $\quad\square$

As usual with weak semantics [Gla93a], further variations are possible. In particular, there are the orthogonal aspects of Sections 4.4 and 4.6–4.9 (such as congruence for + and divergence), which one may wish to take into account. Consider also the definition of a stopped process; in the connotation given above, the processes $\mathbf{0}$, $\tau.\mathbf{0}$, Ω_τ and $\tau + \Omega_\tau$ are all stopped. Yet, only the first cannot do anything; the second thinks for a while before doing nothing; the third thinks forever, and the fourth may or may not think forever. One may prefer a different meaning for 'stopped' in which (some of) these behaviours are distinguished. Similarity, in weak ready simulation, on related processes *P* and *Q* one may want to take into account the ready sets of processes reachable from *P* and *Q* via internal moves. Further, in such cases observing ready sets or refusal sets matters, so that the weak versions of ready similarity and *failure similarity* may differ (we noticed in Section 6.2 that they coincide for strong LTSs).

The significance of the refinements of simulation, however, in the weak case is less compelling than in the strong case, notably in the motivations for the relations as the congruences induced by certain SOS formats, for the reasons mentioned at the end of Section 5.12. This criticism does not apply to the coupled simulation of the next section, which makes a refinement of simulation specific to weak semantics as it only concerns internal activity.

6.5 Coupled simulation

We now discuss *coupled simulation*. It was introduced by Parrow and Sjödin in [PS92], and then refined in [Gla93a, PS94]. It has also been advocated, and studied, by Nestmann and Pierce [NP00] in the π-calculus, and by Fournet [Fou98] in the Join-calculus.

Parrow and Sjödin [PS92] proposed coupled simulation equivalence to prove the correctness of a distributed implementation of multi-way synchronisations in an environment supporting only asynchronous binary communications. The multi-party synchronisation was achieved through the cooperation of several processes. The specification, in contrast, was formalised, more abstractly, through a centralised synchroniser. In the specification the centralised synchroniser is capable of selecting all participants of a synchronisation in a single internal move. In the implementation more steps are needed to gradually narrow down the possible combinations. The implementation was not correct with respect to the specification under weak bisimilarity. The reason is the bisimulation game on internal

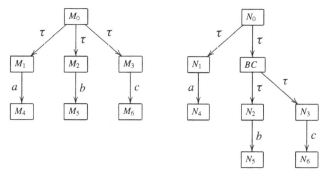

Fig. 6.1 Atomic vs gradual commitment

moves: if a process in one step resolves certain internal choices, then a weakly bisimilar process should perform some internal moves that resolve exactly the same choices. The obvious alternative to weak bisimilarity would have been a behavioural equivalence less sensitive than bisimulation to the branching structure of processes. An example is the testing equivalence of Section 5.4. Adopting testing would, however, imply reverting to the coinduction proof method, in particular to the locality of the checks in proofs. Parrow and Sjödin managed to stick to coinduction by adopting coupled simulation, which relaxes the demand of weak bisimulation on internal choice points. More generally, coupled simulation can be an alternative to weak bisimulation when reasoning on processes that have sequences of internal moves in which some of the derivatives attained are not bisimilar with the initial and the final processes. The example below, from [PS92, NP00], which is a (very) simplified version of the multiway synchronisation in [PS92], illustrates the case.

Consider the processes M_0 and N_0:

$$M_0 \stackrel{\text{def}}{=} \tau.a + \tau.b + \tau.c,$$
$$N_0 \stackrel{\text{def}}{=} (\nu e, f)(e.f \mid \overline{e}.a \mid \overline{e}.(\overline{f}.b \mid \overline{f}.c)).$$

Their behaviour is depicted in Figure 6.1, where symbolic names are used for the derivatives. Both M_0 and N_0 internally commit to one out of three possible future behaviours. However, the specification, M_0, does so *atomically*, in one internal move. In contrast, the commitment of the implementation, N_0, is *gradual*, through competitions between pairs of processes for the inputs at e and f. Thus N_0 may need two steps to complete the commitment, which appear as distinguished choice points in the LTS for N_0.

The difference between M and N matters in all forms of weak bisimilarity examined in Chapter 4: the transition of $N_0 \Longrightarrow BC$ cannot be matched by M_0. (We may consider an exception: the variant of weak bisimilarity without the bisimulation game on τ-actions, in Definition 4.6.1, which does relate M_0 and N_0. We however discarded this variant because it is not preserved by important operators such as parallel composition.)

Exercise 6.5.1 Are M_0 and N_0 weakly ready similar? □

Remark 6.5.2 The sensitiveness of weak bisimilarities to internal choice points may indeed be disturbing in practice. For instance, we might be unable to use bisimulation to prove that an implementation and a specification of a system are equal if a certain atomic step in the specification requires some negotiations among components in the implementation. Situations like this, involving a gradual pre-emption or a gradual commitment, are particularly relevant in protocols for distributed systems.   □

Nevertheless M_0 and N_0 are simulation equivalent, as witnessed by the two relations

$$S_1 \stackrel{\text{def}}{=} \bigcup_{0 \leq i \leq 6}\{(M_i, N_i)\}\},$$
$$S_2 \stackrel{\text{def}}{=} \{(M_0, BC)\} \cup S_1.$$

It is easy to see that S_1 and S_2^{-1} are simulations. (Note that S_1 and S_2 are different; were they equal then we would have a bisimulation.) A result about simulation equivalence is in itself not satisfactory, having rejected simulation equivalence as a behavioural equivalence for processes. We can, however, prove that M and N are a bit more than simulation equivalent: they are coupled simulation equivalent. Coupled simulation equivalence refines simulation equivalence by adding check points that force certain ties between the two simulations. These ties also remedy the deadlock problems of simulation equivalence.

Definition 6.5.3 (Coupled simulation)   A *coupled simulation* is a pair $(\mathcal{R}_1, \mathcal{R}_2)$ in which $\mathcal{R}_1$ and $\mathcal{R}_2^{-1}$ are simulations and such that:

(1) $P \mathrel{\mathcal{R}_1} Q$ implies there is Q' with $Q \Longrightarrow Q'$ and $P \mathrel{\mathcal{R}_2} Q'$;
(2) the converse on $\mathcal{R}_2$, that is: $P \mathrel{\mathcal{R}_2} Q$ implies there is P' with $P \Longrightarrow P'$ and $P' \mathrel{\mathcal{R}_1} Q$.

Coupled similarity is the union of all coupled simulations. Two processes P and Q are *coupled simulation equivalent*, written $P \approx_{\text{cs}} Q$, if there is a coupled simulation $(\mathcal{R}_1, \mathcal{R}_2)$ with (P, Q) both in $\mathcal{R}_1$ and $\mathcal{R}_2$.   □

The coupling property of a coupled simulation $(\mathcal{R}_1, \mathcal{R}_2)$ is, pictorially, thus:

If P and Q are related in $\mathcal{R}_1$ then Q must exhibit a derivative Q' that is related with P in $\mathcal{R}_2$; in turn, P must exhibit a derivative P'' that is related to Q' in $\mathcal{R}_1$; and so forth. Note that pairs of stable processes should appear in both relations.

The pair of relations (S_1, S_2) above, used to prove that M_0 and N_0 are simulation equivalent, is nearly a coupled simulation. The only pair that does not appear in both relations is the pair (M_0, BC) of S_2; so this is the only case in which the coupling requirement has to be checked. We have to find a derivative M' of M_0 with $(M', BC) \in S_1$. This forces us to add an extra pair to S_1; we can add either (M_2, BC), or (M_3, BC), or both. Suppose we add the first one. Then we have to check the coupling requirement also on it. The check is successful because for the derivative N_2 of BC we have $M_2 \, S_2 \, N_2$. Moreover, S_1 remains a simulation after the addition of the pair. We can therefore conclude that M_0 and N_0 are coupled simulation equivalent. We write $\leq_{cs}$ for the 'one-way' coupled similarity, where $P \leq_{cs} Q$ if $P \, \mathcal{R} \, Q$ for some coupled simulation $(\mathcal{R}, \mathcal{R}')$, and $\geq_{cs}$ for the inverse of $\leq_{cs}$.

Exercise 6.5.4 Show that $(\leq_{cs}, \geq_{cs})$ is the largest coupled simulation, and that $\approx_{cs} = \leq_{cs} \cap \geq_{cs}$. □

Exercise 6.5.5 ($\hookrightarrow$) Show that $\approx_{cs}$ is transitive. □

Lemma 6.5.6 *Coupled simulation equivalence is an equivalence relation.* □

Exercise 6.5.7 Show that $(P \oplus Q) \oplus R \approx_{cs} P \oplus (Q \oplus R)$, where $\oplus$ is the internal choice operator of Exercise 5.8.10. □

Exercise 6.5.8 (Recommended, $\hookrightarrow$) Show that the axiom of testing equivalence in Exercise 5.8.9 (namely, $\mu.P + \mu.Q = \mu.(\tau.P + \tau.Q)$) is not valid for weak ready simulation or coupled simulation equivalence. Can we, however, use coupled similarity? □

Exercise 6.5.9 Define a fixed-point characterisation of coupled simulation equivalence, akin to Theorem 2.10.3 for strong bisimilarity; prove also the analogue of Lemma 2.10.1. □

As usual, to obtain a full congruence in CCS we have to add a 'root' condition. It can be formulated differently with respect to the ordinary root conditions for bisimilarities, in terms of stability. We recall that a process is *stable* if it cannot perform τ-actions.

Definition 6.5.10 (Rooted coupled simulation) Two processes P and Q are *rooted coupled simulation equivalent* if

(1) $P \approx_{cs} Q$;
(2) P is stable iff Q is stable. □

Exercise 4.4.13 shows that the analogous characterisation for weak bisimilarity fails.

Exercise 6.5.11 ($*$, $\hookrightarrow$)

(1) Show that coupled simulation equivalence is preserved by all CCS operators but summation, and rooted coupled simulation equivalence is preserved by all CCS operators. (The interesting and novel part here is to show that rooted coupled simulation equivalence is preserved by summation, so the reader may want to try this point only.)
(2) Show that rooted coupled simulation equivalence is strictly included in coupled simulation equivalence. □

Exercise 6.5.12 ($\hookrightarrow$) Show that rooted coupled simulation equivalence is the largest congruence included in coupled simulation equivalence. (Hint: follow the same proof strategy as in the analogous result for rooted weak bisimilarity and weak bisimilarity.) □

Exercise 6.5.13 Show that $\tau.(\tau.P + Q) = \tau.P + Q$ is valid for rooted coupled simulation equivalence but not for rooted weak bisimilarity.   □

The axiom in Exercise 6.5.13 tells us that certain internal choices in processes are irrelevant: precisely, a τ-move may be ignored if the derivative has a further τ-move. In the axiomatisation of rooted coupled simulation equivalence over finite CCS processes [PS94], the above axiom captures precisely the difference between the rooted versions of coupled simulation equivalence and weak bisimilarity.

The original definition of coupled similarity [PS92] requires the coupling only on stable processes. It is also called *S-coupled simulation equivalence*, to remind us that it is 'coupled by stability'.

Definition 6.5.14 (S-coupled simulation) An *S-coupled simulation* is a pair $(\mathcal{R}_1, \mathcal{R}_2)$ in which $\mathcal{R}_1$ and $\mathcal{R}_2^{-1}$ are simulations and such that:

(1) $P \mathcal{R}_1 Q$ and P stable implies $P \mathcal{R}_2 Q$;
(2) the converse on $\mathcal{R}_2$, that is: $P \mathcal{R}_2 Q$ and Q stable implies $P \mathcal{R}_1 Q$.

S-coupled similarity is the union of all S-coupled simulations. Two processes P and Q are *S-coupled simulation equivalent*, written $P \approx_{\text{Scs}} Q$, if P and Q are related by both components of an S-coupled simulation.   □

In clause (1), P alone is stable. Without divergences, coupled and S-coupled simulation equivalences coincide. We write $\leq_{\text{Scs}}$ the 'one-way' S-coupled similarity where $P \leq_{\text{Scs}} Q$ if $P \mathcal{R} Q$ for some S-coupled simulation $(\mathcal{R}, \mathcal{R}')$.

Exercise 6.5.15 $(*, \hookrightarrow)$ On divergence-free LTSs, show that:

(1) $\leq_{\text{cs}}$ does not imply $\leq_{\text{Scs}}$;
(2) $\approx_{\text{cs}}$ implies $\approx_{\text{Scs}}$;
(3) $\approx_{\text{Scs}}$ implies $\approx_{\text{cs}}$.   □

In applications, however, S-coupled simulations may be more convenient to use than coupled simulations because the former may have fewer pairs. For instance, on the processes M_0 and N_0 of Figure 6.1, exactly the same relations $\mathcal{S}_1$ and $\mathcal{S}_2$ that we used to prove that the processes are simulation equivalent also prove that they are S-coupled simulation equivalent. For proving that they are coupled-simulation equivalent, in contrast, we had to add at least one pair to $\mathcal{S}_1$.

The problem with $\approx_{\text{Scs}}$ is that it does not work well outside divergence-free LTSs. In particular, transitivity can break.

Exercise 6.5.16 Show that transitivity of $\approx_{\text{Scs}}$ may break without the assumption on divergence. (Hint: you may show that $a.b \approx_{\text{Scs}} a.b + a.\Omega_\tau \approx_{\text{Scs}} a.b + a$, but $a.b \not\approx_{\text{Scs}} a.b + a$.)   □

Exercise 6.5.17 Show that $a.b + a.\Omega_\tau \approx_{\text{Scs}} a.(\Omega_\tau + b)$.   □

On divergence-free LTSs, $\approx_{\text{Scs}}$ is actually transitive, as follows from Exercises 6.5.5 and 6.5.15. However, $\leq_{\text{Scs}}$ is not transitive even on divergent-free LTSs.

Exercise 6.5.18 Show that $0 \leq_{\text{Scs}} \tau \leq_{\text{Scs}} \tau + a$, but not $0 \leq_{\text{Scs}} \tau + a$. □

Coupled simulation equivalence is strictly coarser than weak bisimilarity and, on divergence-free LTSs, it is strictly finer than testing equivalence. It is, however, incomparable with weak ready simulation equivalence and weak two-nested simulation equivalence. On LTSs without internal moves, coupled simulation equivalence degenerates to bisimilarity and is therefore strictly finer than ready and two-nested simulation equivalences. However, on non-stable processes, the simulation game of coupled simulation may not be sufficient to guarantee, for instance, that related processes have the same ready sets, see for instance Exercise 6.5.7.

In comparison with bisimilarity, coupled simulation requires us to work with two relations. Proofs can therefore be more tedious. Proofs can also be conceptually more complex, especially when coinductive arguments have to be combined with inductive ones. A good example is the completeness proof of axiomatisations (for coupled simulation in [PS94], for weak bisimulation in Theorem 4.5.3 or in [Mil89]).

Exercise 6.5.19 (∗, ↪) **(Stable bisimulation and contrasimulation, continuing Exercise 4.6.4)** Consider the following refinement of the bisimulation in Exercise 4.6.4, using s for a sequence of visible actions. A process relation $\mathcal{R}$ is a *stable bisimulation* if, whenever $P \mathcal{R} Q$, for all s we have:

- for all P' with $P \overset{s}{\Rightarrow} P'$ and P' is stable, there is Q' such that $Q \overset{s}{\Rightarrow} Q'$ and $P' \mathcal{R} Q'$,

and the converse on the actions from Q. *Stable bisimilarity* is the union of all stable bisimulations. Show that on divergence-free LTSs:

(1) stable bisimilarity is an equivalence relation;
(2) the axiom $\mu.P + \mu.Q = \mu.(\tau.P + \tau.Q)$ of Exercise 6.5.8 is valid for stable bisimilarity;
(3) coupled simulation equivalence implies stable bisimilarity;
(4) if $(\mathcal{S}_1, \mathcal{S}_2)$ is an S-coupled simulation, then $\mathcal{S}_1 \cap \mathcal{S}_2$ is a stable bisimulation;
(5) stable bisimilarity is strictly between coupled simulation equivalence and testing equivalence. □

As a note, the problems of stable bisimilarity of the above exercise are that it is defined on sequences of transitions and therefore may be difficult to verify, and it is not transitive on LTSs with divergences. A possible remedy to the latter problem is to use *contrasimulations*. A contrasimulation $\mathcal{R}$ is a kind of simulation in which the simulation game on a pair $(P, Q) \in \mathcal{R}$ requires that a challenge $P \overset{s}{\Rightarrow} P'$ be matched by a transition $Q \overset{s}{\Rightarrow} Q'$ with $Q' \mathcal{R} P'$ (the order on the derivatives is reversed). The equivalence induced by the largest

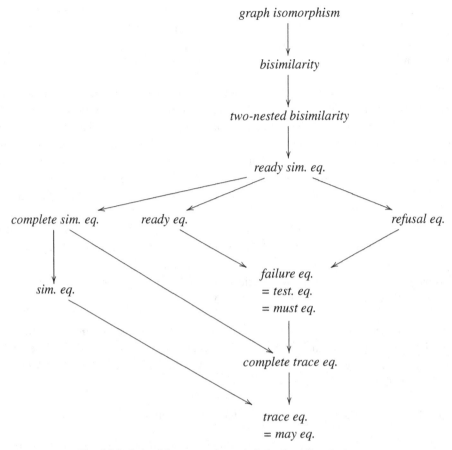

Fig. 6.2 Relationship among the main behavioural equivalences.

contrasimulation (which, as usual, is also the union of all contrasimulations) is contrasimulation equivalence. Both stable bisimulation and contrasimulation are due to van Glabbeek [Gla88, Gla93a].

6.6 The equivalence spectrum

Figure 6.2 summarises the relationship among the equivalences for (strong) LTSs that we have considered in this chapter and in the previous ones. An arrow from a relation to another one means that the former is strictly finer than the latter. Recall that the non-coinductive equivalences have been presented and discussed under the assumption of image-finiteness for the LTSs. Hence this assumption applies to Figure 6.2.

On weak LTSs the full picture is more complicated: there are various ways of taking into account silent transitions in the simulation or bisimulation game (e.g., delay, η, branching, dynamic, coupled); there are congruence issues for the choice operator that bring in additional language-specific relations (the largest congruence included in the equivalences); and finally there may be different ways of dealing with divergence (e.g., weak bisimulation versus divergence-sensitive weak bisimulation). The effect of each of these aspects has been discussed in the dedicated sections. On divergence-free (and image-finite) weak LTSs, Figure 6.2 remains unchanged. Further details on comparisons among behavioural equivalences and preorders may be found in [Gla01a, Gla93a].

7

Basic observables

A transition $P \xrightarrow{\mu} P'$ of an LTS intuitively describes a pure synchronisation between the process P and its external environment along port μ. In concurrent systems one finds many other forms of interaction: asynchronous, with exchange of values, via broadcast, and so on.

Therefore the question naturally arises about how to tune the schema of ordinary bisimulation (Definition 1.4.2) to other interaction models. The issue is relevant also outside concurrency theory. For instance, one may wish to define equality between terms of the λ-calculus as a bisimilarity relation, so as to be able to exploit coinductive techniques. We can then view the computation mechanism of the λ-calculus – functional application – as a special form of interaction, between the function and its argument (see [Pit12]). Similarly, we may want to use bisimulation on list-like structures, as we did in Section 2.6.4. In this case, interaction is given by the operations available on lists, such as the extraction of the head of a list.

However, not only do we look for a notion of equality based on bisimulation that can be used on different interaction models. We also wish such an equality to be a *natural* one. The distinctions on states that it makes must be justifiable in terms of observations that an environment in which the states run can make. When the states are part of a term language, this means that there should be contexts of the language that can separate the states.

In this chapter we present a method for deriving bisimilarity relations that can be applied to virtually all languages whose terms are described by means of a grammar. The idea is to set a bisimulation game in which the observer has a minimal ability to observe actions and/or states. This yields a bisimilarity, namely indistinguishability under such observations, which in turn induces a congruence over terms, namely bisimilarity in all contexts. The bisimilarity is called *barbed bisimilarity*, the congruence *barbed congruence*.

The main assumption underpinning barbed bisimilarity and congruence is the existence, in the language, of a *reduction relation* that expresses an evolution step of a term in which no intervention from the environment is required. In CCS, this relation is $\xrightarrow{\tau}$. The reduction relation represents the most basic and fundamental notion in the operational semantics of a language. In fact, there is an approach to the operational semantics of processes, referred to as *reduction semantics*, which, borrowing ideas from term-rewriting systems, only gives meaning to reductions; that is, it only explains how a system can evolve independently of its environment. This approach is in contrast with the *labelled transition semantics*, which explains both the activity within a system and interaction between a systems and its environment, by describing all actions that processes can perform. A reduction semantics can be more tedious than a labelled transition semantics to work with, but makes it easier to grasp the meaning of a calculus or language. See [Mil99, SW01] for details and comparisons of the two approaches. Another advantage of barbed congruence is that it fits well in a reduction semantics.

In barbed bisimilarity the bisimulation game is only played on reductions. Equal processes should, however, also exhibit the same *barbs* – certain predicates representing basic observables of the states. The barbs are needed to obtain the appropriate discriminating power. Barbed congruence is a contextual equivalence: it is the context-closure of barbed bisimilarity. As we shall see, however, tuning the basic observables so to yield an equality that is natural and robust (i.e., it is the 'desired' equality in all languages) requires some care.

In Section 7.1 we further discuss why a method for uniformly deriving bisimilarity in different languages is desirable. We show that adapting the bisimulation schema of Definition 1.4.2 to a given language in an ad hoc manner may be troublesome. It may be that different choices for a bisimulation are possible. Or it may be that a form of bisimulation that looks reasonable turns out to be overdiscriminating or to lack desirable mathematical properties such as congruence.

We begin to move towards barbed congruence in Section 7.2, with *reduction congruence*, which is is an even simpler form of contextual bisimilarity than barbed congruence, as no barbs are considered. We show that reduction congruence does not give the desired discriminating power and this will pave the way to the introduction of barbed congruence. We present barbed congruence in Section 7.3. The main result is the characterisation of barbed congruence in terms of the ordinary labelled bisimilarity, on image-finite processes. In Section 7.4 we show a Context Lemma that allows us to reduce the set of contexts in the definition of barbed congruence. We also discuss, in Sections 7.5–7.6, variants of barbed congruence, notably weak versions, intended to capture weak bisimilarity (and its rooted variant), and *reduction-closed barbed congruence*, where the closure under contexts is part of the definition itself of bisimilarity. Finally, Section 7.7 contains some concluding remarks on the use and meaning of barbed congruence.

In the remainder of this section we use the term *labelled bisimilarity* to indicate a bisimilarity that, as the ordinary one of Definition 1.4.2, is not contextual (i.e., it does not use quantification over contexts) and has a bisimulation game in which the labels of the transitions matter. The term serves to contrast these bisimilarities with barbed congruence, which is contextual and its bisimulation game, being only played on reductions, does not involve labels.

As the relations in this chapter are mostly contextual, they depend on the process language chosen. It is intended that the language for the whole chapter is CCS (the choice of the set of constants for infinite behaviour, in contrast, is not important; the set could also be empty).

7.1 Labelled bisimilarities: examples of problems

To see the kind of problem that one may encounter in the quest of a satisfactory labelled bisimilarity for a given language, we briefly discuss two cases: CCS with value passing and higher-order process languages.

7.1.1 CCS with value passing

The difficulties already show up if we add a very simple form of value passing to CCS, where boolean values may be communicated. The basic operators of CCS remain the same but the input and output prefixes now take the form $a(x).P$ and $\overline{a}\langle e\rangle.P$, and a conditional construct if e then P else Q is added. The input $a(x).P$ indicates a process that is willing to receive at a a value that will replace the variable x in the continuation P. The output $\overline{a}\langle e\rangle.P$ indicates a process that is willing to emit at a the result of evaluating the boolean expression e, with P being the derivative. Concerning the transitions that such prefixes originate, a common approach is to stipulate that they are, respectively,

$$a(x).P \xrightarrow{a(x)} P \qquad \text{and} \qquad \overline{a}\langle v\rangle.P \xrightarrow{\overline{a}\langle v\rangle} P,$$

where v ranges over the boolean values $\texttt{true}$ and $\texttt{false}$. Accordingly, the input clause for bisimilarity could be (we only examine the input clause because it is the delicate one):

- if $P \mathrel{\mathcal{R}} Q$ and $P \xrightarrow{a(x)} P'$, then there is Q' such that $Q \xrightarrow{a(x)} Q'$ and for all v it holds that $P\{v/x\} \mathrel{\mathcal{R}} Q\{v/x\}$.

However, the order of the quantifiers following the transition from the challenger P could be swapped:

- if $P \mathrel{\mathcal{R}} Q$ and $P \xrightarrow{a(x)} P'$, then for all v there is Q' such that $Q \xrightarrow{a(x)} Q'$ and $P\{v/x\} \mathrel{\mathcal{R}} Q\{v/x\}$.

The bisimilarity resulting from the first choice is called *late bisimilarity*, the other *early bisimilarity*. To see that the choice matters, consider the terms

$$P \stackrel{\text{def}}{=} a(x).\overline{b}\langle x\rangle.0 + a(x).0,$$

$$\begin{aligned} Q \stackrel{\text{def}}{=} \ & a(x).\overline{b}\langle x\rangle.0 + a(x).0 \\ & + a(x).\,\text{if } x = \texttt{true} \text{ then } \overline{b}\langle x\rangle.0 \text{ else } 0. \end{aligned}$$

The two processes are early, but not late, bisimilar. In the early bisimilarity, the transition

$$Q \xrightarrow{a(x)} \text{if } x = \texttt{true} \text{ then } \overline{b}\langle x\rangle.0 \text{ else } 0$$

can be matched by P using the transition $P \xrightarrow{a(x)} \overline{b}\langle x\rangle.0$ or $P \xrightarrow{a(x)} 0$, depending on whether the value v that should instantiate x is $\texttt{true}$ or $\texttt{false}$. This is not possible with late bisimilarity, where P is required to exhibit a single transition, to be used for all values v. In general late bisimilarity is strictly included in the early one.

The example shows that in CCS with value passing it may not be clear which labelled bisimilarity should be adopted. In languages such as the π-calculus, besides late and early, other formats are possible, for instance the *open bisimilarity* [SW01]. In such situations, barbed congruence can guide us in the choice of a bisimilarity. Incidentally, in CCS and π-calculus barbed congruence corresponds to early bisimilarity, see [SW01].

7.1.2 Higher-order process languages

In ordinary bisimulation, as by Definition 1.4.2, two processes are *bisimilar* if any action by one of them can be matched by an equal action from the other in such a way that the resulting derivatives are again bisimilar. The two matching actions must be syntactically *identical*. This condition is too strong in higher-order languages, where the values exchanged may contain processes. Consider a simple process-passing calculus with operators similar to those of CCS and an output primitive $\overline{a}\langle P\rangle.Q$ to indicate a term that can perform an output action at a emitting a process P and then continues as Q. Now, if R_1 and R_2 are two syntactically different processes, then the bisimilarity of Definition 1.4.2 would distinguish processes $\overline{a}\langle R_1 \mid R_2\rangle.0$ and $\overline{a}\langle R_2 \mid R_1\rangle.0$, since the transitions they perform, namely

$$\overline{a}\langle R_1 \mid R_2\rangle.0 \xrightarrow{\overline{a}\langle R_1 \mid R_2\rangle} 0 \quad \text{and} \quad \overline{a}\langle R_2 \mid R_1\rangle.0 \xrightarrow{\overline{a}\langle R_2 \mid R_1\rangle} 0,$$

have different labels. This means that a basic algebraic law such as the commutativity of parallel composition would not hold. (Furthermore, the bisimilarity so obtained would not be a congruence relation.)

One might think of resolving the above problem by requiring that the processes emitted in an output action be *bisimilar*, rather than *identical*. (This is the approach taken by Thomsen [Tho90], following earlier ideas by Astesiano and Boudol [AGR88, Bou89].) This form of bisimilarity, called *higher-order bisimilarity*, in general remains unsatisfactory: it still gives congruence problems, and is over-discriminating. We refer to [San96] for more details.

In summary, in a higher-order process language it is not at all clear what the clauses of a labelled bisimilarity should be, as matching transitions might have quite different labels. Again, a contextually-defined equivalence such as barbed congruence can serve as a guide; see [San92, JR03, MZ05, SKS07a, RS08] for examples of labelled bisimilarities that characterise barbed congruence in higher-order process calculi.

7.2 Reduction congruence

In this section we address the following question, in CCS. What minimal power of observation on processes is needed so as to obtain a relation whose induced congruence coincides with the familiar bisimilarity $\sim$?

We examine first the case in which only the silent action, the simplest forms of action, appears.

Definition 7.2.1 (Reduction bisimulation) A process relation $\mathcal{R}$ is *reduction bisimulation* if whenever $P \, \mathcal{R} \, Q$:

(1) for all P' with $P \xrightarrow{\tau} P'$, there is Q' such that $Q \xrightarrow{\tau} Q'$ and $P' \, \mathcal{R} \, Q'$;
(2) the converse, on the τ-transitions emanating from Q, i.e., for all Q' with $Q \xrightarrow{\tau} Q'$, there is P' such that $P \xrightarrow{\tau} P'$ and $P' \, \mathcal{R} \, Q'$.

Reduction bisimilarity, written $\dot{\sim}^\tau$, is the union of all reduction bisimulations.   □

As a process equivalence, reduction bisimilarity is seriously defective: for instance, it relates any two processes that have no τ transitions, such as $a.\mathbf{0}$ and $\mathbf{0}$. Moreover it is not even preserved by parallel composition.

Example 7.2.2 For $P \stackrel{\text{def}}{=} a.\mathbf{0}$ and $Q \stackrel{\text{def}}{=} b.\mathbf{0}$, it holds that $P \dot{\sim}^\tau Q$, but

$$P \,|\, \overline{a} \not\dot{\sim}^\tau Q \,|\, \overline{a}.$$ □

The congruence induced by $\dot{\sim}^\tau$, in contrast, is more interesting.

Definition 7.2.3 (Reduction congruence) Two processes P and Q are *reduction congruent*, written $P \sim^\tau Q$, if for each context C, it holds that $C[P] \dot{\sim}^\tau C[Q]$.   □

Reduction congruence distinguishes, for instance, between $a.\mathbf{0}$ and $b.\mathbf{0}$: a context that distinguishes them is $C \stackrel{\text{def}}{=} [\cdot] \,|\, \overline{a}.\mathbf{0}$.

Notation 7.2.4 In this chapter we use a dot to denote an equivalence that is not necessarily a congruence; so in this case, and for future equivalences, the absence of a dot means a congruence.   □

Lemma 7.2.5 $\sim \, \subseteq \, \sim^\tau$.

Proof Clearly, $\sim \, \subseteq \, \dot{\sim}^\tau$. Since $\sim$ is a congruence, $P \sim Q$ implies $C[P] \sim C[Q]$, which in turns implies $C[P] \dot{\sim}^\tau C[Q]$, for every context C.   □

The converse of Lemma 7.2.5 is, however, false. For instance, reduction congruence does not distinguish between Ω_τ and $\Omega_\tau \,|\, a.\mathbf{0}$. Indeed since $\Omega_\tau \xrightarrow{\tau} \Omega_\tau$, for any P the process $\Omega_\tau \,|\, P$ is reduction congruent to Ω_τ. More generally, reduction congruence does not distinguish between always-divergent processes.

Definition 7.2.6 The set of *always-divergent* processes is the largest set S of processes such that $P \in S$ implies $P \xrightarrow{\tau} P'$, for some P', and $P \xrightarrow{\mu} P''$ implies $P'' \in S$, for any μ, P''.   □

Exercise 7.2.7 Show that a process is always-divergent iff all its multi-step derivatives are divergent.   □

Processes that are always-divergent are not necessarily bisimilar (see the proof of Corollary 7.2.10). However, they are reduction congruent; intuitively since any state they can reach is divergent, no CCS context can make the distinction between them as long as only τ actions are taken into account.

Theorem 7.2.8 *If P and Q are always-divergent, then $P \sim^\tau Q$.*

Proof [Sketch] We prove that

$$\mathcal{R} \stackrel{\text{def}}{=} \{(C[P], C[Q]) \mid C \text{ is a context, and } P, Q \text{ are always-divergent}\}$$

is a reduction bisimulation.

Let $C[P] \, \mathcal{R} \, C[Q]$. Suppose that $C[P] \stackrel{\tau}{\to} C'[P]$ and C itself has produced the τ-action (i.e. P has not been 'used'): then also $C[Q] \stackrel{\tau}{\to} C'[Q]$ and $C'[P] \, \mathcal{R} \, C'[Q]$.

Suppose now that $C[P] \stackrel{\tau}{\to} C'[P']$ and P has contributed to such action (either with an interaction with C or by simply performing itself the τ-action): then P' cannot appear as a subterm in a summation and hence it cannot be discharged by C'. Since P' is always-divergent, this means that also $C'[P']$ is always-divergent. It remains to find a process R always-divergent such that $C[Q] \stackrel{\tau}{\to} R$, as this would yield $C'[P'] \, \mathcal{R} \, R$ (in the definition of $\mathcal{R}$ take the empty context $[\cdot]$).

Now, since P has contributed to the action of $C[P]$, P is not underneath a prefix in $C[P]$. Therefore the same is true for Q, which can perform actions. Therefore if $Q \stackrel{\tau}{\to} Q'$, then for some C'', also $C[Q] \stackrel{\tau}{\to} C''[Q']$. Moreover, for the same reason as $C'[P']$, also $C''[Q']$ is always-divergent. For $R \stackrel{\text{def}}{=} C''[Q']$, this concludes the proof. $\qquad\square$

Exercise 7.2.9 Refine and complete the details of the proof sketch above. $\qquad\square$

Corollary 7.2.10 $\sim^\tau \, \not\subseteq \, \sim$.

Proof Take Ω_τ and the constant K with transitions $K \stackrel{a}{\to} \Omega_\tau$ and $K \stackrel{\tau}{\to} K$. Then K is always-divergent. By Theorem 7.2.8, $\Omega_\tau \sim^\tau K$; however $\Omega_\tau \not\sim K$. $\qquad\square$

Exercise 7.2.11 (Recommended, $\hookrightarrow$) Show that reduction congruence would distinguish the processes Ω_τ and K in the proof of Corollary 7.2.10 if we add to CCS a *disabling* operator $\rhd$, very similar in the intent to Lotos's disrupting operator [BB89], and described by the following rules:

$$\frac{Q \stackrel{\mu}{\to} Q'}{P \rhd Q \stackrel{\mu}{\to} P \rhd Q'} \qquad\qquad \frac{P \stackrel{\mu}{\to} P' \quad Q \stackrel{\bar{u}}{\to} Q'}{P \rhd Q \stackrel{\tau}{\to} P'}$$

$\qquad\square$

In the case of weak bisimilarities, where we abstract from internal activity by allowing a τ-transition of one process to be matched by any number (even 0) of τ-transitions of another, the problem with reduction congruence is worse: it makes no distinctions among processes, and coincides with the universal relation.

7.3 Barbed congruence

To obtain a satisfactory notion in the vein of reduction congruence it is therefore necessary to allow some properties of the states to be observable. It is natural in concurrency that the extra power provided is in terms of action observability. We allow the observer to detect whether a process can perform an observable action; this gives barbed bisimilarity. We recall that ℓ ranges over CCS names and conames (the visible actions).

Definition 7.3.1 (Observability predicates, barb-preserving relation)

(1) For each visible action ℓ, the *observability predicate* (or *barb*) $\downarrow_\ell$ holds on a process P if $P \xrightarrow{\ell}$.

(2) A process relation $\mathcal{R}$ is *barb preserving* if whenever $P \mathcal{R} Q$, for all ℓ it holds that $P \downarrow_\ell$ iff $Q \downarrow_\ell$. $\qquad\square$

For instance, $a.c.\mathbf{0} + b.\mathbf{0}$ has observables a and b – it is capable of receiving via a and via b – while $\overline{a}.b.\mathbf{0}$ has observable $\overline{a}$ – it can send via a. The restricted composition $\nu a\,((a.c.\mathbf{0} + b.\mathbf{0})\,|\,\overline{a}.b.\mathbf{0})$ of these processes has only the observable b; its continuation after a reduction, $\nu a\,(c.\mathbf{0}\,|\,b.\mathbf{0})$ has the observables c and b.

We modify reduction bisimilarity to take observability into account in the following definition.

Definition 7.3.2 (Barbed bisimilarity) A reduction bisimulation $\mathcal{R}$ is a *barbed bisimulation* if it is barb preserving. *Barbed bisimilarity*, written $\overset{\cdot}{\sim}$, is the union of all barbed bisimulations. $\qquad\square$

Thus a relation is a barbed bisimulation just if it is a reduction bisimulation that respects observability. That is, $P \overset{\cdot}{\sim} Q$ holds if P and Q have the same observables, and to each τ transition of one there corresponds a τ transition of the other to a barbed-bisimilar process. For example,

$$\nu b\,(\overline{b}.\mathbf{0}\,|\,b.c.\mathbf{0}) \overset{\cdot}{\sim} \tau.c.\mathbf{0}.$$

Like reduction bisimilarity, barbed bisimilarity is unsatisfactory as a process equivalence. For instance, we have $a.b.\mathbf{0} \overset{\cdot}{\sim} a.c.\mathbf{0}$. Barbed bisimilarity, however, underpins barbed congruence, which is a satisfactory equivalence.

Exercise 7.3.3 ($\hookrightarrow$)

(1) Show that $\overset{\cdot}{\sim}$ is an equivalence relation, and is preserved by the CCS operators of prefixing, sum, and restriction.

(2) Show that, however, $\overset{\cdot}{\sim}$ is not preserved by parallel composition. $\qquad\square$

Definition 7.3.4 (Barbed congruence) Processes P and Q are *barbed congruent*, written $P \simeq Q$, if $C[P] \stackrel{.}{\sim} C[Q]$ for every context C. □

Directly from the definition:

Lemma 7.3.5 $\simeq$ *is the largest congruence included in* $\stackrel{.}{\sim}$. □

Exercise 7.3.6 Show that $\sim \,\subseteq\, \simeq$. □

The proof that $P \simeq Q$ is contained in $\sim$ is more difficult. The proof below requires image-finiteness so as to be able to use the stratification of bisimilarity, that is, the fact that $\sim$ is the same as $\sim_\omega$. The crux of the proof is showing by induction on n that if $P \not\sim_n Q$ then $C[P] \not\stackrel{.}{\sim} C[Q]$ for some context C (Lemma 7.3.7).

We recall that $\Sigma_{i \in I} P_i$ abbreviates summation $P_{i_1} + \cdots + P_{i_r}$ where $I = \{i_1, \ldots, i_r\}$. We use M, N to range over summations. In a statement, we say that a name a is *fresh* if it does not occur in the sort of the processes in the statement.

Lemma 7.3.7 *Suppose that, for $n \geq 0$, $P \not\sim_n Q$ and P, Q are image-finite. Then there is a summation M such that for any fresh c,*

$$P \,|\, (M + c) \not\stackrel{.}{\sim} Q \,|\, (M + c).$$

Proof By induction on n. For $n = 0$ there is nothing to prove, so suppose that $n > 0$. Then there are μ and P' such that $P \stackrel{\mu}{\rightarrow} P'$ but $P' \not\sim_{n-1} Q'$ for all Q' such that $Q \stackrel{\mu}{\rightarrow} Q'$ (or vice versa, the argument is the same). Since $\stackrel{\mu}{\rightarrow}$ is image-finite, $\{Q' \,|\, Q \stackrel{\mu}{\rightarrow} Q'\} = \{Q_i \,|\, i \in I\}$ for some finite set I. Appealing to the induction hypothesis, for each $i \in I$ let M_i be a summation such that for any fresh name d,

$$P' \,|\, (M_i + d) \not\stackrel{.}{\sim} Q_i \,|\, (M_i + d). \tag{7.1}$$

We distinguish the case in which μ is a visible action and that of τ-action.

Case 1 Suppose that μ is a visible action. Let c_i ($i \in I$) be fresh names, and set

$$M \stackrel{\text{def}}{=} \overline{\mu}.\Sigma_{i \in I} \, \tau.(M_i + c_i).$$

We show that M is as required in the claim. So suppose that c is fresh. Let $A \stackrel{\text{def}}{=} P \,|\, (M + c)$ and $B \stackrel{\text{def}}{=} Q \,|\, (M + c)$, and suppose, for a contradiction, that $A \stackrel{.}{\sim} B$. We have

$$A \stackrel{\tau}{\rightarrow} A' \stackrel{\text{def}}{=} P' \,|\, \Sigma_{i \in I} \, \tau.(M_i + c_i).$$

Since $A \stackrel{.}{\sim} B$ there is B' such that $B \stackrel{\tau}{\Rightarrow} B' \stackrel{.}{\sim} A'$. Since $A' \downarrow_c$ does not hold, $B' \downarrow_c$ should not hold either. The only way this is possible is if $I \neq \emptyset$ and

$$B' \stackrel{\text{def}}{=} Q_j \,|\, \Sigma_{i \in I} \, \tau.(M_i + c_i)$$

for some $j \in I$. We now exploit the inductive hypothesis on P', Q_j and M_j. We have

$$A' \xrightarrow{\iota} A''_j \overset{\text{def}}{=} P' \,|\, (M_j + c_j).$$

Since $A' \overset{\centerdot}{\sim} B'$ there is B''_j such that $B' \xrightarrow{\tau} B''_j \overset{\centerdot}{\sim} A''_j$. In particular, since $A''_j \downarrow_{c_j}$ we must have $B''_j \downarrow_{c_j}$. The only possibility is

$$B''_j \overset{\text{def}}{=} Q_j \,|\, (M_j + c_j).$$

But $A''_j \not\overset{\centerdot}{\sim} B''_j$ by (7.1), a contradiction. Hence $A \not\overset{\centerdot}{\sim} B$, as required.

Case 2 Suppose that μ is τ. Let c_i ($i \in I$) be fresh names, and set

$$M \overset{\text{def}}{=} \Sigma_{i \in I} \,\tau.(M_i + c_i).$$

The argument is then similar.

$\square$

Exercise 7.3.8 Complete case (2) of the above proof. $\square$

Theorem 7.3.9 (Characterisation Theorem for barbed congruence) *On image-finite processes, relations $\simeq$ and $\sim$ coincide.*

Proof The inclusion $\sim \subseteq \simeq$ is in Exercise 7.3.6. For the opposite inclusion, suppose that $P \not\sim Q$. Then by Exercise 2.10.18, $P \not\sim_n Q$ for some n. Then let M be as given by Lemma 7.3.7, let c be fresh, and set $C \overset{\text{def}}{=} [\cdot] \,|\, (M + c)$. Then $C[P] \not\overset{\centerdot}{\sim} C[Q]$, and so $P \not\simeq Q$. $\square$

Exercise 7.3.10 ($\hookrightarrow$) Prove the variant of Theorem 7.3.9 on the set of processes that are image-finite up-to $\sim$ rather than just image-finite. $\square$

It is not known whether Theorem 7.3.9 holds without the image-finiteness (or image-finiteness up-to $\sim$) hypothesis. The hypothesis can, however, be dropped if we assume that for each P the set

$$\{P' \mid P \xrightarrow{\mu} P' \text{ for some } \mu\}$$

is countable and allow infinite sums in the calculus. That is, we replace the sum $P + P'$ by

$$\Sigma_{i \in I} P_i,$$

where I is a countable set, as in the original CCS language of [Mil89]. See [SW01, Section 2.4.2] for more details. The main difference in the Characterisation Theorem 7.3.9 is that one needs to apply the stratification of bisimilarity over the ordinals, rather than the natural numbers.

Although the construction in the proof of Theorem 7.3.9 employs many observables, a *single observable* is sufficient to establish the theorem, at least for processes that have a finite sort. Let us write $P \downarrow$ to mean $P \downarrow_\ell$ for some visible action ℓ. Consider the relation defined like barbed congruence except that in the Definition 7.3.1(2) of barb preserving, the clause '$P \downarrow_\ell$ iff $Q \downarrow_\mu$' is replaced by '$P \downarrow$ iff $Q \downarrow$'. The proof of Theorem 7.3.9 can be adapted to the relation so obtained.

Exercise 7.3.11 $(*, \hookrightarrow)$ Prove the claim above. ☐

The proofs of Lemma 7.3.7 and Theorem 7.3.9 extensively use the $+$ *operator*. This operator is, however, not needed. What *is* needed is a form of internal choice, where a process decides autonomously to follow one of several possible paths, and this can be expressed via other operators (see the internal choice operator of Exercise 5.8.10). This fact is important when one seeks similar results on calculi that lack $+$; for instance, asynchronous calculi such as the asynchronous π-calculus or the Join calculus.

Exercise 7.3.12 $(*)$ Show that on processes that are image-finite and divergence-free (that is, none of their derivatives is divergent) relations $\sim^\tau$ and $\sim$ coincide. (Hint: try to modify the proof of Lemma 7.3.7. The role of the fresh names used in the proof of the lemma can be played by processes of the form $\tau^n.\mathbf{0}$. Note also that under the hypothesis of the exercise, for each process P there is n such that P cannot perform more than n consecutive τ-steps.) ☐

7.4 Barbed equivalence

A way of reducing the quantification over contexts in the definition of barbed congruence is to prove *context lemmas* for it, that is, to show that a subset of all contexts is sufficient to give all discriminating power. This may be useful in languages in which a characterisation theorem in terms of a labelled bisimilarity akin to Theorem 7.3.9 is hard to obtain.

An example of context lemma, for CCS, is the following result. It asserts that two processes are barbed congruent iff the systems obtained by composing with an arbitrary process are barbed bisimilar.

Definition 7.4.1 (Barbed equivalence) Two processes P and Q are *barbed equivalent*, written $P \simeq^e Q$, if $P \mid R \stackrel{.}{\sim} Q \mid R$, for all R. ☐

Theorem 7.4.2 (Context Lemma for barbed congruence) *Relations $\simeq$ and $\simeq^e$ coincide.* ☐

We can re-use the proof of Theorem 7.3.9 to show that $\simeq^e = \sim$, and then from this and Theorem 7.3.9 itself conclude that $\simeq$ and $\simeq^e$ coincide. This would, however, prove the result for image-finite processes, as this condition appears in Theorem 7.3.9. We can, however, discard the condition by directly comparing $\simeq$ and $\simeq^e$.

Exercise 7.4.3 (Recommended, $\hookrightarrow$) Prove Theorem 7.4.2. (Hint: proceed by induction on the structure of the context used in $\simeq$.) ☐

7.5 The weak barbed relations

We briefly discuss how to adapt the barbed machinery to the weak case. The definition of the weak relations is the expected one.

Definition 7.5.1 (Weak barbed bisimilarity and congruence) The definitions of *weak barbed bisimulation* and *weak barbed bisimilarity*, written $\overset{\cdot}{\approx}$, are obtained by replacing, in Definition 7.3.2, 'reduction bisimulation' with 'weak reduction bisimulation', and 'barb preserving' with 'weak-barb preserving', where: 'weak reduction bisimulation' modifies 'reduction bisimulation' by replacing, in Definition 7.2.1(1) the strong transition $Q \overset{\tau}{\to} Q'$ with the weak transition $Q \Longrightarrow Q'$, and similarly in clause (2) of the definition; 'weak-barb preserving' modifies 'barb preserving' by replacing, in Definition 7.3.1(2), the strong observability predicates $\downarrow_\ell$ with the weak predicates $\Downarrow_\ell$ defined as $\Downarrow_\ell \overset{\text{def}}{=} \Longrightarrow \downarrow_\ell$.

Processes P and Q are *weakly barbed congruent*, written $P \cong Q$, if $C[P] \overset{\cdot}{\approx} C[Q]$ for every context C. □

Exercise 7.5.2 Show that in Definition 7.5.1, weak-barb preserving can be set thus: a weak reduction bisimulation $\mathcal{R}$ is weak-barb preserving if whenever $P \mathcal{R} Q$, for all ℓ:

(1) $P \downarrow_\ell$ implies $Q \Downarrow_\ell$;
(2) conversely, $Q \downarrow_\ell$ implies $P \Downarrow_\ell$. □

Since weak barbed congruence is, by definition, preserved by all operators, in CCS it corresponds to rooted weak bisimilarity ($\approx^c$), rather than weak bisimilarity ($\approx$), as the latter is not preserved by the choice operator.

To recover weak bisimilarity we have to restrain the quantification over contexts, disallowing, in summands, holes that are not underneath a prefix. It is more common, however, to simply consider parallel composition contexts, i.e., contexts of the form $[\cdot] \mid R$. This is both mathematically handy (these contexts are easy to handle in proofs) and observationally satisfactory (the process R acts as a tester for the processes compared, akin to the testers in the testing equivalence of Section 5.4).

Definition 7.5.3 (Weak barbed equivalence) Two processes P and Q are *weakly barbed equivalent*, written $P \cong^e Q$, if $P \mid R \overset{\cdot}{\approx} Q \mid R$, for all R. □

Exercise 7.4.3 showed that, in the strong case, barbed equivalence and congruence coincide. In the weak case this only holds if we remove the sum operator, or we only allow guarded forms of sum (see the discussion before Lemma 4.4.3).

Theorem 7.5.4

(1) $P \approx Q$ *implies* $P \cong^e Q$.
(2) $P \approx^c Q$ *implies* $P \cong Q$.

Proof The first assertion follows from Lemma 4.4.1, and the fact that weak bisimilarity is included in weak barbed bisimilarity. The second is similar, using Exercise 4.4.9. □

The proof of the converse of Theorem 7.5.4 is very similar to that of the corresponding result in the strong case: see Theorem 7.3.9. We indicate the main points of difference. Corresponding to Lemma 7.3.7 we have:

Lemma 7.5.5 *Suppose that for $n \geq 0$, $P \not\approx_n Q$, and P, Q are image-finite under weak transitions. Then there is a summation M such that for any fresh name c, one of the following holds:*

(1) $P' | (M + c) \not\approx Q | (M + c)$ *for all P' such that $P \Longrightarrow P'$;*
(2) $P | (M + c) \not\approx Q' | (M + c)$ *for all Q' such that $Q \Longrightarrow Q'$.*

Proof By induction on n. For $n = 0$ there is nothing to prove, so suppose that $n > 0$. Then there are μ and P' such that $P \xrightarrow{\mu} P'$ but $P' \not\approx_{n-1} Q''$ for all Q'' such that $Q \xrightarrow{\hat{\mu}} Q''$ (or vice versa, with the roles of P and Q swapped). By image-finiteness, $\{Q'' \mid Q \xrightarrow{\hat{\mu}} Q''\} = \{Q_i \mid i \in I\}$ for some finite set I. We prove that assertion (2) of the claim holds (in the case when the roles of P and Q are swapped, one would prove assertion (1)). Appealing to the induction hypothesis, for each $i \in I$ let M_i be a summation such that P', Q_i, M_i satisfy the assertion of the lemma.

The argument is similar to that in Lemma 7.3.7. We give the details for the case when μ is a visible action, and show the definition of the process M when $\mu = \tau$.

Case 1 Suppose that μ is a visible action. Let c_i $(i \in I)$ and c' be fresh names, and set

$$M \stackrel{\text{def}}{=} \overline{\mu}.(c' + \Sigma_{i \in I} \, \tau.(M_i + c_i)).$$

Suppose that c is fresh, and let Q' be any process such that $Q \Longrightarrow Q'$. Let $A \stackrel{\text{def}}{=} P | (M + c)$ and $B \stackrel{\text{def}}{=} Q' | (M + c)$, and suppose, for a contradiction, that $A \approx B$. We have

$$A \xrightarrow{\tau} A' \stackrel{\text{def}}{=} P' | (c' + \Sigma_{i \in I} \, \tau.(M_i + c_i))$$

and $A' \Downarrow_{c'}$ but not $A' \Downarrow_c$. Since $A \approx B$ there is B' such that $B \Longrightarrow B' \approx A'$. In particular it must be that $B' \Downarrow_{c'}$ but not $B' \Downarrow_c$. The only way this is possible is if $I \neq \emptyset$ and

$$B' \stackrel{\text{def}}{=} Q_j | (c' + \Sigma_{i \in I} \, \tau.(M_i + c_i))$$

for some $j \in I$ (a derivative of Q' under $\xrightarrow{\mu}$ is also a derivative of Q).

By the induction hypothesis, either (1) or (2) of the claim holds for P', Q_j and M_j. Suppose that (2) holds. We have

$$A' \xrightarrow{\tau} A''_j \stackrel{\text{def}}{=} P' | (M_j + c_j)$$

and $A''_j \Downarrow_{c_j}$ but not $A''_j \Downarrow_{c'}$. Then $B' \Longrightarrow B''_j$ for some B''_j with $B''_j \approx A''_j$. We must have

$$B''_j \stackrel{\text{def}}{=} Q'_j | (M_j + c_j)$$

for some Q'_j such that $Q_j \Longrightarrow Q'_j$. But $A''_j \overset{\cdot}{\approx} B''_j$ contradicts that (2) of the claim holds for P', Q_j and M_j.

Dually, if (1) of the claim holds for P', Q_j and M_j, then we obtain a contradiction by considering how A' can match the transition

$$B' \overset{\tau}{\to} B''_j \overset{\text{def}}{=} Q_j \mid (M_j + c_j).$$

Case 2 Suppose that $\mu = \tau$. Let c_i ($i \in I$) be fresh names, and set

$$M \overset{\text{def}}{=} \Sigma_{i \in I} \, \tau.(M_i + c_i).$$

$\square$

Exercise 7.5.6 ($\hookrightarrow$) Show that $\cong$ is the largest congruence included in $\cong^e$. $\square$

Theorem 7.5.7 (Characterisation Theorem, weak case) *On processes image-finite on weak transitions,*

(1) $\cong^e$ *and* $\approx$ *coincide;*
(2) $\cong$ *and* $\approx^c$ *coincide.*

Proof The first assertion follows from Theorem 7.5.4(1) and Lemma 7.5.5, via the stratification of $\approx$.

The second item follows from (1) since weak barbed congruence is the largest congruence included in weak barbed equivalence, and rooted weak bisimilarity is the largest congruence included in weak bisimilarity. $\square$

As in the strong case, so here Theorem 7.5.7 can be strengthened using the hypothesis of image-finiteness up-to $\approx$. In contrast, it is not known whether in the weak case having a *single observable* is sufficient to establish the theorem (the analogue of Exercise 7.3.11 in the strong case).

Exercise 7.5.8 ($\hookrightarrow$) In the weak case, barbed congruence and barbed equivalence are different, due to the congruence problems with the choice operator. Propose and prove a context lemma for $\cong$, in replacement of the Context Theorem 7.4.2 for the strong case. $\square$

7.6 Reduction-closed barbed congruence

We briefly discuss a variant of barbed congruence in which the quantification over contexts is pushed inside the definition of barbed bisimulation.

Definition 7.6.1 (Reduction-closed barbed bisimilarity) A reduction bisimulation $\mathcal{R}$ is a *reduction-closed barbed bisimulation* if it is barb preserving and context-closed (i.e., $P \, \mathcal{R} \, Q$ implies $C[P] \, \mathcal{R} \, C[Q]$, for all contexts). *Reduction-closed barbed congruence*, written $\simeq_{\text{rc}}$, is the union of all reduction-closed barbed bisimulations. $\square$

Reduction-closed barbed congruence is, essentially by definition, both a congruence and a barbed bisimulation; indeed, it is the largest barbed bisimulation that is a congruence.

The main advantage of reduction-closed barbed congruence over barbed congruence is that a characterisation theorem in terms of labelled bisimilarity can be proved for all processes, without the need of the image-finiteness hypothesis. This can be done using reasoning similar to (in fact, simpler than) that in Theorem 7.3.9. Such a proof is possible because the context surrounding the processes being compared can be changed at any point in the reduction-closed barbed bisimulation game.

Theorem 7.6.2 *Relations $\simeq_{\mathrm{rc}}$ and $\sim$ coincide.*

Proof As usual, the inclusion $\sim \subseteq \simeq_{\mathrm{rc}}$ is easy: $\sim$ is a bisimulation hence it is a reduction bisimulation, preserves barbs, and is a congruence, hence is context-closed.

For the opposite inclusion, we show that $\simeq_{\mathrm{rc}}$ is a bisimulation. Suppose $P \simeq_{\mathrm{rc}} Q$ and $P \xrightarrow{\mu} P'$, for $\mu \neq \tau$. We have to find Q' such that $Q \xrightarrow{\mu} Q'$ and $P' \simeq_{\mathrm{rc}} Q'$. Consider the context $C \overset{\text{def}}{=} [\cdot] \mid (\overline{\mu}.\mathbf{0} + a.\mathbf{0})$ where a is not in the sort of P, Q. We have $C[P] \downarrow_a$ and $C[P] \xrightarrow{\tau} P' \mid \mathbf{0} \not\downarrow_a$. Since $P \simeq_{\mathrm{rc}} Q$, process $C[Q]$ should be able to reduce without producing at the end a barb at a. This can only happen if the reduction consists of an interaction between Q and $\overline{\mu}.\mathbf{0}$ in which Q makes a transition $Q \xrightarrow{\mu} Q'$, for some Q'. We then obtain

$$P' \mid \mathbf{0} \simeq_{\mathrm{rc}} Q' \mid \mathbf{0}. \tag{7.2}$$

We know that for any R, we have $R \mid \mathbf{0} \sim R$ and $\sim \subseteq \simeq_{\mathrm{rc}}$; hence also $R \mid \mathbf{0} \simeq_{\mathrm{rc}} R$. Using this property on (7.2) we conclude $P' \simeq_{\mathrm{rc}} Q'$, and we are done. We leave the case $\mu = \tau$ to the reader. $\qquad\square$

The main disadvantage of reduction-closed barbed congruence is to be less robust than barbed congruence. In some calculi the former is indeed stronger and, arguably, less natural than the latter. This happens for instance in the π-calculus [SW01]. It also happens for weak bisimilarities in languages with dynamic operators such as choice that disappear after producing an action (the weak version of reduction-closed barbed congruence is defined in the expected way). For instance, in CCS, weak reduction-closed barbed congruence violates the equation

$$\mu.\tau.P = \mu.P.$$

Indeed, in CCS weak reduction-closed barbed congruence gives dynamic bisimilarity, rather than the ordinary (rooted) weak bisimilarity. The reason why barbed congruence is more robust is that it keeps the intervention of the external observer to a minimum. (Recall that we started from reduction bisimilarity in Section 7.2.) In reduction-closed barbed congruence, in contrast, the observer has the power to change the context surrounding the processes being tested. Further, as we explain in Section 7.7, the fact that $P \simeq Q$ implies $P \sim Q$ for a large class of processes (though not all processes) is satisfactory: the important point is that $P \sim Q$ implies $P \simeq Q$ for all P and Q.

A way to remedy the problems of weak reduction-closed barbed congruence in languages with the choice operator is to move to reduction-closed barbed equivalence where, analogously to Definition 7.4.1, one only closes barbed bisimilarity with parallel composition contexts. In CCS, we thus obtain weak bisimilarity.

Remark 7.6.3 (Other variations)   The barbed relations have been used in the literature to recover bisimilarity and weak bisimilarity, in various languages. The definitions of the barbed relations can be rectified, in the expected way, to recover other coinductive labelled relations examined in previous chapters. For instance, to recover the similarity preorder it suffices to omit the symmetric clause (2) from Definition 7.2.1, and to replace the 'iff' demand of Definition 7.3.1(2) (barb preserving) with an 'implies'. If the definition of barb preserving is left unchanged, then we recover ready similarity. The changes in the proofs are straightforward.

Somewhat more delicate are the modifications in the proofs needed to recover branching bisimilarity (and the related η and delay bisimilarities). See Exercise 7.6.4 to get a flavour of the kind of reasoning needed.   □

Exercise 7.6.4 ($\hookrightarrow$)   Propose a 'branching' version of weak barbed congruence, in which the bisimulation game on reductions of Definition 7.2.1 is replaced by the bisimulation game on τ-actions as in branching bisimulation. Show that in the resulting branching barbed congruence, the third τ-law, **T3**, is not valid.   □

Remark 7.6.5   If in the definition of weak barbed congruence we omitted the requirement about weak reduction bisimulation, that is, we took the context closure of weak barbed preserving relations, then we would obtain essentially Morris's contextual equivalence [Mor68], generally taken as the reference equality in sequential languages such as the λ-calculus. In CCS, this modified weak barbed congruence would coincide with trace equivalence.   □

7.7 Final remarks

Barbed congruence intuitively says that two processes are equal if they 'evolve in the same way in all contexts'. This is formalised using a bisimulation game – the barbed bisimilarity – on the steps that the two systems, thought of as closed systems, may take. Along the game the two systems must be able to produce the same success signals (the barbs).

Being the bisimulation game played only on internal action – the simplest form of action – barbed congruence can be applied to virtually all languages, both concurrent and sequential, including imperative and object-oriented programming languages. Several examples of such applications can be found in the literature. They also serve us as evidence of the robustness of barbed congruence: it gives us the desired discriminating power. Further, being contextually defined, barbed congruence is 'observational', in the sense that the distinctions it makes on processes can be explained in terms of the existence of suitable contexts that can tell the processes apart.

The quantification over contexts also represents the main drawback of barbed congruence: it makes it difficult to understand the meaning of the equality; and it can make it awkward to prove equalities by applying the definition directly. These problems are motivations for establishing characterisations on barbed congruence in terms of labelled bisimilarities, as we did in Theorem 7.3.9 for CCS.

In general, one actually goes the opposite way: one first defines barbed congruence as *the* behavioural equality on processes. Then one looks for a labelled bisimilarity that characterises it, or approximates it as best as possible. It even becomes an excellent test for the operators of the language to see whether they can express such labelled characterisations.

In certain languages, the labelled bisimilarity that characterises barbed congruence may be quite different from that of Definition 1.4.2. For instance, it may be that the matching transitions of two equal processes be syntactically quite different from each other. This occurs when processes are first-class values, as discussed in Section 7.1. It may also happen that only certain transitions of the processes are observable. That is, there may be transitions that the processes can perform that should not be taken into account in the labelled bisimilarity.

The above phenomena are prominent in languages with information hiding mechanisms, such as polymorphic types, capability types, encryption, data abstraction or store. The reason has to do with multiple 'points of view' about the values exchanged in a program. For instance, in the case of typed π-calculus, when a value is transmitted from one process to another, the receiver may have less type information about it – and so may use fewer of its actual capabilities – than the sender. For this, in a labelled bisimilarity one has to explicitly record, in each pair of related processes, the *observer's perspective* – that is, the observer's current knowledge about the values he/she has acquired through interactions with the process. Examples of this kind of labelled bisimilarity may be found, e.g., in [BS98, PS00, AG98, BDP99a, SP04, SP05, KW06, SKS07a].

Finally, we comment on the image-finite hypothesis in the Characterisation Theorem 7.3.9 (similar remarks apply to its weak counterpart Theorem 7.5.7). It is often very hard to prove the theorem without such a hypothesis. Even though the theorem does not cover all processes, the result expressed is important and satisfactory for two reasons. First, Exercise 7.3.6 shows that bisimilarity is sound, in that it can be used to obtain proof techniques for barbed congruence. Soundness alone, however, does not tell us whether the techniques are applicable to many processes. (For instance, the identity relation is included in barbed congruence and is therefore sound, but it does not give us interesting proof techniques.) This is where we can appeal to Theorem 7.3.9 and Exercise 7.3.10, which show that the techniques do apply to a very large class of processes. Second, the characterisation holds for processes that are image-finite up-to $\sim$; processes not in this class tend to arise rarely in practice.

An analogy can be drawn between barbed congruence and the *testing* approach to behavioural equivalence examined in Section 5.4. In the testing theory, the basis for comparing processes is the emission of success signals during experiments in which the processes are tested by composing them with special terms, the testers. The contexts that appear in the definition of barbed congruence play the role of the testers; and the observability predicates of barbed bisimilarity play the role of the success signals of an experiment. In testing, however, one considers linear runs of the experiments, whereas in barbed congruence one can follow the branching structure of the tree of the possible evolutions of an experiment by virtue of the bisimulation game. As we saw in Section 5.2, the same discriminating power can also be obtained in the testing approach, but one needs rather sophisticated testers. Another difference between barbed congruence and testing equivalence is in the set of contexts used. Barbed congruence is defined by quantification over *all* contexts, whereas testing equivalence only uses parallel composition contexts. Thus testing equivalence requires the existence of the CCS parallel composition operator in the language, and the equivalence produced need not be a congruence. Definitions of testing-like relations that are fully contextual are proposed in [BDP99b]; with respect to barbed congruence, the bisimulation game on internal moves is removed, and the barbs are *may* and *must* observables along the lines of the may and must predicates of testing equivalence.

Appendix A

Solutions to selected exercises

The reader can find in this appendix solutions to most of the exercises in the book. Often a solution is not fully worked out, but should anyhow be sufficient for the reader to fill in the missing details.

Exercises in Chapter 1

Exercise 1.4.10 Take

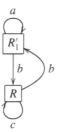

A bisimulation is $\{(R_1, R_1'), (R_2, R), (R_3, R)\}$. We omit the details that show this relation is a bisimulation. $\square$

Exercise 1.4.11 Here the initial guess could be

$$\{(R_1, Q_1), (R_2, Q_4), (R_3, Q_3)\}.$$

In this way, the transitions emanating from (R_1, Q_1) and (R_3, Q_3) are matched. But when examining the transitions emanating from (R_2, Q_4) one is forced to add the pair (R_3, Q_5) first, and then also (R_2, Q_2). The resulting relation is a bisimulation, as the reader can easily check.

In this exercise, when looking for the match for a given transition, there may be choices possible, because a state may have different outgoing transitions with the same label; in these cases, following the existential quantifier in the definition of bisimulation, we are asked to pick one, and we have to be careful to pick a good one. For instance, the transition $R_1 \xrightarrow{a} R_3$ is matched by $Q_1 \xrightarrow{a} Q_3$; it cannot be matched by $Q_1 \xrightarrow{a} Q_4$, as (R_3, Q_4) cannot be in a bisimulation because R_3 has a c-transition whereas Q_4 has not. $\square$

Exercise 1.4.12 Bisimilarity would become the universal relation. In the case when the process P has transitions with a label μ, whereas Q has no such transitions, the set $\{Q' \mid Q \xrightarrow{\mu} Q'\}$ is empty and therefore the demand

- "for all P' with $P \xrightarrow{\mu} P'$, and for all Q' such that $Q \xrightarrow{\mu} Q'$, we have $P' \mathcal{R} Q'$"

becomes trivially true. $\hfill\square$

Exercise 1.4.13

(1) We show that if each $\mathcal{R}_i$ is a bisimulation then also $\mathcal{R} \stackrel{\text{def}}{=} \cup_i \mathcal{R}_i$ is a bisimulation. Suppose $P \mathcal{R} Q$ and $P \xrightarrow{\mu} P'$. As $P \mathcal{R} Q$, then also $P \mathcal{R}_i Q$, for some $\mathcal{R}_i$. As $\mathcal{R}_i$ is a bisimulation, Q can match the transition from P, thus there is Q' with $Q \xrightarrow{\mu} Q'$ and $P' \mathcal{R}_i Q'$. Hence also $P' \mathcal{R} Q'$, and we are done. The case of transition from Q is similar.

(2) Consider the following processes:

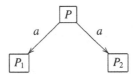

Both $\mathcal{I}$ (the identity relation) and $\{(P, P), (P_1, P_2), (P_2, P_1)\}$ are bisimulations. Their intersection, however, is $\{(P, P)\}$, and this is not a bisimulation. $\hfill\square$

Exercise 1.4.16 If a pair (P, Q) satisfies the clauses in the exercise, on sequences of actions, then it also satisfies the bisimulation clauses, on single actions, as a single action is a special case of a sequence.

The converse is proved by induction on the length of a sequence s. If $s = \epsilon$, then there is nothing to prove. Otherwise, $s = s'\mu$, for some sequence s' and action μ. If $P \xrightarrow{s'\mu} P'$ then this means that there is P'' with $P \xrightarrow{s'} P''$ and $P'' \xrightarrow{\mu} P'$. By induction, there is Q'' with $Q \xrightarrow{s'} Q''$ and $P'' \mathcal{R} Q''$, where $\mathcal{R}$ is the bisimulation given. Now, as $\mathcal{R}$ is a bisimulation and $P'' \xrightarrow{\mu} P'$, there is Q' with $Q'' \xrightarrow{\mu} Q'$ and $P' \mathcal{R} Q'$. Thus we have found that $Q \xrightarrow{s'\mu} Q'$, for some Q' with $P' \mathcal{R} Q'$, and we are done.

The case when Q launches the challenge is similar. $\hfill\square$

Exercise 1.4.17

(1) Easy.
(2) For any such P and Q, the singleton relation $\{(P, Q)\}$ is a simulation. There is nothing to prove, as the process on the left, P, has no transitions.
(3) Easy.
(4) The converse of none of the points holds. In the case of P_2 and Q_2, it suffices to note that P_2 has an a-transition to a state in which both b and c can be performed. Q cannot evolve into a state with both such observables.
(5) Similar to the analogous proof for bisimulation.

(6) The inclusion follows from point (1). For the strictness, one can show that processes in Figure 1.4 are simulation equivalent but not bisimilar.

(7) First one shows, by induction on the length of a sequence s of actions, that if $P \leq Q$ and $P \xrightarrow{s}$, then also $Q \xrightarrow{s}$. One can thus conclude that simulation equivalence implies trace equivalence.

For the strictness, the processes P_2, Q_2 of Figure 1.7 are trace equivalent: the sequences of actions they can perform are the same, namely ϵ, a, ab, ac. We have seen at point (4) that they are not simulation equivalent. □

Exercise 1.4.18 We prove that $S \stackrel{\text{def}}{=} \sim \mathcal{R} \sim$ is a bisimulation. Take $P \, S \, Q$ and suppose $P \xrightarrow{\mu} P'$. We have to find a matching transition from Q. If $P \, S \, Q$ then this means that there are P_1, Q_1 with $P \sim P_1$, $P_1 \, \mathcal{R} \, Q_1$ and $Q_1 \sim Q$. As $\sim$ is a bisimulation and $P \xrightarrow{\mu} P'$, there is P_1' with $P_1 \xrightarrow{\mu} P_1'$ and $P' \sim P_1'$. Similarly, as $\mathcal{R}$ is a bisimulation up-to $\sim$, Q_1 can answer the transition $P_1 \xrightarrow{\mu} P_1'$ with $Q_1 \xrightarrow{\mu} Q_1'$, for some Q_1' with $P_1' \sim \mathcal{R} \sim Q_1'$. Finally, again from the fact that $\sim$ is a bisimulation and $Q_1 \xrightarrow{\mu} Q_1'$, we deduce that there is Q' with $Q \xrightarrow{\mu} Q'$ and $Q_1' \sim Q'$.

In summary, we have found Q' with $Q \xrightarrow{\mu} Q'$ and $P' \sim P_1' \sim \mathcal{R} \sim Q_1' \sim Q'$. As $\sim$ is transitive, this means $P' \sim \mathcal{R} \sim Q'$; thus $P' \, S \, Q'$ and we are done.

The case when Q moves first is similar. □

Exercises in Chapter 2

Exercise 2.1.2 Let

$$\mathcal{R} \stackrel{\text{def}}{=} \{(e, e') \mid e \Downarrow e' \text{ and } e' \text{ is an abstraction}\}.$$

We prove $\Downarrow \subseteq \mathcal{R}$ by showing that $\mathcal{R}$ is closed forward under the rules for $\Downarrow$. We have two rules to check. The first rule is immediate: for any abstraction e we do have $e \, \mathcal{R} \, e$. In the case of the second rule, suppose $e_1 \, \mathcal{R} \, \lambda x. e_0$ and $e_0\{e_2/x\} \, \mathcal{R} \, e'$. This means that e' is abstraction; it also means that $e_1 \Downarrow \lambda x. e_0$ and $e_0\{e_2/x\} \Downarrow e'$, from which we derive $e_1 \, e_2 \Downarrow e'$. We can thus conclude $e_1 \, e_2 \, \mathcal{R} \, e'$. □

Exercise 2.1.4 Let

$$\mathcal{R} \stackrel{\text{def}}{=} \{(e, e') \mid e \Downarrow e' \text{ and } e \Uparrow \text{ does not hold}\}.$$

One proves $\Downarrow \subseteq \mathcal{R}$ by showing that $\mathcal{R}$ is closed forward under the rules for $\Downarrow$. The reasoning is similar to that for Exercise 2.1.2. If e is an abstraction, then indeed $e \, \mathcal{R} \, e$; moreover not $e \Uparrow$, as the rules for $\Uparrow$ require the conclusion to be an application. Suppose now $e_1 \, \mathcal{R} \, \lambda x. e_0$ and $e_0\{e_2/x\} \, \mathcal{R} \, e'$. This means that $e_1 \, e_2 \Downarrow e'$ (by definition of $\mathcal{R}$ and the rules for $\Downarrow$). It also means that:

- not $e_1 \Uparrow$;
- $e_1 \Downarrow \lambda x. e_0$ and not $e_0\{e_2/x\} \Uparrow$.

These two facts mean that we cannot apply, backwards, any of the rules for $\Uparrow$ on $e_1 \, e_2$, hence not $e_1 \, e_2 \Uparrow$. We can thus conclude $e_1 \, e_2 \, \mathcal{R} \, e'$.

Note that the reasoning we have made corresponds to a proof of the statement by induction on the depth of a proof of $e \Downarrow e'$ (the induction *on derivation proofs* of Section 2.7.1), which is the proof strategy that a reader with some familiarity with induction would have naturally followed if presented with the two rules for $\Downarrow$. □

Exercise 2.1.6 For $e_2 \, e_2$, use the set $S \overset{\text{def}}{=} \{e_2 \, e_2 \, , \, (e_2 \, e_2) \, e_2)\}$. For $e_1 \, e_2$ use $S \cup \{e_1 \, e_2\}$, for $e_2 \, e_1$ use $\{e_2 \, e_1 \, , \, (e_1 \, e_1) \, e_1 \, , \, e_1 \, e_1\}$. □

Exercise 2.3.3 Take the set of processes, quotiented by simulation equivalence. This is a well-defined quotient because simulation equivalence is an equivalence relation. Define an ordering on the resulting equivalence classes using similarity; the ordering can be given on representatives of the classes, exploiting again the equivalence properties of simulation equivalence. Using Exercise 1.4.17(5) it is easy to see that this is indeed a poset. □

Exercise 2.3.14 It is a lattice but not a complete lattice, as it does not have top and bottom elements. It suffices to add two points, for top and bottom elements, to obtain a complete lattice. □

Exercise 2.3.15 The meet is the usual intersection of relations. The join of relations is the transitive closure of the union of the relations. The bottom element is the identity relation (any equivalence relation is reflexive and therefore includes the identity); the top element is the universal relation, that includes all pairs of points. □

Exercise 2.3.17 Let L be the complete lattice and X a set of points in the lattice. We have to show that X has a meet. Consider the set

$$Y \overset{\text{def}}{=} \{y \mid y \leq x, \forall x \in X\}.$$

Note that if X is empty, then $Y = L$. We show that the join of Y, say z, is also the meet of X. First, it holds that $z \leq x$, for all $x \in X$. Indeed, if there were a point in X for which the relation failed, then z could not be the join of Y (as the join of a set is smaller than all upper bounds of that set). Further, z is the greatest point with this property, as any other points with the property belong to Y and are therefore smaller than z, by definition of join. □

Exercise 2.3.19
(1) In this proof we sometimes use an infix notation for the join. By definition of join, $x \leq x \cup y$, therefore, as F is monotone, also $F(x) \leq F(x \cup y)$. From this and using the hypothesis that x is a post-fixed point, we get $x \leq F(x \cup y)$. Similarly we derive $y \leq F(x \cup y)$. Therefore $F(x \cup y)$ is an upper bound for $\{x, y\}$, hence $x \cup y \leq F(x \cup y)$, by definition of join.
(2) In the case of a set $\{x_i\}_i$ of post-fixed points the reasoning is similar. Let $z = \cup \{x_i\}_i$. We first derive, for all i, $F(x_i) \leq F(z)$: for this we use the definition of join, which gives us $x_i \leq z$, and the monotonicity of F. As x_i is a post-fixed point, we then obtain

$x_i \leq F(z)$. As this holds for all i, $F(z)$ is an upper bound for the set $\{x_i\}_i$. As z is the join (i.e., the least upper bound) we can finally conclude $z \leq F(z)$.

The dual statement for pre-fixed points is: given a set S of pre-fixed points, $\cap S$ is a pre-fixed point too. The proof is obtained by dualising that of post-fixed points above.

(3) Consider the complete lattice with five distinct points related as follows:

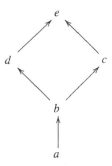

and a function F that is the identity everywhere except that $F(b) = a$. Then F is monotone, c and d are post-fixed points, but $\cap\{c, d\}$ is not.

For another counterexample see Exercise 1.4.13(2), since, as we show in Section 2.10, the bisimulations are the post-fixed points of a monotone endofunction on the complete lattice of the binary relations on processes. □

Exercise 2.3.20 We consider one part of the statement, namely

$$\mathtt{gfp}(F) \stackrel{\text{def}}{=} \bigcup \{S \mid S \subseteq F(S)\}$$

(the other part is similar). Set $T \stackrel{\text{def}}{=} \bigcup \{S \mid S \subseteq F(S)\}$. We first show that $T \subseteq F(T)$, then the converse.

- $T \subseteq F(T)$ is proved as in Exercise 2.3.19(2).
- From $T \subseteq F(T)$ and monotonicity of F, we derive $F(T) \subseteq F(F(T))$, hence $F(T)$ is a post-fixed point. We conclude $F(T) \subseteq T$ by definition of join of the post-fixed points.

Finally, T is the greatest among the fixed points: any other fixed point is a post-fixed point, hence below T by definition of join. □

Exercise 2.3.22 Here are the missing details for the proof.

We have to show that S is a complete lattice in itself, therefore it is non-empty, and it has a join for all its subsets. We show the latter, as in doing so we will also prove the former.

Consider X and Y as defined in the exercise, and the meet z of Y. Note that, for $x \in X$ and $y \in Y$, as the points in X are fixed points and F monotone, $x \leq y$ implies also $x \leq F(y)$. To show that z is also the join of X in S, we prove that z is a fixed point; this is sufficient, because all points of X are below z (by definition of meet, as each point of X is below all points of Y), thus showing that z is an upper bound; and any other fixed points with the same property would be in Y and therefore would be above z, thus showing that z is the least upper bound.

The proof that z is a fixed point is similar to the proof of Exercise 2.3.20 (the part on least fixed points). We first show $F(z) \le z$. This holds if $F(z) \le y$ for all $y \in Y$. This in turn holds if $F(z) \le F(y)$ (as $F(y) \le y$, the pre-fixed point property), which then holds if $z \le y$ (as F is monotone). Now we are done, as $z \le y$ is true by definition of z.

Now the converse. From $F(z) \le z$, by monotonicity, we infer that $F(z)$ is a pre-fixed point of L. Moreover, as z is an upper bound of X, again by monotonicity (and the fixed-point property for X), we infer that also $F(z)$ is an upper bound of X. Hence $F(z) \in Y$, from which we can conclude $z \le F(z)$.

The above construction precisely shows that the meet of the pre-fixed points that are above X is a fixed point, and it is exactly the least fixed point that is above X. Thus when X is empty the construction shows that L has a least fixed point, which is obtained as the meet of all pre-fixed points of L. □

Exercise 2.5.3 In one direction, it has already been shown that rule functionals give rise to monotone functions. For the opposite, let F be the monotone function. If $F(S) = T$, then add the rules (S, t) for all $t \in T$. The associated functional coincides with F, exploiting the fact that F is monotone.

We can try to be more restrictive, or precise, adding the following constraint. For each t, suppose there are sets S_i such that, for each i, $F(S_i) = t$ and S_i is minimal, in that there is no set S_i' smaller than S_i with $F(S_i') = t$ (such sets S_i need not exist, though). Then the only rules whose conclusion is t are (S_i, t), for each i. Being more restrictive can be useful for obtaining rules that are finite in the premises or in the conclusions, as by Definitions 2.9.1 and 2.9.3. □

Exercise 2.6.2 Let S be the set of all processes P for which there are P_i ($i \ge 0$) with $P_0 = P$ and, for each i, $P_i \overset{\mu}{\to} P_{i+1}$. One shows that S is a post-fixed point of $\Phi_{\mathcal{R}_{\restriction\mu}}$, and that any post-fixed point only contains processes in S. □

Exercise 2.6.3 The set of all finite lists plus the infinite lists that are almost constant (meaning that all their elements are identical except for a finite number of them) also satisfies the equation for Φ_{Alist}. The important property is that the set of almost constant lists is closed under append and tail operations; that is, if s is an almost constant list then also $\langle a \rangle \bullet s$ is almost constant, for any a; and conversely if $\langle a \rangle \bullet s$ is almost constant then s is so too. □

Exercise 2.6.4 The empty set and the set of all infinite lists. □

Exercise 2.6.10 First one shows that, for all $n \ge 0$, we have

$$(\text{map} +_1)^n \text{nats} = \langle n \rangle \bullet (\text{map} +_1)^{n+1} \text{nats}$$

using induction on n. For $n = 0$, we have $(\text{map} +_1)^0 \text{nats} = \text{nats}$, and then

$$\text{nats} = \langle 0 \rangle \bullet \text{map} +_1 \text{nats}$$

by definition of nats. For $n > 0$, we have:

$$(\text{map} +_1)^n \text{nats} =$$
$$\text{map} +_1 (\text{map} +_1)^{n-1} \text{nats} = \text{(by induction)}$$
$$\text{map} +_1 \langle n - 1 \rangle \bullet (\text{map} +_1)^n \text{nats} = \text{(by definition of map)}$$
$$\langle n \rangle \bullet \text{map} +_1 (\text{map} +_1)^n \text{nats} =$$
$$\langle n \rangle \bullet (\text{map} +_1)^{n+1} \text{nats}.$$

Using this property, we show that $\mathcal{R}$ is a bisimulation. Take $(\text{map} +_1)^n \text{nats} \; \mathcal{R} \; \text{from} \, (n)$. We have

$$(\text{map} +_1)^n \text{nats} = \langle n \rangle \bullet (\text{map} +_1)^{n+1} \text{nats} \xrightarrow{n} (\text{map} +_1)^{n+1} \text{nats}$$

and

$$\text{from} \, (n) = \langle n \rangle \bullet \text{from} \, (n + 1) \xrightarrow{n} \text{from} \, (n + 1).$$

Since $(\text{map} +_1)^{n+1} \text{nats} \; \mathcal{R} \; \text{from} \, (n + 1)$, we are done. $\qquad \square$

Exercise 2.6.11 In this exercise, for readability, we omit the parentheses '⟨' and '⟩' in lists, for instance writing $b \bullet s$ for $\langle b \rangle \bullet s$. We also recall that by our bracketing conventions, expressions such as $n \bullet (\text{map} +_1)^{n+1} \text{nats}$ read as $n \bullet ((\text{map} +_1)^{n+1} \text{nats})$.

First, using the property

$$(\text{map} +_1)^n \text{nats} = n \bullet (\text{map} +_1)^{n+1} \text{nats}$$

shown in the proof of Exercise 2.6.10, and the definition of map, we derive, for $n \geq 0$,

$$\text{map} \, f \, ((\text{map} +_1)^n \text{nats}) = \text{map} \, f \; n \bullet (\text{map} +_1)^{n+1} \text{nats}$$
$$= f(n) \bullet \text{map} \, f \, ((\text{map} +_1)^{n+1} \text{nats}) \qquad \text{(A.1)}$$

Now, consider the function h, from natural numbers to lists of natural numbers, defined by recursion on $n \geq 1$ as follows:

$$h(1) \stackrel{\text{def}}{=} \text{plus} \, (\text{fibs}, \text{tail} \, (\text{fibs})),$$
$$h(n) \stackrel{\text{def}}{=} \text{plus} \, (f(n - 1) \bullet h(n - 1), h(n - 1)) \quad \text{(for } n > 1\text{)}.$$

We prove that, for $n \geq 1$

$$h(n) = f(n + 1) \bullet h(n + 1). \qquad \text{(A.2)}$$

The proof is by induction on n. For $n = 1$ we have

$$h(1) = \text{plus} \, (\text{fibs}, \text{tail} \, (\text{fibs}))$$
$$= \text{plus} \, (0 \bullet 1 \bullet \text{plus} \, (\text{fibs}, \text{tail} \, (\text{fibs})), 1 \bullet \text{plus} \, (\text{fibs}, \text{tail} \, (\text{fibs})))$$
$$= 1 \bullet \text{plus} \, (1 \bullet \text{plus} \, (\text{fibs}, \text{tail} \, (\text{fibs})), \text{plus} \, (\text{fibs}, \text{tail} \, (\text{fibs})))$$
$$= f(2) \bullet \text{plus} \, (f(1) \bullet h(1), h(1))$$
$$= f(2) \bullet h(2).$$

For $n > 1$ we have, using induction,

$$
\begin{aligned}
h(n) &= \mathtt{plus}\ (f(n-1) \bullet h(n-1), h(n-1)) \\
&= \mathtt{plus}\ (f(n-1) \bullet f(n) \bullet h(n), f(n) \bullet h(n)) \\
&= f(n+1) \bullet \mathtt{plus}\ (f(n) \bullet h(n), h(n)) \\
&= f(n+1) \bullet h(n+1).
\end{aligned}
$$

Now we are ready to define the list bisimulation:

$$
\mathcal{R} \overset{\text{def}}{=} \{\ (\,\mathtt{fibs}\,,\ \mathtt{map}\ f\ \mathtt{nats}\,),\ (\,1 \bullet h(1)\,,\ \mathtt{map}\ f\ (\mathtt{map}\ +_1\ \mathtt{nats})\,)\ \}
$$
$$
\bigcup\nolimits_{n \geq 1} \{(h(n), \mathtt{map}\ f\ ((\mathtt{map}\ +_1)^{n+1}\mathtt{nats}))\}.
$$

We have to show that $\mathcal{R}$ is a list bisimulation. We consider the three kinds of pair in $\mathcal{R}$:

- $(\mathtt{fibs}, \mathtt{map}\ f\ \mathtt{nats})$. We have

$$
\begin{aligned}
\mathtt{fibs} &= 0 \bullet 1 \bullet \mathtt{plus}\ (\mathtt{fibs}, \mathtt{tail}\,(\mathtt{fibs})) \\
&\overset{0}{\to} 1 \bullet \mathtt{plus}\ (\mathtt{fibs}, \mathtt{tail}\,(\mathtt{fibs})) \\
&= 1 \bullet h(1)
\end{aligned}
$$

and, using (A.1),

$$
\begin{aligned}
\mathtt{map}\ f\ \mathtt{nats} &= \mathtt{map}\ f\ ((\mathtt{map}\ +_1)^0\mathtt{nats}) \\
&= f(0) \bullet \mathtt{map}\ f\ ((\mathtt{map}\ +_1)\mathtt{nats}) \\
&\overset{0}{\to} \mathtt{map}\ f\ ((\mathtt{map}\ +_1)\mathtt{nats})
\end{aligned}
$$

which closes the case, as $1 \bullet h(1)\ \mathcal{R}\ \mathtt{map}\ f\ ((\mathtt{map}\ +_1)\mathtt{nats})$.
- $(1 \bullet h(1), \mathtt{map}\ f\ (\mathtt{map}\ +_1\ \mathtt{nats}))$. Similar to the previous one.
- $(h(n), \mathtt{map}\ f\ ((\mathtt{map}\ +_1)^{n+1}\mathtt{nats}))$. We have, using (A.2):

$$
h(n) = f(n+1) \bullet h(n+1) \xrightarrow{f(n+1)} h(n+1)
$$

and, again using (A.1),

$$
\begin{aligned}
\mathtt{map}\ f\ ((\mathtt{map}\ +_1)^{n+1}\mathtt{nats}) \quad &= \quad f(n+1) \bullet \mathtt{map}\ f\ ((\mathtt{map}\ +_1)^{n+2}\mathtt{nats}) \\
&\xrightarrow{f(n+1)} \mathtt{map}\ f\ ((\mathtt{map}\ +_1)^{n+2}\mathtt{nats})
\end{aligned}
$$

and we are done, as $h(n+1)\ \mathcal{R}\ \mathtt{map}\ f\ ((\mathtt{map}\ +_1)^{n+2}\mathtt{nats})$. □

Exercise 2.7.1 We use the property, discussed in Section 0.5, that given any well-founded relation $\mathcal{R}$ on X, in any non-empty subset of X there is at least a minimal element.

Now, assume that the condition of well-founded induction holds for the well-founded relation $\mathcal{R}$ on the set X and the property T on X and yet the set $\{y \mid y \in X \text{ and } y \notin T\}$ is non-empty. By the observation above, the set has at least one minimal element, say z. Thus for all z' with $z'\ \mathcal{R}\ z$ we have $z' \in T$, however $z \notin T$. This contradicts the assumption that the well-founded induction holds. □

Exercise 2.7.3 Rule induction says that if a property holds for the empty string, and whenever it holds at s it also holds at $a.s.b$, and whenever it holds at s_1 and s_2 it also holds at $s_1.s_2$, then the property holds in all strings inductively produced by the rules. One can show that the number of a and b is the same by structural induction or rule induction.

The set S inductively defined by the rules is the set of all strings s in which the number of a and b symbols is the same and, moreover, in any prefix of s the number of bs is always less than, or equal to, the number of as.

In the coinductive case, the results is the set of all strings. To see this, consider the backward closure: given a string s, we can match it against the conclusion of the rule $(\{s_1, s_2\}, s_1.s_2)$, taking $s_1 = \epsilon$ and $s_2 = s$. When the rule $(\emptyset, \epsilon)$ is replaced by the rule $(\emptyset, a.b)$: in the assertion of rule induction the assumption "a property holds for the empty string" is replaced by "a property holds at $a.b$"; the only other thing that changes is that ϵ itself is not anymore in the set S inductively defined by the rules (in contrast, ϵ remains in the set coinductively defined, for in the backward closure we can expand ϵ as $\epsilon.\epsilon$, which then is matched against the conclusion of the third rule). Suppose now that we also have $\epsilon \notin X$. The set S does not change further, but the set T coinductively defined does change, as we cannot play the above trick with the backward closure anymore. For instance, no finite string beginning with a b is in T; indeed the only finite strings in T are those that are also in the inductive set. In contrast, all infinite strings remain in T, using the fact that on an infinite string s we have $s.s' = s$ for any s'. □

Exercise 2.7.7 The schema of the proof is as for Theorem 2.7.6. Thus the crux is proving $x \cup y \leq F(x \cup y)$, under the assumption that $x \leq F(x) \cup y$, and we only show the details for this. We prove that $F(x \cup y)$ is an upper bound for both x and y. For the case of y, use the monotonicity of F and the hypothesis $y \leq F(y)$. For the case of x, since $x \leq F(x) \cup y$ it is sufficient to prove that $F(x \cup y)$ is an upper bound for $F(x)$ and for y. Both cases follow the monotonicity of F and the hypothesis on y being a post-fixed point (the latter case had in fact been already considered earlier in the proof). □

Exercise 2.7.9 Referring to the proof of Theorem 2.7.8, the only points that need modification are the proof of (i) and of $\mathtt{gfp} \leq \mathtt{gfp} \bullet \mathtt{gfp}$. The latter is the new assumption. In place of (i) we prove that $x \leq F(x)$ implies there is z with $x \leq z$ and $z \leq F(\mathtt{gfp} \bullet z \bullet \mathtt{gfp})$. It suffices to take $z = \mathtt{gfp}$ (by the Fixed-point Theorem, $x \leq \mathtt{gfp}$). Then the conclusion is derived using assumption (1) and the property $\mathtt{gfp} = \mathtt{gfp} \bullet \mathtt{gfp}$. □

Exercise 2.7.10 One shows that $x \cap y$ is a pre-fixed point of F, i.e., $F(x \cap y) \leq x \cap y$, proving that $F(x \cap y)$ is a lower bound for both x and y. The remaining details are similar to those of the proof of Theorem 2.7.6. □

Exercise 2.8.2 We consider cocontinuity. Suppose $x \geq y$. We have $\cap\{x, y\} = y$, hence $F(\cap\{x, y\}) = F(y)$.

Consider now the sequence $x, y, y, y, \dots$. It is decreasing, therefore we can apply cocontinuity and infer $F(\cap\{x, y\}) = \cap\{F(x), F(y)\}$. Since we have $\cap\{F(x), F(y)\} \leq F(x)$, we derive $F(\cap\{x, y\}) \leq F(x)$.

We have therefore showed $F(y) = F(\cap\{x, y\}) \leq F(x)$, which proves the monotonicity of F. □

Exercise 2.8.3 Cocontinuity does not imply continuity. Example: take the integers plus the points ω, $\omega + 1$, $-\omega$, with the ordering $-\omega \leq n \leq \omega$, for all n, and $\omega \leq \omega + 1$. This is a complete lattice. Now take a function that is the identity on all points, except ω that is mapped onto $\omega + 1$.   □

Exercise 2.8.4 We consider part (1), as (2) is similar. For each α_i, we have $\alpha_i \leq \bigcup_i \alpha_i$; hence, since F is monotone, $F(\alpha_i) \leq F(\bigcup_i \alpha_i)$. Thus $F(\bigcup_i \alpha_i)$ is an upper bound for each $F(\alpha_i)$, and we can then conclude $\bigcup_i F(\alpha_i) \leq F(\bigcup_i \alpha_i)$.   □

Exercise 2.8.6 First we show that $\bigcap_{n \geq 0} F^n(\mathsf{T})$ is a fixed point. It is easy to check that $F^0(\mathsf{T}), \ldots, F^n(\mathsf{T}), \ldots$ is a sequence of decreasing points, using the monotonicity of F. Therefore, by cocontinuity:

$$F\left(\bigcap_{n \geq 0} F^n(\mathsf{T})\right) = \bigcap_{n \geq 0} F(F^n(\mathsf{T})) = \bigcap_{n > 0} F^n(\mathsf{T})$$

and also

$$= \bigcap_{n \geq 0} F^n(\mathsf{T}).$$

Now, if y is any fixed point of the lattice, from $\mathsf{T} \geq y$ and monotonicity of F it follows that also $F^n(\mathsf{T}) \geq y$, for any n. Thus y is a lower bound for the set $\{F^n(\mathsf{T})\}_n$, hence it is below its meet.   □

Exercise 2.8.9

(1) For the decreasing sequence, use monotonicity. By cocontinuity, and reasoning as in Exercise 2.8.6, $F(F^{\cap\omega}(x)) = \bigcap_n F(F^n(x))$, which is also $= \bigcap_n F^n(x)$ (since $F^0(x)$ is above each $F^n(x)$), and, by definition, this is $F^{\cap\omega}(x)$.

(2) Each fixed point of L below x is also below $F^n(x)$, for each n (by monotonicity), hence also below their meet.

(3) Let $Y \stackrel{\text{def}}{=} \{y \mid y \leq x \text{ and } y \leq F(y)\}$. If $y \in Y$, then $y \leq F^n(x)$, for each n (which is proved by induction on n, using the monotonicity of F and the hypothesis $y \leq x$ and $y \leq F(y)$). Hence, y is also below the meet of these points, i.e., $y \leq F^{\cap\omega}(x)$. Since this holds for each y, it also holds for their join, i.e., $\bigcup Y \leq F^{\cap\omega}(x)$.

For the converse, we know (from point (2)) that $F^{\cap\omega}(x)$ is a fixed point below x, hence it is in Y. Therefore $F^{\cap\omega}(x)$ is below the join of Y, i.e., $F^{\cap\omega}(x) \leq \bigcup Y$.   □

Exercise 2.8.13 We use two facts:

- if $\{R_i\}_i$ is a set of equivalence relations, then also $\bigcap_i R_i$ is so;
- if R is an equivalence relation, then also $F(R)$ is an equivalence relation.

The first expresses a general property of relations, whose proof is simple and left to the reader. To prove the second fact we need the properties (1)–(3) of the exercise.

For reflexivity, suppose $\mathcal{I} \subseteq R$; then by monotonicity of F, also $F(\mathcal{I}) \subseteq F(R)$, from which we derive $\mathcal{I} \subseteq F(R)$ using property (1).

For transitivity, suppose $\mathcal{R}$ is transitive, i.e., $\mathcal{R}\mathcal{R} \subseteq \mathcal{R}$. Using this, monotonicity and property (2), we derive:

$$F(\mathcal{R})F(\mathcal{R}) \subseteq F(\mathcal{R}\mathcal{R}) \subseteq F(\mathcal{R}),$$

thus showing that $F(\mathcal{R})$ is transitive too.

For symmetry, suppose $\mathcal{R}^{-1} \subseteq \mathcal{R}$. Then we have, using property (3),

$$(F(\mathcal{R}))^{-1} \subseteq F(\mathcal{R}^{-1})$$

and, from $\mathcal{R}^{-1} \subseteq \mathcal{R}$ and monotonicity of F,

$$\subseteq F(\mathcal{R}),$$

thus showing that also $F(\mathcal{R})$ is symmetric.

Having the above two facts, the exercise is proved by applying Theorem 2.8.8. The theorem tells us that

$$\mathtt{gfp}(F) = F^{\infty}(\top) = \bigcap_{\lambda} F^{\lambda}(\top).$$

Using the first of the facts above, it is then sufficient to prove that for all ordinal λ, relation $F^{\lambda}(\top)$ is an equivalence. This is done by reasoning by (transfinite) induction, following the definition of $F^{\lambda}(\top)$. The single steps are straightforward consequences of the two facts above. $\qquad\square$

Exercise 2.9.2 Take a sequence of increasing sets S_i. We need to show that $\Phi_{\mathcal{R}}(\cup_i S_i) = \cup_i \Phi_{\mathcal{R}}(S_i)$.

Suppose $x \in \Phi_{\mathcal{R}}(\cup_i S_i)$. This means that there is $(S, x) \in \mathcal{R}$ and $S \subseteq \cup_i S_i$. As $\mathcal{R}$ is FP, S is finite, and since the sequence S_i is increasing there must be S_n with $S \subseteq S_m$ for all $m \geq n$. Hence $x \in \Phi_{\mathcal{R}}(S_m)$, and therefore also $x \in \cup_i \Phi_{\mathcal{R}}(S_i)$.

Conversely, if $x \in \cup_i \Phi_{\mathcal{R}}(S_i)$ then $x \in \Phi_{\mathcal{R}}(S_n)$, for some n, and hence also $x \in \Phi_{\mathcal{R}}(\cup_i S_i)$, as $S_n \subseteq \cup_i S_i$ and $\Phi_{\mathcal{R}}$ is monotone. (This implication also follows from Exercise 2.8.3(1) and monotonicity of $\Phi_{\mathcal{R}}$.)

Having continuity, the assertion $\mathtt{lfp}(\Phi_{\mathcal{R}}) = \Phi_{\mathcal{R}}^{\cup\omega}(\emptyset)$ follows from Theorem 2.8.5. $\qquad\square$

Exercise 2.9.5 Consider a sequence $S_0, \ldots, S_n, \ldots$ of decreasing sets. We have to show that

$$\Phi_{\mathcal{R}}(\cap_n S_n) = \cap_n \Phi_{\mathcal{R}}(S_n).$$

First, the inclusion $\subseteq$. Suppose $x \in \Phi_{\mathcal{R}}(\cap_n S_n)$. This means that there is S' such that $(S', x) \in \mathcal{R}$ and $S' \subseteq S_n$, for all n. Hence x is also in $\Phi_{\mathcal{R}}(S_n)$, for each n. (The inclusion can also be derived from Exercise 2.8.3(2), since $\Phi_{\mathcal{R}}$ is monotone.)

Now, the converse inclusion $\supseteq$. Suppose $x \in \cap_n \Phi_{\mathcal{R}}(S_n)$. This means that, for each n, there is $S'_n \subseteq S_n$ with $(S'_n, x) \in \mathcal{R}$. Since $\mathcal{R}$ is FC and the S_ns are decreasing, there is some S'_i that is contained in each S_n. Hence $S'_i \subseteq \cap_n S_n$, and $x \in \Phi_{\mathcal{R}}(\cap_n S_n)$. $\qquad\square$

Exercise 2.9.7 Both $\Phi_{\mathcal{R}_1}$ and $\Phi_{\mathcal{R}_{1\mu}}$ are continuous. To see that we need image-finiteness for the cocontinuity of $\Phi_{\mathcal{R}_{1\mu}}$, we use the notation in Example 2.10.11. Let $S_i \stackrel{\text{def}}{=} \cup_{n \geq i}\{a^n\}$. Then P is in $\cap_i \Phi_{\mathcal{R}_{1a}}(S_i)$ but not in $\Phi_{\mathcal{R}_{1a}}(\cap_i S_i)$. We also have P in $\Phi^{\cap\omega}_{\mathcal{R}_{1a}}(Pr)$ but not in $\mathrm{gfp}(\Phi_{\mathcal{R}_{1a}})$.   □

Exercise 2.9.8 Both assertions are proved by induction on n.   □

Exercise 2.9.9 Call S the set of all P for which there are $n \geq 0$, processes $P_0, \ldots, P_n$ and actions $\mu_1, \ldots, \mu_n$ such that $P = P_0 \xrightarrow{\mu_1} P_1 \cdots \xrightarrow{\mu_n} P_n$ and P_n is stopped.

One can either use the continuity of $\Phi_{\mathcal{R}_1}$ and prove, using Exercise 2.9.8, that S is the least fixed point via the iterative construction in (the first part of) Theorem 2.8.5; or one can first show $\mathrm{lfp}(\Phi_{\mathcal{R}_1}) \subseteq S$ by proving that S is pre-fixed point of $\Phi_{\mathcal{R}_1}$, and then show the converse by proving that any pre-fixed point of $\Phi_{\mathcal{R}_1}$ must contain S (for this, reason by mathematical induction on the shortest trace of actions that a process in S can perform before reaching a stopped process).   □

Exercise 2.9.11 We consider the assertion for the greatest fixed point, that for the least fixed point being similar.

We can exploit the cocontinuity of Φ_{Alist}, and show that for all $n \geq 0$, $\Phi^n_{\text{Alist}}(X)$ is the set of all finite lists with a number of elements less than or equal to n plus the elements of the form

$$\langle a_1 \rangle \bullet \langle a_2 \rangle \bullet \cdots \langle a_n \rangle \bullet x$$

for some $x \in X$. Then one concludes from the definition of $\Phi^{\cap\omega}_{\text{Alist}}$.

Alternatively, one can show $\mathrm{FinInfLists}_A \subseteq \mathrm{gfp}(\Phi_{\text{Alist}})$ by proving that $\mathrm{FinInfLists}_A$ is a post-fixed point, and then the converse by showing that any post-fixed point may only contain elements in $\mathrm{FinInfLists}_A$ (for this, one uses mathematical induction to show that for all n, the n-th character of an element in a post-fixed point, if it exists, is correct; we also need to know that if $\langle a_1 \rangle \bullet \langle a_2 \rangle \bullet \cdots \langle a_m \rangle \bullet x$ is in the post-fixed point then x is there too).   □

Exercise 2.10.4 For (2), one needs the fact that if, for each i in a set I, relation $\mathcal{R}_i$ is an equivalence relation, then also $\cap_{i \in I} \mathcal{R}_i$ is so. We used this fact also in Exercise 2.8.13.

For (3) the hypotheses of Exercise 2.8.13 are indeed satisfied.   □

Exercise 2.10.5 We can use Lemmas 2.10.1 and 2.10.2 so as to derive Exercise 1.4.13(1) from Exercise 2.3.19(1)–(2).   □

Exercise 2.10.6 The set $\{(P, Q) \mid P \sim Q$ and P, Q are finite$\}$. Hence on finite LTSs, least and greatest fixed points of $F_\sim$ coincide.   □

Exercise 2.10.7 A relation $\mathcal{R}$ is a 'bisimulation up-to $\cup$' if there is a bisimulation $\mathcal{S}$ such that whenever $P \mathcal{R} Q$, for all μ we have:

(1) for all P' with $P \xrightarrow{\mu} P'$, there is Q' such that $Q \xrightarrow{\mu} Q'$ and either $P' \mathcal{R} Q'$ or $P' \mathcal{S} Q'$;

and similarly for the converse clause. The most interesting case is for $S = \sim$, since $\sim$ is the largest bisimulation. ☐

Exercise 2.10.12 We use the process notations in Example 2.10.11. For $i \geq 1$, consider the relations

$$\mathcal{S}_i \stackrel{\text{def}}{=} \bigcup_{n \geq i} \{(a^n, a^\omega)\} \cup \{(P, Q)\}.$$

We have:

- $\{\mathcal{S}_i\}_i$ is a decreasing sequence of relations;
- $F_\sim(\mathcal{S}_i) = \mathcal{S}_{i+1}$;
- $\bigcap_i \mathcal{S}_i = \{(P, Q)\}$;
- $\bigcap_i F_\sim(\mathcal{S}_i) = \{(P, Q)\}$;
- $F_\sim(\bigcap_i \mathcal{S}_i) = \emptyset$.

☐

Exercise 2.10.20 The additional fact needed is that whenever $P \sim_n Q$ and $Q \sim Q'$, then also $P \sim_n Q'$. ☐

Exercise 2.10.22 See the beginning of Section 2.13. ☐

Exercise 2.10.23 Finitely-branching implies that the possible matches among the derivatives of two processes are finite. This need not hold with image-finiteness, for instance with two processes that may perform transitions with infinitely many labels and with, for each label, at least two different derivatives. In this case there are infinitely many rules whose conclusion is that pair of processes. ☐

Exercise 2.10.24 Given an LTS with processes Pr, call a set S of processes image-finite if, for all $P \in S$ and all μ, the set of μ-derivatives of P is finite and contained in S. Now call a process P image-finite if $P \in S$ for some image-finite set S of processes.

This is a coinductive definition: the complete lattice is $\wp(Pr)$, the endofunction F has $P \in F(S)$ if the above clause of image-finiteness holds. The image-finite sets are the post-fixed points of F.

The definition can also be given by means of rules. We then have rules of the form (S_P, P), where P is a processes whose set of μ-derivatives is finite and contained in S_P, for each μ.

The coinductive set so defined is the largest set of processes each of which is image-finite according to Definition 1.2.5. ☐

Exercise 2.10.26 It is the function $F : \wp(Pr \times Pr) \to \wp(Pr \times Pr)$ where $F(\mathcal{R})$ is the set of all pairs (P, Q) such that:

- for all P' with $P \stackrel{\mu}{\to} P'$, there is Q' such that $Q \stackrel{\mu}{\to} Q'$ and $P' \mathcal{R} Q'$.

☐

Exercise 2.11.4 The FP hypothesis allows us to prove the result from the Continuity Theorem 2.8.5 (via Exercise 2.9.2) and Lemma 2.11.3.   □

Exercise 2.14.1 Suppose V has a winning strategy. Consider all pairs (P_i, Q_i) that represent the current pair of a play

$$(P_0, Q_0), (P_1, Q_1), \ldots, (P_i, Q_i)$$

in which V has applied the strategy. Show that this is a bisimulation.

   Conversely, given a bisimulation containing (P, Q) it is easy to define a winning strategy for V. The strategy simply says that whenever the last pair in a play, say (P', Q'), is in the bisimulation and R proposes a challenge transition $P' \xrightarrow{\mu} P''$ or $Q' \xrightarrow{\mu} Q''$, then V chooses the answer transition suggested by the bisimulation clauses, so as to make sure that the two final derivatives are again in the bisimulation. One then proves that this is indeed a winning strategy. Call the bisimulation S, and consider a play of the game and a pair (P_i, Q_i) in the play. One shows, by induction on i, that the pair is also in S and moreover either both P_i and Q_i are stopped and therefore R has no further move, or both R and V can move and therefore there is another pair in the play.   □

Exercise 2.14.2 Suppose R has a winning strategy for (P, Q). Then we cannot have a bisimulation containing (P, Q) because otherwise, by Exercise 2.14.1, there would be a winning strategy for V (which is impossible, given the hypothesis and the definition of winning strategy, as the set of plays for a game is always non-empty).

   Conversely, suppose $P \not\sim Q$. We define a winning strategy for R. Given a pair (P_1, P_2) with $P_1 \not\sim P_2$, by Theorem 2.8.8 (or Theorem 2.10.21) define $\mathrm{ord}(P_1, P_2)$ as the smallest ordinal α such that $P_1 \not\sim_\alpha P_2$. This means that there is a transition $P_1 \xrightarrow{\mu} P_1'$ or $P_2 \xrightarrow{\mu} P_2'$ that the other process cannot match in $\sim_{\alpha-1}$. The strategy for R picks such a transition. We can show by transfinite induction that the strategy so defined is winning for all games in which the initial processes (P, Q) are not bisimilar. To see this, let $\alpha = \mathrm{ord}(P, Q)$. The case $\alpha = 1$ is straightforward. Otherwise, $\alpha > 1$, and consider the following pair (P', Q') in the game, obtained from the moves by R and V. As R has followed the strategy, we have $\mathrm{ord}(P', Q') < \alpha$. Hence we can apply induction and infer that any play beginning with (P', Q') ends with a win for R.

   Note that we cannot immediately infer Exercise 2.14.2 from Exercise 2.14.1 because we would need to prove first that in any game either R or V has a winning strategy. And for this we need to know that R has a winning strategy whenever $P \not\sim Q$, which is indeed what we have done above.   □

Exercises in Chapter 3

Exercise 3.4.3

(1) Take $P = a$.
(2) See Example 3.3.1. The process cannot be in *finCCS*. One can show that if a process P is in *finCCS*, then there is n such that P has a trace of transitions $P \xrightarrow{\mu_1} P_1 \cdots \xrightarrow{\mu_n} P_n$

of length n but no traces of length greater than n. Then $P \mid P$ is capable of performing a trace of length $2n$. A bisimulation cannot relate processes with traces of different lengths. □

Exercise 3.4.6 Counterexample: $P = a$, $Q = \bar{a}$. Having distributed the restriction, we break the possibility of interactions between components. □

Exercise 3.4.9 The bisimulation consists of $\mathcal{I} \cup \{(P \mid P', Q)\}$, where

$$Q \stackrel{\text{def}}{=} \Sigma_i \mu_i.(P_i \mid P') + \Sigma_j \mu'_j.(P \mid P'_j) + \Sigma_{\mu_i \text{ opp } \mu'_j} \tau.(P_i \mid P'_j).$$

Suppose $P \mid P' \stackrel{\mu}{\to} R$. This can have been derived from one of the rules PARL, PARR, or COM. We only consider the case of COM. Thus $P \stackrel{\mu}{\to} P_i$ and $P' \stackrel{\bar{\mu}}{\to} P'_j$, for some i, j, and $R = P_i \mid P'_j$. This means that $\mu.P_i$ is a summand of P and $\bar{\mu}.P'_j$ a summand of P'. Since μ opp $\bar{\mu}$ holds, $\tau.(P_i \mid P'_j)$ is a summand of Q, and we have $Q \stackrel{\tau}{\to} P_i \mid P'_j$. This closes the case, since $(P_i \mid P'_j, P_i \mid P'_j) \in \mathcal{I}$.

The challenge transitions from Q are treated similarly. □

Exercise 3.4.10 None of the laws is valid. As a counterexample to the first, we can use again the processes $a.(b + c)$ and $a.b + a.c$. For the second, take $P = a$, $Q = b$, $R = c$. Then $(P \mid R) + (Q \mid R) \stackrel{c}{\to} P \mid \mathbf{0}$, where b has been pre-empted, whereas the only c-transition from $(P + Q) \mid R$ takes to $(P + Q) \mid \mathbf{0}$, and b is still available. □

Exercise 3.5.6 We need *n-hole contexts*. An n-hole context is a process expression that may contain the holes $[\cdot]_1, \ldots, [\cdot]_n$, each of which may appear several (and possibly zero) times; that is, the grammar for n-hole contexts is the same as the grammar for processes with the addition of productions that make $[\cdot]_1, \ldots, [\cdot]_n$ process expressions. If C is an n-hole context then $C[P_1, \ldots, P_n]$ is the process obtained by replacing each $[\cdot]_i$ in C by P_i for each i. If $n < m$, then an n-hole context is also an m-hole context. In the remainder, in context expressions such as $C[P_1, \ldots, P_n]$ it is intended that C is an n-hole context; moreover, in $\tilde{P} \sim \tilde{Q}$ it is intended that the vectors $\tilde{P}$ and $\tilde{Q}$ are of equal length and pairwise bisimilar.

To prove the result, we take the relation

$$\mathcal{R} \stackrel{\text{def}}{=} \{(C[\tilde{P}], C[\tilde{Q}]) \mid C \text{ is an } n\text{-hole context, for some } n, \text{ and } \tilde{P} \sim \tilde{Q}\}$$

and show that $\mathcal{R}$ is a bisimulation (we do not need $\mathcal{I}$, as an expression without holes is an n-hole context). Consider a transition $C[\tilde{P}] \stackrel{\mu}{\to} R$ (the case of a move from $C[\tilde{Q}]$ is similar). One finds a matching transition from $C[\tilde{Q}]$ proceeding by induction on the structure of C. The base of the induction is when C is an atomic expression; then the interesting case is $C = [\cdot]_i$, for some i, and can be dealt with using the hypothesis $P_i \sim Q_i$. In the inductive case, $C = f(C_1, \ldots, C_m)$, for some m. For simplicity of presentation we assume that $m = 1$ and that the rule applied for the transition $f(C_1[\tilde{P}]) \stackrel{\mu}{\to} R$ is as follows:

$$\frac{C_1[\tilde{P}] \xrightarrow{\mu'} R'}{f(C_1[\tilde{P}]) \xrightarrow{\mu} D[R']}$$

where D is some one-hole context. Exploiting the inductive assumption, $C_1[\tilde{Q}] \xrightarrow{\mu'} S'$ and there are $\tilde{P}'$, $\tilde{Q}'$, with $\tilde{P}' \sim \tilde{Q}'$ and some r-hole context D' such that $R' = D'[\tilde{P}']$ and $S' = D'[\tilde{Q}']$. We can therefore also infer

$$f(C_1[\tilde{Q}]) \xrightarrow{\mu} D[S']$$

and $D[R'] \mathcal{R} D[S']$, using the r-hole context $D[D']$.   □

Exercise 3.5.10

(1) The bisimulation contains the identity and has all pairs of the form $((P + Q)[f], (P[f]) + (Q[f]))$. The details are easy.
(2) It is not true. A counterexample is $P = a$ and $Q = b$ with $f(a) = a$ and $f(b) = a$. Then $(P \mid Q)[f]$ may not do a τ-transition, whereas $(P[f]) \mid (Q[f])$ can. A condition for recovering the equality is the injectivity of f.
(3) This is not true either. As a counterexample, take $P = b$ and $f(b) = a$. To recover the equality we can impose $f(a) = a$ and $f(b) \neq a$ whenever $b \neq a$.   □

Exercise 3.5.11 Take $P \stackrel{\text{def}}{=} a \mid \bar{b}$ and $Q \stackrel{\text{def}}{=} a.\bar{b} + \bar{b}.a$. We have $P \sim Q$. However, if we substitute b with a in P and Q we obtain, respectively, $a \mid \bar{a}$ and $a.\bar{a} + \bar{a}.a$, and these processes are not bisimilar.   □

Exercise 3.5.12 As a counterexample to associativity, consider $(\bar{a}.c \parallel a) \parallel \bar{a}.b$ versus $\bar{a}.c \parallel (a \parallel \bar{a}.b)$. Only in the former case is the sequence of transitions $\xrightarrow{\tau}\xrightarrow{c}$ possible.   □

Exercises in Chapter 4

Exercise 4.1.4 To prove image-finiteness, proceed by structural induction. As a counterexample to image-finiteness under weak transitions, take the process K defined before Lemma 4.2.10.   □

Exercise 4.2.4 Use the bisimulation $\{(P, Q)\} \cup \approx$.   □

Exercise 4.2.5 Use $\mathcal{R} \stackrel{\text{def}}{=} \{(P, R)\} \cup \approx$ to show that $P \approx R$. The details are easy (it is a simplified version of the Stuttering Lemma for branching bisimilarity, Lemma 4.9.2). Then conclude by transitivity that $R \approx Q$ holds too.   □

Exercise 4.2.6 They are not, as $\tau.0 + \tau.\bar{a}.0 \stackrel{\tau}{\Rightarrow} 0$, thus terminating without producing any visible action. Hence one can derive that no weak bisimulation exists that contains the given pair of processes.   □

Exercise 4.2.7 No. For instance, one would equate $\tau.b + a$ and $b + a$. However, the meaning of deterministic process given in Definition 1.2.4 is questionable on weak LTSs: one may well argue that a process such as $\tau.b + a$ should not be considered deterministic, as the action a can be pre-empted by a silent transition. $\qquad\square$

Exercise 4.2.11 If we take as the definition of weak bisimulation that in Lemma 4.2.9 there is nothing to prove, as weak bisimilarity becomes a form of strong bisimilarity.

More interestingly, we can take other definitions of weak bisimilarity, notably that in Lemma 4.2.10. Then the functional $F_{\approx}$ associated with weak bisimulation is defined thus: $F_{\approx}(\mathcal{R})$ is the set of all pairs (P, Q) such that:

(1) for all P' with $P \xrightarrow{\mu} P'$, there is Q' such that $Q \xoverset{\widehat{\mu}}{\Longrightarrow} Q'$ and $P' \mathcal{R} Q'$;
(2) for all Q' with $Q \xrightarrow{\mu} Q'$, there is P' such that $P \xoverset{\widehat{\mu}}{\Longrightarrow} P'$ and $P' \mathcal{R} Q'$.

Little modification is needed in the proof of Theorem 2.10.3. The modifications for the game interpretations are similar. $\qquad\square$

Exercise 4.2.12 Reason as in the corresponding result for strong bisimilarity, Exercise 1.4.16. $\qquad\square$

Exercise 4.2.13 One shows:

(1) $P \xrightarrow{\mu} P'$ in $\mathcal{L}'$ implies $P \xoverset{\widehat{\mu}}{\Longrightarrow} P'$ in $\mathcal{L}$;
(2) $P \Longrightarrow P'$ in $\mathcal{L}$ implies $P \xrightarrow{\tau} P'$ in $\mathcal{L}'$;
(3) $P \xoverset{\mu}{\Longrightarrow} P'$ in $\mathcal{L}$ implies $P \xrightarrow{\mu} P'$ in $\mathcal{L}'$.

From the last two points we derive that

- $P \xoverset{\widehat{\mu}}{\Longrightarrow} P'$ in $\mathcal{L}$ implies $P \xrightarrow{\mu} P'$ in $\mathcal{L}'$.

We can thus conclude that strong bisimilarity in $\mathcal{L}'$ is precisely weak bisimilarity in $\mathcal{L}$, using the characterisation of weak bisimilarity in Lemma 4.2.9. $\qquad\square$

Exercise 4.2.15 First one shows that if $\mathcal{R}$ is a weak bisimulation up-to $\approx$, $P \mathcal{R} Q$, and $P \Longrightarrow P'$ then there is Q' such that $Q \Longrightarrow Q'$ and $P' \sim\mathcal{R}\approx Q'$. This is proved by induction on a weight for $P \Longrightarrow P'$.

Then this result is extended to transitions $P \xoverset{\mu}{\Longrightarrow} P'$: there is Q' such that $Q \xoverset{\widehat{\mu}}{\Longrightarrow} Q'$ and $P' \sim\mathcal{R}\approx Q'$. This is proved by decomposing the relation $\xoverset{\mu}{\Longrightarrow}$ as $\Longrightarrow \xrightarrow{\mu} \Longrightarrow$.

Finally, using such results, one proves that $\approx \mathcal{R} \approx$ is a bisimulation. $\qquad\square$

Exercise 4.3.2 Show that the set of all pairs of the form $\{(P \mid \Omega_\tau, P)\}$ is a bisimulation. $\quad\square$

Exercise 4.3.4 We have $a + \Omega_\tau \approx a + \tau$, as can be shown using the weak bisimulation $\{(a + \Omega_\tau, a + \tau), (\mathbf{0}, \mathbf{0}), (\Omega_\tau, \mathbf{0})\}$. $\qquad\square$

Exercise 4.3.6 First we check what the transitions from BW are. Set

$$B_1 \overset{\text{def}}{=} \boldsymbol{\nu}\,\texttt{timeout}\,(\Omega_{\texttt{timeout}} \mid B);$$
$$C_1 \overset{\text{def}}{=} \boldsymbol{\nu}\,\texttt{timeout}\,(\Omega_{\texttt{timeout}} \mid C);$$
$$D \overset{\text{def}}{=} \boldsymbol{\nu}\,\texttt{timeout}\,(\Omega_{\texttt{timeout}} \mid \mathbf{0}).$$

Then we have $BW \xrightarrow{\text{init}} B_1$, $BW \xrightarrow{\text{init}} C_1$, $B_1 \overset{b}{\to} D$, $B_1 \overset{\tau}{\to} C_1$, $C_1 \overset{b}{\to} D$, $C_1 \overset{\tau}{\to} B_1$. The weak bisimulation to use is

$$\mathcal{R} \overset{\text{def}}{=} \{(P, BW), (b+c, B_1), (b+c, C_1), (\mathbf{0}, D)\}.$$

Note that the transition $B_1 \overset{\tau}{\to} C_1$ is matched by $b + c \Longrightarrow b + c$, and similarly for $C_1 \overset{\tau}{\to} B_1$. $\qquad\square$

Exercise 4.4.4 We have $\tau.a \approx a$, but not $\tau.a \parallel b \approx a \parallel b$, as only the former can do a b-transition before an a-transition. $\qquad\square$

Exercise 4.4.9 We only show the case of summation. Suppose $P \approx^c Q$; we wish to prove $P + R \approx^c Q + R$. Consider $P + R$ and the transition it can take. The case of transitions from R poses no problem. Suppose $P + R \overset{\mu}{\to} P'$ because $P \overset{\mu}{\to} P'$. From $P \approx^c Q$ we infer that there is Q' with $Q \overset{\mu}{\Longrightarrow} Q'$ and $P' \approx Q'$. Hence also $Q + R \overset{\mu}{\Longrightarrow} Q'$ and we are done. $\qquad\square$

Exercise 4.4.11 The implication from right to left is easy. For the converse, suppose $P \approx Q$. Recall that the difference between $\approx$ and $\approx^c$ is only the initial clause for τ-transitions. Suppose there is P' such that $P \overset{\tau}{\to} P'$ and $P' \approx Q$. Then one can show that $P \approx^c \tau.Q$, the details are simple. Conversely, if there is Q' such that $Q \overset{\tau}{\to} Q'$ and $P \approx Q'$, then $\tau.P \approx^c Q$. If neither case holds, then one derives $P \approx^c Q$. Suppose in fact $P \overset{\tau}{\to} P'$. As $P \approx Q$, there is Q' such that $Q \Longrightarrow Q'$ and $P' \approx Q'$. The weight of $Q \Longrightarrow Q'$ cannot be 0, otherwise we would be in one of the two previous cases; hence the weight is at least 1, as required by the definition of $\approx^c$. One reasons similarly when the challenge τ-transition originates from Q. $\qquad\square$

Exercise 4.4.13 Take $P \overset{\text{def}}{=} \tau + a$, and $Q \overset{\text{def}}{=} \Omega_\tau \mid P$. Then P and Q are not stable and are both in $\approx$, but not in $\approx^c$. $\qquad\square$

Exercise 4.5.6

(1) The equality

$$\nu d\,(P' \mid d.d.Q) \approx^c a.(b.\overline{c}.Q + \overline{c}.b.Q) + \overline{c}.a.b.Q$$

may be proved by applying Corollary 3.4.11(1) and a few algebraic laws as follows. As $P' \overset{\text{def}}{=} a.b.\overline{d} \mid \overline{c}.\overline{d}$, the only initial actions for $\nu d\,(P' \mid d.d.Q)$ are a and $\overline{c}$, thus

$$\nu d\,(P' \mid d.d.Q) \sim$$
$$a.\nu d\,(b.\overline{d} \mid \overline{c}.\overline{d} \mid d.d.Q) + \overline{c}.\nu d\,(a.b.\overline{d} \mid \overline{d} \mid d.d.Q) \overset{\text{def}}{=} R.$$

Call the first summand R_1 and the second R_2. Consider R_1; its only initial actions are b and c, hence

$$R_1 \sim b.vd \, (\overline{d} \mid \overline{c}.\overline{d} \mid d.d.Q) + \overline{c}.vd \, (b.\overline{d} \mid d \mid d.d.Q).$$

Call the two summands of R_1 so obtained R_1' and R_1''. Consider now the subterm $vd \, (\overline{d} \mid \overline{c}.\overline{d} \mid d.d.Q)$ of R_1'. Reasoning similarly, and garbage-collecting $\mathbf{0}$ processes in parallel, we have

$$vd \, (\overline{d} \mid \overline{c}.\overline{d} \mid d.d.Q) \sim$$
$$\overline{c}.vd \, (\overline{d} \mid d \mid d.d.Q) + \tau.vd \, (\overline{c}.\overline{d} \mid d.Q) \sim$$
$$\overline{c}.\tau.\tau.vd \, Q + \tau.\overline{c}.\tau.vd \, Q.$$

As d is fresh, we can apply the first law of Lemma 3.6.9 and eliminate the restriction. Using also the first and second τ-laws, we continue

$$\approx^c \overline{c}.Q + \tau.\overline{c}.Q$$
$$\approx^c \overline{c}.Q.$$

By the compositionality properties of $\sim$ and $\approx^c$ and the inclusion $\sim \, \subseteq \, \approx^c$, we can derive:

$$R \sim R_1 + R_2$$
$$\approx^c a.(b.\overline{c}.Q + R_1'') + R_2.$$

The final result is obtained by continuing the development of R_1'' and R_2.

(2) Here is an encoding:

$$[\![\mathbf{0}]\!]_d \stackrel{\mathrm{def}}{=} \overline{d};$$
$$[\![a.P]\!]_d \stackrel{\mathrm{def}}{=} a.[\![P]\!]_d;$$
$$[\![P_1 \mid P_2]\!]_d \stackrel{\mathrm{def}}{=} ve \, ([\![P_1]\!]_e \mid [\![P_2]\!]_e \mid e.e.\overline{d}) \qquad \text{where name } e \text{ is fresh};$$
$$[\![va \, P]\!]_d \stackrel{\mathrm{def}}{=} va \, [\![P]\!]_d.$$

The proof of the laws for sequential composition indicated can be derived by reasoning as at point (1).

The proof of the final two laws is delicate. We outline an argument. For a *finCCS* process P, write $P^\#$ for the LTS generated by P, whose states are the multi-step derivatives of P (Definition 1.2.3). In $P^\#$, we call the state P *root* and the states whose syntax has no prefix *leaves* (for instance $va \, (\mathbf{0} \mid \mathbf{0})$ and $\mathbf{0}$ are leaves, but $va \, a.\mathbf{0}$ is not). Call LTSs of this kind, where a state is identified as a root and certain states without outgoing transitions are considered leaves, a *rooted LTS*. If A, B are rooted LTSs, write $A : B$ for the rooted LTS obtained by attaching onto the leaves of A the root of B (if A has n leaves, we need n copies of B); in $A : B$, the root is that of A and the leaves those of B.

One can now prove that for $P \in finCCS$ and d,

$$[\![P]\!]_d \approx P^\# : \overline{d}. \tag{A.3}$$

This is proved by structural induction on P; in the case of parallel composition, one needs to show that for all finite Q_1 and Q_2, and name e fresh,

$$ve\,(Q_1^{\#} : \overline{e} \,|\, Q_2^{\#} : \overline{e} \,|\, e.e.\overline{d}) \approx (Q_1 \,|\, Q_2)^{\#} : d$$

(we take here the CCS operators and their SOS rules of Section 3.1 as general operator on LTSs, rather than on CCS processes); the result can be established either by induction on the sum of the number of prefixes in Q_1 and Q_2, or by directly proving a bisimulation. One also needs the property that $va\,(P^{\#}) \sim (va\,P)^{\#}$.

Having (A.3) at hand, one can now prove that for any P and Q,

$$P; Q = vd\,(\llbracket P \rrbracket_d \,|\, d.Q) \approx P^{\#} : Q^{\#}.$$

The proof is simple, also bearing in mind that if d is fresh and A is a rooted LTS, then $A : \overline{d} \xrightarrow{d}$ only if A has no transitions.

Finally, having reduced the sequential composition on processes to an operator on graphs, the required properties, namely

$$(P; Q); R \approx^c P; (Q; R),$$
$$P; 0 \approx^c P,$$

are immediate.   □

Exercise 4.6.2 We have $\tau.a + b \approx_\tau a + b$, but not $(\tau.a + b)\,|\,c \approx_\tau (a + b)\,|\,c$; the former process has a $\xRightarrow{c}$-transition to $a\,|\,0$, which the latter process can only match with a $\xRightarrow{c}$-transition to $(a + b)\,|\,0$. The derivatives are not $\approx_\tau$-bisimilar because only $(a + b)\,|\,0$ has a b-transition. Similarly, we have not $a.(\tau.a + b) \approx_\tau a.(a + b)$, because only the former process has an $\xRightarrow{a}$-transition to a.   □

Exercise 4.6.3 Write $\approx_\tau^c$ for the congruence induced by $\approx_\tau$. First of all, it is immediate to derive $\approx^c \subseteq \approx_\tau^c$, as $\approx^c \subseteq \approx_\tau$ holds and $\approx^c$ is a congruence (and as such contained in the largest congruence contained in $\approx_\tau$). We prove now the converse.

We begin by showing that $\approx_\tau^c \subseteq \approx$. Take some processes in $\approx_\tau$ that do not have a in their sort. Recall that Ω_a is the constant whose only transition is $\Omega_a \xrightarrow{a} \Omega_a$. We show that the set of all pairs (P, Q), without a in the sort of P and Q, and with $P\,|\,\Omega_a \approx_\tau Q\,|\,\Omega_a$, is a weak bisimulation.

Suppose $P \xrightarrow{\mu} P'$; we must show that there is Q' such that $Q \xRightarrow{\widehat{\mu}} Q'$, and $P'\,|\,\Omega_a \approx_\tau Q'\,|\,\Omega_a$. The case when $\mu \neq \tau$ is easy: we have $P\,|\,\Omega_a \xrightarrow{\mu} P'\,|\,\Omega_a$, and since Ω_a may only perform a-transitions and may not communicate with Q, the matching transition from $Q\,|\,\Omega_a$ must be of the form $Q\,|\,\Omega_a \xRightarrow{\mu} Q'\,|\,\Omega_a$, for some Q' with $Q \xRightarrow{\mu} Q'$ and $P'\,|\,\Omega_a \approx_\tau Q'\,|\,\Omega_a$.

Suppose now $\mu = \tau$. In this case we have $P\,|\,\Omega_a \xRightarrow{a} P'\,|\,\Omega_a$; from $P\,|\,\Omega_a \approx_\tau Q\,|\,\Omega_a$ there should be R such that $Q\,|\,\Omega_a \xRightarrow{a} R$ and $P'\,|\,\Omega_a \approx_\tau R$. By the transition rules for parallel composition, and since Q and Ω_a may not communicate, R must be of the form $Q'\,|\,\Omega_a$, for some Q' such that $Q \Longrightarrow Q'$. Thus we have found the transition from Q

matching the challenge from P. We can conclude that the relation defined above is a weak bisimulation.

We now know that $\approx^c_\tau$ is included in $\approx$; but the latter is not a congruence. The largest congruence included in $\approx$ is $\approx^c$. Hence also $\approx^c_\tau \subseteq \approx^c$, as $\approx^c_\tau$ is a congruence too. □

Exercise 4.7.3

(1) As $P \Uparrow$, clause (2.b) of Definition 4.7.1 is not applicable, hence $\{(P, P + Q)\} \cup \mathcal{I}$ is a prebisimulation with divergence.

(2) $\{(\Omega_\tau, P)\}$ is a prebisimulation with divergence. A transition $\Omega_\tau \xrightarrow{\tau} \Omega_\tau$ is matched by $P \Longrightarrow P$; transitions from P are not examined because $\Omega_\tau \Uparrow$. The property is not true for $\mathbf{0}$, which is not divergent, hence clause (2.b) of Definition 4.7.1 can be used.

(3) By showing that $\{(a.(b + \Omega_\tau), a.(b + \Omega_\tau) + a.\Omega_\tau)\} \cup \mathcal{I}$ is a prebisimulation with divergence. The proof is easy; as $a.(b + \Omega_\tau) \Uparrow_a$, the transition $a.(b + \Omega_\tau) + a.\Omega_\tau \xrightarrow{a} \Omega_\tau$ is not considered in the challenges.

(4) Use the following prebisimulation with divergence:

$$\leq_\Uparrow \cup \{(P, Q + R) \mid P \Uparrow, \text{ and } P \leq_\Uparrow Q, \text{ and}$$
$$\text{there is no } P' \text{ with } (P \xrightarrow{\tau} P' \text{ and not } P' \Uparrow) \}.$$

As a counterexample for the condition, take $P = \tau + \Omega_\tau$, $Q = \mathbf{0}$, and $R = a$. □

Exercise 4.8.5 They are not. For the first law, take $P = a$, and the transition $\tau.a \xrightarrow{\tau} a$, that a cannot match. For the second law, take $P = a$, $Q = b$ and the transition $a \mid \tau.b \xrightarrow{a} \mathbf{0} \mid \tau.b$, that could only be matched by $\tau.(a \mid b) \xrightarrow{a} \mathbf{0} \mid b$. Now, the transition $\mathbf{0} \mid \tau.b \xrightarrow{\tau} \mathbf{0} \mid b$, on the first derivative, cannot be matched by the second one. □

Exercise 4.9.3 To see that Lemma 4.9.2 is an immediate consequence of the branching bisimilarity version of Exercise 4.2.4, it is sufficient to note that for each i, $P_0 \Longrightarrow P_i \approx_{\text{br}} P_i$ and $P_i \Longrightarrow P_n \approx_{\text{br}} P_0$. □

Exercise 4.9.10

(1) First one shows that the law is valid for $\approx_{\text{br}}$, then that the clause of $\approx^c_{\text{br}}$ on initial actions is respected. The details are easy.

(2) The relation $\{(P + \tau.P, \tau.P)\} \cup \approx_{\text{br}}$ is a branching bisimulation (one needs the fact that $\approx_{\text{br}}$ is reflexive). As a counterexample for $\approx^c_\eta$, take $P = a$, and the move $a + \tau.a \xrightarrow{a} \mathbf{0}$.

(3) Take $a.(b + \tau.c)$ and $a.(b + \tau.c) + a.c$, and the move $a.(b + \tau.c) + a.c \xrightarrow{a} c$.

□

Exercise 4.9.11 For the first question, take $P = \mathbf{0}$ in **B**, and use the axioms for choice in Figure 3.2 (in particular **S1**). For the second item, we have, using **T2**, the axioms for choice in Figure 3.2 (in particular **S4**), again **T2**, and finally **T1**:

$$\mu.(\tau.(P+Q)+P) = \mu.(\tau.(P+Q)+P+Q+P)$$
$$= \mu.(\tau.(P+Q)+P+Q)$$
$$= \mu.\tau.(P+Q)$$
$$= \mu.(P+Q).$$

$\square$

Exercises in Chapter 5

Exercise 5.2.3 The two assertions are proved simultaneously, by induction on the structure of the tests. The base case is when T is SUCC or FAIL, and is immediate. We consider a couple of cases in the induction, leaving the others to the reader.

Suppose $T = \mu.T'$; then $\overline{T} = \widetilde{\mu}.\overline{T'}$. We have $\top \in \mathcal{O}_{\text{den}}(T, P)$ if there is P' with $P \xrightarrow{\mu} P'$ and $\top \in \mathcal{O}_{\text{den}}(T', P')$. By induction $\bot \in \mathcal{O}_{\text{den}}(\overline{T'}, P')$. Hence also $\bot \in \mathcal{O}_{\text{den}}(\widetilde{\mu}.\overline{T'}, P)$.

On the other hand, $\bot \in \mathcal{O}_{\text{den}}(\mu.T', P)$ means that either there is P' with $P \xrightarrow{\mu} P'$ and $\bot \in \mathcal{O}_{\text{den}}(T', P')$, or $P \operatorname{ref}(\mu)$; in the former case, reason as above, in the latter case we immediately get $\top \in \mathcal{O}_{\text{den}}(\widetilde{\mu}.\overline{T'}, P)$.

Suppose now $T = \forall T'$. Then $\overline{T} = \exists\overline{T'}$. We have $\top \in \mathcal{O}_{\text{den}}(T, P)$ if $\bot \notin \mathcal{O}_{\text{den}}(T', P)$. By induction, this means that $\top \notin \mathcal{O}_{\text{den}}(\overline{T'}, P)$. Hence $\bot \in \mathcal{O}_{\text{den}}(\exists\overline{T'}, P)$.

In contrast, we have $\bot \in \mathcal{O}_{\text{den}}(\forall T', P)$ if $\bot \in \mathcal{O}_{\text{den}}(T', P)$. By induction, this means that $\top \in \mathcal{O}_{\text{den}}(\overline{T'}, P)$. Hence $\top \in \mathcal{O}_{\text{den}}(\exists\overline{T'}, P)$. $\square$

Exercise 5.2.5 Take the test $T \stackrel{\text{def}}{=} a.b.\text{SUCC}$. Then $\mathcal{O}_{\text{den}}(T, P_2) = \{\top\}$ and $\mathcal{O}_{\text{den}}(T, Q_2) = \{\top, \bot\}$. $\square$

Exercise 5.2.8 Only Q_3 passes the test $a.((\exists b.\widetilde{c}.\text{FAIL}) \wedge (\exists b.\widetilde{d}.\text{FAIL}))$. $\square$

Exercise 5.2.9 Use the test $a.(\widetilde{b}.\text{FAIL} \wedge a.\widetilde{a}.\text{FAIL})$; only P_4 can give $\top$. $\square$

Exercise 5.7.5

Example 5.6.2. For the $\simeq_{\text{may}}$ results, one checks that the processes are trace equivalent, the details are easy. To see that $P_3 \simeq_{\text{must}} Q_3$, suppose that P_3 after s must A; this holds in one of the following cases:

- $s = \epsilon$ and $a \in A$;
- $s = a$ and $b \in A$;
- $s = ab$ and $\{c, d\} \subseteq A$.

These are also exactly the cases in which Q_3 after s must A holds.

In any of the above choices for s and A, also R_3 after s must A holds, which gives $P_3 \leq_{\text{must}} R_3$ and $Q_3 \leq_{\text{must}} R_3$. There are additional possibilities, however, for R_3 (e.g., with $s = ab$ and $A = \{c\}$), hence the converse is false.

Example 5.6.3. For the $\simeq_{\text{may}}$ relations, and $Q_2 \simeq_{\text{must}} R_2$, reason as above. We have $P_2 \not\leq_{\text{must}} Q_2$ because only on the former process the predicate after a must $\{b\}$ holds.

Example 5.6.4. $P \leq_{\text{must}} Q$ holds because P after s must A in one of the following cases:

- $s = \epsilon$ and $a \in A$;
- $s = a$ and $\{b, c\} \subseteq A$.

In all these cases, we have Q after s must A.

We also have Q after a must $\{b, d\}$, which fails for P, hence $Q \not\leq_{\text{must}} P$.

Example 5.6.5. $P \leq_{\text{must}} Q$ because P after s must A in one of the following cases:

- $s = \epsilon$ and $a \in A$;
- $s = a$ and $\{b, c\} \subseteq A$. In all these cases, we also have Q after s must A. The converse is false, as Q after a must $\{b\}$ but not P after a must $\{b\}$.

□

Exercise 5.7.6 The law is valid under $\simeq_{\text{may}}$, but not under $\simeq_{\text{must}}$, as shown in Example 5.6.3.

$a.P + a.Q \leq_{\text{must}} a.(P + Q)$ is true. Suppose after s must A holds with the former process. Distinguishing the cases $s = a$ and $s \neq a$, one proves that the same would hold also on the latter process. □

Exercise 5.7.7 We use the characterisation of $\leq_{\text{must}}$ as $\leq'_{\text{must}}$.

Writing $P \leq''_{\text{must}} Q$ if for all s and Q' such that $Q \xrightarrow{s} Q'$ there is P' with $P \xrightarrow{s} P'$ and readies$(P') \subseteq$ readies(Q'), we have to show $\leq'_{\text{must}} = \leq''_{\text{must}}$.

We first show that $\leq''_{\text{must}}$ implies $\leq'_{\text{must}}$. Suppose P after s must A, and not Q after s must A. This means that there is Q' with $Q \xrightarrow{s} Q'$ and Q' is unable to perform an action in A; but from $P \leq''_{\text{must}} Q$ it follows that there is also an s-derivative of P with the same property, against the assumption P after s must A.

Conversely, assume $P \leq'_{\text{must}} Q$ and $Q \xrightarrow{s} Q'$, for some Q'. The set P after s cannot be empty; otherwise P after s must $\emptyset$ would be true, whereas Q after s must $\emptyset$ is not (as Q has at least one s-derivative). Let $\{P_i\}_i = P$ after s. If none of the P_i had readies included in those of Q', we could find actions μ_i such that P after s must $\{\mu_i\}_i$ whereas not Q after s must $\{\mu_i\}_i$, against the initial assumption. □

Exercise 5.8.2 Under any test, both processes may yield an infinite run, originated by the term Ω_τ. Such a run has $\perp$ as a result. In the "must" semantics, additional $\top$ results are ignored. □

Exercise 5.8.4 We consider the assertion for weak bisimilarity.

Exercise 4.2.12 is useful here, showing that whenever $P \approx Q$ and $P \xRightarrow{s} P'$, where s is a sequence of visible actions, we have $Q \xRightarrow{s} Q'$, for some Q' with $P' \approx Q'$.

From Exercise 4.2.12 it follows that bisimilar processes perform the same sequences of visible actions, hence $P \approx Q$ implies $P \simeq_{\text{may}} Q$.

We now prove that $P \approx Q$ also implies $P \simeq_{\text{must}} Q$ if the LTS has no divergences. As the processes are divergent-free, the predicates $\Downarrow s$ in the definition of $\leq'_{\text{must}}$ are not needed. Thus it is sufficient to prove that for all visible sequences s and sets A of visible actions: if whenever $P \xRightarrow{s} P'$ there is $\ell \in A$ with $P' \xRightarrow{\ell}$, then the same holds for Q. Suppose this were not true. There would be Q' with $Q \stackrel{s}{\Rightarrow} Q'$ and not $Q' \stackrel{\ell}{\Rightarrow}$, for all $\ell \in A$. As $P \approx Q$, there must be a derivative P' of P with $P \stackrel{s}{\Rightarrow} P'$ and $P' \approx Q'$ (again by Exercise 4.2.12). Moreover, as $P' \approx Q'$, also not $P' \stackrel{\ell}{\Rightarrow}$ for all $\ell \in A$. This contradicts the initial assumption on the s-derivatives of P. □

Exercise 5.8.5 Bisimilarity implies $\simeq_{may}$, also on weak LTSs (see Exercise 5.8.4) Thus from $P \approx BW$ we can derive $P \simeq_{may} BW$.

The equality fails under $\simeq_{must}$ and $\simeq_{test}$ because process BW only may diverge, via a computation along the internal channel timeout. Must and testing semantics are sensitive to divergences. □

Exercise 5.8.6 The two processes have the same visible traces (ϵ, a, b), hence they are in the relation $\simeq_{may}$. To see that they are also in $\simeq_{must}$, first note that they do not contain divergences. The only predicates of the form "after s must A" they satisfy have $s = \epsilon$ and $b \in A$. Note that in the must semantics the presence of the a-transition in the processes is completely irrelevant, hence it could be replaced by any other label, except τ. □

Exercise 5.8.8 It is sufficient to prove the result for processes in full standard form, because, by Lemma 3.6.6, any *finCCS* process can be rewritten in such a form using the laws of Figure 3.2 (which are also the laws needed for the exercise; actually not all of them are needed), and the laws are also valid for testing (as strong bisimilarity implies testing).

Thus suppose P is in full standard form. We prove the assertion using induction on the number n of prefixes that appear in P. The case $n = 0$ is trivial. Consider now the inductive case, with $n > 1$. In this case P is of the form $\Sigma_i \mu_i.P_i$. When all μ_i are different from τ, or they are all τ, the result is immediate: there is no hybrid non-determinism at the outermost level, and we only have to apply induction on the subterms P_i to make sure that also the inner hybrid non-determinism is removed.

Suppose now that there is some hybrid non-determinism at the outermost level. Then, using the monoidal laws of sum, we can rewrite P as $\tau.R + S$. Using axiom (5.1), we then have:

$$P = \tau.(R + S) + \tau.R.$$

Now, as the number of prefixes in $R + S$ and in R is smaller than n, we can conclude using induction on these terms. □

Exercise 5.8.10 For the second question, set

$$P \oplus Q \stackrel{\text{def}}{=} \nu a \, (\bar{a} \mid a.P \mid a.Q),$$

where a is fresh. □

Exercise 5.11.2 The processes have the same sets of failures, namely

- (ϵ, A) for all A with $a \notin A$;
- (a, A) for all A with $\{b, c\} \not\subseteq A$;
- (ab, A) and (ac, A), for all A.

However, R_2 has an a-derivative in which both b and c are observables, whereas Q_2 has not. Hence they are not ready equivalent. □

Exercise 5.11.3

(1) The two processes have the same nine ready pairs. A test that distinguishes them is $T \stackrel{\text{def}}{=} a.\vec{b}.c.e.\omega$, which only the process on the left may pass.

(2) We sketch the argument. Call the process on the left P and that on the right Q. As the processes initially have the same action available, and Q has more non-determinism, a run of P on a given test can also be mimicked by Q. Hence the results obtained by runs of tests on P are also obtained with Q.

For the converse, consider a run of Q on a test where the run exploits the branch $a.(b+c)$ that P does not have. Suppose this produces a success. This means that in the test, before the success signal, we can only meet some refusals, different from $\vec{a}$, then a, then some refusals not mentioning b and c, then b or c. In any case there is at least one branch of P that can be used to reproduce the success.

Finally one shows that the extra branch of Q cannot produce a failure on tests that only produce successes when run on P. In order to produce only successes on P the test can only possibly have, before the final success signal: first refuses that do not mention a, then an a prefix, then refuses that do not mention b and c (otherwise one of the branches of P would yield a failure). Such a test yields only successes also when run on Q, even if Q makes use of its extra branch.

The processes are not ready equivalent, as Q has an a-derivative in which both b and c are observable, whereas P has not. □

Exercises in Chapter 6

Exercise 6.2.7 One can show $K_1 \leq_{\text{rs}} K_2$ using the ready simulation

$$\mathcal{R}_1 \stackrel{\text{def}}{=} \{(K_1, K_2), (d.\bar{v}.K_1 + d.z.K_1, d.\bar{v}.K_2 + d.z.K_2),$$
$$(\bar{v}.K_1, \bar{v}.K_2), (z.K_1, z.K_2)\}.$$

To prove the converse, we can use the ready simulation

$$\mathcal{R}_2 \stackrel{\text{def}}{=} \mathcal{R}_1^{-1} \cup \{(d.z.K_2, d.\bar{v}.K_1 + d.z.K_1)\},$$

where in the latter pair the specific v chosen is irrelevant. □

Exercise 6.3.2 (2). The problem is that the process on the right has an a-transition with derivative $b.d$. The only a-transition of the process on the left yields $b.c + b.d$. Now, $b.d$ and $b.c + b.d$ are not simulation equivalent (only the latter has c in its sort). □

Exercise 6.3.3 The implication from left to right is immediate. For the converse, we proceed by induction on n. For $n = 0$, the assertion holds because $(\leq_{0n})^{-1} = \sim_{0n} = Pr \times Pr$. Suppose the assertion holds for $n - 1$, and that there is a simulation $\mathcal{R} \subseteq (\leq_{nn})^{-1}$. We have to show that we also have $\mathcal{R} \subseteq \leq_{n\,n}$. By induction, this is true if $\mathcal{R} \subseteq (\leq_{n-1\,n})^{-1}$. In turn, this holds from the hypothesis $\mathcal{R} \subseteq (\leq_{n\,n})^{-1}$ and the inclusion $(\leq_{n\,n})^{-1} \subseteq (\leq_{n-1\,n})^{-1}$ (which is a straightforward consequence of the definition of the $\leq_{m\,n}$ relations).   □

Exercise 6.3.4

(1) $P \sim_{n\,n} Q$ means that P and Q should be able to match each other's transitions in a way that the derivatives are in $\sim_{n-1\,n}$. Now, on the processes of the exercise, the transition $Q \xrightarrow{a} b.c$ may only be matched by $P \xrightarrow{a} b.c + b$. Thus, if P and Q were three-nested simulation equivalent, $b.c$ and $b.c + b$ should be two-nested simulation equivalent. This, in turn, would mean that the transition $b.c + b \xrightarrow{b} 0$ is matched by $b.c \xrightarrow{b} c$ and that 0 and c are simulation equivalent. But the last claim is impossible, as c has a transition whereas 0 has none.

However, we do have $P \leq_{3\,n} Q$, as the simulation $\mathcal{R} \stackrel{\text{def}}{=} \{(P, Q)\} \cup \mathcal{I}$ is in $\sim_{2\,n}$.

(2) Reasoning as above, one shows that $a.Q$ and $a.P + a.Q$ are not four-nested simulation equivalent: the transition $a.P + a.Q \xrightarrow{a} P$ may only be matched by $a.Q \xrightarrow{a} Q$, and we would need $P \sim_{3\,n} Q$, which at point (1) we have established to be false.

We prove that $a.Q \sim_{3\,n} a.P + a.Q$. Consider the two simulations

$$\mathcal{R}_1 \stackrel{\text{def}}{=} \{(a.Q, a.P + a.Q)\} \cup \mathcal{I},$$
$$\mathcal{R}_2 \stackrel{\text{def}}{=} \{(a.P + a.Q, a.Q), (P, Q)\} \cup \mathcal{I}.$$

We need $\mathcal{R}_i \subseteq \sim_{2\,n}, i = 1, 2$. It is easy to see that $\mathcal{R}_i \subseteq \sim_{1\,n}$. Therefore also $\mathcal{R}_i \subseteq \leq_{2\,n}$. This means $a.Q \sim_{2\,n} a.P + a.Q$ (as the pair appears in both relations), and similarly $\mathcal{I} \subseteq \sim_{2\,n}$. There remains the pair (P, Q), which we have established to be in $\sim_{2\,n}$ in Exercise 6.3.2(1).   □

Exercise 6.3.5 They are two-nested simulation equivalent, but not three-nested simulation equivalent, hence also not bisimilar.

We prove that they are two-nested simulation equivalent. We call $A \stackrel{\text{def}}{=} a.(b + c) + a.b$, and $B \stackrel{\text{def}}{=} a.(b + c)$. Consider the two simulations

$$\mathcal{R}_1 \stackrel{\text{def}}{=} \{(P, Q)\} \cup \mathcal{I},$$
$$\mathcal{R}_2 \stackrel{\text{def}}{=} \{(Q, P), (B, A)\} \cup \mathcal{I}.$$

As both relations are simulations, $\mathcal{R}_1 \subseteq \sim_{1\,n}$. One can also prove, separately, that $A \sim_{1\,n} B$ (the details are simple). Hence also $\mathcal{R}_2 \subseteq \sim_{1\,n}$. From this we deduce $P \sim_{2\,n} Q$.

The reason why the processes are not three-nested simulation equivalent is that the transition $Q \xrightarrow{a} B$ is only matched by $P \xrightarrow{a} A$, but we do not have $A \sim_{2\,n} B$, which can be established by reasoning as in earlier exercises.   □

Exercise 6.3.6 Show that the relation

$$\{(P, Q) \mid \text{ for all } n \text{ there is a simulation } \mathcal{R}_n \subseteq \sim_{n\,n} \text{ with } P \mathcal{R} Q\}$$

is a bisimulation. The details are similar to the stratification result for bisimilarity (Theorem 2.10.13 and Exercise 2.10.18), using the fact that relations $\sim_{0n}$, $\sim_{1n}$, ... form a decreasing sequence of relations with respect to set containment. □

Exercise 6.4.3 Surprisingly, weak similarity is indeed a precongruence, and weak simulation equivalence is indeed a congruence. The usual counterexample for choice (τ and $\mathbf{0}$ related, but $\tau + a$ and $\mathbf{0} + a$ unrelated) does not apply. We omit the details. □

Exercise 6.4.4 We only explain the case for two-nested simulation equivalence. The first clause does not apply, for otherwise we would not identify $\tau.a + \tau.b$ with itself (a simulation would have to relate a and $\tau.a + \tau.b$, which are not simulation equivalent). This would break the reflexivity property of two-nested simulation equivalence.

With the second clause we would identify $\tau.a. + \tau.b$ and $a + b$, which are not two-nested simulation equivalent. □

Exercise 6.4.5 We can apply the usual counterexample: τ and $\mathbf{0}$ are related but not $\tau + a$ and $\mathbf{0} + a$. The former can evolve into $\mathbf{0}$, which is stopped, and this cannot be matched by the latter. □

Exercise 6.5.5 Suppose $P \approx_{cs} Q$ and $Q \approx_{cs} R$. This means that there are coupled simulations $(\mathcal{S}_1, \mathcal{S}_2)$ and $(\mathcal{R}_1, \mathcal{R}_2)$ with $(P, Q) \in \mathcal{S}_1 \cap \mathcal{S}_2$ and $(Q, R) \in \mathcal{R}_1 \cap \mathcal{R}_2$. Take the pair of relations $(\mathcal{S}_1 \mathcal{R}_1, \mathcal{S}_2 \mathcal{R}_2)$. Clearly $(P, R) \in \mathcal{S}_1 \mathcal{R}_1 \cap \mathcal{S}_2 \mathcal{R}_2$. So we have to show that $(\mathcal{S}_1 \mathcal{R}_1, \mathcal{S}_2 \mathcal{R}_2)$ is a coupled simulation. Relations $\mathcal{S}_1 \mathcal{R}_1$ and $(\mathcal{S}_2 \mathcal{R}_2)^{-1}$ are simulations: this follows from the fact that the composition of simulations is a simulation (note that $(\mathcal{S}_2 \mathcal{R}_2)^{-1} = \mathcal{R}_2^{-1} \mathcal{S}_2^{-1}$).

Now, the coupling property; we consider clause (1) of Definition 6.5.3, as (2) is analogous. Since $(\mathcal{S}_1, \mathcal{S}_2)$ is a coupled simulation, there is Q' with $Q \Longrightarrow Q'$ and $(P, Q') \in \mathcal{S}_2$. Since $(Q, R) \in \mathcal{R}_1$ and $\mathcal{R}_1$ is a simulation, there is R' with $R \Longrightarrow R'$ and $(Q', R') \in \mathcal{R}_1$. By the coupling requirement, however, there is also R'' with $R' \Longrightarrow R''$ and $(Q', R'') \in \mathcal{R}_2$. Thus we have found a derivative R'' of R with $(P, R'') \in \mathcal{S}_2 \mathcal{R}_2$, as required. □

Exercise 6.5.8 Take $P = a$ and $Q = b$. In both cases the problem is matching the transition $\mu.(\tau.a + \tau.b) \xrightarrow{\mu} \tau.a + \tau.b$. We cannot even use coupled similarity: if μ is a visible action, both processes are stable, hence coupled similarity (or its inverse) would imply coupled simulation equivalence, yielding the same simulation problems as above. □

Exercise 6.5.11 In this exercise, we write $\approx_{cs}^c$ for rooted coupled simulation equivalence.

(1) We only consider the proof that $\approx_{cs}^c$ is preserved by summation, as the other proofs are along the lines of the analogous results for weak bisimilarity and its rooted version. Let

$$\mathcal{S}_1 \stackrel{\text{def}}{=} \leq_{cs}$$
$$\cup \{(P + R, Q + R) \mid P \approx_{cs}^c Q\}$$
$$\cup \{(P, Q + R) \mid P \leq_{cs} Q \text{ and } Q \text{ is not stable}\}$$

and S_2 be defined symmetrically. We show that (S_1, S_2) is a coupled simulation. This proves the assertion, because if $P \approx_{cs}^c Q$ then we would have $(P + R, Q + R) \in S_1 \cap S_2$ and, obviously, when (P is stable iff Q is stable) then also ($P + R$ is stable iff $Q + R$ is stable). We consider S_1, as the case for S_2 is symmetric. The proof that S_1 is a simulation is easy. We only examine the coupling requirement.

For $\leq_{cs}$, coupling holds because $\geq_{cs} \subseteq S_2$. For $(P + R, Q + R)$ it holds because the pair is also in S_2. Thus we are left with $(P, Q + R)$, where $P \leq_{cs} Q$ and Q is not stable. Since $P \leq_{cs} Q$, by the coupling condition for $\leq_{cs}$ there is Q' such that $Q \Longrightarrow Q'$ and $P \geq_{cs} Q'$. If Q' is reached by performing some τs, then also $Q + R \Longrightarrow Q'$ and we are then done, as $\geq_{cs} \subseteq S_2$.

Thus suppose $Q' = Q$. As Q is not stable, there is Q'' with $Q \overset{\tau}{\Rightarrow} Q''$. Hence also $Q + R \overset{\tau}{\Rightarrow} Q''$. We use this transition for the coupling; i.e., we have to show that $P \geq_{cs} Q''$ holds. For this we have to check the simulation and the coupling conditions.

- The simulation condition holds: if $Q'' \overset{\mu}{\Rightarrow} Q'''$ then, since $P \geq_{cs} Q$ (obtained from $P \geq_{cs} Q'$ and $Q' = Q$) and $Q \overset{\tau}{\Rightarrow} Q''$, there is P' such that $P \overset{\mu}{\Rightarrow} P'$ and $P' \geq_{cs} Q'''$.
- Now the coupling condition. Since $P \geq_{cs} Q$ and $Q \overset{\tau}{\Rightarrow} Q''$, there is P' with $P \Longrightarrow P'$ and $P' \geq_{cs} Q''$. By the coupling requirement on $P' \geq_{cs} Q''$ there is P'' such that $P' \Longrightarrow P'' \leq_{cs} Q''$. We have thus derived the existence of some P'' with $P \Longrightarrow P''$ and $P'' \leq_{cs} Q''$, which concludes the case.

(2) We can take the usual example: $\tau.a$ versus a. $\qquad\square$

Exercise 6.5.12 Suppose P is stable, and Q is not, and that for all R we have $P + R \approx_{cs} Q + R$. Take now $R \overset{\text{def}}{=} a$, where a is not in the sort of P and Q. We have $Q + a \overset{\tau}{\rightarrow} Q'$, for some Q' with $Q \overset{\tau}{\rightarrow} Q'$. As $P + a \geq_{cs} Q + a$ and both P and R are stable, it must be that $P + R \geq_{cs} Q'$. By the coupling requirement, there is Q'' with $Q' \Longrightarrow Q''$ and $P + a \leq_{cs} Q''$. This is, however, impossible, as $P + a$ can take an a-transition, and a is not in the sort of Q''. $\qquad\square$

Exercise 6.5.15

(1) A counterexample is given by the processes a and $\tau.a + \tau.b$, which is easy to prove that are in the relation $\leq_{cs}$ but not in $\leq_{Scs}$.
(2) We show that (R_1, R_2) is an S-coupled simulation, for

$$R_1 \overset{\text{def}}{=} \{(P, Q) \mid P \leq_{cs} Q \text{ and } (P \text{ stable implies } Q \text{ stable})\},$$
$$R_2 \overset{\text{def}}{=} \{(P, Q) \mid P \geq_{cs} Q \text{ and } (Q \text{ stable implies } P \text{ stable})\}.$$

We focus on R_1, as the reasoning for R_2 is symmetric. First we show that R_1 is a simulation.

Suppose $P \, R_1 \, Q$ and $P \overset{\mu}{\rightarrow} P'$. As $P \leq_{cs} Q$, we have $Q \overset{\widehat{\mu}}{\Rightarrow} Q'$, for some Q' with $P' \leq_{cs} Q'$. If P' is not stable, there is nothing else to prove. Otherwise, (P', Q') is not in R_1. However, by the coupling requirement, there is Q'' such that $Q' \Longrightarrow Q''$ and $P' \geq_{cs} Q''$. Since the LTS is not divergent, there is Q''' stable with $Q'' \Longrightarrow Q'''$, moreover $P' \geq_{cs} Q'''$, as P' is stable and $\geq_{cs}$ is a simulation. Again, by the coupling requirement and the stability of P' also $P' \leq_{cs} Q'''$; as Q''' is stable too, $P' \mathcal{R}_1 Q'''$. Summarising, we have found Q''' such that $Q \stackrel{\hat{\mu}}{\Longrightarrow} Q'''$ and $P' \mathcal{R}_1 Q'''$.

The S-coupling requirement for $\mathcal{R}_1$ is straightforward, as the stability of the first process in the pair implies that of the second. The pair is thus related by $\approx_{cs}$ and is also in $\mathcal{R}_2$.

(3) We show that $(\mathcal{R}_1, \mathcal{R}_2)$ is a coupled simulation, for

$$\mathcal{R}_1 \stackrel{\text{def}}{=} \leq_{Scs} \cup \{(P, Q) \mid \exists Q' \text{ with } Q \Longrightarrow Q' \text{ and } P \approx_{Scs} Q'\},$$
$$\mathcal{R}_2 \stackrel{\text{def}}{=} \geq_{Scs} \cup \{(P, Q) \mid \exists P' \text{ with } P \Longrightarrow P' \text{ and } P' \approx_{Scs} Q\},$$

where $\geq_{Scs}$ is the inverse of $\leq_{Scs}$.

As usual, we focus on $\mathcal{R}_1$, as the reasoning for $\mathcal{R}_2$ is symmetric. The proof that $\mathcal{R}_1$ is a simulation is straightforward. We consider the coupling requirement. If $(P, Q) \in \mathcal{R}_1$ because there is Q' with $Q \Longrightarrow Q'$ and $P \approx_{Scs} Q'$ then we can take $Q \Longrightarrow Q'$ to be the coupling transition, as $P \mathcal{R}_2 Q'$ holds.

Otherwise, suppose $(P, Q) \in \mathcal{R}_1$ because $P \leq_{Scs} Q$. If P is stable, then also $P \geq_{Scs} Q$, so $Q \Longrightarrow Q$ can be the coupling transition.

If P is not stable, as the LTS is divergence-free there is P' stable with $P \Longrightarrow P'$; there is also Q' with $Q \Longrightarrow Q'$ and $P' \leq_{Scs} Q'$. As P' is stable, we actually have $P' \approx_{Scs} Q'$. Summarising, we have $P \Longrightarrow P' \approx_{Scs} Q'$; thus $P \mathcal{R}_2 Q'$ holds, and $Q \Longrightarrow Q'$ is a coupling transition. $\qquad\square$

Exercise 6.5.19

(1) We only discuss transitivity. One shows that the composition of two stable bisimulations $\mathcal{R}_1, \mathcal{R}_2$ is again a stable bisimulation. Suppose $P \mathcal{R}_1 Q$, $Q \mathcal{R}_2 R$ and $P \stackrel{s}{\Rightarrow} P'$ with P' stable; we have to find R' with $R \stackrel{s}{\Rightarrow} R'$ and $P'\mathcal{R}_1\mathcal{R}_2R'$. Since $\mathcal{R}_1$ is a stable bisimulation, there is Q' with $Q \stackrel{s}{\Rightarrow} Q'$ and $P' \mathcal{R}_1 Q'$. Since Q' is not divergent there is Q'' stable with $Q' \Longrightarrow Q''$. From $P' \mathcal{R}_1 Q'$, and since P' is stable, taking s to be the empty sequence we derive $P' \mathcal{R}_1 Q''$. As $Q \stackrel{s}{\Rightarrow} Q''$, there is R' with $R \stackrel{s}{\Rightarrow} R'$ and $Q'' \mathcal{R}_2 R'$. Thus also $P'\mathcal{R}_1\mathcal{R}_2R'$, and we are done.

(2) The relation $\{\mu.P + \mu.Q, \mu.(\tau.P + \tau.Q)\} \cup \mathcal{I}$ is a stable bisimulation.

(3) By showing that $\approx_{cs}$ is a stable bisimulation. Suppose $P \approx_{cs} Q$ and $P \stackrel{s}{\Rightarrow} P'$ with P' stable. Since $\approx_{cs}$ is a simulation, there is Q' with $Q \stackrel{s}{\Rightarrow} Q'$ and $P' \leq_{cs} Q'$; by the coupling requirement, there is also Q'' with $Q' \Longrightarrow Q''$ and $P' \geq_{cs} Q''$. As P' is stable, we derive $P' \approx_{cs} Q''$. Thus $Q \stackrel{s}{\Rightarrow} Q''$ and $P' \approx_{cs} Q''$, and we are done.

The assertion is actually simpler using the characterisation of $\approx_{cs}$ in terms of $\approx_{Scs}$ for divergent-free LTSs, as the following point of the exercise shows.

(4) Straightforward, as the coupling requirement in S-coupled simulations is on stable processes.

(5) The previous points show that coupled simulation equivalence implies stable bisimilarity. We show that stable bisimilarity implies testing equivalence. We make use of the weak version of Theorem 5.7.3, discussed in Section 5.8. Thus suppose P and Q are stable bisimilar. Then they have the same visible traces. If $P \overset{s}{\Rightarrow} P'$ then, as the LTSs are divergent-free, also $P \overset{s}{\Rightarrow} P''$, for some P'' stable. Therefore also $Q \overset{s}{\Rightarrow}$, and s is in the traces of Q. Now suppose P after s must A and not Q after s must A. This means that Q has a stable derivative under s, say Q' (the existence of such a stable derivative uses the divergence-free hypothesis), and Q' is unable to perform any action in A. There is also P' with $P \overset{s}{\Rightarrow} P'$ and P' stable bisimilar with Q'. We have earlier shown that stable bisimilarity implies trace equivalence, hence also P' is unable to perform any action in A, contradicting the assumption P after s must A.

For the strictness of the inclusions: for coupled simulation equivalence, use the axiom at point (2); for testing, we can use the examples that distinguish bisimilarity and testing on strong LTSs.

Note that on LTSs with divergences, stable bisimilarity does not even imply may testing, as the former equates, for instance, Ω_τ^a and Ω_τ^b. □

Exercises in Chapter 7

Exercise 7.2.11 For Ω_τ and K as defined in Corollary 7.2.10 it holds that $\overline{a}.0 \rhd \Omega_\tau \overset{\centerdot}{\not\simeq}{}^\tau$ $\overline{a}.0 \rhd K$. □

Exercise 7.3.3 (2) We have $a.b \overset{\centerdot}{\sim} a.c$, but not $a.b \mid \overline{a}.\overline{b} \overset{\centerdot}{\sim} a.c \mid \overline{a}.\overline{b}$. □

Exercise 7.3.10 We only have to make a few modifications to Lemma 7.3.7. In its assertion, P, Q are image-finite up-to $\sim$. In the proof there are two places to modify. First since $\overset{\mu}{\rightarrow}$ is image-finite up-to $\sim$, $\{Q' \mid Q \overset{\mu}{\rightarrow} Q'\}$ is finite when quotiented by $\sim$. We can write this quotient as

$$\{Q_i \mid i \in I\} \tag{A.4}$$

for some finite set I, where the processes Q_i are representatives for each class in the quotient.

Second, in Case 1 of the proof (and similarly in Case 2), we have to rectify the definition of B'. We have

$$B' \overset{\text{def}}{=} Q' \mid \Sigma_{i \in I} \, \tau.(M_i + c_i)$$

for some Q' such that $Q \overset{\mu}{\rightarrow} Q'$. Let Q_j be the representative of the equivalence class that Q' belongs to, according to (A.4). Thus $Q' \sim Q_j$. As $\sim \subseteq \overset{\centerdot}{\sim}$ and $\overset{\centerdot}{\sim}$ is transitive, it must also be $A' \overset{\centerdot}{\sim} B'_\star$, for

$$B'_\star \overset{\text{def}}{=} Q_j \mid \Sigma_{i \in I} \, \tau.(M_i + c_i).$$

Then the proof continues as before, with $B'_\star$ in place of B'. □

Exercise 7.3.11 Suppose that the finite set A contains all names that appear in the sorts of P_1 and P_2, and let a be a fresh name. The idea is to hide all the names in A via restrictions (that we write νA, with some abuse of notation), and then to define, using the visible name a, a sequence of processes R_i ($i \geq 0$) such that for all processes Q_1, Q_2 whose sorts use only names in A we have: $\nu A\,(Q_1 \mid R_i) \stackrel{\cdot}{\sim} \nu A\,(Q_2 \mid R_j)$ implies $i = j$. The processes $\{R_i\}_i$ will play the roles of the signal names used in the proof of Lemma 7.3.7 (e.g., name c in the assertion of the lemma).

For this we can set

$$R_i \stackrel{\text{def}}{=} \underbrace{\tau.\ldots.\tau}_{i}.a.$$

$\square$

Exercise 7.4.3 Obviously $\simeq\ \subseteq\ \simeq^{\mathrm{e}}$. For the converse, we show that for each context C and processes P, Q, if $P \simeq^{\mathrm{e}} Q$ then $C[P] \simeq^{\mathrm{e}} C[Q]$, that is, $C[P] \mid R \stackrel{\cdot}{\sim} C[Q] \mid R$ for all R. We do this by structural induction on C.

The base case is when $C = [\cdot]$ and follows from the definition of $\simeq^{\mathrm{e}}$. For the inductive cases, we only show the details for parallel composition, the other operators are easy. Then $C = C' \mid S$ (the case C of the form $S \mid C'$ is similar). We have to show that, for all R,

$$(C'[P] \mid S) \mid R \stackrel{\cdot}{\sim} (C'[Q] \mid S) \mid R.$$

Since $\sim\ \subseteq\ \stackrel{\cdot}{\sim}$ and we know that the law of associativity of parallel composition is valid for $\sim$, we infer

$$C'[P] \mid (S \mid R) \stackrel{\cdot}{\sim} (C'[Q] \mid (S \mid R)$$

and then we can appeal to the inductive hypothesis on C'. $\square$

Exercise 7.5.6 Write $\cong^{\mathrm{e}}_{\star}$ for the largest congruence included in $\cong^{\mathrm{e}}$, thus $P \cong^{\mathrm{e}}_{\star} Q$ holds if for all C, $C[P] \cong^{\mathrm{e}} C[Q]$. As $\cong^{\mathrm{e}}$ implies $\stackrel{\cdot}{\approx}$, $\cong^{\mathrm{e}}_{\star}$ implies $\cong$.

For the converse, suppose $P \cong Q$, we have to show that $P \cong^{\mathrm{e}}_{\star} Q$, that is, for all contexts C, $C[P] \cong^{\mathrm{e}} C[Q]$. This means ensuring that, for all R, $C[P] \mid R \stackrel{\cdot}{\approx} C[Q] \mid R$. This holds by definition of $\cong$, taking $C \mid R$ as a context. $\square$

Exercise 7.5.8 The context lemma uses contexts of the form $([\cdot] + P) \mid Q$. The details of the proof are similar to those for Exercise 7.4.3. $\square$

Exercise 7.6.4 We sketch the definition of branching barbed bisimulation. In the definition of weak reduction bisimulation, the bisimulation clause becomes:

- for all P' with $P \stackrel{\tau}{\rightarrow} P'$, either

  (1) $P' \mathrel{\mathcal{R}} Q$, or
  (2) there are Q', Q_1, Q_2 such that $Q \Longrightarrow Q_1$, $Q_1 \stackrel{\tau}{\rightarrow} Q_2$, and $Q_2 \Longrightarrow Q'$ with $P \mathrel{\mathcal{R}} Q_1$, $P' \mathrel{\mathcal{R}} Q_2$, and $P' \mathrel{\mathcal{R}} Q'$.

Moreover, the definition of weak-barb preserving in Exercise 7.5.2 becomes: whenever $P \mathrel{\mathcal{R}} Q$, for all ℓ:

(1) $P \downarrow_\ell$ implies $Q \Longrightarrow Q' \downarrow_\ell$ for some Q' with $P \mathcal{R} Q'$;

(2) conversely, $Q \downarrow_\ell$ implies $P \Longrightarrow P' \downarrow_\ell$ for some P' with $P' \mathcal{R} Q$.

The τ-law **T3**, $\mu.(P + \tau.Q) = \mu.(P + \tau.Q) + \mu.Q$, fails for branching barbed congruence when we use a context $[\cdot] \mid \overline{\mu}$; in this context, the latter process has a reduction to $Q \mid \mathbf{0}$; the former process, in the same context, to match such a reduction may need to go through the intermediate state $(P + \tau.Q) \mid \mathbf{0}$ whose observables may be different from those of $Q \mid \mathbf{0}$ (take $P = a$ and $Q = b$). $\square$

Notation

We report here the main notation under the following headings: miscellaneous, processes, preorders and equivalences. The page number refers to the first occurrence of the notation.

Miscellaneous

$S_1 \cup S_2, \cup_i S_i$	set union	7
$S_1 \cap S_2, \cap_i S_i$	set intersection	7
$S_1 - S_2$	set difference	7
$S \times S', S^n$	cartesian product of sets	7
$\wp$	powerset construct	7
$\mathcal{R}, \mathcal{S}$	relations	7
$\mathcal{R}^{-1}$	inverse of a relation	7
$\mathcal{R} \subseteq \mathcal{S}$	relation inclusion	7
$\mathcal{R}\mathcal{S}$	composition of relations	7
$P \mathcal{R} Q$	infix notation for relations	7
$\mathcal{I}$	identity relation	8
$\nleftrightarrow$	complement of relation $\leftrightarrow$	8
$\mathcal{R}^+$	transitive closure of relation $\mathcal{R}$	8
$\mathcal{R}^\star$	reflexive and transitive closure of relation $\mathcal{R}$	8
$=$	syntactic equality	7
$e \Downarrow$	convergent term in the λ-calculus	34
$e \Uparrow$	divergent term in the λ-calculus	35
$\leq$	partial order relation	40
$\geq$	inverse of $\leq$	41
$\cup S$	join of S in a complete lattice	42
$\cap S$	meet of S in a complete lattice	42
$\mathsf{gfp}(F)$	greatest fixed points of F	42
$\mathsf{lfp}(F)$	least fixed points of F	42
$\bot$	bottom element of a complete lattice	43
$\top$	top element of a complete lattice	43

Processes

References

[Abr87] S. Abramsky. Observation equivalence as a testing equivalence. *Theoretical Computer Science*, **53**:225–241, 1987.

[Abr10] S. Abramsky. Coalgebras, chu spaces, and representations of physical systems. In *25th Symposium on Logic in Computer Science (LICS'10)*, 411–420. IEEE Computer Society, 2010.

[ABS99] S. Abiteboul, P. Buneman and D. Suciu. *Data on the Web: from Relations to Semistructured Data and XML*. Morgan Kaufmann, 1999.

[ABV94] L. Aceto, B. Bloom and F. Vaandrager. Turning SOS rules into equations. *Information and Computation*, **111**(1):1–52, 1994.

[AC93] R. M. Amadio and L. Cardelli. Subtyping recursive types. *ACM Transactions on Programming Languages and Systems*, **15**(4):575–631, 1993.

[Acz77] P. Aczel. An introduction to inductive definitions. In Jon Barwise, ed., *Handbook of Mathematical Logic*, 739–782. North-Holland, 1977.

[Acz88] P. Aczel. *Non-well-founded Sets*. CSLI lecture notes; no. 14, 1988.

[AFV01] L. Aceto, W. Fokkink and I. C. Verhoef. Structural operational semantics. In A. Ponse, J. Bergstra and S. Smolka, ed., *Handbook of Process Algebra*, 197–292. Elsevier, 2001.

[AFvGI04] L. Aceto, W. Fokkink, R. J. van Glabbeek and A. Ingólfsdóttir. Nested semantics over finite trees are equationally hard. *Information and Computation*, **191**(2):203–232, 2004.

[AG98] M. Abadi and A. D. Gordon. A bisimulation method for cryptographic protocols. In C. Hankin, ed., *ESOP'98: European Symposium on Programming*, volume 1381 of *Lecture Notes in Computer Science*, 12–26. Springer Verlag, 1998.

[AGR88] E. Astesiano, A. Giovini and G. Reggio. Generalized bisimulation in relational specifications. In *STACS'88: Symposium on Theoretical Aspects of Computer Science*, volume 294 of *Lecture Notes in Computer Science*, 207–226. Springer Verlag, 1988.

[AH92] L. Aceto and M. Hennessy. Termination, deadlock, and divergence. *J. ACM*, **39**(1):147–187, 1992.

[AI08] L. Aceto and A. Ingólfsdóttir. On the expressibility of priority. *Inf. Process. Lett.*, **109**(1):83–85, 2008.

[AILS07] L. Aceto, A. Ingólfsdóttir, K. Guldstrand Larsen and J. Srba. *Reactive Systems: Modelling, Specification and Verification*. Cambridge University Press, 2007.

[AIS12] L. Aceto, A. Ingólfsdóttir and J. Srba. The algorithmics of bisimilarity. In Sangiorgi and Rutten [SR12].

[AV93] S. Abramsky and S. Vickers. Quantales, observational logic and process semantics. *Mathematical Structures in Computer Science*, 3(2):161–227, 1993.

[AvGFI96] L. Aceto, R. J. van Glabbeek, W. Fokkink and A. Ingólfsdóttir. Axiomatizing prefix iteration with silent steps. *Information and Computation*, 127(1):26–40, 1996.

[Bas96] T. Basten. Branching bisimilarity is an equivalence indeed! *Inf. Process. Lett.*, 58(3):141–147, 1996.

[BB89] T. Bolognesi and E. Brinksma. Introduction to the ISO specification language LOTOS. In P. H. J. van Eijk, C. A. Vissers and M. Diaz, eds., *The Formal Description Technique LOTOS*. North Holland, 1989.

[BBK87a] J. C. M. Baeten, J. A. Bergstra and J. W. Klop. On the consistency of Koomen's fair abstraction rule. *Theoretical Computer Science*, 51:129–176, 1987.

[BBK87b] J. C. M. Baeten, J. A. Bergstra and J. W. Klop. Ready-trace semantics for concrete process algebra with the priority operator. *Comput. J.*, 30(6):498–506, 1987.

[BC04] Y. Bertot and P. Casteran. *Interactive Theorem Proving and Program Development. Coq'Art: The Calculus of Inductive Constructions*. EATCS Series. Springer Verlag, 2004.

[BDHS96] P. Buneman, S. B. Davidson, G. G. Hillebrand and D. Suciu. A query language and optimization techniques for unstructured data. In H. V. Jagadish and I. S. Mumick, eds., *Proc. ACM Int. Conf. on Management of Data*, 505–516. ACM Press, 1996.

[BDP99a] M. Boreale, R. De Nicola and R. Pugliese. Proof techniques for cryptographic processes. In *14th Symposium on Logic in Computer Science (LICS'99)*, 157–166. IEEE Computer Society, 1999.

[BDP99b] M. Boreale, R. De Nicola and R. Pugliese. Basic observables for processes. *Information and Computation*, 149(1):77–98, 1999.

[BG96] R. N. Bol and J. F. Groote. The meaning of negative premises in transition system specifications. *J. ACM*, 43:863–914, 1996.

[BGMM99] E. Bertino, G. Guerrini, I. Merlo and M. Mesiti. An approach to classify semi-structured objects. In *ECOOP'99: European Conference on Object-Oriented Programming*, volume 1628 of *Lecture Notes in Computer Science*, 416–440. Springer, 1999.

[BH97] M. Brandt and F. Henglein. Coinductive axiomatization of recursive type equality and subtyping. In R. Hindley, ed., *TLCA'97: Typed Lambda Calculi and Applications*, volume 1210 of *Lecture Notes in Computer Science (LNCS)*, 63–81. Springer-Verlag, April 1997.

[BHR84] S. D. Brookes, C. A. R. Hoare and A. W. Roscoe. A theory of communicating sequential processes. *J. ACM*, 31(3):560–599, 1984.

[BIM95] B. Bloom, S. Istrail and A. R. Meyer. Bisimulation can't be traced. *J. ACM*, 42(1):232–268, 1995.

[BK84] J. A. Bergstra and J. W. Klop. Process algebra for synchronous communication. *Information and Computation*, 60:109–137, 1984.

[BK86] J. A. Bergstra and J. W. Klop. Verification of an alternating bit protocol by means of process algebra. In *Proc. Int. Spring School on Mathematical*

Methods of Specification and Synthesis of Software Systems '85, volume 215, 9–23. Springer Verlag, 1986.

[BKO87] J. A. Bergstra, J. W. Klop and E.-R. Olderog. Failures without chaos: a process semantics for fair abstraction. In M. Wirsing, ed., *IFIP Formal Description of Programming Concepts – III*, pages 77–101. Elsevier Science Publishers B.V., 1987.

[BKO88] J. A. Bergstra, J. Willem Klop and E.-R. Olderog. Readies and failures in the algebra of communicating processes. *SIAM J. Comput.*, **17**(6):1134–1177, 1988.

[Blo89] B. Bloom. *Ready Simulation, Bisimulation, and the Semantics of CCS-like Languages*. Ph.D. thesis, Massachusetts Institute of Technology, 1989.

[BM96] J. Barwise and L. Moss. *Vicious Circles: on the Mathematics of Non-Wellfounded Phenomena*. CSLI (Center for the Study of Language and Information), 1996.

[Bou89] G. Boudol. Towards a lambda calculus for concurrent and communicating systems. In *TAPSOFT'89: Theory and Practice of Software Development*, volume 351 of *Lecture Notes in Computer Science*, 149–161, Springer Verlag, 1989.

[BPS01] J. Bergstra, A. Ponse and S. Smolka, eds. *Handbook of Process Algebra*. Elsevier, 2001.

[BR84] S. D. Brookes and A. W. Roscoe. An improved failures model for communicating processes. In S. D. Brookes, A. W. Roscoe and G. Winskel, eds., *Seminar on Concurrency*, volume 197 of *Lecture Notes in Computer Science*, 281–305. Springer Verlag, 1984.

[Bri99] E. Brinksma. Cache consistency by design. *Distrib. Comput.*, **12**(2/3):61–74, 1999.

[BRV01] P. Blackburn, M. de Rijke and Y. Venema. *Modal Logic*. Cambridge University Press, 2001.

[BS98] M. Boreale and D. Sangiorgi. Bisimulation in name-passing calculi without matching. In *Proc. 13th Symposium on Logic in Computer Science (LICS'98)*, 411–420. IEEE, Computer Society Press, 1998.

[BvG87] J. C. M. Baeten and R. J. van Glabbeek. Another look at abstraction in process algebra (extended abstract). In T. Ottmann, ed., *ICALP'87: Automata, Languages and Programming*, volume 267 of *Lecture Notes in Computer Science*, 84–94. Springer Verlag, 1987.

[Cas01] I. Castellani. Process algebras with localities. In A. Ponse, J. Bergstra and S. Smolka, eds., *Handbook of Process Algebra*, 945–1045. Elsevier, 2001.

[CC79] P. Cousot and R. Cousot. Constructive versions of Tarski's fixed point theorems. *Pacific Journal of Mathematics*, **81**(1):43–57, 1979.

[CH93] R. Cleaveland and M. Hennessy. Testing equivalence as a bisimulation equivalence. *Formal Asp. Comput.*, **5**(1):1–20, 1993.

[CHM93] S. Christensen, Y. Hirshfeld and F Moller. Decomposability, decidability and axiomatisability for bisimulation equivalence on basic parallel processes. In *Proc. 8th Symposium on Logic in Computer Science (LICS'93)*, 386–396. IEEE Computer Society, 1993.

[Chr93] S. Christensen. *Decidability and Decomposition in Process Algebras*. Ph.D. thesis, Department of Computer Science, University of Edinburgh, 1993.

[Coq94] T. Coquand. Infinite objects in type theory. In H. Barendregt and T. Nipkow, eds., *1st Int. Workshop TYPES*, volume 806 of *Lecture Notes in Computer Science*, 62–78. Springer Verlag, Berlin, 1994.

[DD91] P. Darondeau and P. Degano. About semantic action refinement. *Fundam. Inform.*, **14**(2):221–234, 1991.

[De87] R. De Nicola. Extensional equivalences for transition systems. *Acta Informatica*, **24**:211–237, 1987.

[Den07] Y. Deng. A simple completeness proof for the axiomatisations of weak behavioural equivalences. *Bulletin of the EATCS*, **93**:207–219, 2007.

[DH84] R. De Nicola and R. Hennessy. Testing equivalences for processes. *Theoretical Computer Science*, **34**:83–133, 1984.

[DP02] B. A. Davey and H. A. Priestley. *Introduction to Lattices and Order.* Cambridge University Press, 2002.

[DS85] R. De Simone. Higher level synchronising devices in MEIJE-SCCS. *Theoretical Computer Science*, **37**:245–267, 1985.

[DV95] R. De Nicola and F. W. Vaandrager. Three logics for branching bisimulation. *J. ACM*, **42**(2):458–487, 1995.

[DvGHM08] Y. Deng, R. J. van Glabbeek, M. Hennessy and C. Morgan. Characterising testing preorders for finite probabilistic processes. *Logical Methods in Computer Science*, **4**(4), 2008.

[Fio93] M. Fiore. A coinduction principle for recursive data types based on bisimulation. In *Proc. 8th Symposium on Logic in Computer Science (LICS'93)*, 110–119. IEEE Computer Society, 1993.

[Fou98] C. Fournet. *The Join-Calculus: a Calculus for Distributed Mobile Programming.* Ph.D. thesis, Ecole Polytechnique, 1998.

[Gim96] E. Giménez. *Un Calcul de Constructions Infinies et son Application á la Verification des Systemes Communicants.* Ph.D. thesis 96-11, Laboratoire de l'Informatique du Parallélisme, Ecole Normale Supérieure de Lyon, December 1996.

[GK03] E. Grädel and S. Kreutzer. Will deflation lead to depletion? On non-monotone fixed point inductions. In *Proc. 18th IEEE Symposium on Logic in Computer Science (LICS 2003)*, 158–167. IEEE Computer Society, 2003.

[Gla88] R. J. van Glabbeek. De semantiek van eindige, sequentiële processen met interne acties, syllabus processemantieken, deel 2 (in Dutch). Draft, 1988.

[Gla90] R. J. van Glabbeek. *Comparative concurrency semantics and refinement of actions.* Ph.D. thesis, University of Amsterdam, 1990.

[Gla91] R. J. van Glabbeek. Characterisation GSOS congruence. Posting in the concurrency mailing list, May 1991.

[Gla93a] R. J. van Glabbeek. The linear time-branching time spectrum II (the semantics of sequential systems with silent moves). In E. Best, ed., *CONCUR'93: Concurrency Theory*, volume 715. Springer Verlag, 1993.

[Gla93b] R. J. van Glabbeek. A complete axiomatization for branching bisimulation congruence of finite-state behaviours. In A. M. Borzyszkowski and S. Sokolowski, eds., *Proc. 18th Symposium on Mathematical Foundations of Computer Science (MFCS'93)*, volume 711 of *Lecture Notes in Computer Science*, 473–484. Springer Verlag, 1993.

[Gla93c] R. J. van Glabbeek. Full abstraction in structural operational semantics (extended abstract). In M. Nivat, C. Rattray, T. Rus and G. Scollo, eds., *Proc.*

3rd Conf. on Algebraic Methodology and Software Technology (AMAST '93), Workshops in Computing, 75–82. Springer Verlag, 1993.

[Gla01a] R. J. van Glabbeek. The linear time-branching time spectrum I. In A. Ponse, J. Bergstra and S. Smolka, eds., *Handbook of Process Algebra*, 3–99. Elsevier, 2001.

[Gla01b] R. J. van Glabbeek. What is branching time semantics and why to use it? In G. Paun, G. Rozenberg and A. Salomaa, eds., *Current Trends in Theoretical Computer Science*, 469–479. World Scientific, 2001.

[Gla05] R. J. van Glabbeek. A characterisation of weak bisimulation congruence. In A. Middeldorp, V. van Oostrom, F. van Raamsdonk and R. C. de Vrijer, eds., *Processes, Terms and Cycles: Steps on the Road to Infinity, Essays Dedicated to Jan Willem Klop, on the Occasion of His 60th Birthday*, volume 3838 of *Lecture Notes in Computer Science*, 26–39. Springer Verlag, 2005.

[Gro91] J. F. Groote. *Process Algebra and Structured Operational Semantics*. Ph.D. thesis, University of Amsterdam, 1991.

[Gro93] J. F. Groote. Transition system specifications with negative premises. *Theoretical Computer Science*, **118**(2):263–299, 1993.

[GV92] J. F. Groote and F. W. Vaandrager. Structured operational semantics and bisimulation as a congruence. *Information and Computation*, **100**:202–260, 1992.

[GW96] R. J. van Glabbeek and W. P. Weijland. Branching time and abstraction in bisimulation semantics. *J. ACM*, **43**(3):555–600, 1996. An extended abstract appeared in *Information Processing 89*, *IFIP 11th World Computer Congress*, 1989, 613–618.

[HH06] P. Hancock and P. Hyvernat. Programming interfaces and basic topology *Ann. Pure Appl. Logic*, **137**(1–3):189–239, 2006.

[Hen88] M. Hennessy. *Algebraic Theory of Processes*. The MIT Press, Cambridge, Mass., 1988.

[HJ99] Y. Hirshfeld and M. Jerrum. Bisimulation equivalence is decidable for normed process algebra. In J. Wiedermann, P. van Emde Boas and M. Nielsen, eds., *ICALP'99: Automata, Languages and Programming*, , volume 1644 of *Lecture Notes in Computer Science*, 412–421. Springer Verlag, 1999.

[HM85] M. Hennessy and R. Milner. Algebraic laws for nondeterminism and concurrency. *J. ACM*, **32**:137–161, 1985.

[HMU06] J. E. Hopcroft, R. Motwani and J. D. Ullman. *Introduction to Automata Theory, Languages, and Computation (3rd Edn.)*. Addison-Wesley, 2006.

[Hoa85] C. A. R. Hoare. *Communicating Sequential Processes*. Prentice Hall, 1985.

[HP80] M. Hennessy and G. D. Plotkin. A term model for CCS. In P. Dembinski, ed., *Proc. 9th Symposium on Mathematical Foundations of Computer Science (MFCS'80)*, volume 88 of *Lecture Notes in Computer Science*, 261–274. Springer Verlag, 1980.

[JR03] A. Jeffrey and J. Rathke. Contextual equivalence for higher-order pi-calculus revisited. In *Proc. MFPS XIX*, volume 83 of *ENTCS*. Elsevier Science Publishers, 2003.

[KW06] V. Koutavas and M. Wand. Small bisimulations for reasoning about higher-order imperative programs. In J. G. Morrisett and S. L. Peyton Jones, eds., *Proceedings of the 33rd ACM SIGPLAN-SIGACT Symposium on Principles of Programming Languages*, 141–152, 2006.

[Len98]   M. Lenisa. *Themes in Final Semantics*. Ph.D. thesis, Università di Pisa, 1998.

[LG09]   X. Leroy and H. Grall. Coinductive big-step operational semantics *Information and Computation*, **207**(2):284–304, 2009.

[LJWF02] D. Lacey, N. D. Jones, E. Van Wyk and C. C. Frederiksen. Proving correctness of compiler optimizations by temporal logic. In 29th ACM Symposium on Principles of Programming Languages, 283–294, 2002.

[LM92]   K. G. Larsen and R. Milner. A compositional protocol verification using relativized bisimulation. *Information and Computation*, **99**(1):80–108, 1992.

[LS91]   K. G. Larsen and A. Skou. Bisimulation through probabilistic testing. *Information and Computation*, **94**(1):1–28, 1991. Preliminary version in *POPL'89*, 344–352, 1989.

[LvO05]   B. Luttik and V. van Oostrom. Decomposition orders: Another generalisation of the fundamental theorem of arithmetic. *Theoretical Computer Science*, **335**(2–3):147–186, 2005.

[Mai87]   M. G. Main. Trace, failure and testing equivalences for communicating processes. *Int. J. Parallel Program.*, **16**(5):383–400, 1987.

[Mil81]   R. Milner. A modal characterisation of observable machine-behaviour. In E. Astesiano and C. Böhm, eds., *Proc. 6th Colloquium on Trees in Algebra and Programming (CAAP '81)*, volume 112 of *Lecture Notes in Computer Science*, 25–34. Springer Verlag, 1981.

[Mil89]   R. Milner. *Communication and Concurrency*. Prentice Hall, 1989.

[Mil99]   R. Milner. *Communicating and Mobile Systems: the π-Calculus*. Cambridge University Press, 1999.

[MM93]   R. Milner and F. Moller. Unique decomposition of processes. *Theoretical Computer Science*, **107**(2):357–363, 1993.

[Mol89]   F. Moller. *Axioms for concurrency*. Ph.D. thesis, Department of Computer Science, University of Edinburgh, 1989.

[Mol90a] F. Moller. The importance of the left merge operator in process algebras. In M. Paterson, ed., *ICALP'90: Automata, Languages and Programming*, volume 443 of *Lecture Notes in Computer Science*, 752–764. Springer Verlag, 1990.

[Mol90b] F. Moller. The nonexistence of finite axiomatisations for CCS congruences. In *Proc. 5th Symposium on Logic in Computer Science (LICS'90)*, 142–153. IEEE Computer Society, 1990.

[Mor68]   J. H. Morris. *Lambda-Calculus Models of Programming Languages*. Ph.D. thesis MAC-TR-57, MIT, project MAC, Dec. 1968.

[Mos74]   Y. N. Moschovakis. On non-monotone inductive definability. *Fund. Math.*, **LXXXII**(1):39–83, 1974.

[MRG07]   M. R. Mousavi, M. A. Reniers and J. F. Groote. SOS formats and meta-theory: 20 years after. *Theoretical Computer Science*, **373**(3):238–272, 2007.

[MS92]   U. Montanari and V. Sassone. Dynamic congruence vs. progressing bisimulation for CCS. *Fundamenta Informaticae*, **XVI**(2):171–199, 1992.

[MT91]   R. Milner and M. Tofte. Co-induction in relational semantics. *Theoretical Computer Science*, **87**:209–220, 1991.

[MZ05]   M. Merro and F. Z. Nardelli. Behavioral theory for mobile ambients. *J. ACM*, **52**(6):961–1023, 2005.

[NC95] V. Natarajan and R. Cleaveland. Divergence and fair testing. In *ICALP'95: Automata, Languages and Programming*, volume 944 of *Lecture Notes in Computer Science*, 648–659. Springer Verlag, 1995.

[NNH99] F. Nielson, H. R. Nielson and C. Hankin. *Principles of Program Analysis.* Springer-Verlag New York, 1999.

[NP00] U. Nestmann and B. C. Pierce. Decoding choice encodings. *Information and Computation*, **163**(1):1–59, 2000.

[OH86] E.-R. Olderog and C. A. R. Hoare. Specification-oriented semantics for communicating processes. *Acta Informatica*, **23**(1):9–66, 1986.

[Phi87] I. Phillips. Refusal testing. *Theoretical Computer Science*, **50**:241–284, 1987. A preliminary version *in Proc. ICALP'86, Lecture Notes in Computer Science* 226, Springer Verlag.

[Pit93] A. M. Pitts. Tutorial talk on coinduction. *8th Symposium on Logic in Computer Science (LICS'93)*, 1993.

[Pit94] A. M. Pitts. A co-induction principle for recursively defined domains. *Theoretical Computer Science*, **124**:195–219, 1994.

[Pit97] A. M. Pitts. Operationally-based theories of program equivalence. In P. Dybjer and A. M. Pitts, eds., *Semantics and Logics of Computation*, Publications of the Newton Institute, 241–298. Cambridge University Press, 1997.

[Pit12] A. Pitts. Howe's method. In Sangiorgi and Rutten [SR12].

[Plo76] G. D. Plotkin. A powerdomain construction. *SIAM J. Comput.*, **5**(3):452–487, 1976.

[Plo04a] G. D. Plotkin. The origins of structural operational semantics. *J. Log. Algebr. Program.*, **60–61**:3–15, 2004.

[Plo04b] G. D. Plotkin. A structural approach to operational semantics. *J. Log. Algebr. Program.*, **60–61**:17–139, 2004. Reprinted with corrections from Tech. Rep. DAIMI FN-19, Comp. Sci. Dep. Aarhus University, Aarhus, Denmark, 1981.

[Prz88] T. C. Przymusinski. On the declarative semantics of deductive databases and logic programs. In J. Minker, ed. *Foundations of Deductive Databases and Logic Programming.*, 193–216. Morgan Kaufmann, 1988.

[PS92] J. Parrow and P. Sjödin. Multiway synchronizaton verified with coupled simulation. In R. Cleaveland, ed., *CONCUR'92: Concurrency Theory*, volume 630 of *Lecture Notes in Computer Science*, 518–533. Springer Verlag, 1992.

[PS94] J. Parrow and P. Sjödin. The complete axiomatization of cs-congruence. In P. Enjalbert, E. W. Mayr and K. W. Wagner, eds., *STACS'94: Symposium on Theoretical Aspects of Computer Science*, volume 775 of *Lecture Notes in Computer Science*, 557–568. Springer Verlag, 1994.

[PS00] B. Pierce and D. Sangiorgi. Behavioral equivalence in the polymorphic pi-calculus. *J. ACM*, **47**(3):531–584, 2000.

[PS12] D. Pous and D. Sangiorgi. Enhancements of the bisimulation proof method. In Sangiorgi and Rutten [SR12].

[RJ12] J. Rutten and B. Jacobs. (Co)algebras and (co)induction. In Sangiorgi and Rutten [SR12].

[RS08] J. Rathke and P. Sobocinski. Deconstructing behavioural theories of mobility. In G. Ausiello, J. Karhumäki, G. Mauri and C.-H. Luke Ong, eds., *Proc. Fifth IFIP International Conference On Theoretical Computer Science (TCS 2008), IFIP 20th World Computer Congress*, volume 273 of *IFIP*, 507–520. Springer Verlag, 2008.

[RT94]   J. Rutten and D. Turi. Initial algebra and final coalgebra semantics for concurrency. In *Proc. Rex School/Symposium 1993 "A Decade of Concurrency – Reflexions and Perspectives"*, volume 803 of *Lecture Notes in Computer Science*. Springer Verlag, 1994.

[RV07]   A. Rensink and W. Volger. Fair testing. *Information and Computation*, **205**:125–198, 2007.

[Sab03] A. Sabelfeld. Confidentiality for multithreaded programs via bisimulation. In M. Broy and A. V. Zamulin, eds., *Perspectives of Systems Informatics, 5th Ershov Memorial Conference*, volume 2890 of *Lecture Notes in Computer Science*, 260–274. Springer, 2003.

[San92] D. Sangiorgi. *Expressing Mobility in Process Algebras: First-Order and Higher-Order Paradigms*. Ph.D. thesis CST–99–93, Department of Computer Science, University of Edinburgh, 1992.

[San96] D. Sangiorgi. Bisimulation for higher-order process calculi. *Information and Computation*, **131**(2):141–178, 1996.

[San12] D. Sangiorgi. The origins of bisimulation and coinduction. In Sangiorgi and Rutten [SR12].

[SKS07a] D. Sangiorgi, N. Kobayashi and E. Sumii. Environmental bisimulations for higher-order languages. In *Proc. 22nd Symposium on Logic in Computer Science (LICS 2007)*, 293–302. IEEE Computer Society, 2007.

[SKS07b] D. Sangiorgi, N. Kobayashi and E. Sumii. Logical bisimulations and functional languages. In F. Arbab and M. Sirjani, eds., *FSEN'07: Symposium on Fundamentals of Software Engineering*, volume 4767 of *Lecture Notes in Computer Science*, 364–379. Springer Verlag, 2007.

[Smi08] G. Smith. Adversaries and information leaks (tutorial). In G. Barthe and C. Fournet, eds., *TGC'07: Trustworthy Global Computing*, volume 4912 of *Lecture Notes in Computer Science*, 383–400. Springer Verlag, 2008.

[SP04]   E. Sumii and B. C. Pierce. A bisimulation for dynamic sealing. In N. D. Jones and X. Leroy, eds., *31st ACM Symposium on Principles of Programming Languages*, 161–172, 2004.

[SP05]   E. Sumii and B. C. Pierce. A bisimulation for type abstraction and recursion. In J. Palsberg and M. Abadi eds., *32nd ACM Symposium on Principles of Programming Languages*, 63–74, 2005.

[SR12]   D. Sangiorgi and J. Rutten, eds. *Advanced Topics in Bisimulation and Coinduction*. Cambridge University Press, 2012.

[Sti87] C. Stirling. Modal logics for communicating systems. *Theoretical Computer Science*, **49**:311–347, 1987.

[Sti01] C. Stirling. *Modal and Temporal Properties of Processes*. Springer Verlag, 2001.

[Sti12] C. Stirling. Bisimulation and logic. In Sangiorgi and Rutten [SR12].

[SW01]   D. Sangiorgi and D. Walker. *The π-calculus: a Theory of Mobile Processes*. Cambridge University Press, 2001.

[Tho90] B. Thomsen. *Calculi for Higher Order Communicating Systems*. Ph.D. thesis, Department of Computing, Imperial College, 1990.

[Tho93] W. Thomas. On the Ehrenfeucht-Fraïssé game in theoretical computer science. In M.-C. Gaudel and J.-P. Jouannaud, eds., *TAPSOFT'93: Theory and Practice of Software Development*, volume 668 of *Lecture Notes in Computer Science*, 559–568. Springer Verlag, 1993.

[Uli92] I. Ulidowski. Equivalences on observable processes. In *Proc. 7th Symposium on Logic in Computer Science (LICS 1992)*, 148–159. IEEE Computer Society, 1992.

[Val05] S. Valentini. The problem of the formalization of constructive topology. *Arch. Math. Log.*, **44**(1):115–129, 2005.

[Wal90] D. Walker. Bisimulation and divergence. *Information and Computation*, **85**(2):202–241, 1990.

[Wei89] W. P. Weijland. *Synchrony and Asynchrony in Process Algebra*. Ph.D. thesis, University of Amsterdam, 1989.

[Win93] G. Winskel. *The Formal Semantics of Programming Languages*. The MIT Press, 1993.

Index